SITE DESIGN GRAPHICS

TO

Lee Ann Kendall

and

Olivia Rose Kendall

Acknowledgements

Susan Layton has helped with the numerous changes, revisions, adjustments, etc.

Mary James Herold developed the graphic layout for Site Design Graphics.

Homan Wong was the first person to offer to buy a copy of Site Design Graphics.

Tawn Gorbutt received calls in the middle of the night to answer computer questions.

Hellmuth, Obata & Kassabaum, Inc. has provided time and the use of HOK Draw® computer system, without which this project would not have been possible.

Thank you.

Whatever you can do,

or believe you can, begin it.

Boldness has genius, power

and magic in it.

Goethe

During the Summer of 1986, Hellmuth, Obata & Kassabaum, Inc. was preparing design drawings for the Collin County Community College in Plano, Texas. I was designing the recreation fields adjacent to the college. Several fields were researched and drafted at the correct size and scale of the design drawings. I found all the fields would not fit on site and smaller versions of some fields or a reduced program would be required. After drafting several other field types at the appropriate scale, I felt there must be a way to avoid this repetition of drafting. The idea for **Site Design Graphics** was created.

These are 510 pages of 4,000 illustrations. I hope this book can reduce some of the repetitive work in the preparation of design or construction documents and therefore, free time for the actual design process.

This users guide is intended to explain format and describe techniques for using **Site Design Graphics**.

The book is divided into seven sections with each preceded by a matrix. This matrix expands on the listings in the Table of Contents. The matrix quickly and concisely outlines all elements within that section and at what angles of view and scales they are illustrated. Following is an item by item explanation of the matrix.

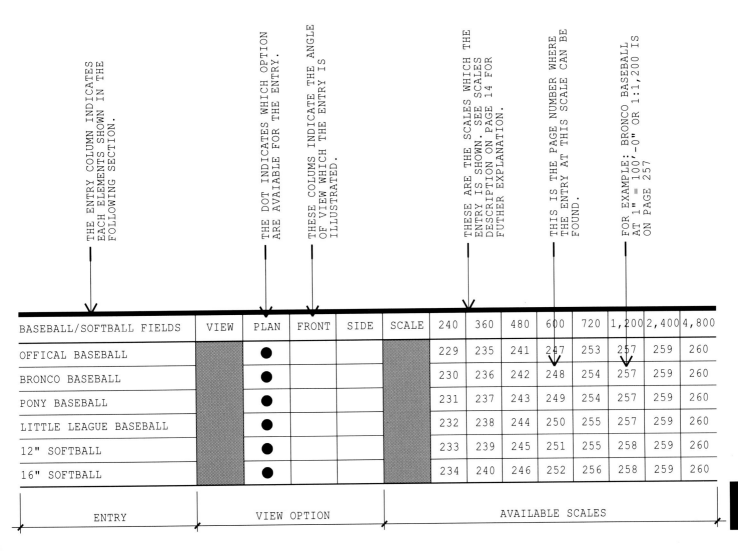

BASEBALL/SOFTBALL FIELDS	VIEW	PLAN	FRONT	SIDE	SCALE	240	360	480	600	720	1,200	2,400	4,800
OFFICAL BASEBALL		●				229	235	241	247	253	257	259	260
BRONCO BASEBALL		●				230	236	242	248	254	257	259	260
PONY BASEBALL		●				231	237	243	249	254	257	259	260
LITTLE LEAGUE BASEBALL		●				232	238	244	250	255	257	259	260
12" SOFTBALL		●				233	239	245	251	255	258	259	260
16" SOFTBALL		●				234	240	246	252	256	258	259	260

ENTRY   VIEW OPTION   AVAILABLE SCALES

Column annotations (top to bottom callouts):
- THE ENTRY COLUMN INDICATES EACH ELEMENTS SHOWN IN THE FOLLOWING SECTION.
- THE DOT INDICATES WHICH OPTION ARE AVAILABLE FOR THE ENTRY.
- THESE COLUMS INDICATE THE ANGLE OF VIEW WHICH THE ENTRY IS ILLUSTRATED.
- THESE ARE THE SCALES WHICH THE ENTRY IS SHOWN. SEE SCALES DESCRIPTION ON PAGE 14 FOR FUTHER EXPLANATION.
- THIS IS THE PAGE NUMBER WHERE THE ENTRY AT THIS SCALE CAN BE FOUND.
- FOR EXAMPLE: BRONCO BASEBALL AT 1" = 100'-0" OR 1:1,200 IS ON PAGE 257

The following scales description is a translation, both written and graphic, for each scale . The first column is a standard written scale. The second column is an actual or whole number ratio with both numbers of the same units of measure. For example, 1"=1,200" is the same as 1:1200 or 1" = 100'-0". The third column is the listing of graphic scale.

WRITTEN SCALE	ACTUAL SCALE	GRAPHIC SCALE	WRITTEN SCALE	ACTUAL SCALE	GRAPHIC SCALE
12" = 1'-0"	1:1	0 .5" 1"	1" = 20'-0"	1:240	0 5 10 20
6" = 1'-0"	1:2	0 1" 2"	1" = 30'-0"	1:360	0 15 30
3" = 1'-0"	1:4	0 2" 4"	1/32" = 1'-0"	1:384	0 8 16 32
1 1/2" = 1'-0"	1:8	0 3" 6"	1" = 40'-0"	1:480	0 10 20 40
1" = 1'-0"	1:12	0 3" 6"	1" = 50'-0"	1:600	0 25 50
3/4" = 1'-0"	1:16	0 6" 1	1" = 60'-0"	1:720	0 15 30 60
1/2" = 1'-0"	1:24	0 1 2	1" = 70'-0"	1:840	0 35 70
3/8" = 1'-0"	1:32	0 1 2	1" = 80'-0"	1:960	0 40 80
1/4" = 1'-0"	1:48	0 1 2 4	1" = 100'-0"	1:1,200	0 50 100
3/16" = 1'-0"	1:64	0 2 4	1" = 120'-0"	1:1,440	0 60 120
1/8" = 1'-0"	1:96	0 2 4 8	1" = 160'-0"	1:1,920	0 80 160
1" = 10'-0"	1:120	0 5 10	1" = 200'-0"	1:2,400	0 100 200
3/32" = 1'-0"	1:128	0 4 8	1" = 400'-0"	1:4,800	0 200 400
1/16" = 1'-0"	1:192	0 4 8 16	1" = 1,200'-0"	1:12,000	0 1000

All the illustrations are shown on typical page formats. Each page has a sub-section title at the top which is so the user can "flip" through a section and easily identify a topic. The page number is located at the outside margin, 2 inches above the bottom of the page, again, so that the user can flip through the numbers to locate the proper page. Each page is titled with a graphic and written scale. See below for further explanation.

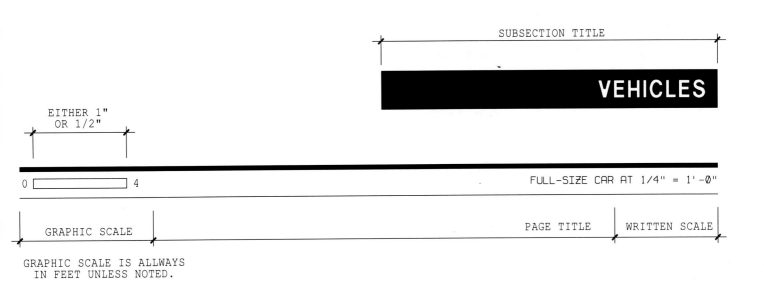

Site Design Graphics has been sewn so that the book can be opened completely flat. Pages can be completely reproduced on a copy machine and laid under an original to be traced or directly on top for a paste-up. The pages can also be copied onto a stickyback or chromatek and placed directly on the original. Use caution when tracing from a copy as all copy machines do not reproduce exactly 100% of originals. Some machines reduce the image by 2% in only one direction. When tracing any items in which accuracy is critical, always double check arithmetically and never rely fully on any graphic image.

The elements are arranged by category and grouped by scale. For example, all paving types are grouped by scale starting with 1/2" = 1'-0". This arrangement is to that all options can be identified and addressed quickly and accurately.

If an entry is not available at a desired sale, use an entry at one-half size and twice the scale. For example, a 40' diameter tree at 1" = 40' is the same as a 20' diameter tree at 1" = 20' scale.

Many entries, such as people, are in generic or schematic form. These entries are guides for drawing and not necessarily actual representations.

BUILDING FOOTPRINTS	VIEW	PLAN	FRONT	SIDE	SCALE	1200	2400	4800
RECTANGLE AT 18,000 SQ. FT.		●	●			5	6	6
RECTANGLE AT 21,000 SQ. FT.		●	●			5	6	6
RECTANGLE AT 24,000 SQ. FT.		●	●			5	6	6

GARAGE FOOTPRINTS	VIEW	PLAN	FRONT	SIDE	SCALE	1200	2400	4800
SLOPED AT 120' x 180'		●	●			5	6	6
SLOPED AT 120' x 180'		●	●			5	6	6
SLOPED AT 120' x 180'		●	●			5	6	6
WITH RAMPS AT 120' x 180'		●	●			6	6	6
WITH CONCENTRIC RAMPS AT 120' x 180'		●	●			6	6	6

0 [========] 100 | BUILDING FOOTPRINTS AND ELEVATIONS AT 1" = 100'-0"

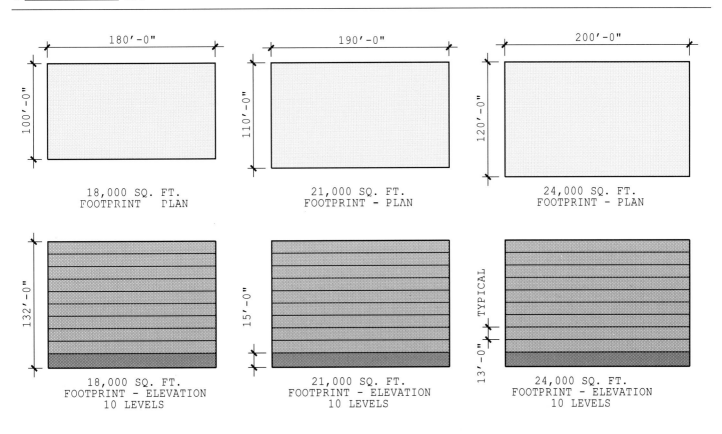

180'-0"
100'-0"
18,000 SQ. FT.
FOOTPRINT PLAN

190'-0"
110'-0"
21,000 SQ. FT.
FOOTPRINT - PLAN

200'-0"
120'-0"
24,000 SQ. FT.
FOOTPRINT - PLAN

132'-0"
18,000 SQ. FT.
FOOTPRINT - ELEVATION
10 LEVELS

15'-0"
21,000 SQ. FT.
FOOTPRINT - ELEVATION
10 LEVELS

13'-0" TYPICAL
24,000 SQ. FT.
FOOTPRINT - ELEVATION
10 LEVELS

0 [========] 100 | GARAGE FOOTPRINTS AND ELEVATIONS AT 1" = 100'-0"

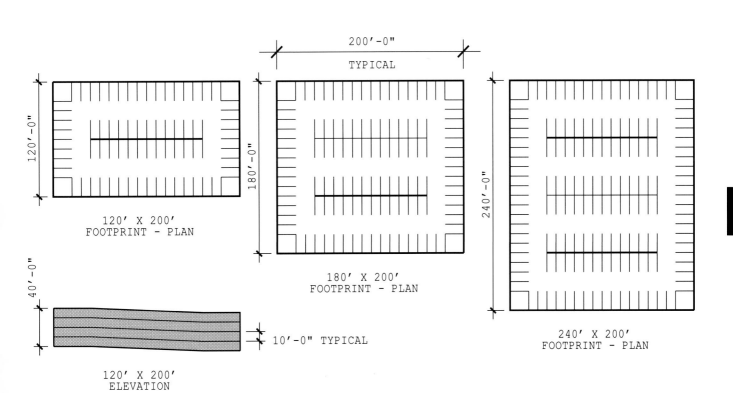

120'-0"
120' X 200'
FOOTPRINT - PLAN

200'-0"
TYPICAL
180'-0"
180' X 200'
FOOTPRINT - PLAN

240'-0"
240' X 200'
FOOTPRINT - PLAN

40'-0"
120' X 200'
ELEVATION

10'-0" TYPICAL

21

GARAGE FOOTPRINTS AND ELEVATIONS AT 1" = 100'-0"   0 ▭ 100

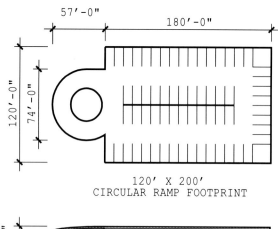

120' X 200'
CIRCULAR RAMP FOOTPRINT

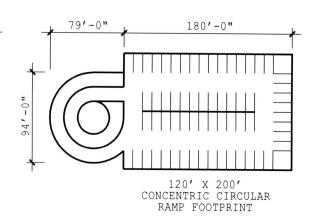

120' X 200'
CONCENTRIC CIRCULAR
RAMP FOOTPRINT

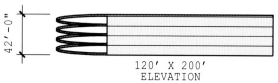

120' X 200'
ELEVATION

FOOTPRINTS AND ELEVATIONS AT 1" = 200'-0"   0 ▭ 200

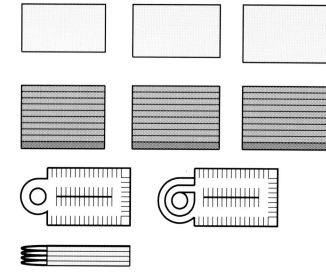

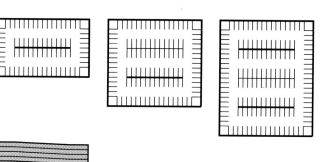

FOOTPRINTS AND ELEVATIONS AT 1" = 400'-0"   0 ▭ 400

PARKING SPACE	VIEW	PLAN	SCALE	240	360	480	600	720	1200	2400
LARGE SPACE ONE-WAY WITH ISLAND AT 60 DEGREE		●		31	40	49	54	59	64	69
LARGE SPACE ONE-WAY WITH ISLAND AT 45 DEGREE		●		31	40	49	54	59	64	69
LARGE SPACE ONE-WAY AT 60 DEGREE		●		32	41	49	54	59	64	69
LARGE SPACE ONE-WAY AT 45 DEGREE		●		32	41	49	54	59	64	69
LARGE SPACE TWO-WAY WITH ISLAND AT 90 DEGREE		●		33	42	50	55	60	65	69
LARGE SPACE TWO-WAY WITH ISLAND AT 60 DEGREE		●		33	42	50	55	60	65	69
LARGE SPACE TWO-WAY WITH ISLAND AT 45 DEGREE		●		34	43	50	55	60	65	70
LARGE SPACE TWO-WAY AT 90 DEGREE		●		34	43	50	55	60	65	70
LARGE SPACE TWO-WAY AT 60 DEGREE		●		35	44	51	56	61	66	70
LARGE SPACE TWO-WAY AT 45 DEGREE		●		35	44	51	56	61	66	70
SMALL SPACE ONE-WAY AT 60 DEGREE		●		36	45	51	56	61	66	70
SMALL SPACE ONE-WAY AT 45 DEGREE		●		36	45	51	56	61	66	70
SMALL SPACE TWO-WAY WITH ISLAND AT 90 DEGREE		●		37	46	52	57	62	67	71
SMALL SPACE TWO-WAY WITH ISLAND AT 60 DEGREE		●		37	46	52	57	62	67	71
SMALL SPACE TWO-WAY WITH ISLAND AT 45 DEGREE		●		38	47	52	57	62	67	71
SMALL SPACE TWO-WAY AT 90 DEGREE		●		38	47	52	57	62	67	71
SMALL SPACE TWO-WAY AT 60 DEGREE		●		39	48	53	58	63	68	71
SMALL SPACE TWO-WAY AT 45 DEGREE		●		39	48	53	58	63	68	71

VEHICLE TURNING RADIUS	VIEW	PLAN	FRONT	SIDE	SCALE	240	360	480	600	720	1200
MID-SIZE CAR		●				72	79	83	86	88	89
FULL-SIZE CAR OR TRUCK		●				72	79	83	86	88	89
VAN		●				73	79	83	86	88	89
BUS		●				74	80	83	86	88	89
WD-40 FIXED TRUCK		●				75	80	83	86	88	89
WD-55 SEMI 45' RADIUS MINIMUM		●				76	81	84	86	88	89
WD-55 SEMI 60' RADIUS		●				77	81	84	87	88	89
WD-55 SEMI 75' RADIUS		●				78	82	84	87	88	89

VEHICLES	VIEW	PLAN	FRONT	SIDE	BACK	SCALE	48	64	96	120	128	192	240	360	480
COMPACT CAR		●	●	●	●		90	98	105	108	110	112	113	114	114
COMPACT - SPORTS CAR		●	●	●	●		90	98	105	108	110	112	113	114	114
MID-SIZE CAR		●	●	●	●		91	99	105	108	110	112	113	114	114
FULL-SIZE CAR		●	●	●	●		91	99	105	108	110	112	113	114	114
MINI-VAN		●	●	●	●		92	100	105	108	110	112	113	114	114
COMPACT TRUCK		●	●	●	●		92	100	106	108	110	112	113	114	114
STANDARD TRUCK		●	●	●	●		93	101	106	108	110	112	113	114	114
MEDIUM TRUCK		●	●	●	●		94	102	106	109	111	112	113	114	114
SEMI-TRUCK		●	●	●	●		95	103	107	109	111	112	113	114	114
SCHOOL BUS		●	●	●	●		97	104	107	109	111	112	113	114	114

PAVING - BRICK	VIEW	PLAN	FRONT	SIDE	SCALE	24	32	48	64	96
RUNNNING BOND		●				115	123	131	135	139
STACKED BOND		●				115	123	131	135	139
HERRINGBONE		●				116	124	131	135	139
BASKETWEAVE VERSION 1		●				116	124	131	135	139
BASKETWEAVE VERSION 2		●				117	125	132	136	139
BASKETWEAVE VERSION 3		●				117	125	132	136	139
BASKETWEAVE VERSION 4		●				118	126	132	136	140

PAVING - PRECAST CONCRETE	VIEW	PLAN	FRONT	SIDE	SCALE	24	32	48	64	96
PAVESTONE UNI-STONE		●				118	126	132	136	140
8" HEXAGONAL		●				119	127	133	137	140
8" SQUARE		●				119	127	133	137	140
12" SQUARE		●				120	128	133	137	140
GRASSCRETE		●				120	128	133	137	140

PAVING STONE	VIEW	PLAN	FRONT	SIDE	SCALE	24	32	48	64	96
4" x 4" RADIAL		●				121	129	134	138	141
4" x 4" FISHSCALE		●				121	129	134	138	141
UNCOARSED RANDOM		●				122	130	134	138	141
COARSED RANDOM		●				122	130	134	138	141

WOOD DECK	VIEW	PLAN	FRONT	SIDE	SCALE	24	32	48	64	96
6" BOARDS		●				142	143	144	144	144
6" AND 2" BOARDS		●				142	143	144	144	144

STEPS	VIEW	PLAN	FRONT	SIDE	SCALE	24	32	48	64	96	120	128	192
7:11				●		145	146	146	147	147	148	148	149
6:14				●		145	146	146	147	147	148	148	149
5:16				●		145	146	146	147	147	148	148	149
4:18				●		145	146	146	147	147	148	148	149
3:20				●		145	146	146	147	147	148	148	149

TREE GRATES	VIEW	PLAN	FRONT	SIDE	SCALE	24	32	48	64	96
ROUND - 72" RADIUS		●				150	151	151	151	151
ROUND - 60" RADIUS W/LIGHT RECESS		●				150	151	151	151	151
ROUND - 42" RADIUS		●				150	151	151	151	151
SQUARE - 72"		●				150	151	151	151	151
SQUARE 72" WITH LIGHT RECESS		●				150	151	151	151	151
SQUARE - 60"		●				150	151	151	151	151
SQAURE - 48"		●				150	151	151	151	151

BOLLARDS	VIEW	PLAN	FRONT	SIDE	SCALE	16	24	32	48	64	96
LIGHT 8" SQUARE		●	●			152	152	153	153	153	153
LIGHT 8" ROUND		●	●			152	152	153	153	153	153
STANDARD 12" ROUND		●	●			152	152	153	153	153	153
STANDARD 24" ROUND		●	●			152	152	153	153	153	153
STANDARD 10" SQUARE		●	●			152	152	153	153	153	153

DRINKING FOUNTAINS	VIEW	PLAN	FRONT	SIDE	SCALE	24	32	48	64	96
METAL VASE		●	●	●		154	155	155	155	156
METAL CYLINDER		●	●	●		154	155	155	155	156
STONE CYLINDER		●	●	●		154	155	155	155	156
METAL		●	●	●		154	155	155	155	156
STONE		●	●	●		154	155	155	155	156

PLANTERS	VIEW	PLAN	FRONT	SIDE	SCALE	24	32	48	64	96
OVAL		●	●			157	163	164	165	166
SAUCERS		●				157	163	164	165	166
VASE		●				157	163	164	165	166
CYLINDER		●				157	163	164	165	166

SEATING	VIEW	PLAN	FRONT	SIDE	SCALE	16	24	32	48	64	96
TRADITIONAL BENCH		●	●	●		167	168	169	169	169	169
CONTEMPORAY BENCH		●	●	●		167	168	169	169	169	169
CONTEMPORAY PLANK BENCH		●	●	●		167	168	169	169	169	169

TRAFFIC SIGNALS	VIEW	PLAN	FRONT	SIDE	SCALE	48	64	96	120	128	192	240	360	480
STANDARD UPRIGHT		●	●	●		170	173	174	175	175	176	176	176	176
STANDARD CANTILEVER		●	●	●		171	173	174	175	175	176	176	176	176
DESIGNER UPRIGHT		●	●	●		172	173	174	175	175	176	176	176	176
DESIGNER CANTILEVER		●	●	●		172	173	174	175	175	176	176	176	176

LIGHT POLES	VIEW	PLAN	FRONT	SIDE	SCALE	96	120	128	192	240	360	480
DECORATIVE		●	●			176	177	178	179	179	180	180
SINGLE POD 20' HEIGHT		●	●			176	177	178	179	179	180	180
FOUR POD 20' HEIGHT		●	●			176	177	178	179	179	180	180
FOUR POD 30' HEIGHT		●	●			176	177	178	179	179	180	180
FOUR POD 40' HEIGHT		●	●			176	177	178	179	179	180	180
FOUR POD 50' HEIGHT		●	●			176	177	178	179	179	180	180
COBRA 35' HEIGHT		●	●			176	177	178	179	179	180	180

FLAGPOLES	VIEW	PLAN	FRONT	SIDE	SCALE	48	64	96	120	128	192	240	360	480
20' HEIGHT		●	●			181	182	183	184	185	186	186	187	187
30' HEIGHT		●	●			181	182	183	184	185	186	186	187	187
40' HEIGHT		●	●				182	183	184	185	186	186	187	187
50' HEIGHT		●	●					183	184	185	186	186	187	187
60' HEIGHT		●	●					183	184	185	186	186	187	187

FENCING	VIEW	PLAN	FRONT	SIDE	SCALE	24	32	48	64	96
6' CHAINLINK		●	●			188	193	198	201	204
6' CHAINLINK WITH BARBES		●	●			188	193	198	201	204
6' ORNAMENTAL IRON VERSION 1		●	●			189	194	198	201	204
6' ORNAMENTAL IRON VERSION 2		●	●			189	194	199	202	205
4' ORNAMENTAL IRON		●	●			190	195	199	202	205
6' WOOD - BOARD ON BOARD		●	●			190	195	199	202	205
6' WOOD - SOLID BOARD		●	●			191	196	200	203	206
6' WOOD - SHADOW BOX		●	●			191	196	200	203	206
4' WOOD - PICKET		●	●			192	197	200	203	206
4' WOOD - SPLIT RAIL		●	●			192	197			

RETAINING WALLS	VIEW	PLAN	FRONT	SIDE	SCALE	24	32	48	64	96
BRICK - RUNNING BOND		●				207	209	211	213	215
BRICK - COMMON BOND		●				207	209	211	213	215
BRICK - GARDEN		●				207	209	211	213	215
BRICK - ENGLISH		●				207	209	211	213	215
BRICK - STACK		●				208	210	212	214	216
BRICK - FLEMISH		●				208	210	212	214	216
STONE		●				208	210	212	214	216
CMU		●				208	210	212	214	216

ARBORS	VIEW	PLAN	FRONT	SIDE	SCALE	24	32	48	64	96
12' x 8'		●				217	219	220	221	221
OVER 6' WALK		●				218	219	220	221	221

29

0 [▭] 20   LARGE SPACE ONE-WAY WITH ISLAND AT 60 DEGREE AT 1" = 20'-0"

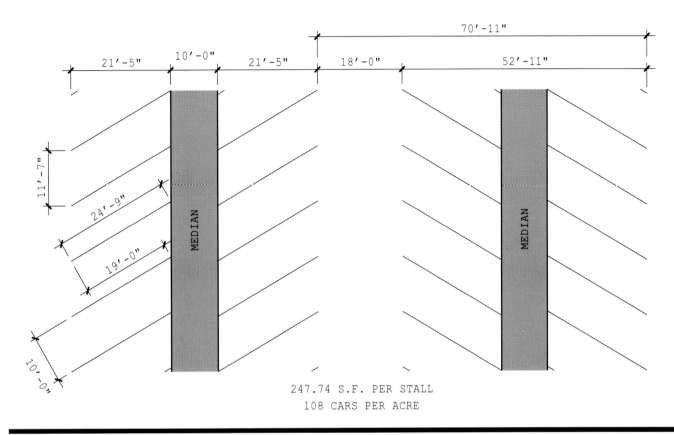

247.74 S.F. PER STALL
108 CARS PER ACRE

0 [▭] 20   LARGE SPACE ONE-WAY WITH ISLAND AT 45 DEGREE AT 1" = 20'-0"

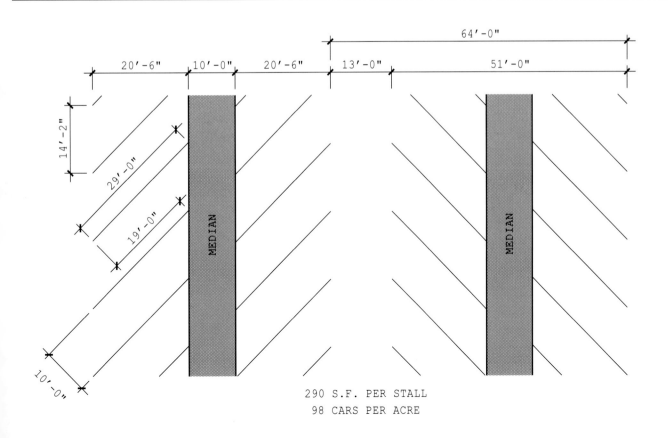

290 S.F. PER STALL
98 CARS PER ACRE

LARGE SPACE ONE-WAY AT 60 DEGREE AT 1" = 20'-0"   0 ▭ 20

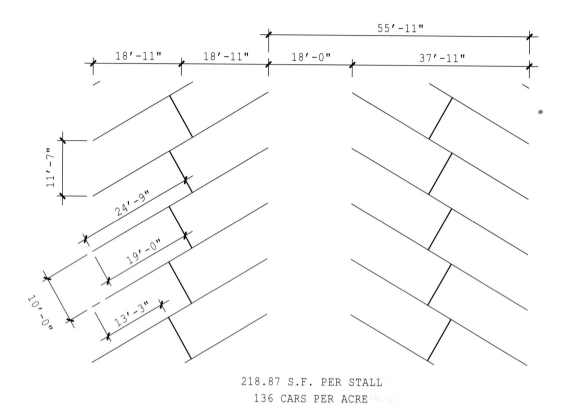

218.87 S.F. PER STALL
136 CARS PER ACRE

LARGE SPACE ONE-WAY AT 45 DEGREE AT 1" = 20'-0"   0 ▭ 20

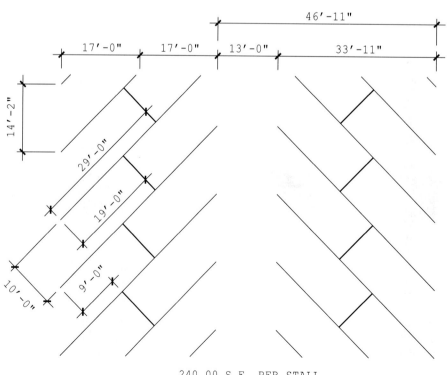

240.00 S.F. PER STALL
132 CARS PER ACRE

32

0 ▭ 20   LARGE SPACE TWO-WAY WITH ISLAND AT 90 DEGREE AT 1" = 20'-0"

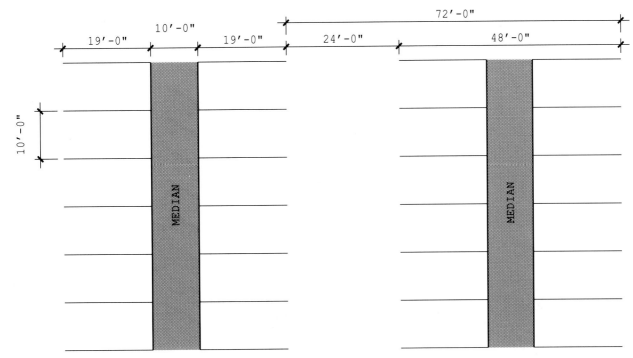

190.00 S.F. PER STALL
122 CARS PER ACRE

0 ▭ 20   LARGE SPACE TWO-WAY WITH ISLAND AT 60 DEGREE AT 1" = 20'-0"

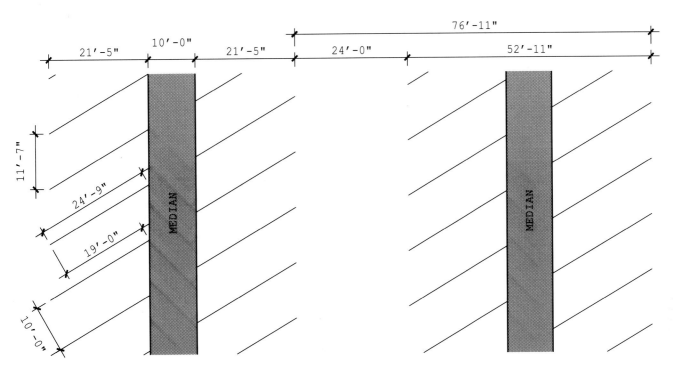

247.74 S.F. PER STALL
100 CARS PER ACRE

33

PARKING SPACE

LARGE SPACE TWO-WAY WITH ISLAND AT 45 DEGREE AT 1" = 20'-0"   0 ▭ 20

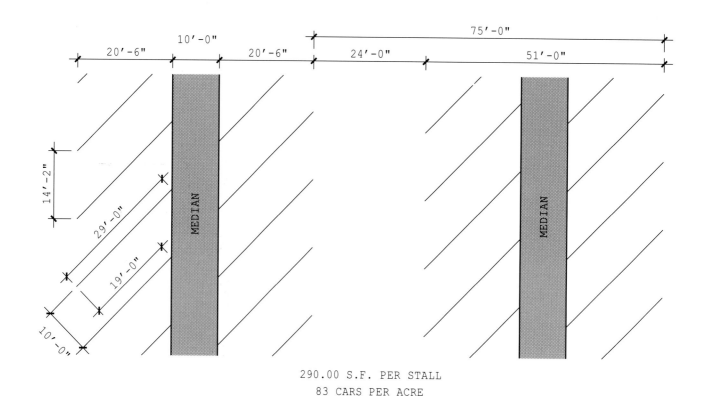

290.00 S.F. PER STALL
83 CARS PER ACRE

LARGE SPACE TWO-WAY AT 90 DEGREE AT 1" = 20'-0"   0 ▭ 20

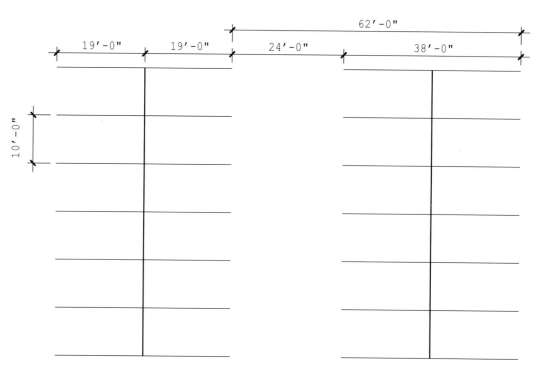

190.00 S.F. PER STALL
140 CARS PER ACRE

0 [========] 20   LARGE SPACE TWO-WAY AT 60 DEGREE AT 1" = 20'-0"

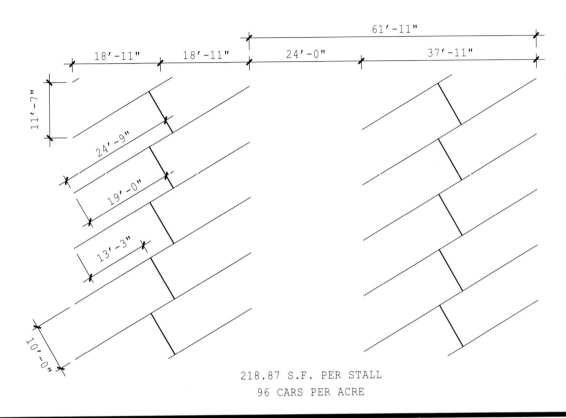

218.87 S.F. PER STALL
96 CARS PER ACRE

0 [========] 20   LARGE SPACE TWO-WAY AT 45 DEGREE AT 1" = 20'-0"

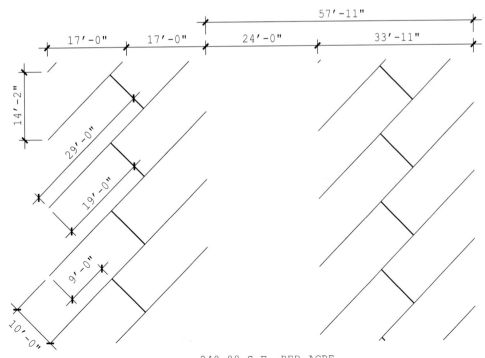

240.00 S.F. PER ACRE
106 CARS PER ACRE

PARKING SPACE

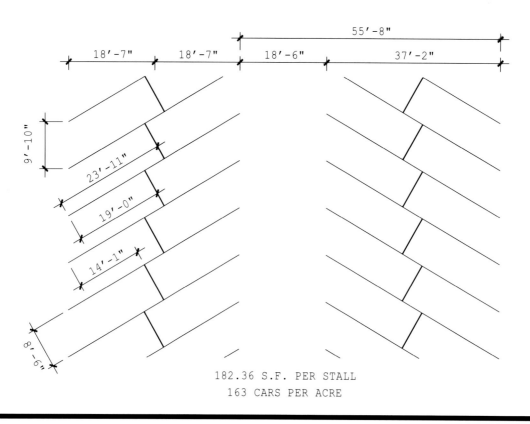

182.36 S.F. PER STALL
163 CARS PER ACRE

36

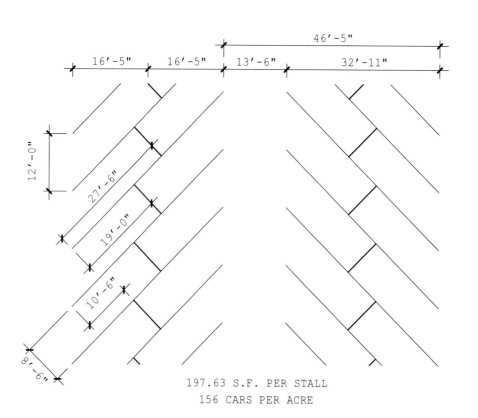

197.63 S.F. PER STALL
156 CARS PER ACRE

0 ☐ 20   SMALL SPACE TWO-WAY WITH ISLAND AT 90 DEGREE AT 1" = 20'-0"

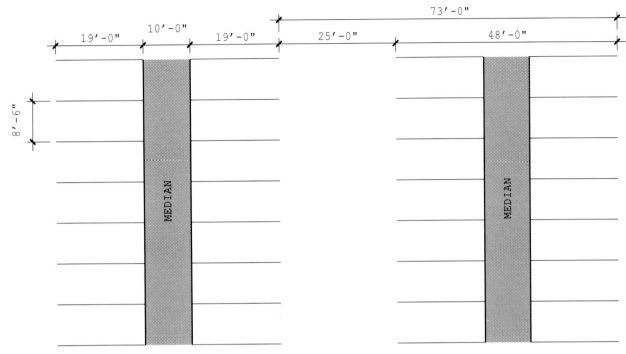

161.50 S.F. PER SPACE
144 CARS PER ACRE

0 ☐ 20   SMALL SPACE TWO-WAY WITH ISLAND AT 60 DEGREE AT 1" = 20'-0"

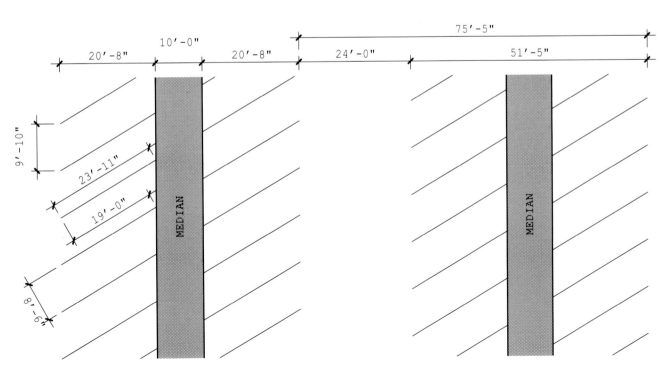

203.21 S.F. PER STALL
120 CARS PER ACRE

PARKING SPACE

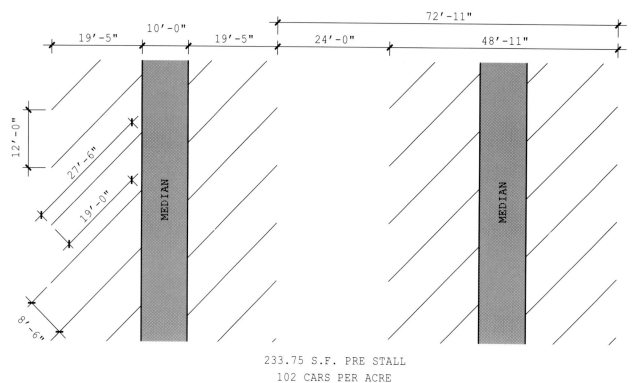

233.75 S.F. PRE STALL
102 CARS PER ACRE

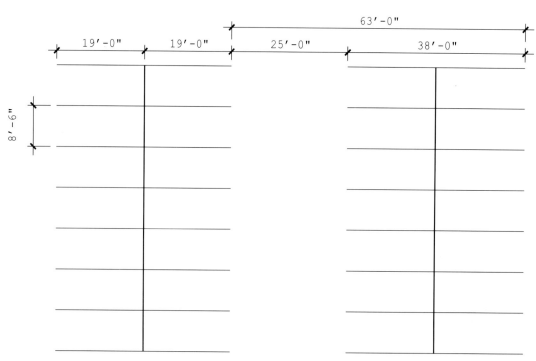

161.50 S.F. PER STALL
164 CARS PER ACRE

0 ▭ 20   SMALL SPACE TWO-WAY AT 60 DEGREE AT 1" = 20'-0"

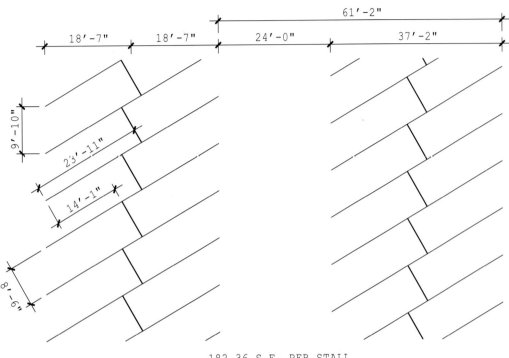

182.36 S.F. PER STALL
146 CARS PER ACRE

0 ▭ 20   SMALL SPACE TWO-WAY AT 45 DEGREE AT 1" = 20'-0"

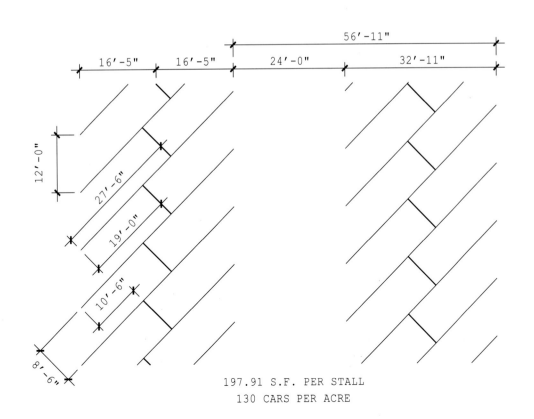

197.91 S.F. PER STALL
130 CARS PER ACRE

39

LARGE SPACE ONE-WAY WITH ISLAND AT 60 DEGREE AT 1" = 30'-0"   0 ▭ 30

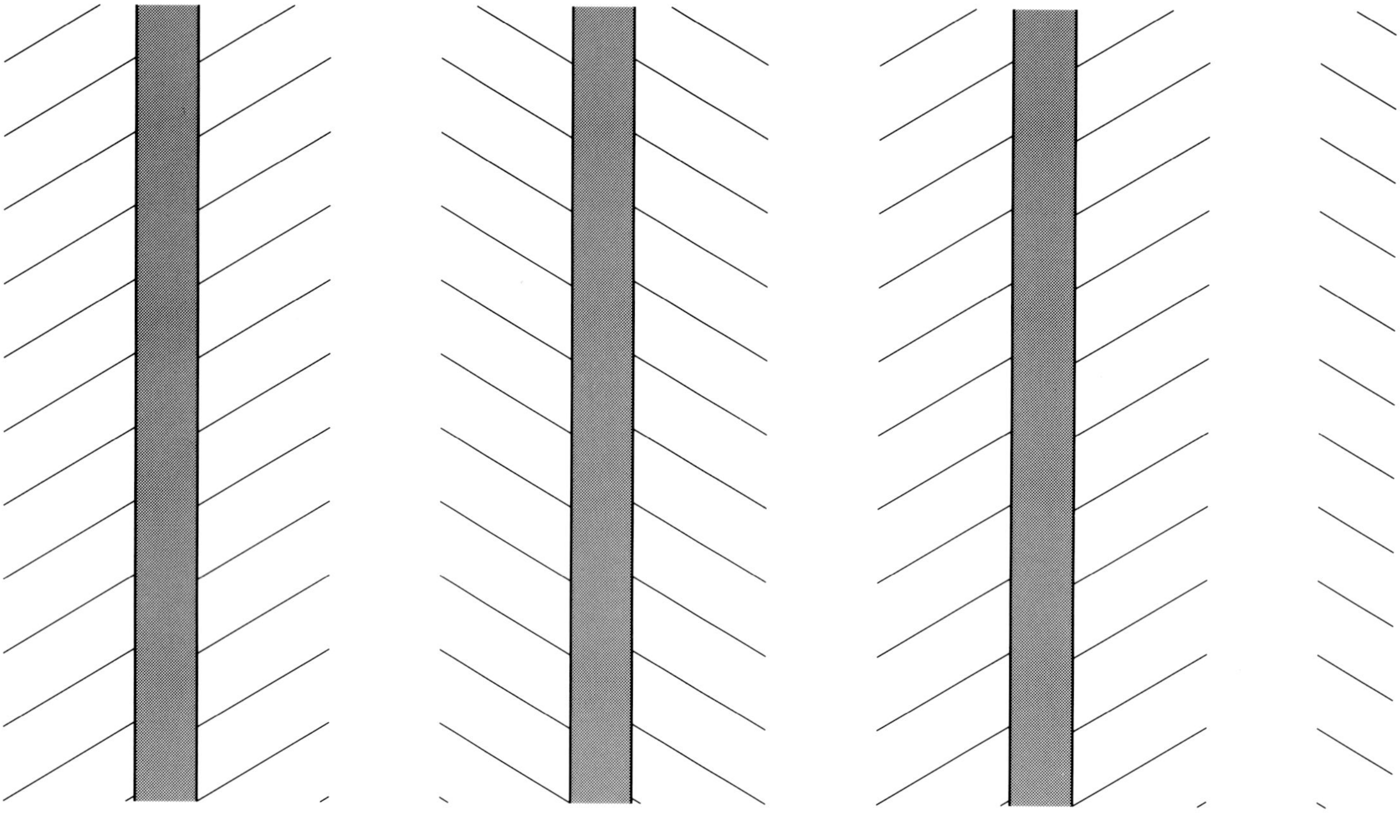

LARGE SPACE ONE-WAY WITH ISLAND AT 45 DEGREE AT 1" = 30'-0"   0 ▭ 30

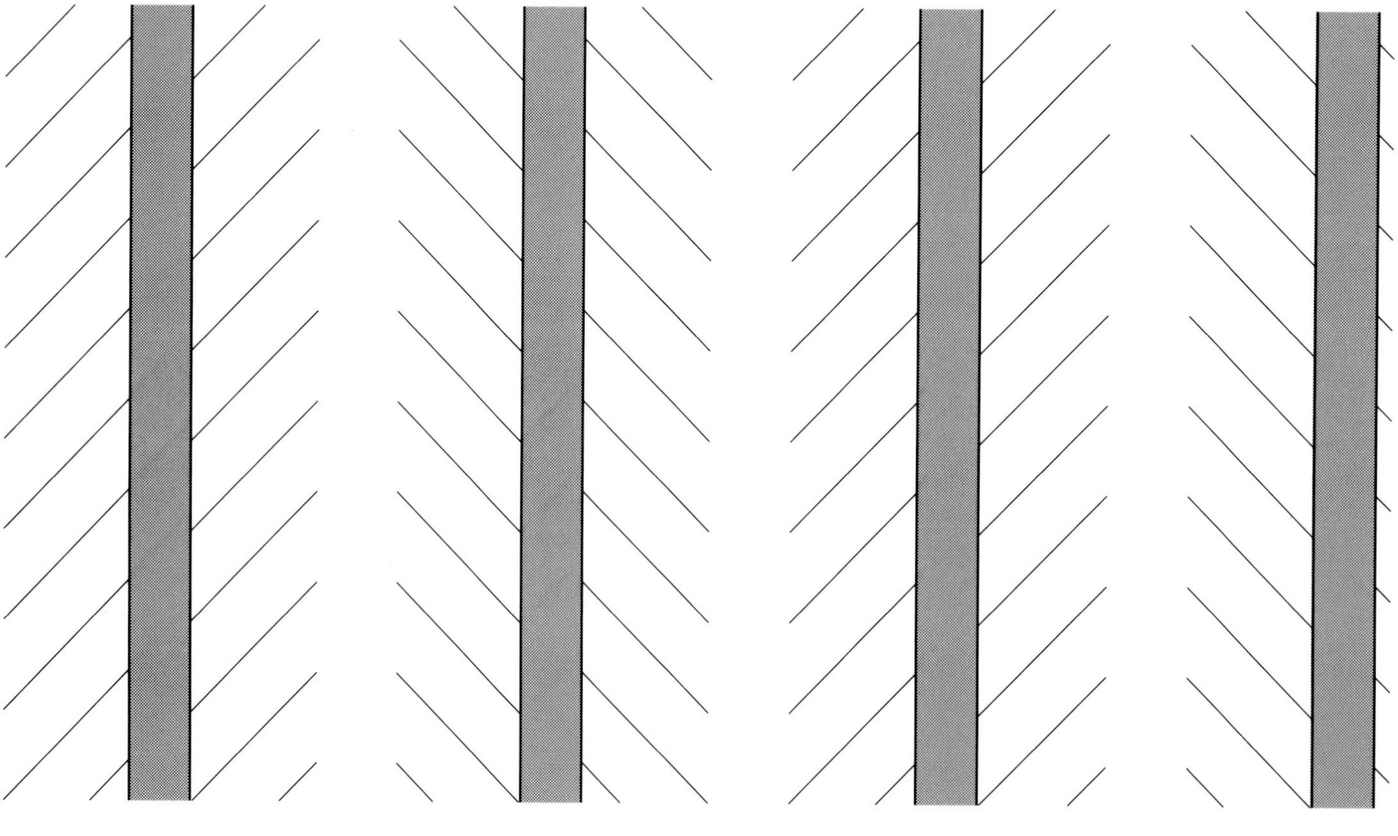

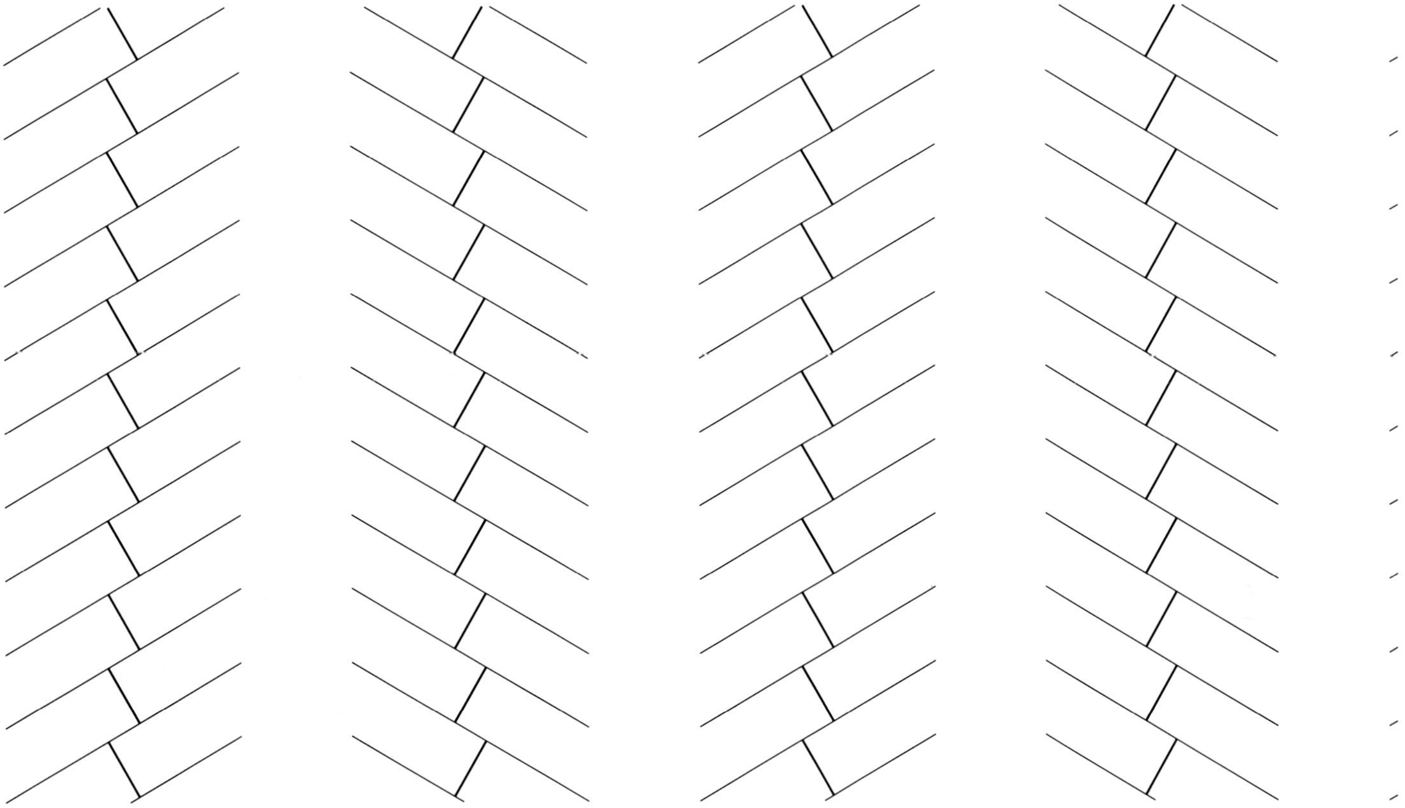

0 [========] 30   LARGE SPACE ONE-WAY AT 60 DEGREE AT 1" = 30'-0"

0 [========] 30   LARGE SPACE ONE-WAY AT 45 DEGREE AT 1" = 30'-0"

PARKING SPACE

LARGE SPACE TWO-WAY WITH ISLAND AT 90 DEGREE AT 1" = 30'-0"   0 [_____] 30

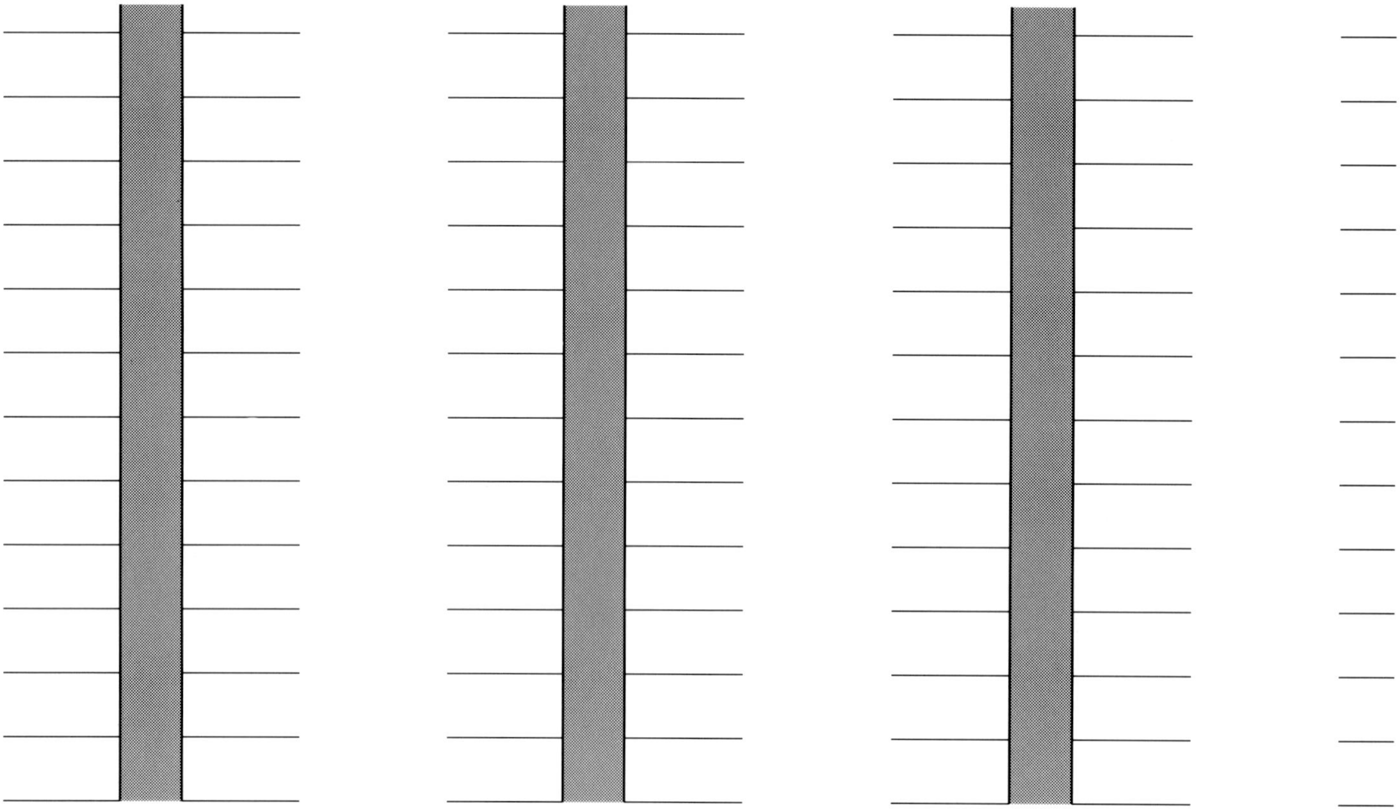

LARGE SPACE TWO-WAY WITH ISLAND AT 60 DEGREE AT 1" = 30'-0"   0 [_____] 30

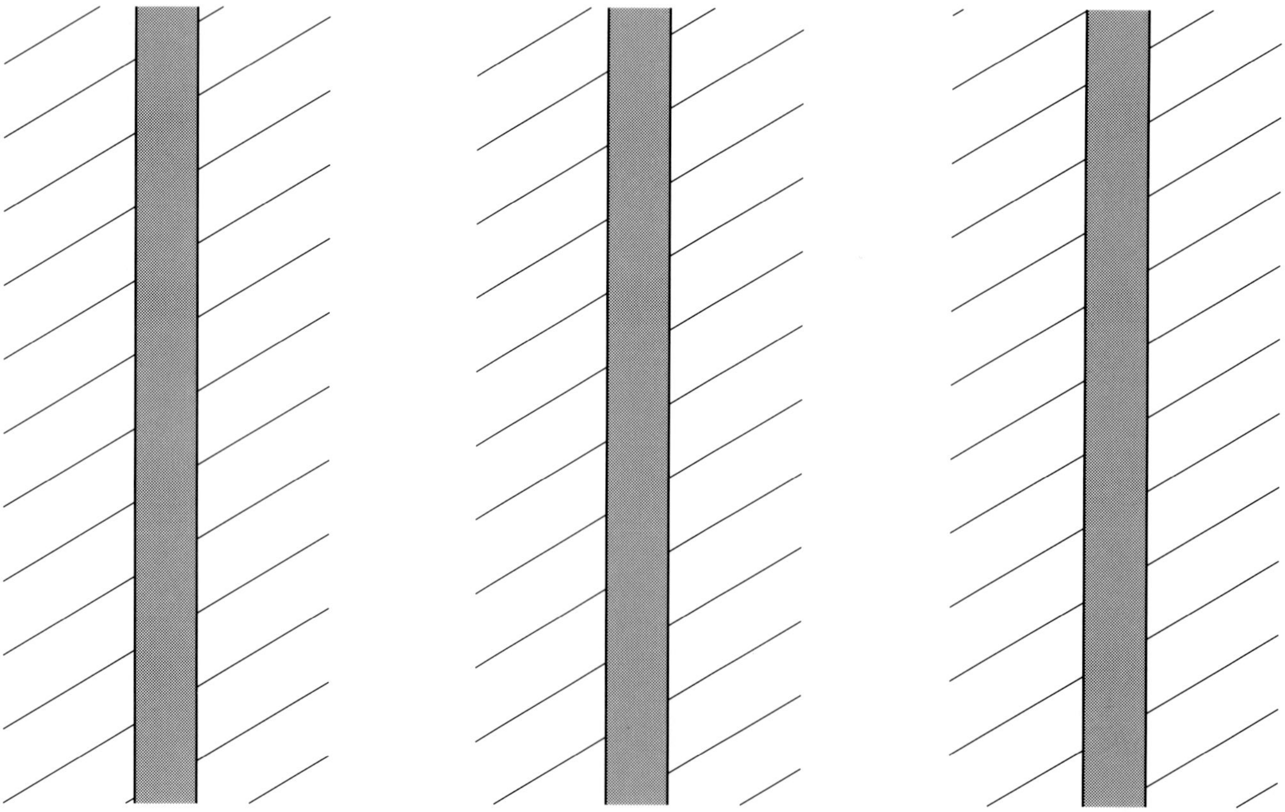

0 [   ] 30   LARGE SPACE TWO-WAY WITH ISLAND AT 45 DEGREE AT 1" = 30'-0"

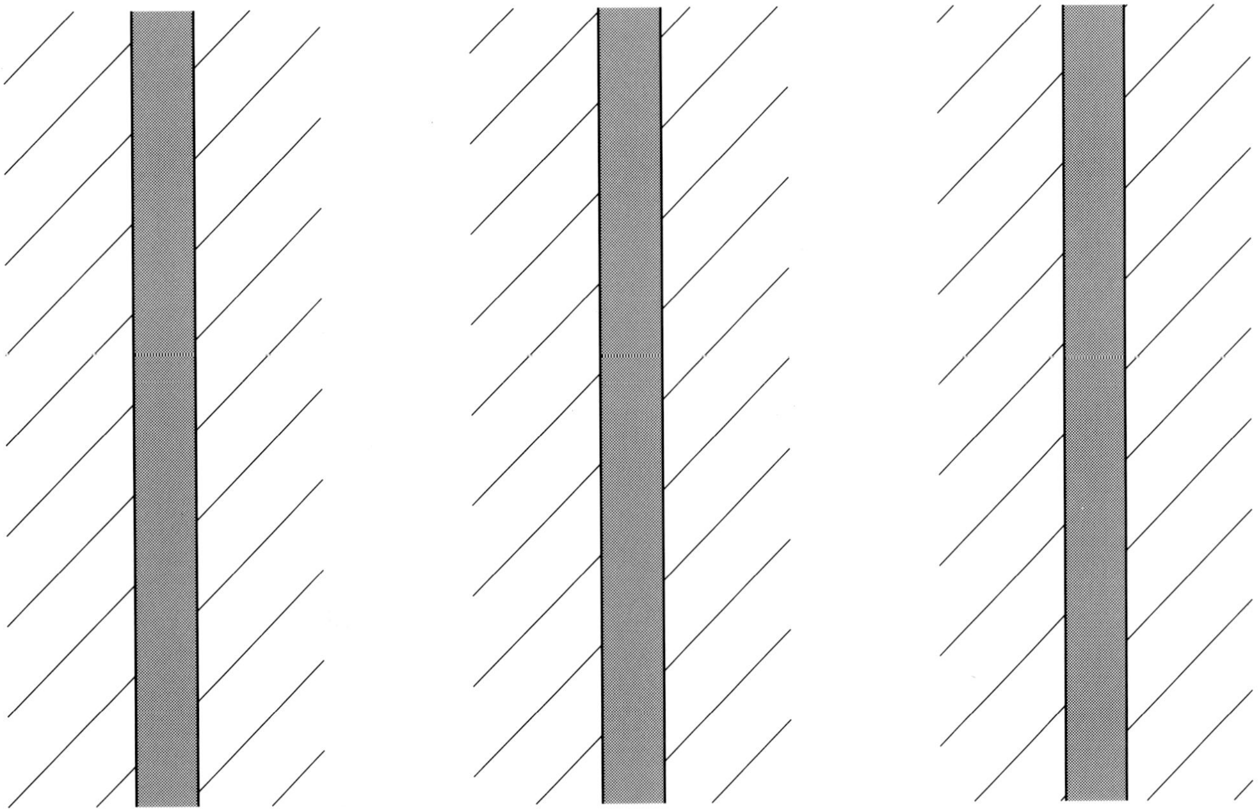

0 [   ] 30   LARGE SPACE TWO-WAY AT 90 DEGREE AT 1" = 30'-0"

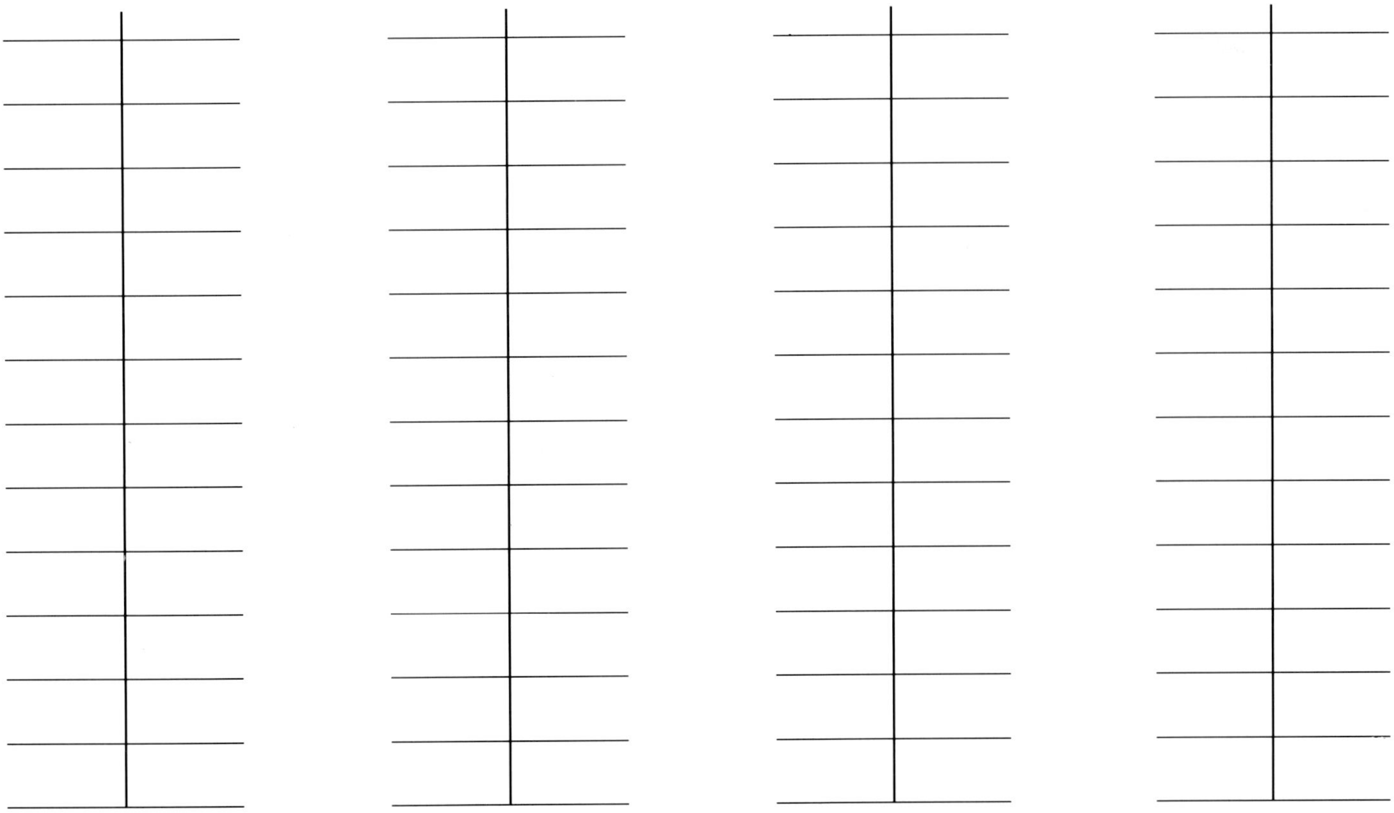

LARGE SPACE TWO-WAY AT 60 DEGREE AT 1" = 30'-0"   0 ▭ 30

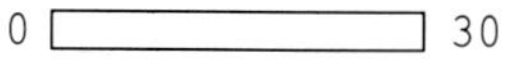

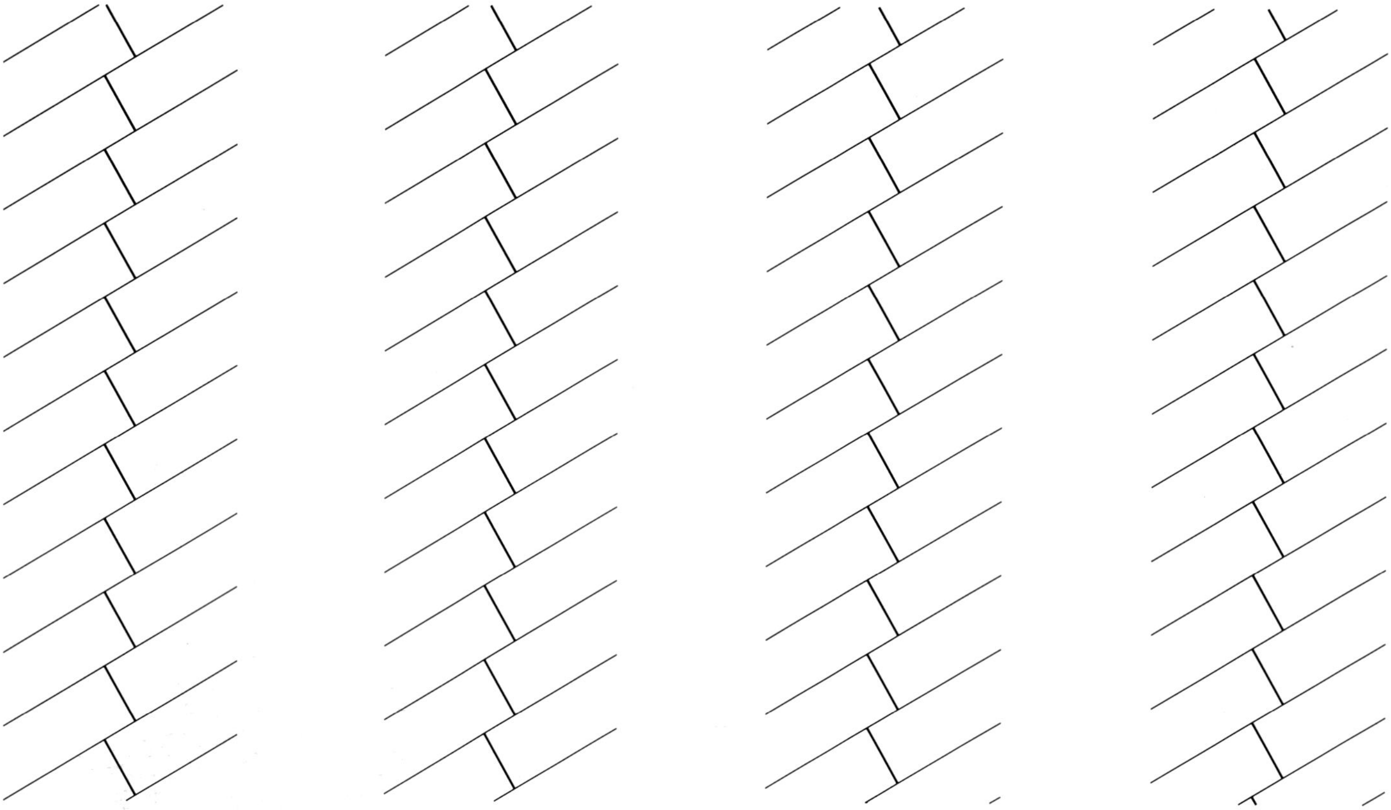

LARGE SPACE TWO-WAY AT 45 DEGREE AT 1" = 30'-0"   0 ▭ 30

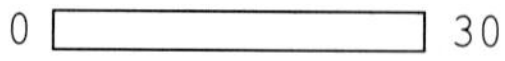

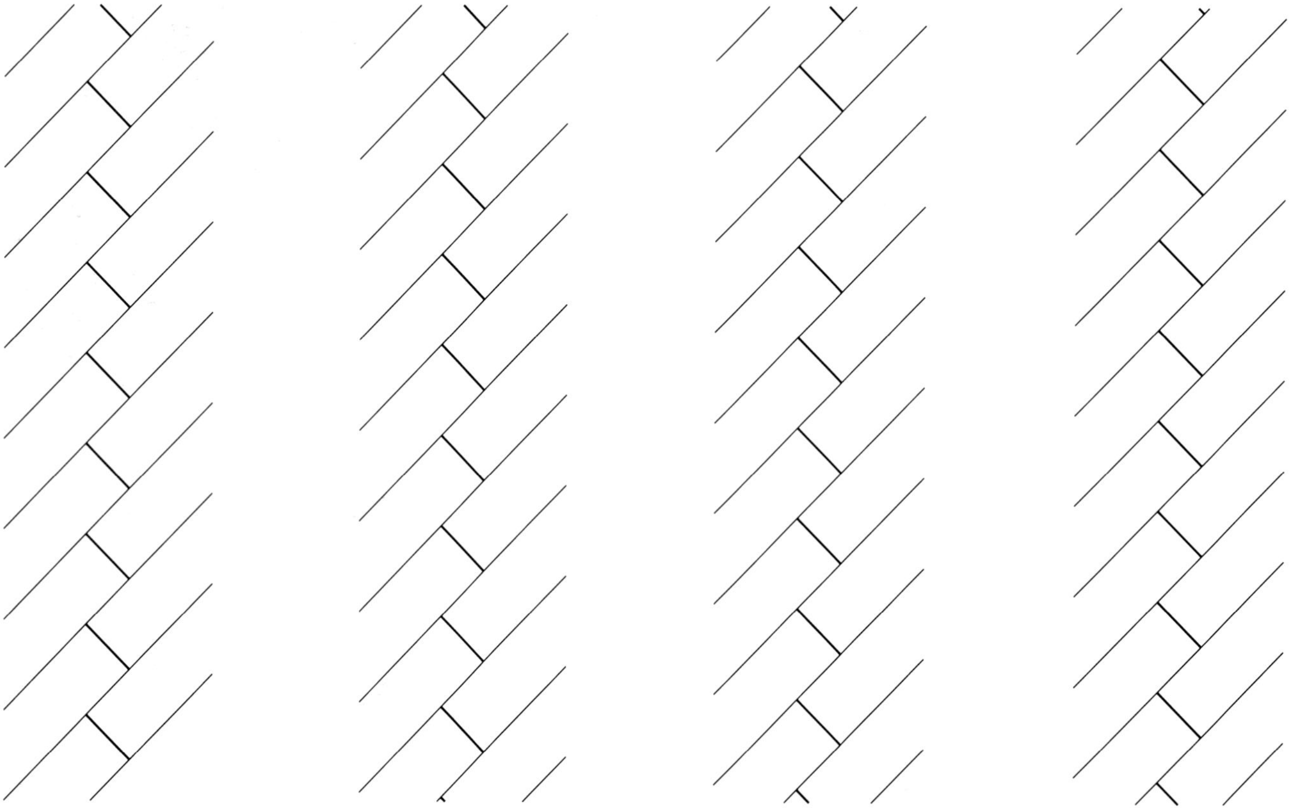

0 [   ] 30   SMALL SPACE ONE-WAY AT 60 DEGREE AT 1" = 30'-0"

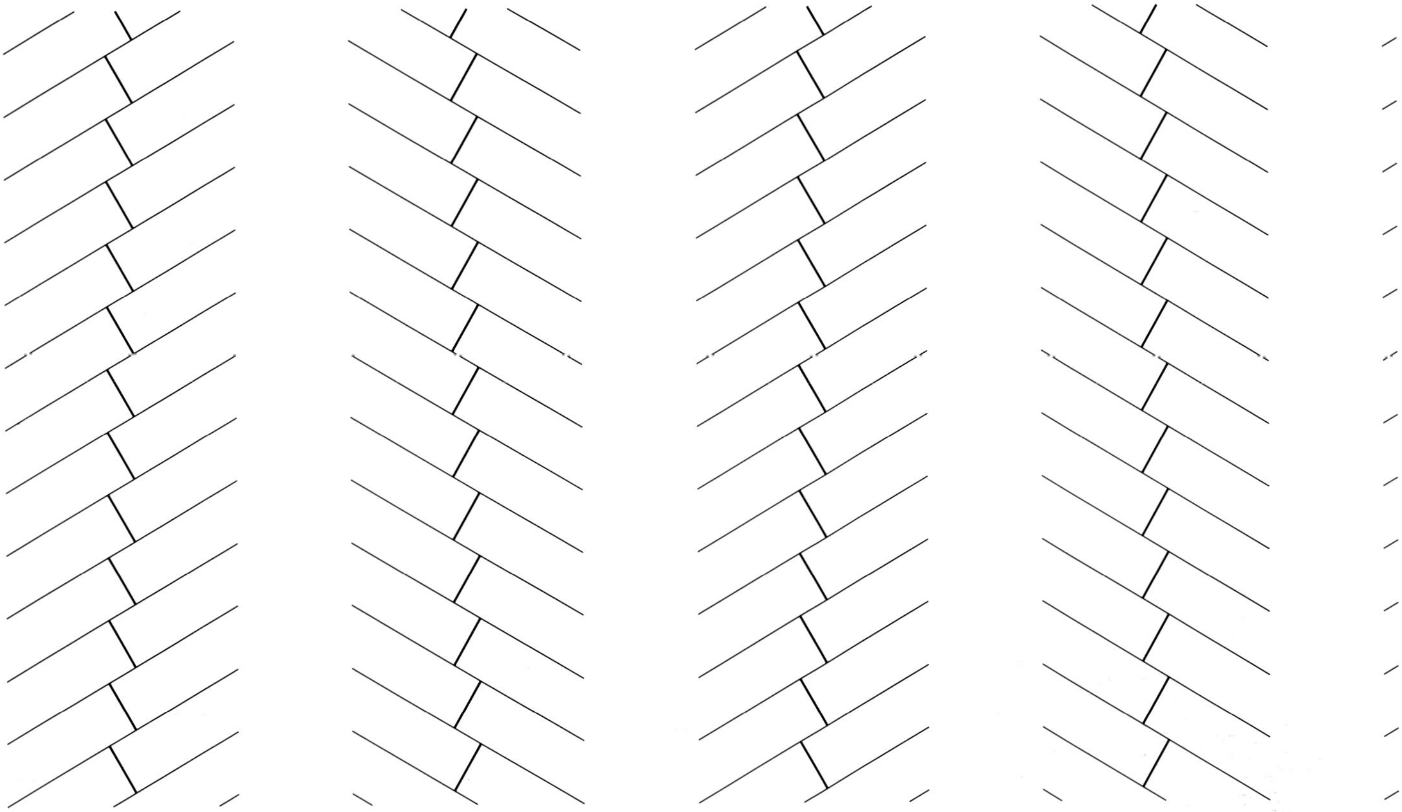

0 [   ] 30   SMALL SPACE ONE-WAY AT 45 DEGREE AT 1" = 30'-0"

45

SMALL SPACE TWO-WAY WITH ISLAND AT 90 DEGREE AT 1" = 30'-0"   0 ⬜ 30

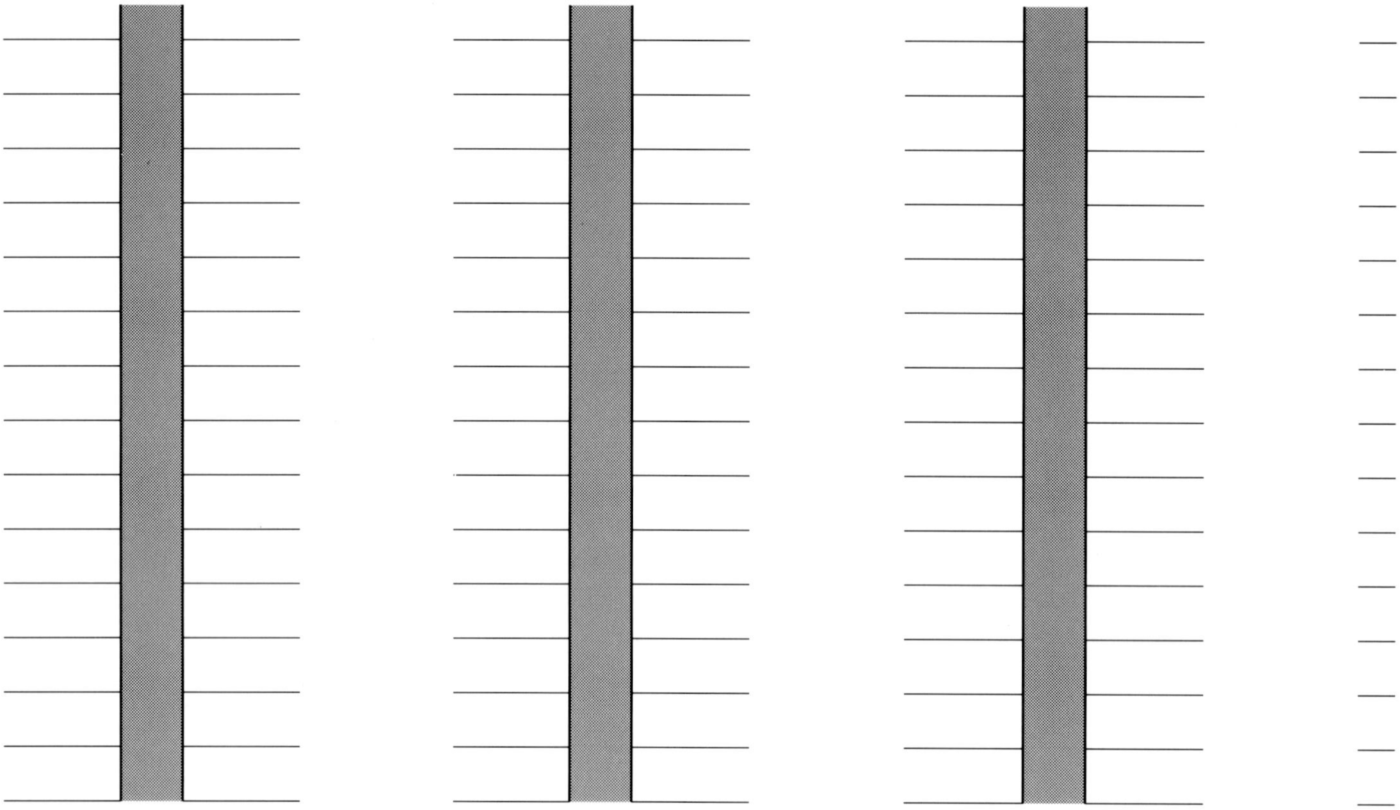

SMALL SPACE TWO-WAY WITH ISLAND AT 60 DEGREE AT 1" = 30'-0"   0 ⬜ 30

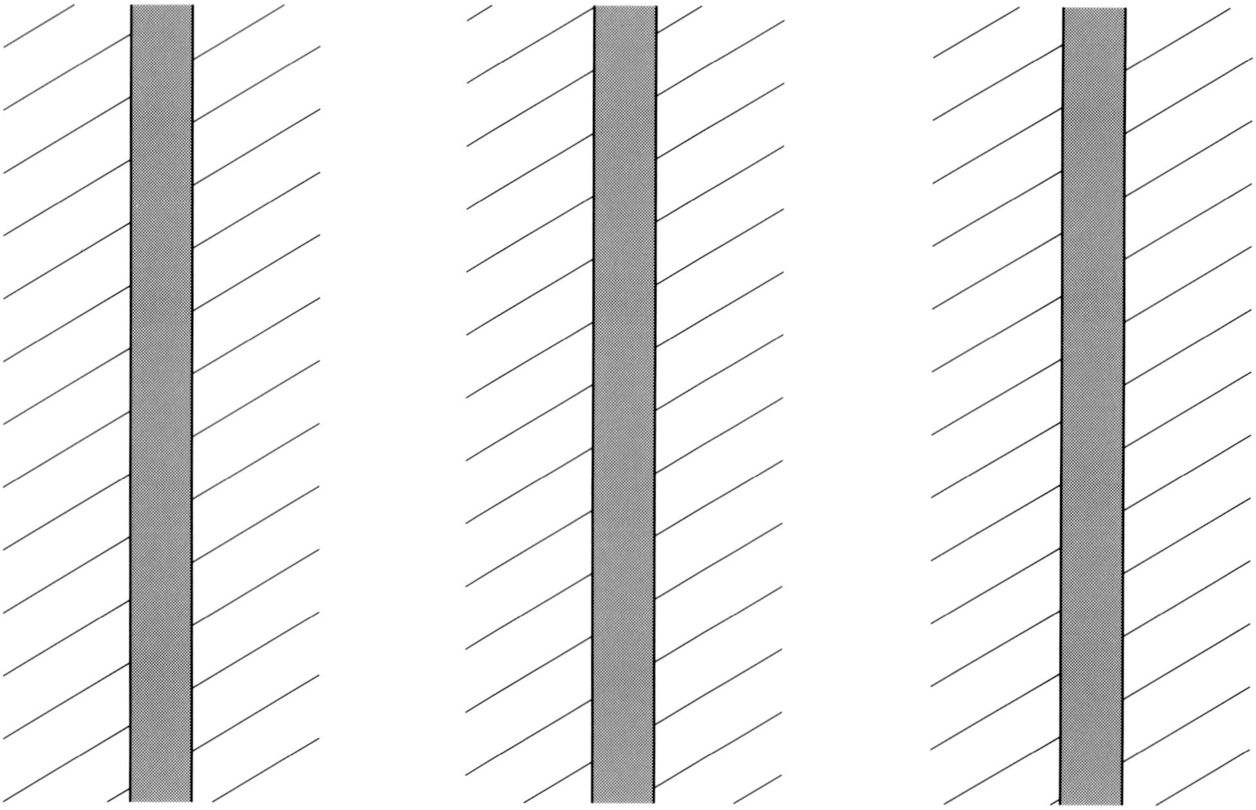

0 ⬛ 30   SMALL SPACE TWO-WAY WITH ISLAND AT 45 DEGREE AT 1" = 30'-0"

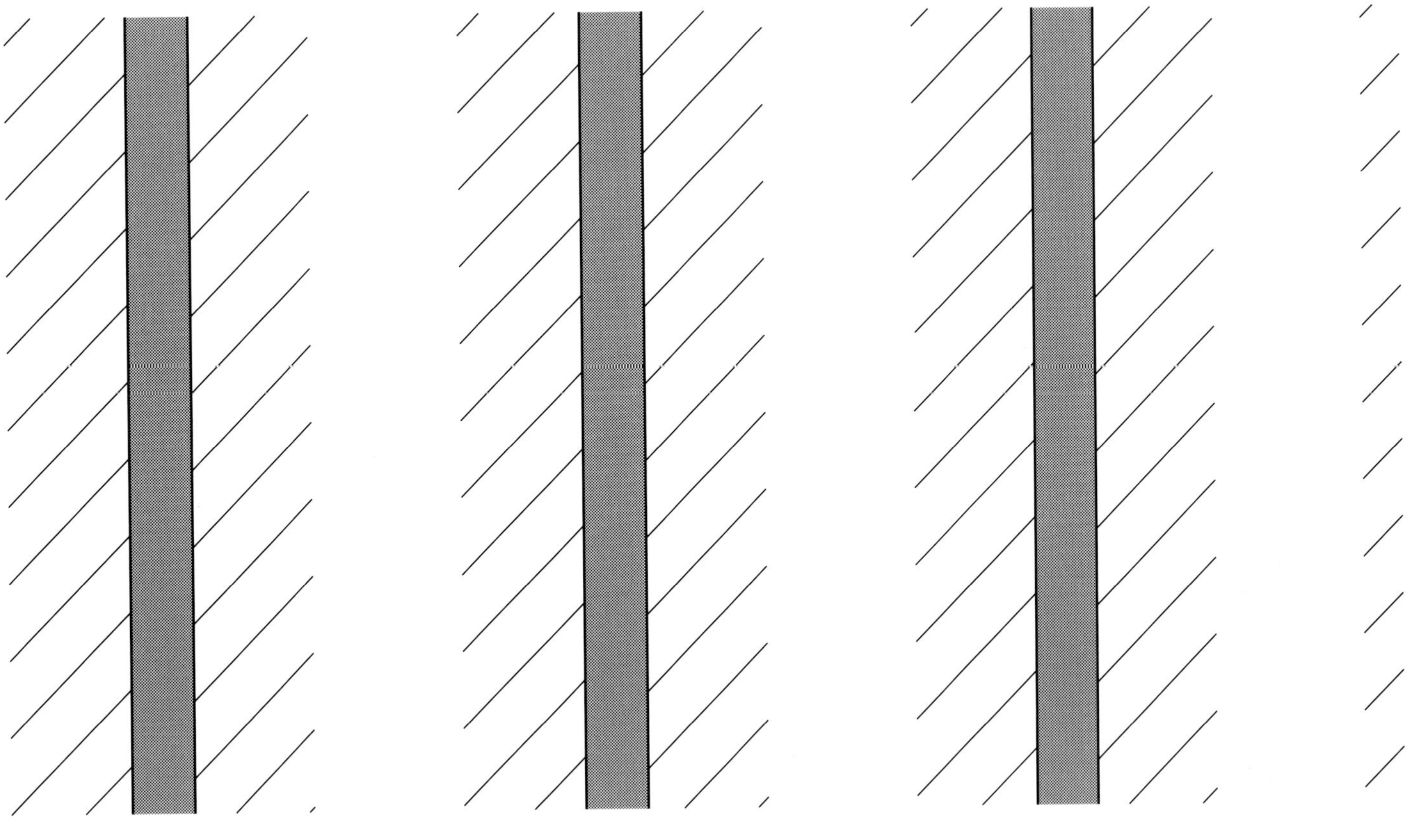

0 ⬛ 30   SMALL SPACE TWO-WAY AT 90 DEGREE AT 1" = 30'-0"

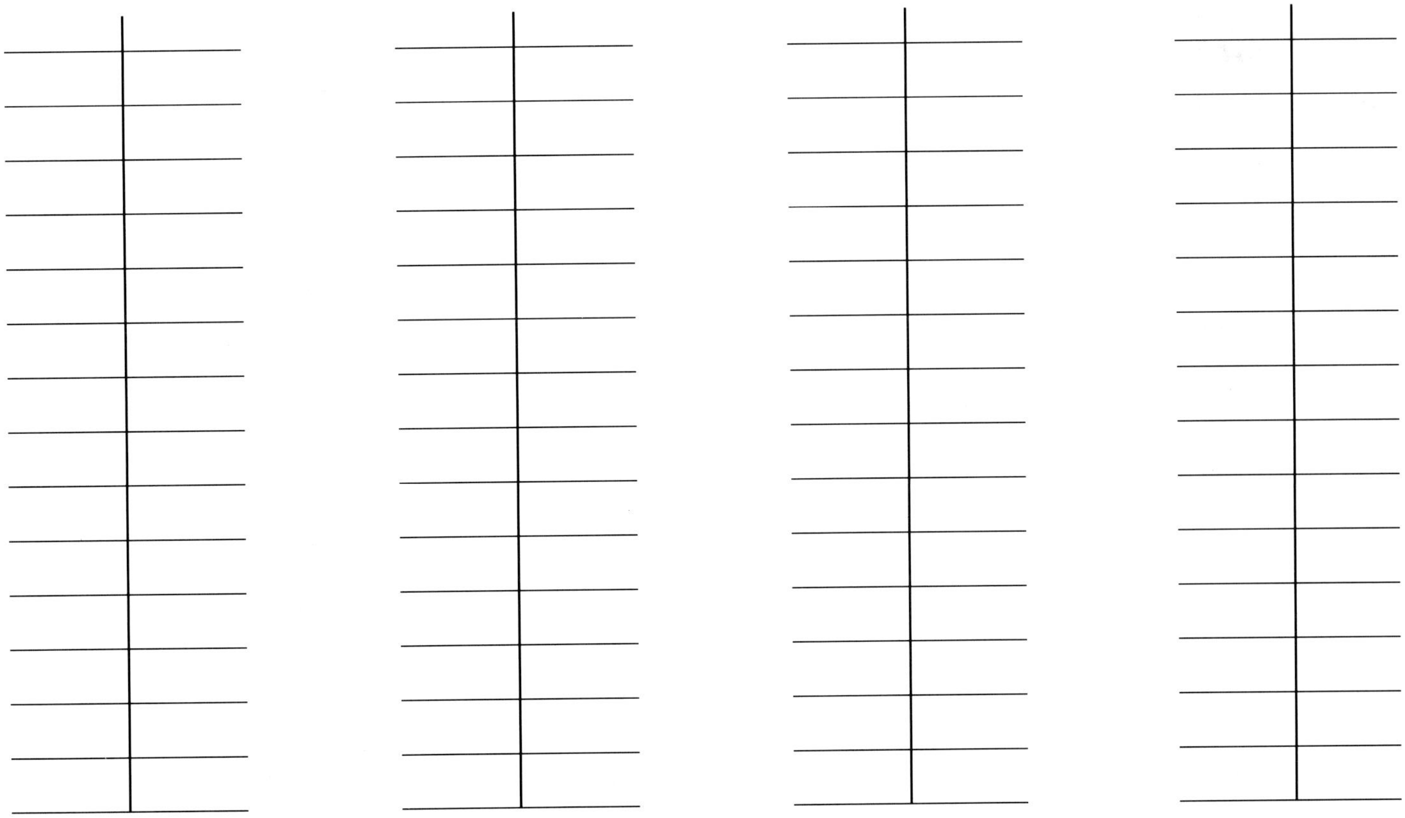

SMALL SPACE TWO-WAY AT 60 DEGREE AT 1" = 30'-0"   0 [   ] 30

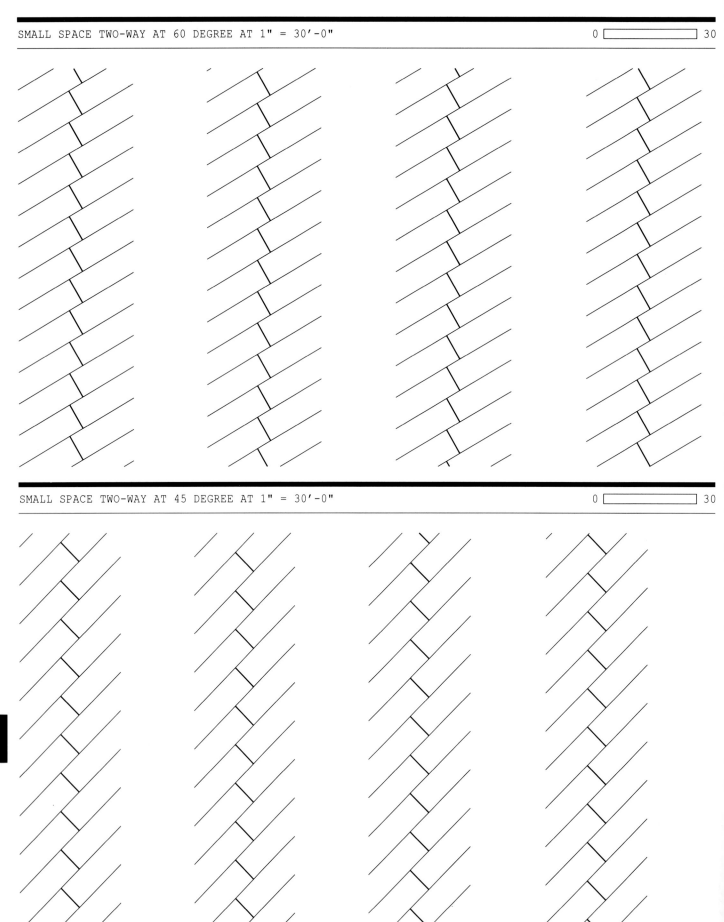

SMALL SPACE TWO-WAY AT 45 DEGREE AT 1" = 30'-0"   0 [   ] 30

48

0 〔▭〕 20   LRG ONE-WAY W/ISL AT 60 DEG AT 1"=40'

0 〔▭〕 20   LRG ONE-WAY W/ISL AT 45 DEG AT 1"=40'

0 〔▭〕 20   LRG SPACE ONE-WAY AT 60 DEG AT 1"=40'

0 〔▭〕 20   LRG SPACE ONE-WAY AT 45 DEG AT 1"=40'

PARKING SPACE

LRG SP TWO-WAY W/ISL AT 90 DEG AT 1"=40' 0 ▭ 20

LRG SP TWO-WAY W/ISL AT 60 DEG AT 1"=40' ▭ 20

LRG SP TWO-WAY W/ISL AT 45 DEG AT 1"=40' 0 ▭ 20

LRG SP TWO-WAY AT 90 DEG AT 1"=40' 0 ▭ 20

0 ▭ 20   LARGE SP TWO-WAY AT 60 DEG AT 1"=40'

0 ▭ 20   LARGE SP TWO-WAY AT 45 DEG AT 1"=40'

0 ▭ 20   SMALL SP ONE-WAY AT 60 DEG AT 1"=40'

0 ▭ 20   SMALL SP ONE-WAY AT 45 DEG AT 1"=40'

PARKING SPACE

SML SP TWO-WAY W/ISL AT 90 DEG AT 1"=40'   0 [＿＿＿] 20

SML SP TWO-WAY W/ISL AT 60 DEG AT 1"=40'   0 [＿＿＿] 20

SML SP TWO-WAY W/ISL AT 45 DEG AT 1"=40'   0 [＿＿＿] 20

SML SP TWO-WAY AT 90 DEG AT 1"=40'   0 [＿＿＿] 20

52

0 [======] 20   SML SP TWO-WAY AT 60 DEG AT 1"=40'

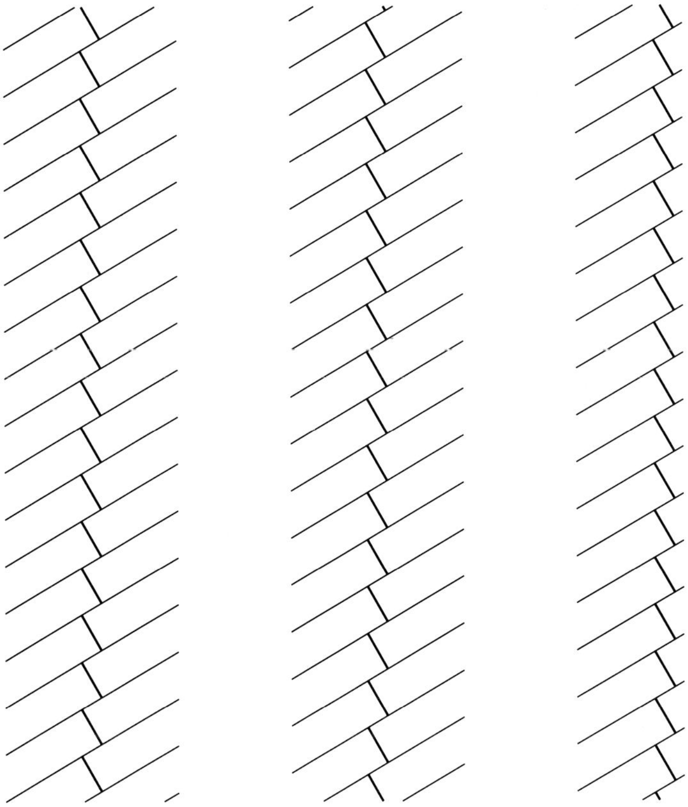

0 [======] 20   SML SP TWO-WAY AT 45 DEG AT 1"=40'

PARKING SPACE

LRG SP ONE-WAY W/ISL AT 60 DEG AT 1"=50'   0 ☐ 25

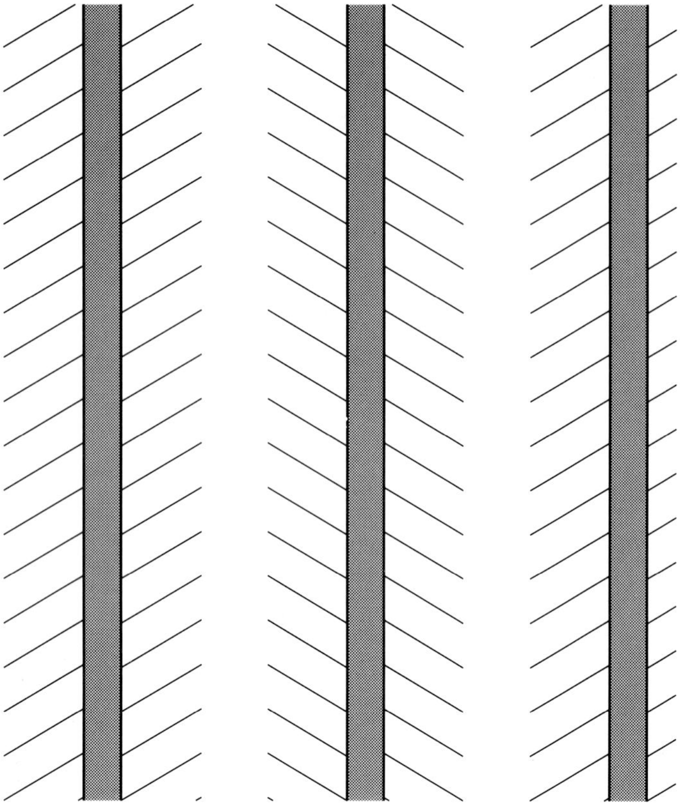

LRG SP ONE-WAY W/ISL AT 45 DEG AT 1"=50'   0 ☐ 25

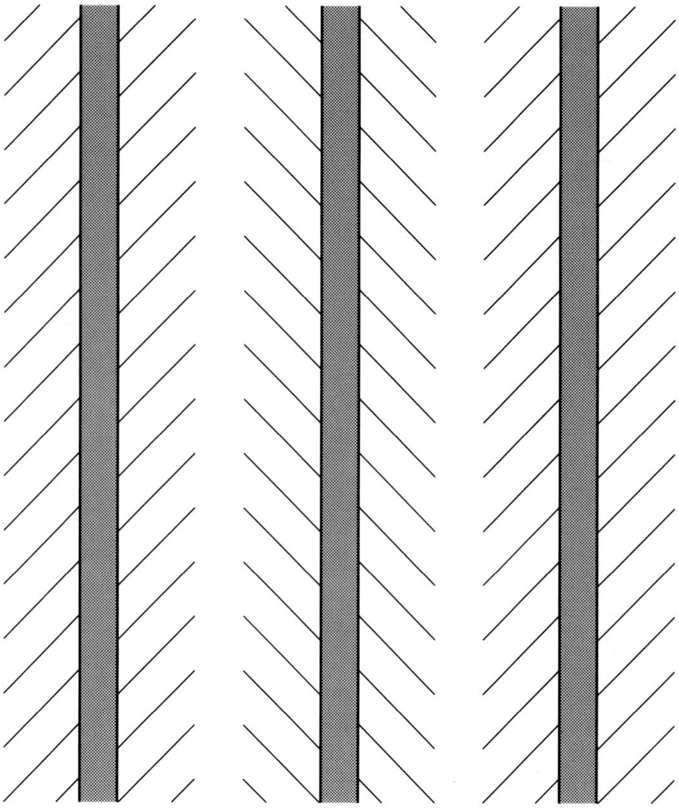

LRG SP ONE-WAY AT 60 DEG AT 1"=50'   0 ☐ 25

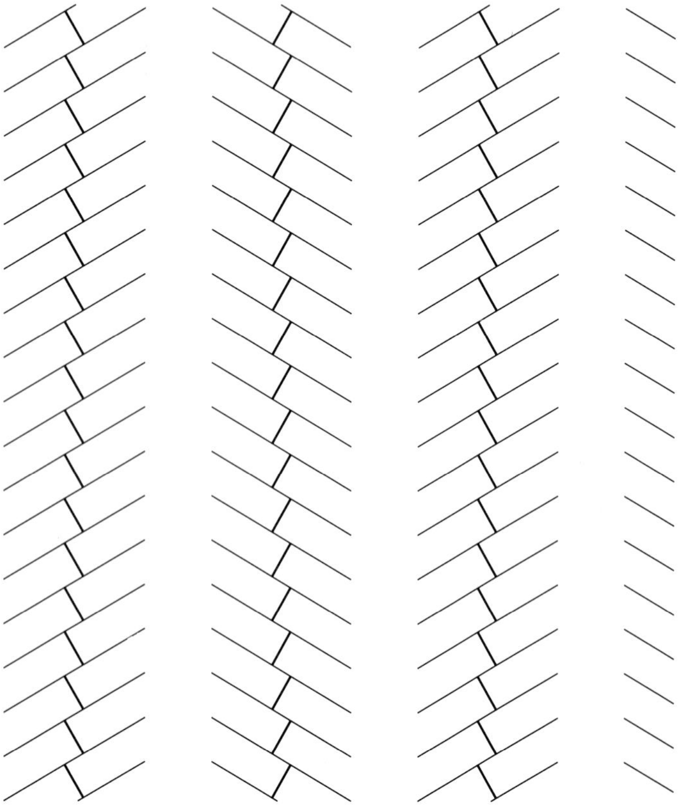

LRG SP ONE-WAY AT 45 DEG AT 1"=50'   0 ☐ 25

0 ⬜ 25   LRG TWO-WAY W/ISL AT 90 DEG AT 1"=50'

0 ⬜ 25   LRG TWO-WAY W/ISL AT 60 DEG AT 1"=50'

0 ⬜ 25   LRG TWO-WAY W/ISL AT 45 DEG AT 1"=50'

0 ⬜ 25   LRG SP TWO-WAY AT 90 DEG AT 1"=50'

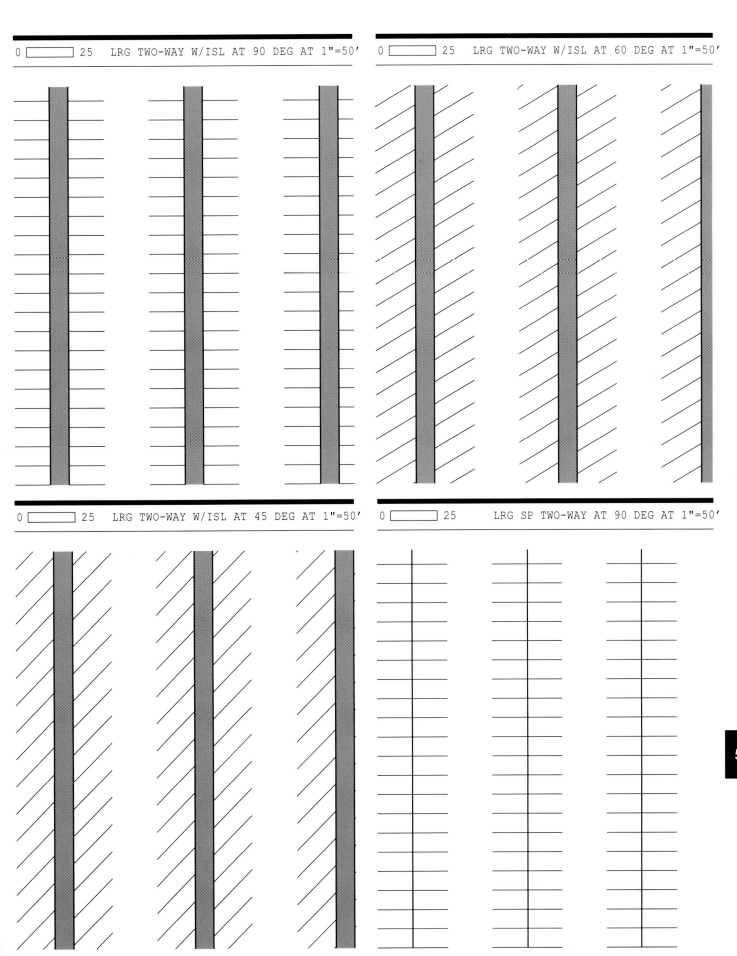

PARKING SPACE

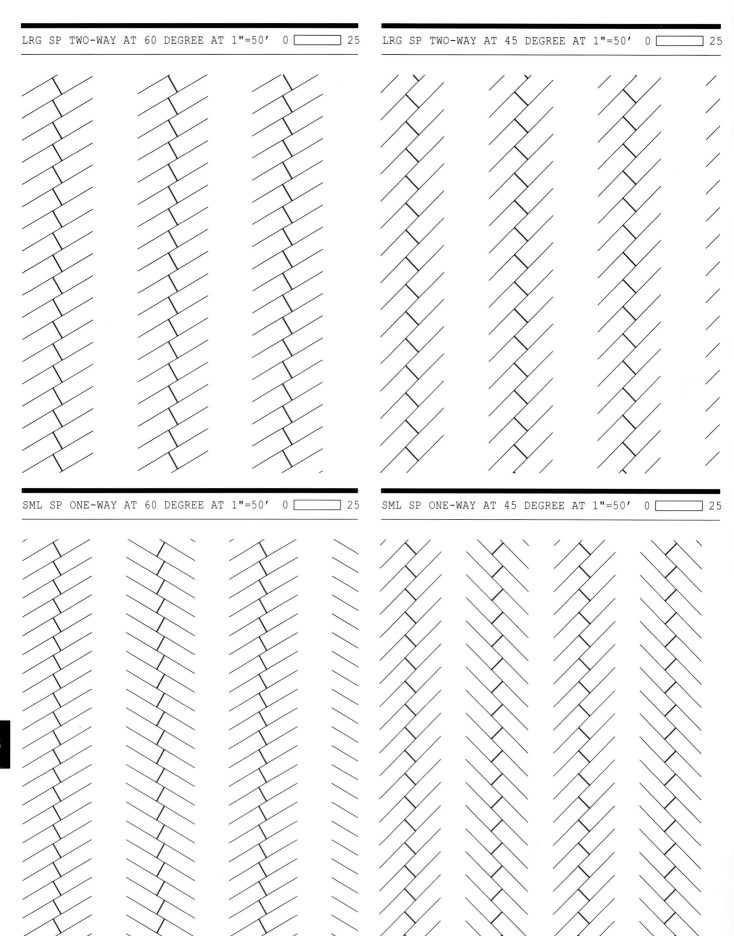

LRG SP TWO-WAY AT 60 DEGREE AT 1"=50' 0 ⬜ 25

LRG SP TWO-WAY AT 45 DEGREE AT 1"=50' 0 ⬜ 25

SML SP ONE-WAY AT 60 DEGREE AT 1"=50' 0 ⬜ 25

SML SP ONE-WAY AT 45 DEGREE AT 1"=50' 0 ⬜ 25

0 ▭ 25   SML TWO-WAY W/ISL AT 90 DEG AT 1"=50'

0 ▭ 25   SML TWO-WAY W/ISL AT 60 DEG AT 1"=50'

0 ▭ 25   SML TWO-WAY W/ISL AT 45 DEG AT 1"=50'

0 ▭ 25   SML SP TWO-WAY AT 90 DEG AT 1"=50'

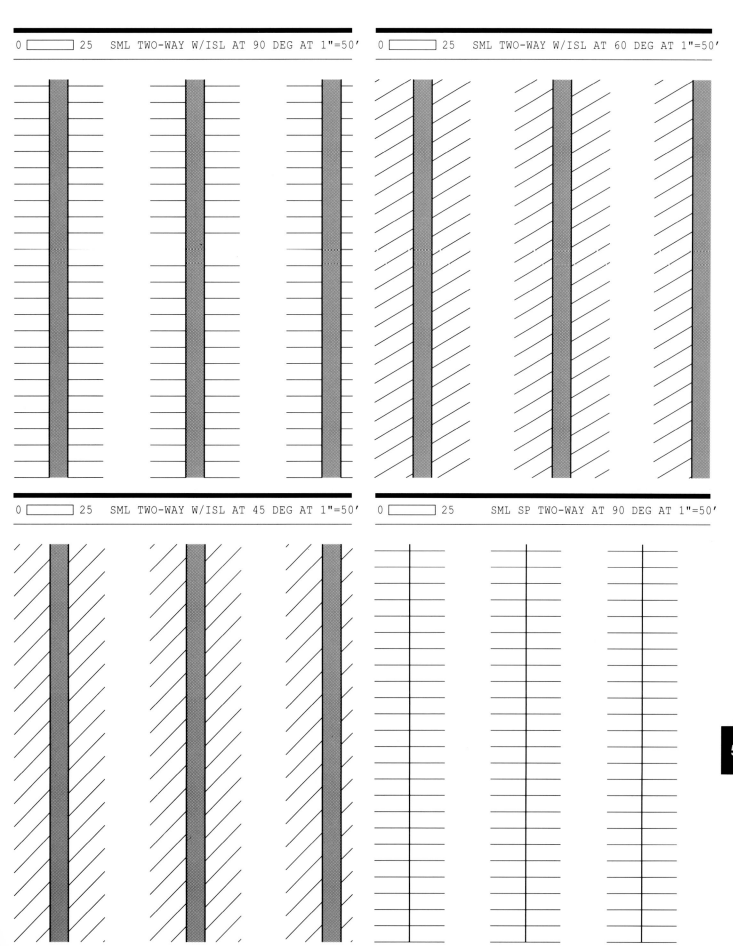

PARKING SPACE

SMALL SP TWO-WAY AT 60 DEG AT 1"=50'   0 [⬚] 25

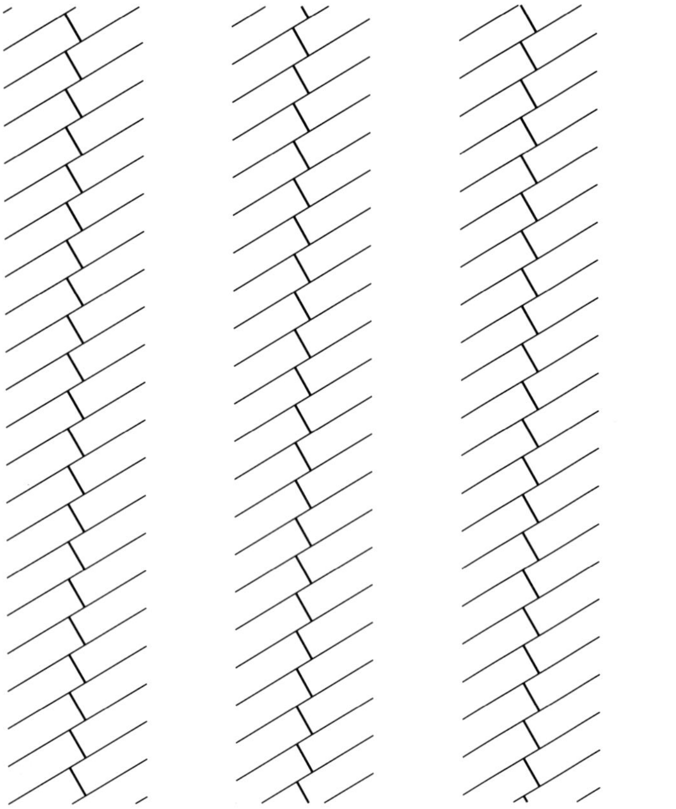

SMALL SP TWO-WAY AT 45 DEG AT 1"=50'   0 [⬚] 25

58

0 ☐ 30   LRG ONE-WAY W/ISL AT 60 DEG AT 1"=60'

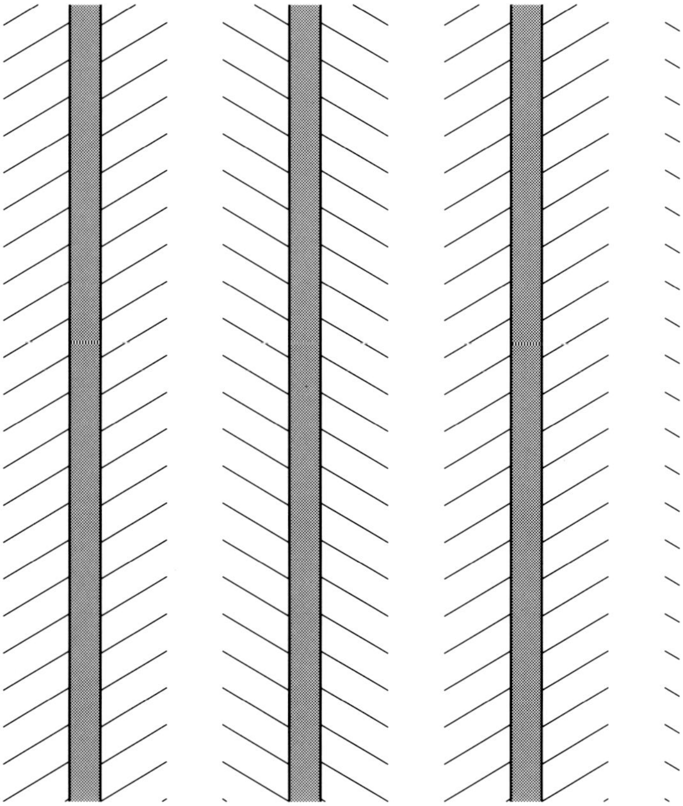

0 ☐ 30   LRG ONE-WAY W/ISL AT 45 DEG AT 1"=60'

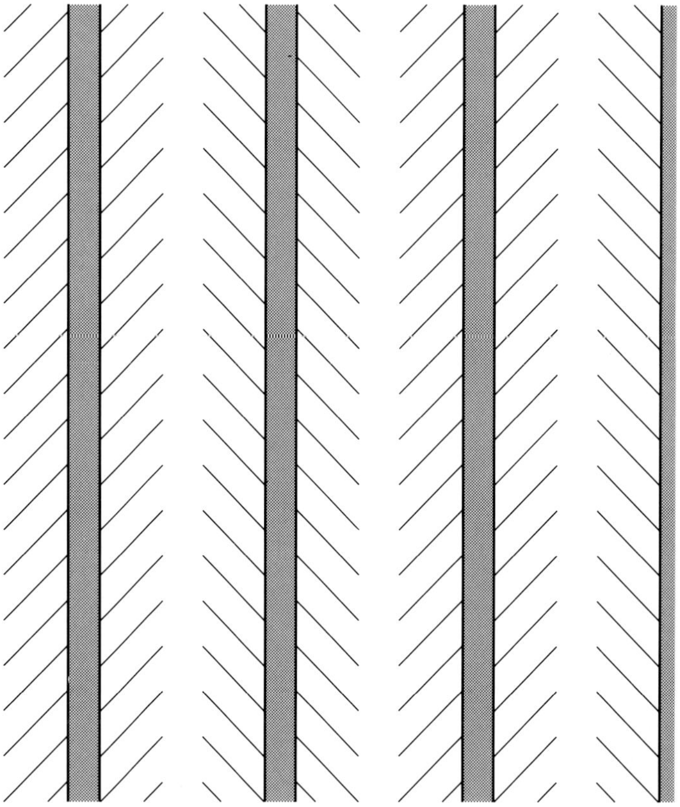

0 ☐ 30   LARGE SP ONE-WAY AT 60 DEG AT 1"=60'

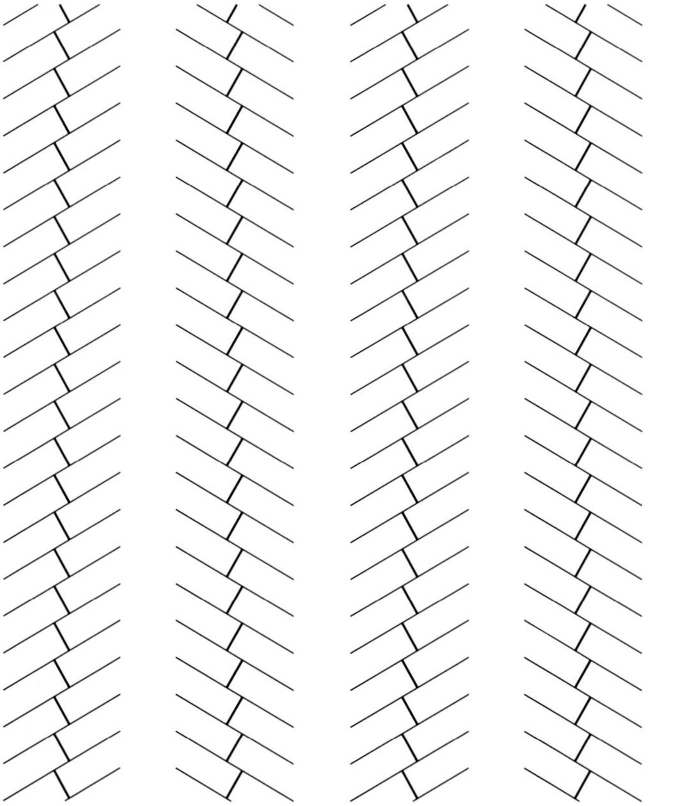

0 ☐ 30   LARGE SP ONE-WAY AT 45 DEG AT 1"=60'

LRG SP TWO-WAY W/ISL AT 90 DEG AT 1"=60' 0 ▭ 30

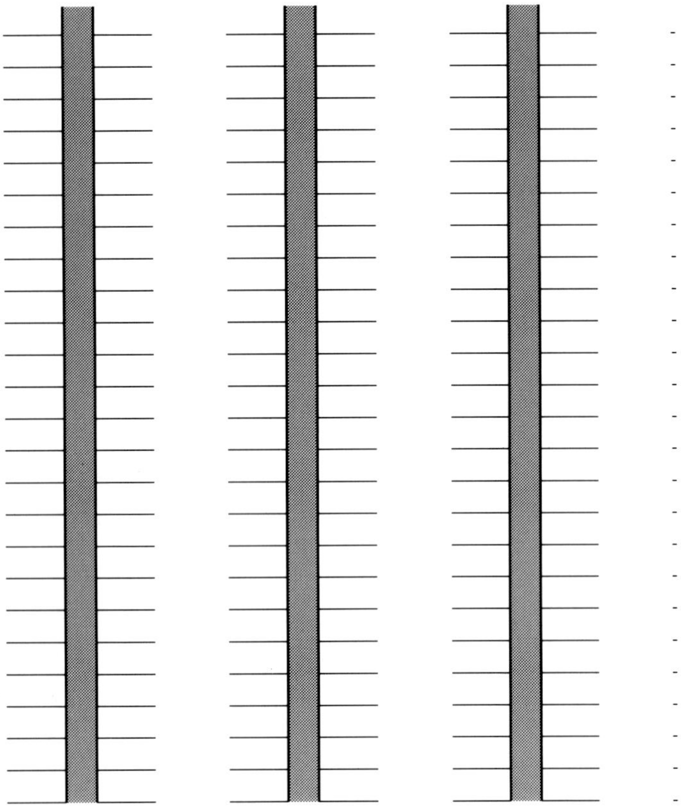

LRG SP TWO-WAY W/ISL AT 60 DEG AT 1"=60' 0 ▭ 30

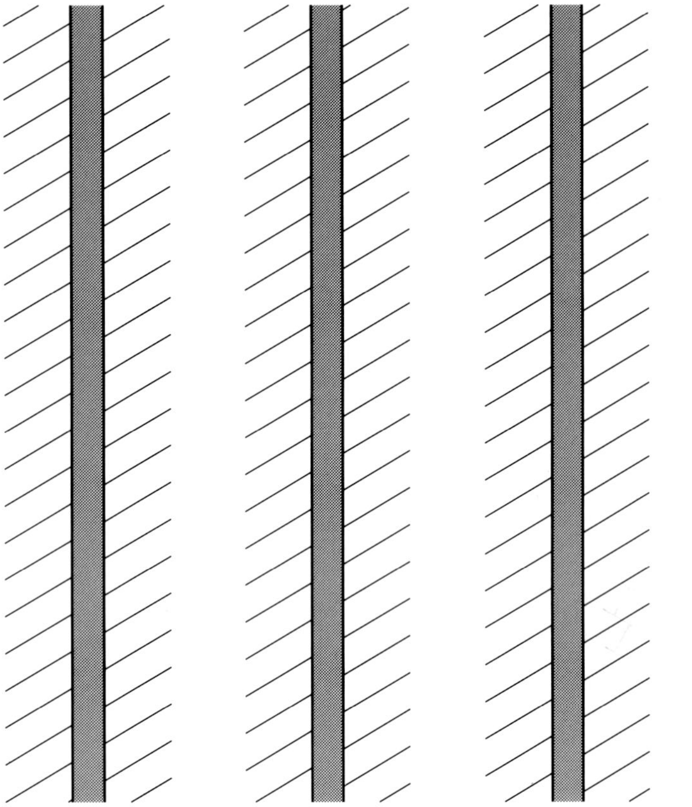

LRG SP TWO-WAY W/ISL AT 45 DEG AT 1"=60' 0 ▭ 30

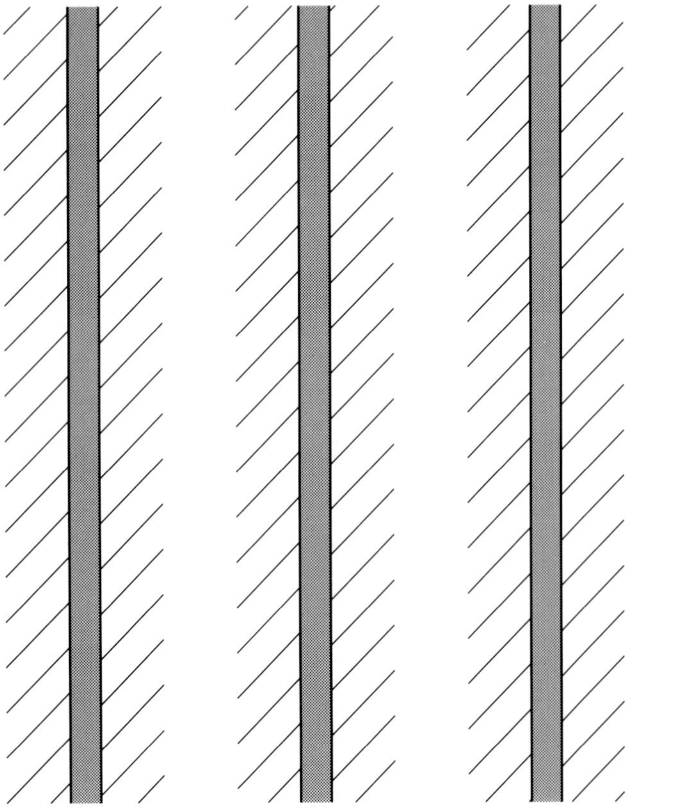

LRG SP TWO-WAY AT 90 DEG AT 1"=60' 0 ▭ 30

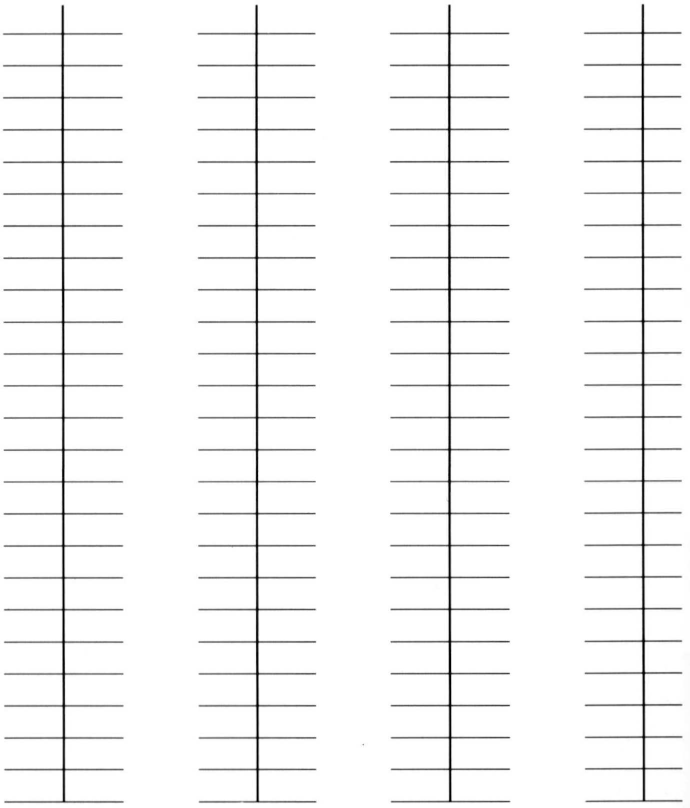

60

0 ⬚ 30   LRG SP TWO-WAY AT 60 DEG AT 1"=60'

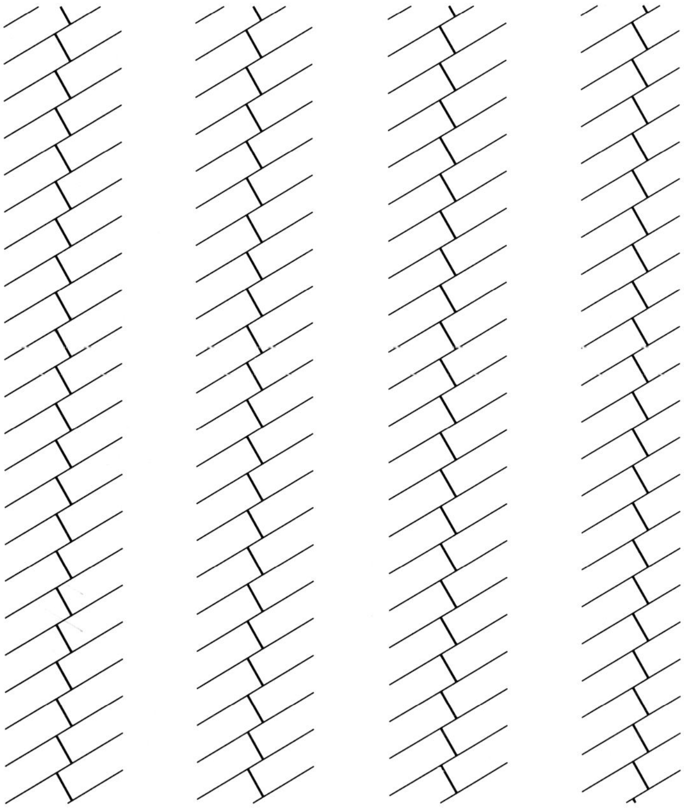

0 ⬚ 30   LRG SP TWO-WAY AT 45 DEG AT 1"=60'

0 ⬚ 30   SML SP ONE-WAY AT 60 DEG AT 1"=60'

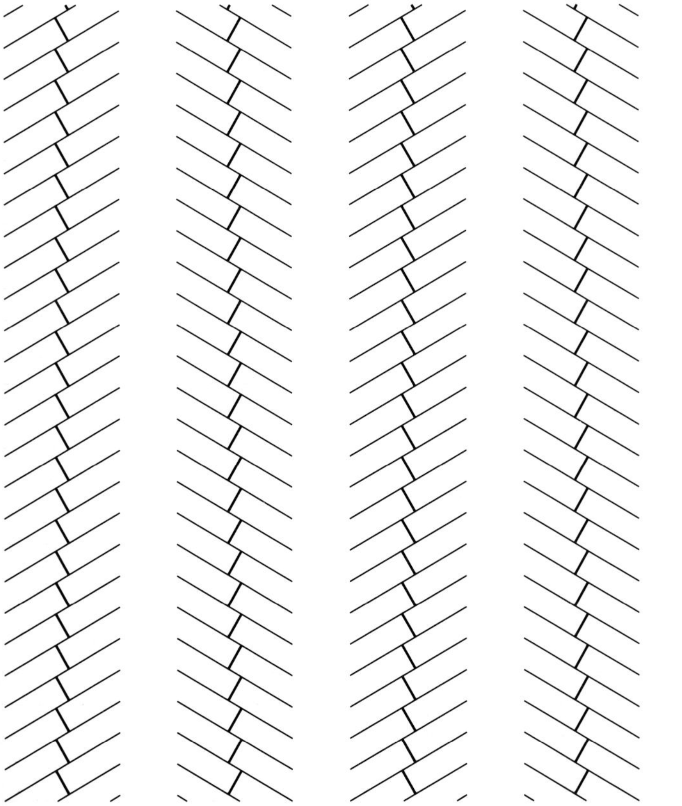

0 ⬚ 30   SML SP ONE-WAY AT 45 DEG AT 1"=60'

61

SML TWO-WAY W/ISL AT 90 DEG AT 1"=60'   0 ☐ 30

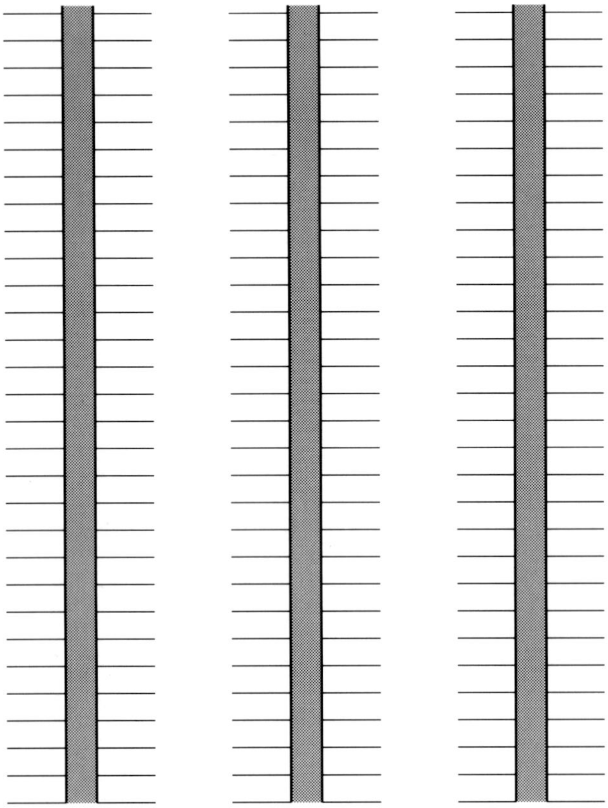

SML TWO-WAY W/ISL AT 60 DEG AT 1"=60'   0 ☐ 30

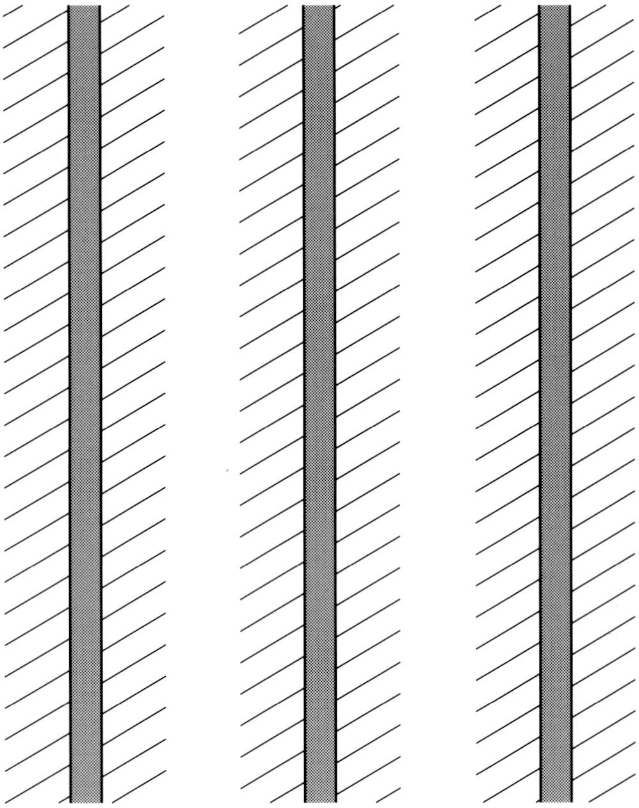

SML TWO-WAY W/ISL AT 45 DEG AT 1"=60'   0 ☐ 30

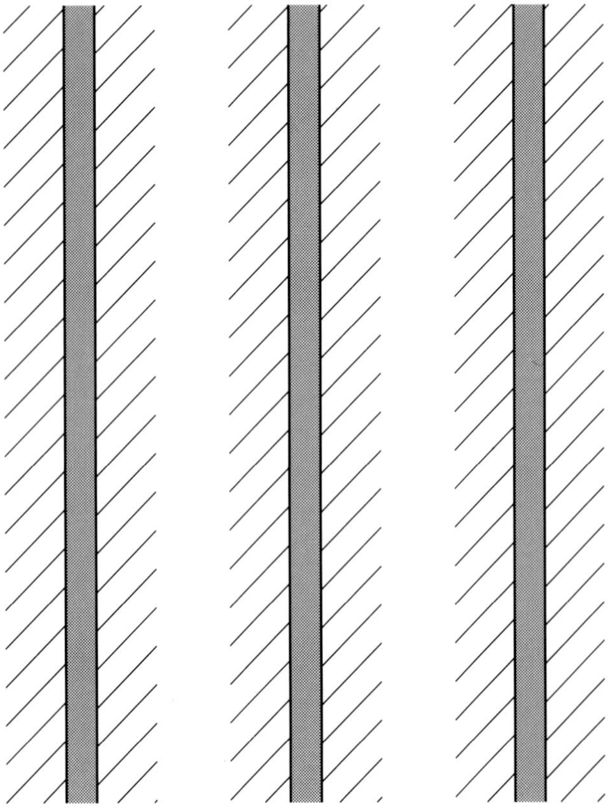

SML TWO-WAY AT 90 DEG AT 1"=60'   0 ☐ 30

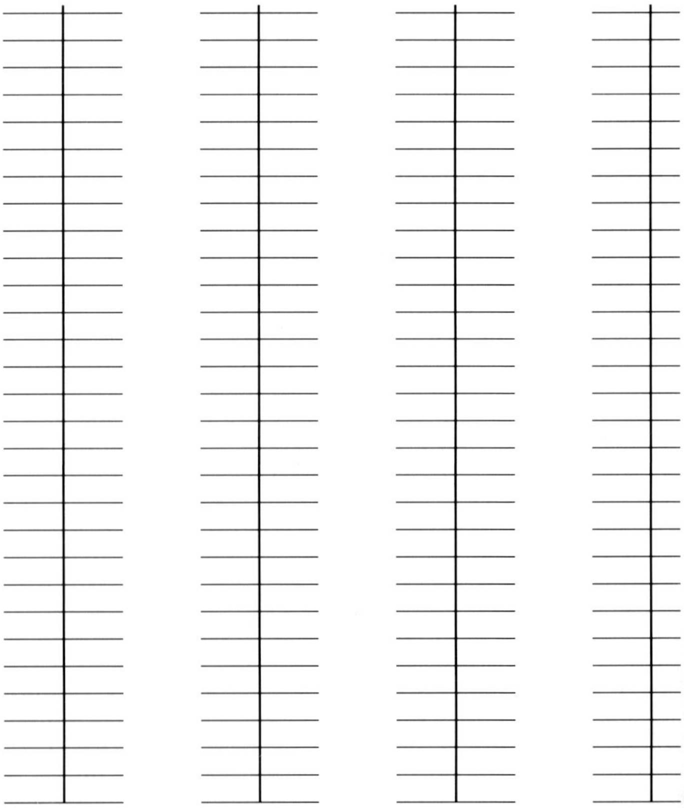

0 [＝＝＝＝] 30   LARGE SP TWO-WAY AT 60 DEG AT 1"=60'   0 [＝＝＝＝] 30   LARGE SP TWO-WAY AT 45 DEG AT 1"=60'

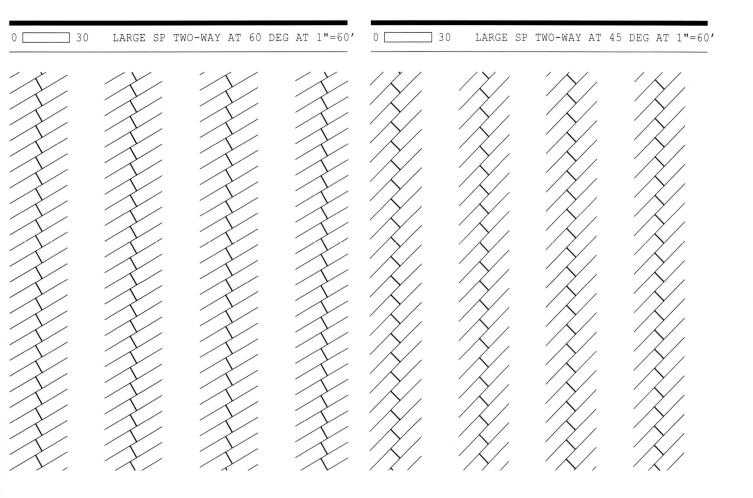

LG SP ONE-WAY W/ISL AT 60 DEG AT 1"=100' 0 ▭ 50

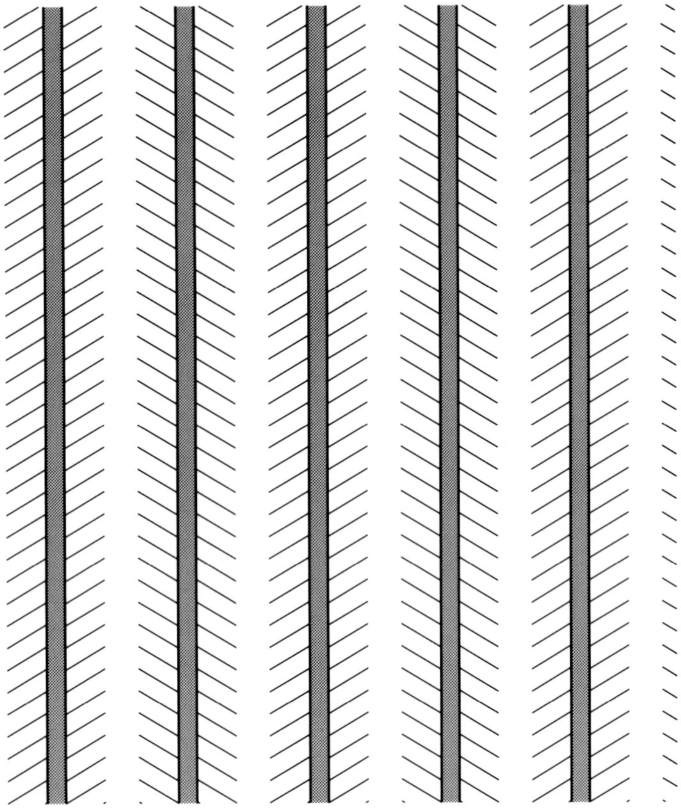

LG SP ONE-WAY W/ISL AT 45 DEG AT 1"=100' 0 ▭ 50

LRG SP ONE-WAY AT 60 DEG AT 1"=100' 0 ▭ 50

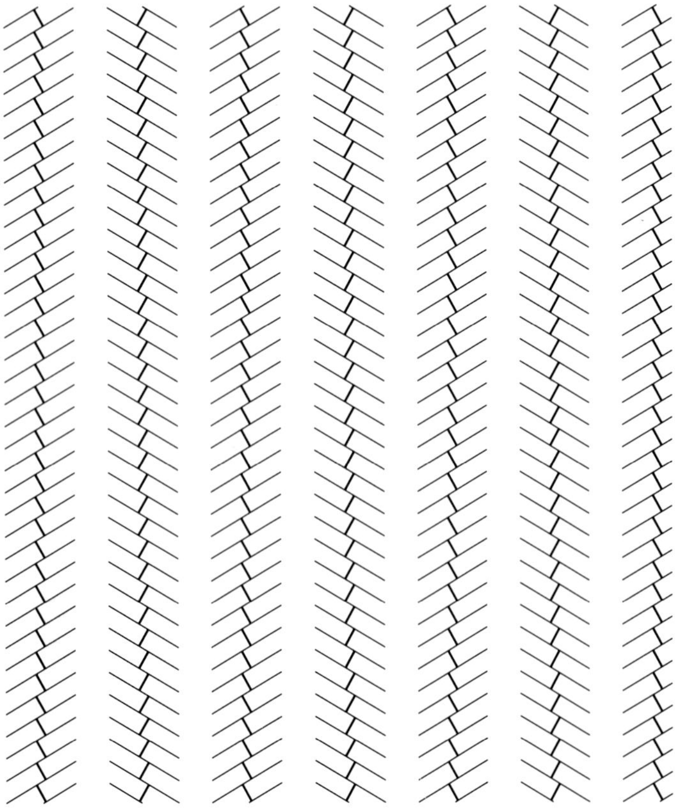

LRG SP ONE-WAY AT 45 DEG AT 1"=100' 0 ▭ 50

0 [========] 50   LRG TWO-WAY W/ISL AT 90 DEG AT 1"=100'

0 [========] 50   LRG TWO-WAY W/ISL AT 60 DEG AT 1"=100'

0 [========] 50   LRG TWO-WAY W/ISL AT 45 DEG AT 1"=100'

0 [========] 50   LRG SP TWO-WAY AT 90 DEG AT 1"=100'

LRG SP TWO-WAY AT 60 DEG AT 1"=100'   0 ▭ 50

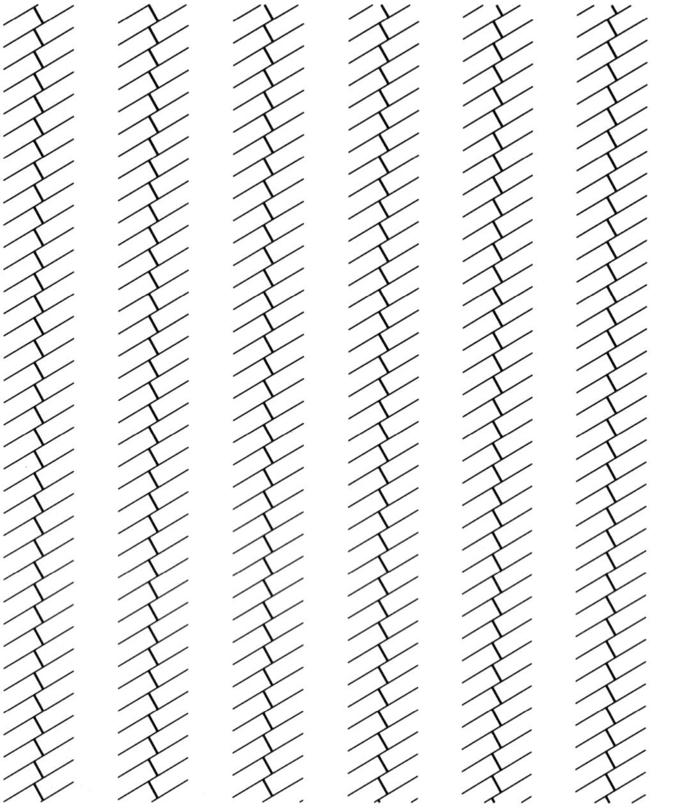

LRG SP TWO-WAY AT 45 DEG AT 1"=100'   0 ▭ 50

SML SP ONE-WAY AT 60 DEG AT 1"=100'   0 ▭ 50

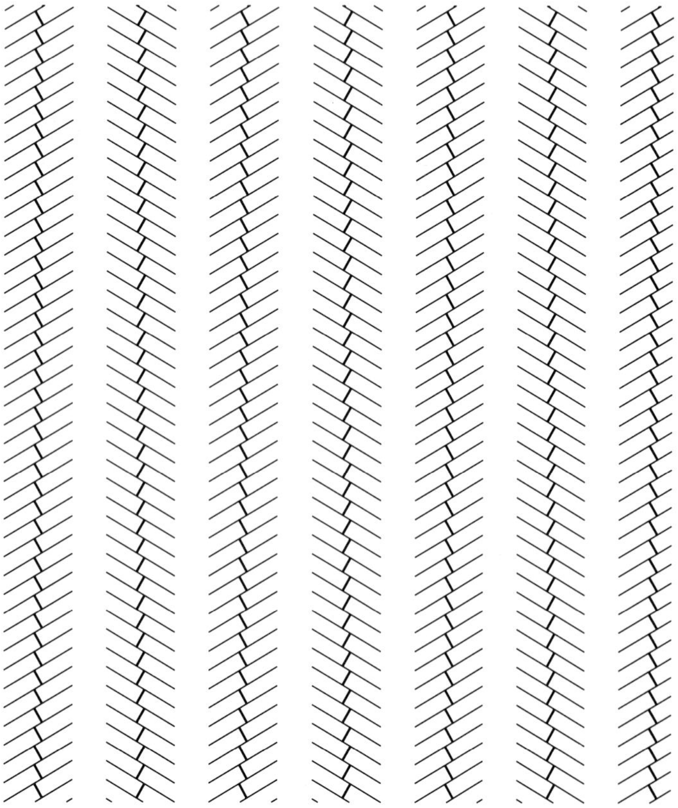

SML SP ONE-WAY AT 45 DEG AT 1"=100'   0 ▭ 50

0 ▭ 50 SML TWO-WAY W/ISL AT 90 DEG AT 1"=100'

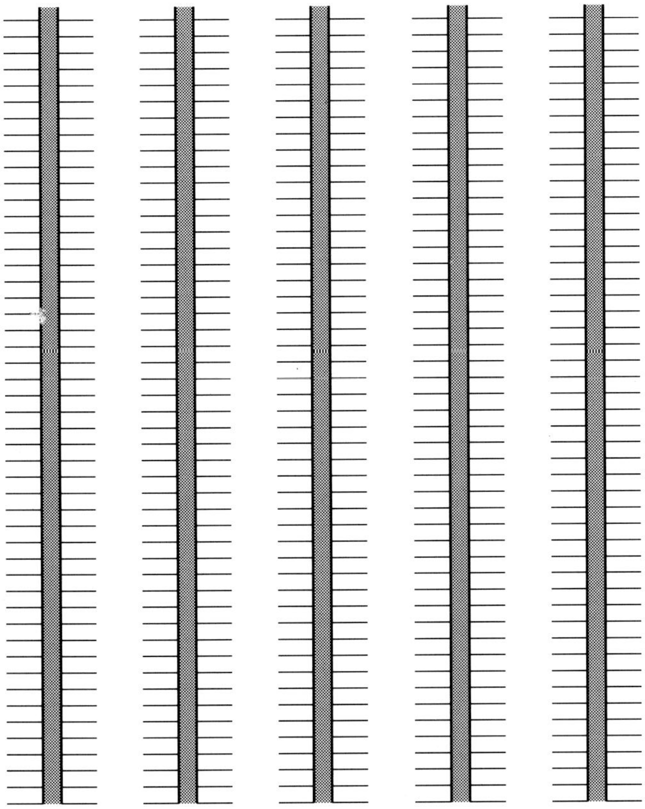

0 ▭ 50 SML TWO-WAY W/ISL AT 60 DEG AT 1"=100'

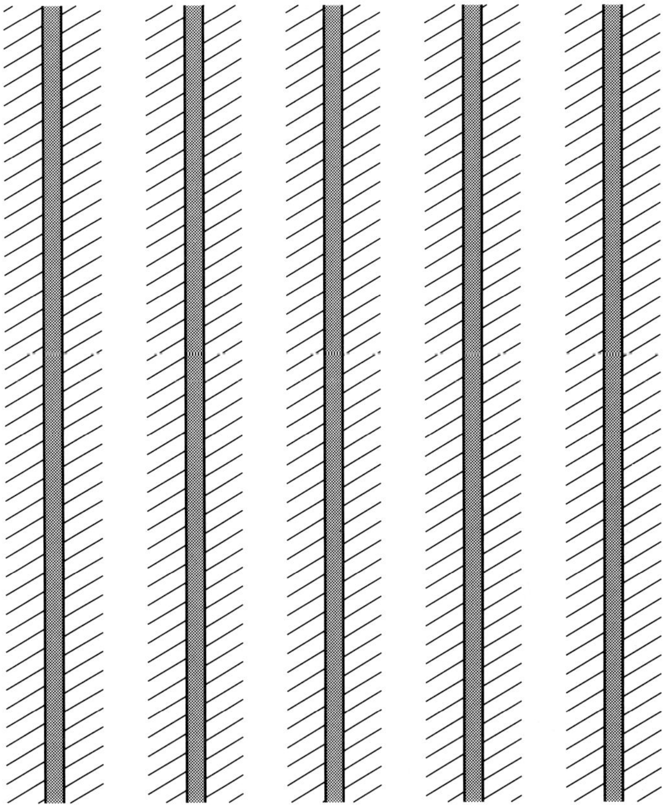

0 ▭ 50 SML TWO-WAY W/ISL AT 45 DEG AT 1"=100'

0 ▭ 50 SML SP TWO-WAY AT 90 DEG AT 1"=100'

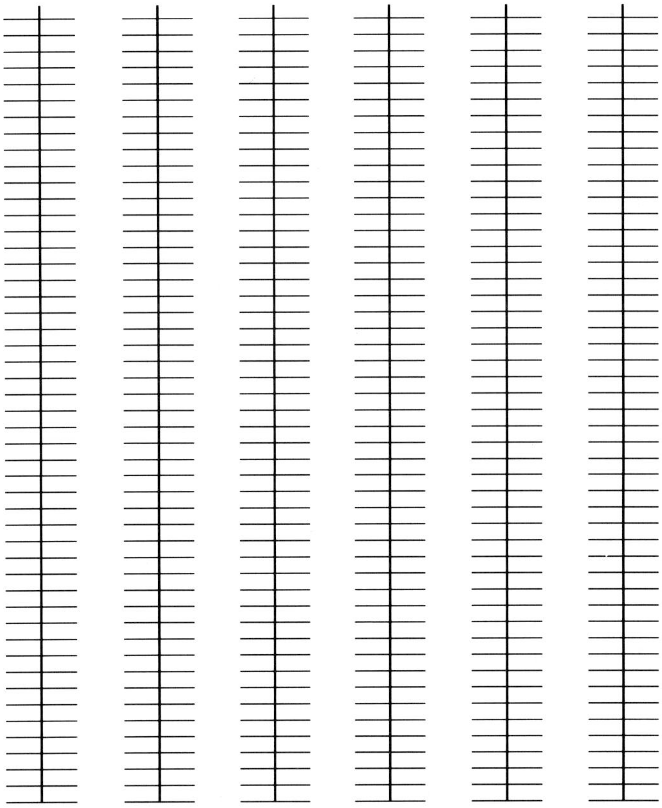

SML SP TWO-WAY AT 60 DEG AT 1"=100'   0 [＿＿] 50

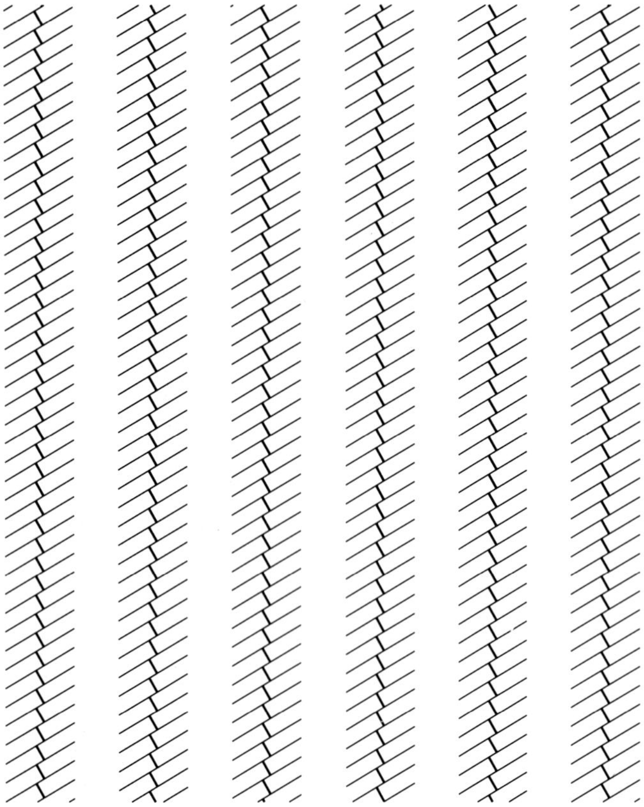

SML SP TWO-WAY AT 45 DEG AT 1"=100'   0 [＿＿] 50

0 ⬚ 100 LRG ONE-WAY W/ISL AT 60 DEG AT 1"=200'

0 ⬚ 100 LRG ONE-WAY W/ISL AT 45 DEG AT 1"=200'

0 ⬚ 100   LRG SP ONE-WAY AT 60 DEG AT 1"=200'

0 ⬚ 100   LRG SP ONE-WAY AT 45 DEG AT 1"=200'

0 ⬚ 100 LRG TWO-WAY W/ISL AT 45 DEG AT 1"=200'

0 ⬚ 100   LRG TWO-WAY AT 90 DEG AT 1"=200'

LRG TWO-WAY W/ISL AT 45 DEG AT 1"=200'   0 [   ] 100

LRG TWO-WAY AT 90 DEG AT 1"=200'   0 [   ] 100

LRG SP TWO-WAY AT 60 DEG AT 1"=200'   0 [   ] 100

LRG SP TWO-WAY AT 45 DEG AT 1"=200'   0 [   ] 100

SML SP ONE-WAY AT 60 DEG AT 1"=200'   0 [   ] 100

SML SP ONE-WAY AT 45 DEG AT 1"=200'   0 [   ] 100

0 [▭] 100 SML TWO-WAY W/ISL AT 90 DEG AT 1"=200'

0 [▭] 100 SML TWO-WAY W/ISL AT 60 DEG AT 1"=200'

0 [▭] 100 SML TWO-WAY W/ISL AT 45 DEG AT 1"=200'

0 [▭] 100   SML SP TWO-WAY AT 90 DEG AT 1"=200'

0 [▭] 100   SML SP TWO-WAY AT 60 DEG AT 1"=200'

0 [▭] 100   SML SP TWO-WAY AT 45 DEG AT 1"=200'

MID-SIZE CAR   AT 1" = 20'-0"   0 ▭ 20

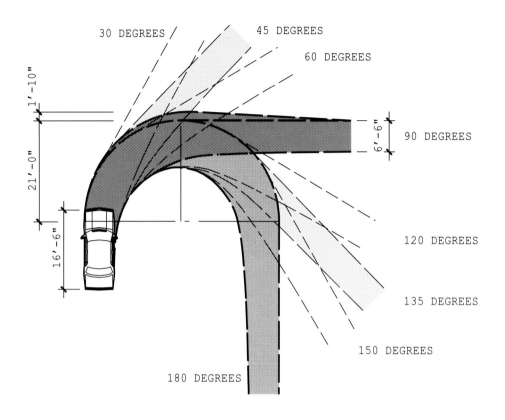

30 DEGREES 45 DEGREES 60 DEGREES

1'-10"
21'-0"
16'-6"
6'-6" 90 DEGREES

120 DEGREES

135 DEGREES

150 DEGREES

180 DEGREES

FULL-SIZE CAR   AT 1" = 20'-0"   0 ▭ 20

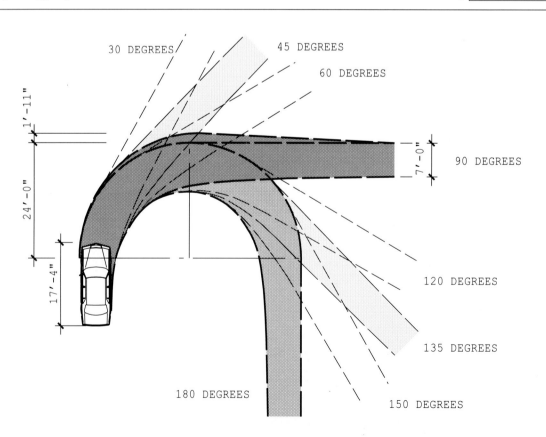

30 DEGREES 45 DEGREES 60 DEGREES

1'-11"
24'-0"
17'-4"
7'-0" 90 DEGREES

120 DEGREES

135 DEGREES

180 DEGREES

150 DEGREES

0 [   ] 20   VAN OR CARGO TRUCK   AT 1" = 20'-0"

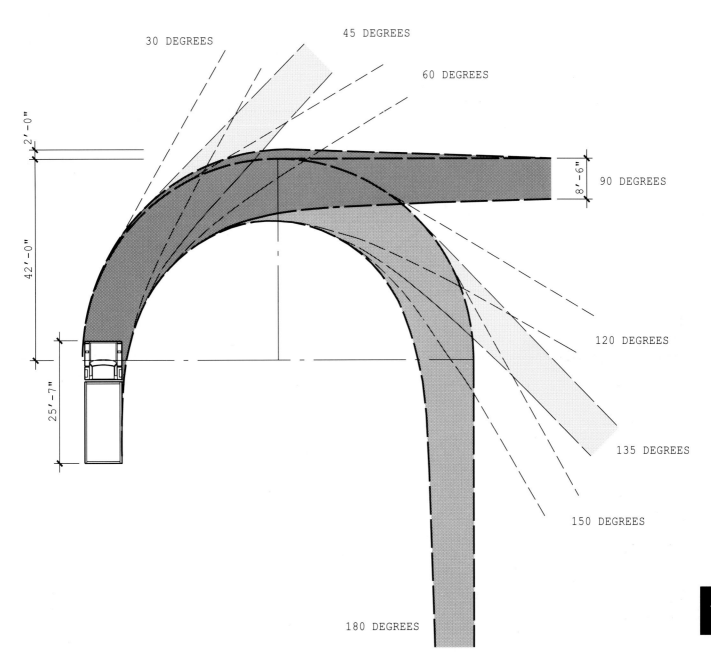

30 DEGREES

45 DEGREES

60 DEGREES

90 DEGREES

120 DEGREES

135 DEGREES

150 DEGREES

180 DEGREES

2'-0"

8'-6"

42'-0"

25'-7"

BUS AT 1" = 20'-0"   0 ▭ 20

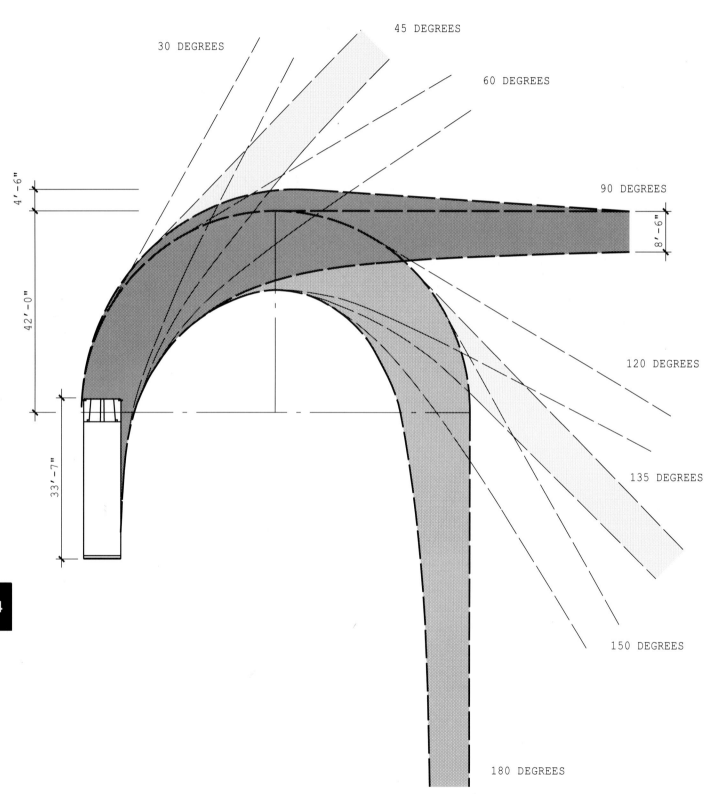

30 DEGREES

45 DEGREES

60 DEGREES

90 DEGREES

120 DEGREES

135 DEGREES

150 DEGREES

180 DEGREES

4'-6"

8'-6"

42'-0"

33'-7"

74

0 ⬚ 20

WD-40 FIXED TRUCK AT 1" = 20'-0"

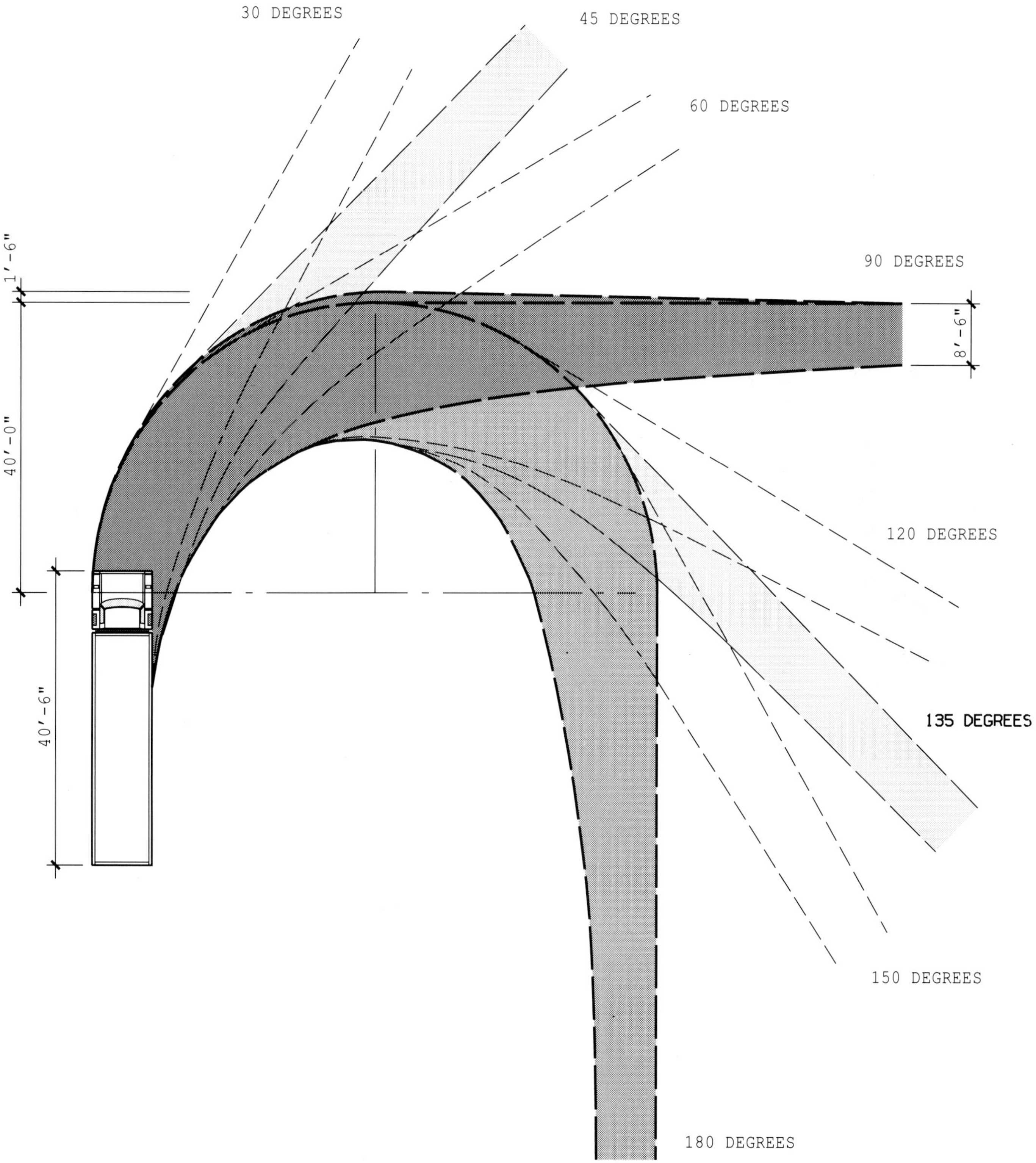

30 DEGREES

45 DEGREES

60 DEGREES

90 DEGREES

1'-6"

8'-6"

40'-0"

120 DEGREES

40'-6"

135 DEGREES

150 DEGREES

180 DEGREES

75

55' SEMI AT 45' RADIUS AT 1" = 20'-0"   0 ▭ 20

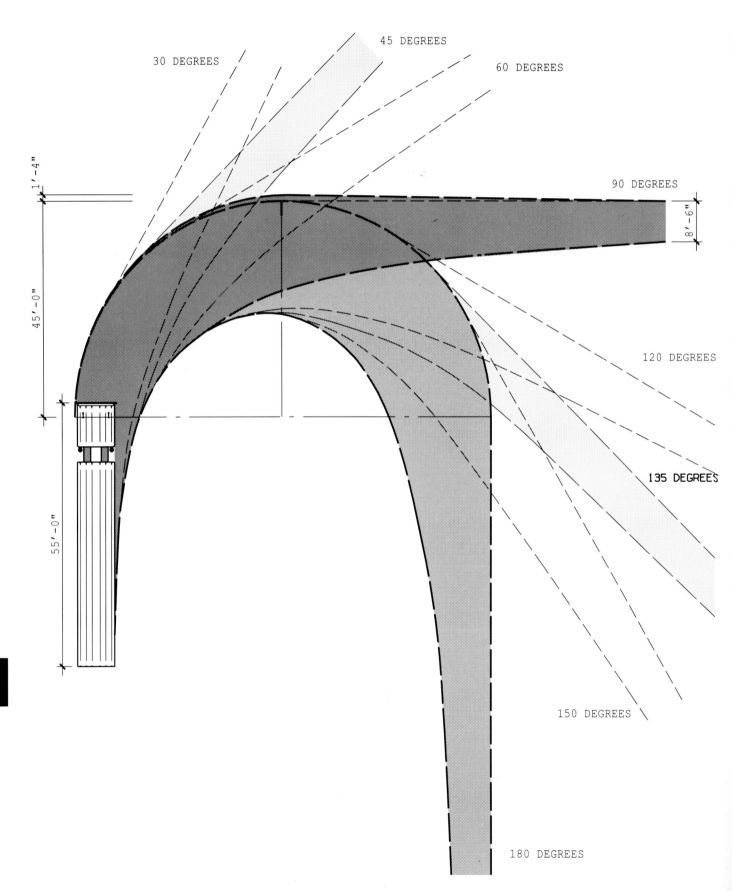

30 DEGREES
45 DEGREES
60 DEGREES
90 DEGREES
120 DEGREES
135 DEGREES
150 DEGREES
180 DEGREES

1'-4"
8'-6"
45'-0"
55'-0"

76

0 [   ] 20

55' SEMI AT 60' RADIUS AT 1" = 20'-0"

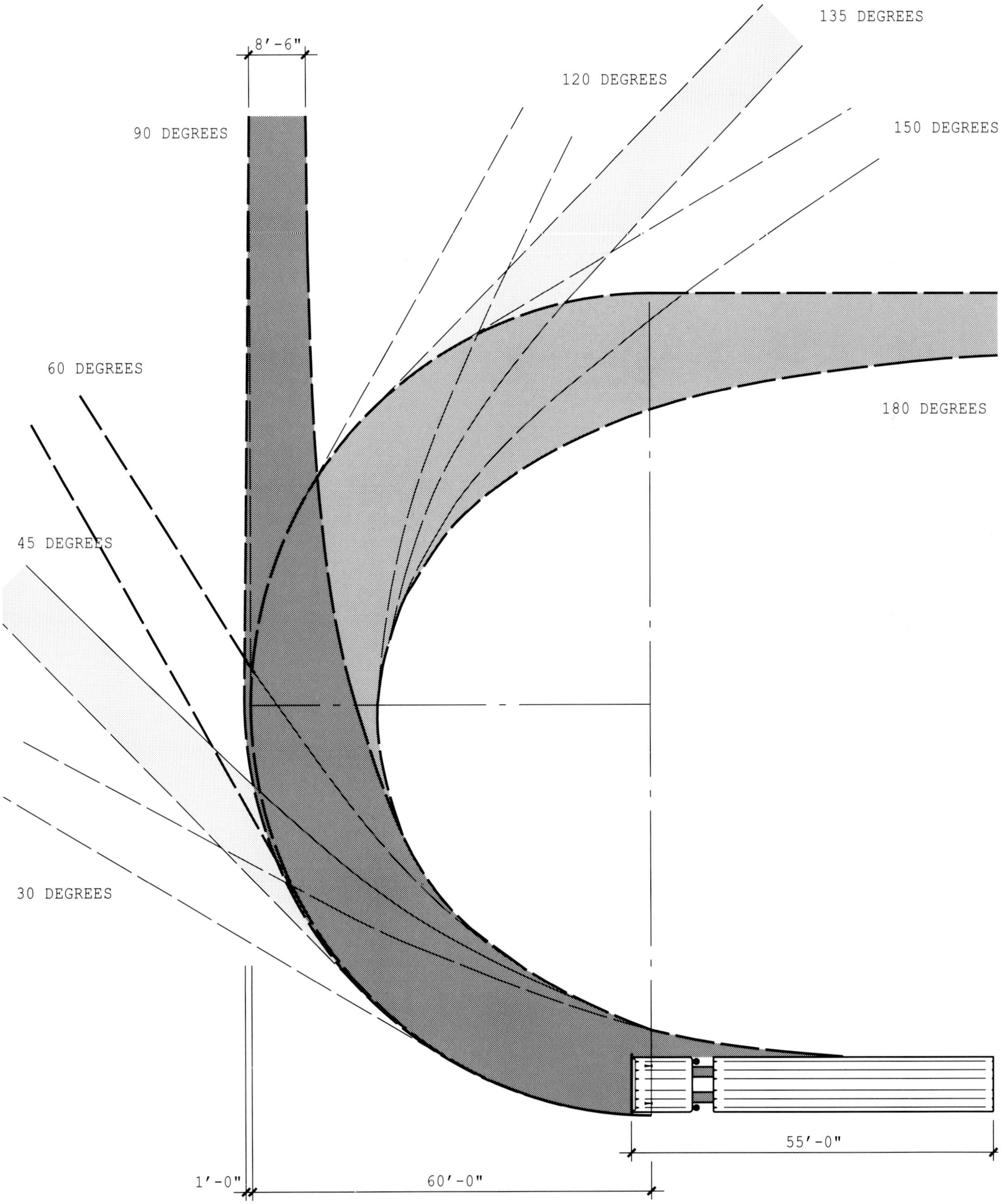

8'-6"

90 DEGREES

135 DEGREES

120 DEGREES

150 DEGREES

60 DEGREES

180 DEGREES

45 DEGREES

30 DEGREES

55'-0"

1'-0"

60'-0"

55' SEMI AT 75' RADIUS AT 1" = 20'-0"   0 [   ] 20

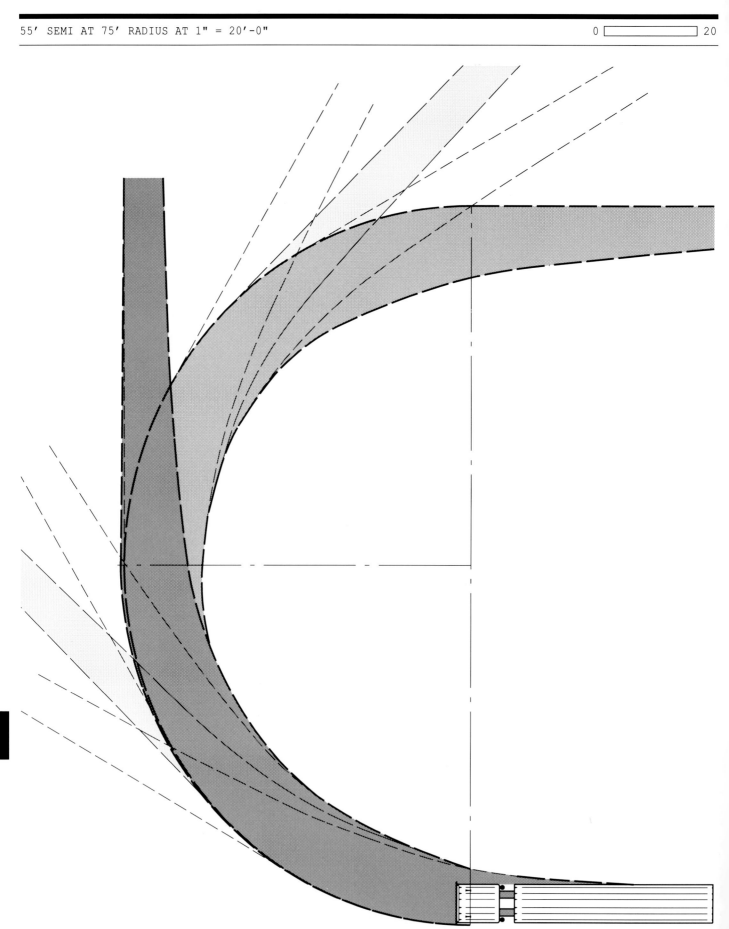

0 ⬜ 30

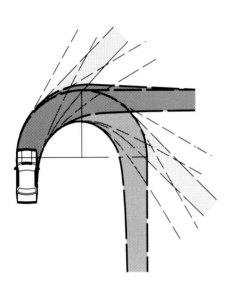

MID-SIZE CAR

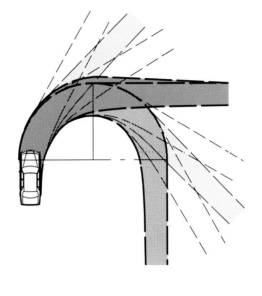

FULL-SIZE CAR

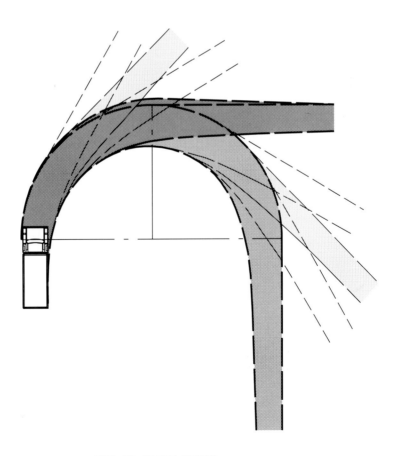

VAN OR CARGO TRUCK

TURNING RADIUS AT 1" = 30'-0"   0 ▭ 30

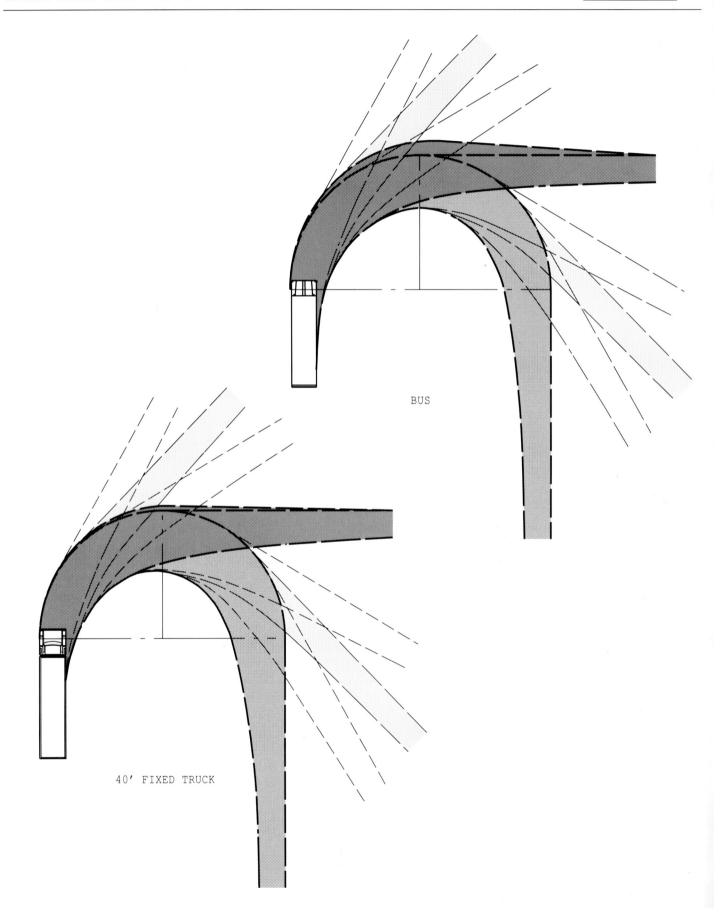

BUS

40' FIXED TRUCK

0 [========] 30

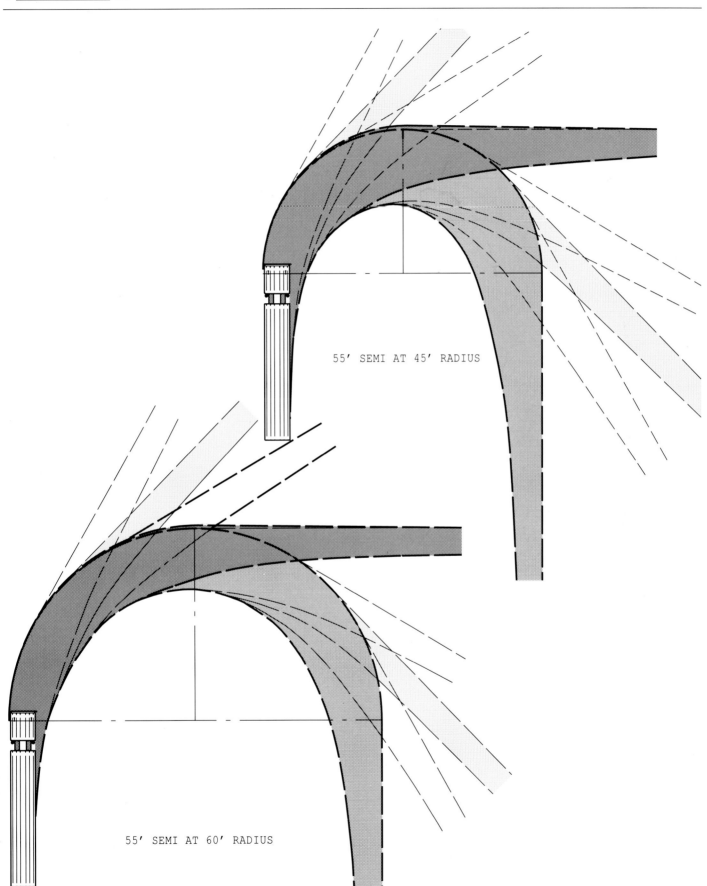

55' SEMI AT 45' RADIUS

55' SEMI AT 60' RADIUS

55' SEMI AT 75' RADIUS AT 1" = 30'-0"   0 ▭ 30

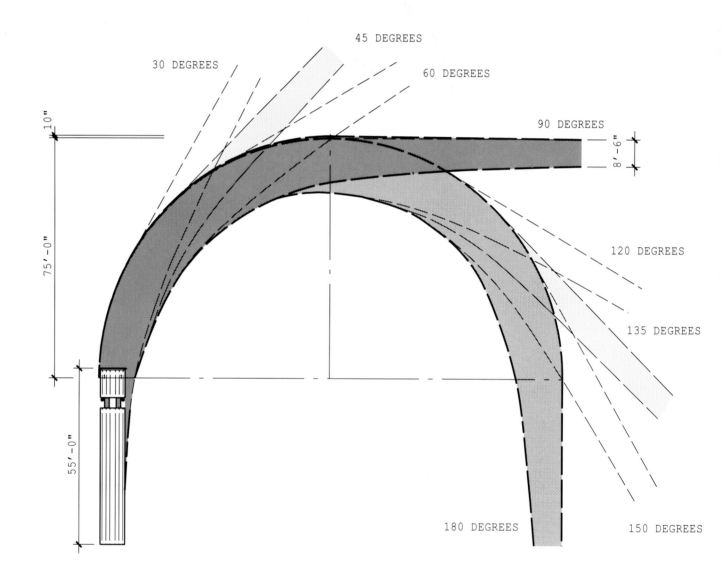

30 DEGREES

45 DEGREES

60 DEGREES

90 DEGREES

8'-6"

120 DEGREES

135 DEGREES

10"

75'-0"

55'-0"

180 DEGREES

150 DEGREES

0 [▭▭▭▭▭▭] 40

TURNING RADIUS AT 1" = 40'-0"

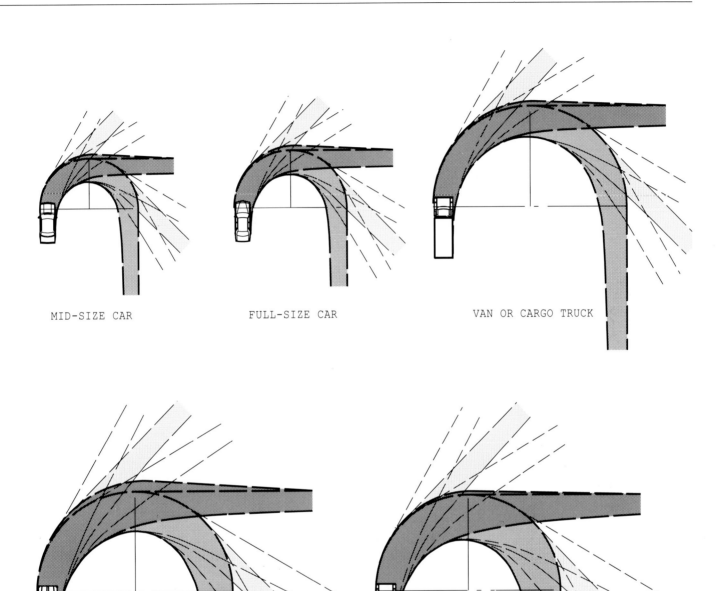

MID-SIZE CAR   FULL-SIZE CAR   VAN OR CARGO TRUCK

BUS   40' FIXED TRUCK

TURNING RADIUS AT 1" = 40'-0"   0 ⬜ 40

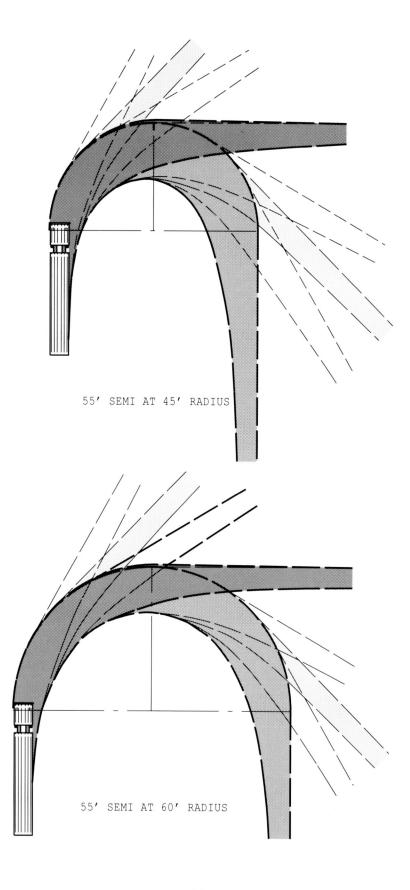

55' SEMI AT 45' RADIUS

55' SEMI AT 60' RADIUS

0 40

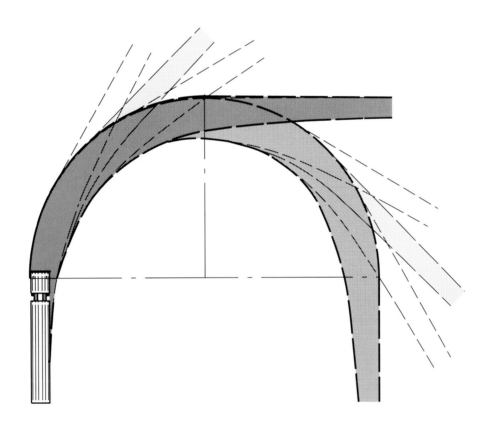

TURNING RADIUS AT 1" = 50'-0"   0 ⬜⬜⬜⬜ 50

MID-SIZE CAR

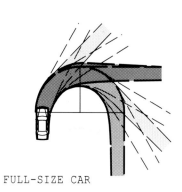

FULL-SIZE CAR

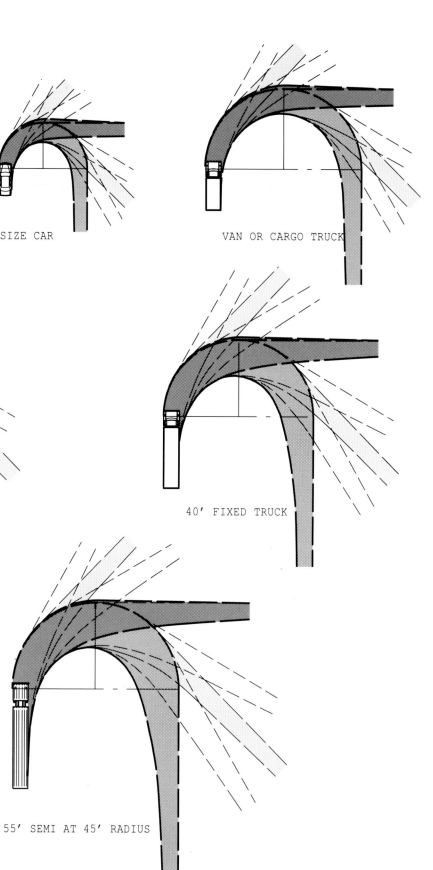

VAN OR CARGO TRUCK

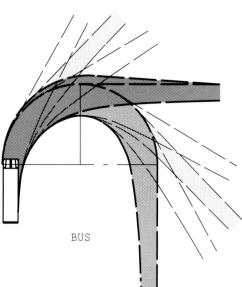

BUS

40' FIXED TRUCK

55' SEMI AT 45' RADIUS

86

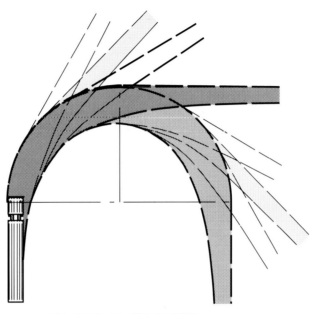

55' SEMI AT 60' RADIUS

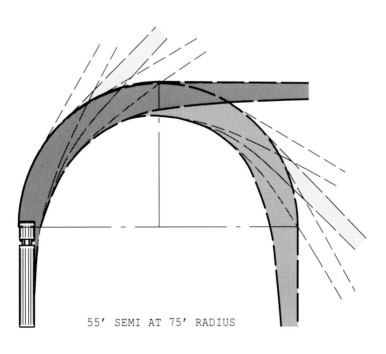

55' SEMI AT 75' RADIUS

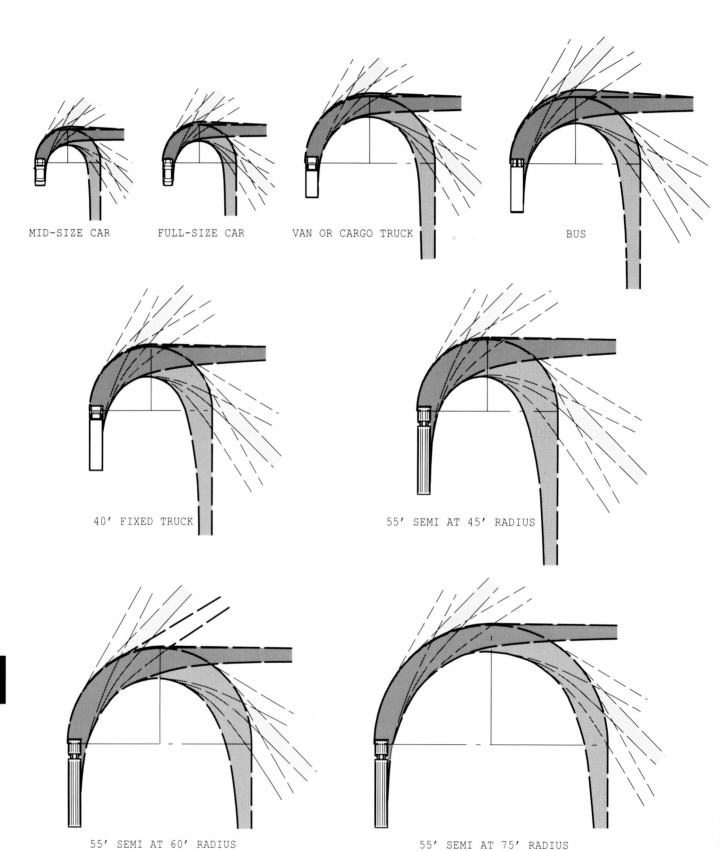

MID-SIZE CAR

FULL-SIZE CAR

VAN OR CARGO TRUCK

BUS

40' FIXED TRUCK

55' SEMI AT 45' RADIUS

55' SEMI AT 60' RADIUS

55' SEMI AT 75' RADIUS

TURNING RADIUS AT 1" = 100'-0"   0 ☐☐☐☐☐ 100

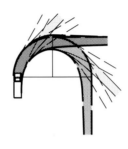
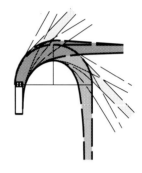

MID-SIZE CAR   FULL-SIZE CAR   VAN OR CARGO TRUCK   BUS

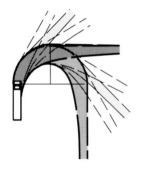
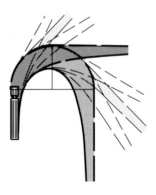

40' FIXED TRUCK   55' SEMI AT 45' RADIUS

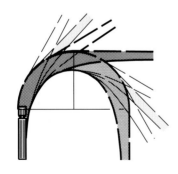
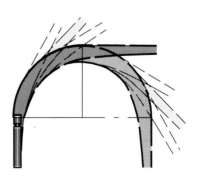

55' SEMI AT 60' RADIUS   55' SEMI AT 75' RADIUS

COMPACT CAR AT 1/4" = 1'-0"   0 ▭ 4

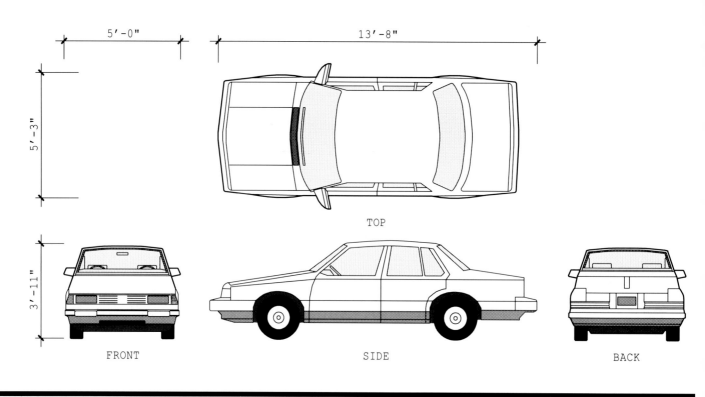

5'-0"   13'-8"

5'-3"

TOP

3'-11"

FRONT   SIDE   BACK

COMPACT SPORTS CAR AT 1/4" = 1'-0"   0 ▭ 4

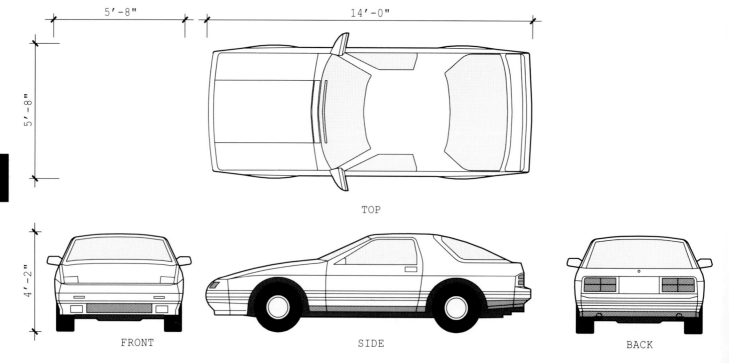

5'-8"   14'-0"

5'-8"

TOP

4'-2"

FRONT   SIDE   BACK

0 ▭ 4   MID-SIZE CAR AT 1/4" = 1'-0"

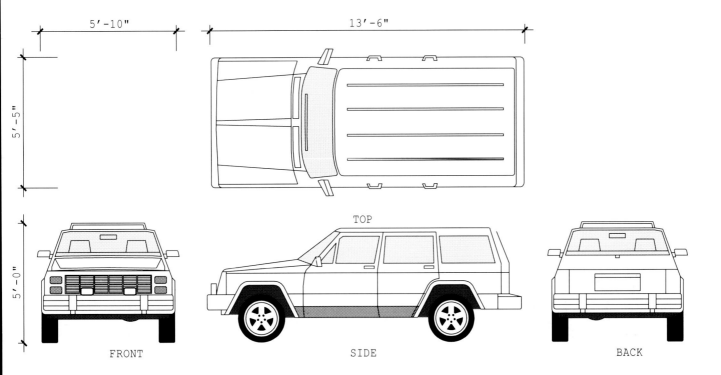

5'-10"   13'-6"

5'-5"

5'-0"

FRONT   TOP / SIDE   BACK

0 ▭ 4   FULL-SIZE CAR AT 1/4" = 1'-0"

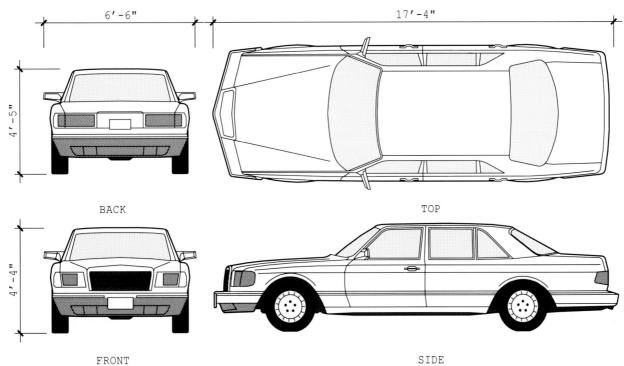

6'-6"   17'-4"

4'-5"

4'-4"

BACK   TOP

FRONT   SIDE

MINI VAN AT 1/4" = 1'-0"

0 ▭ 4

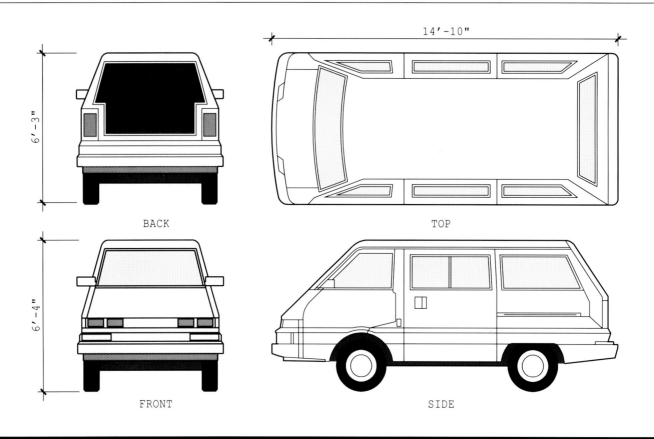

BACK

TOP

14'-10"

6'-3"

FRONT

SIDE

6'-4"

COMPACT TRUCK AT 1/4" = 1'-0"

0 ▭ 4

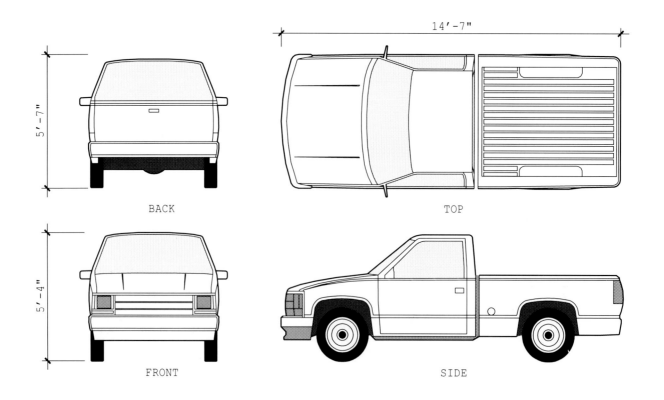

BACK

TOP

14'-7"

5'-7"

FRONT

SIDE

5'-4"

0 [▭▭▭▭] 4   STANDARD TRUCK AT 1/4" = 1'-0"

18'-1"

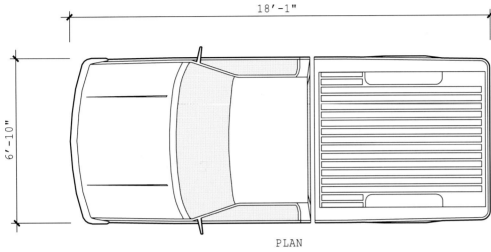

6'-10"

PLAN

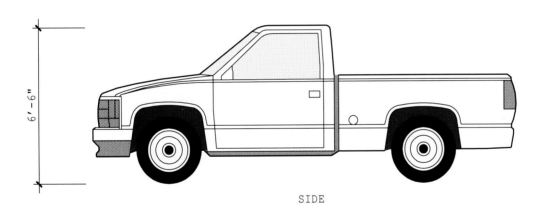

6'-6"

SIDE

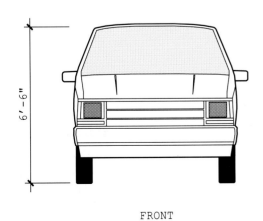

6'-6"

FRONT

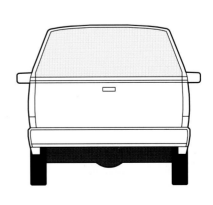

BACK

WD-35 TRUCK AT 1/4" = 1'-0"   0 ⊏━━━━━━━━━━━━⊐ 4

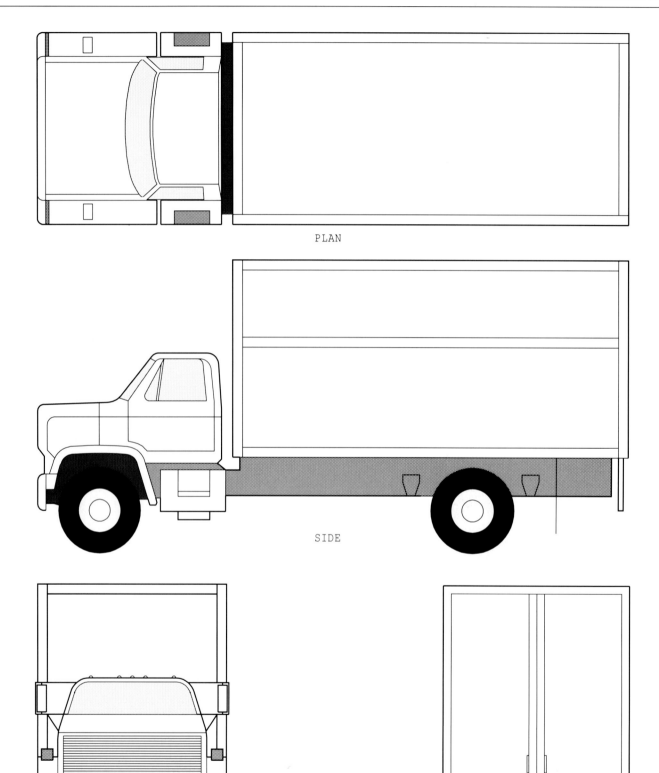

PLAN

SIDE

FRONT

BACK

0 ▭ 4   SEMI-TRUCK AT 1/4" = 1'-0"

SEMI-TRUCK AT 1/4" = 1'-0"   0  4

FRONT

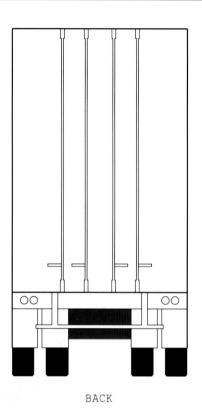

BACK

BUS AT 1/4" = 1'-0"   0 [   ] 4

FRONT

BACK

0 ▭ 4

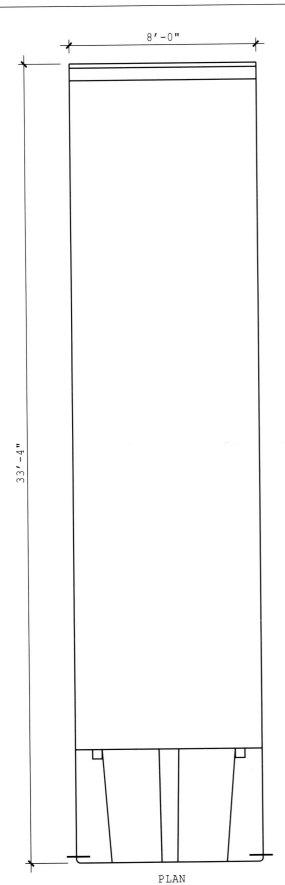

8'-0"

7'-10"

33'-4"

PLAN

SIDE

COMPACT CAR AT 3/16" = 1'-0"   0 [   ] 4

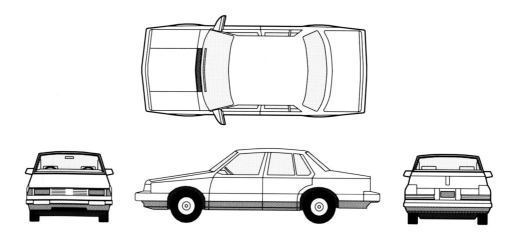

COMPACT SPORTS CAR AT 3/16" = 1'-0"   0 [   ] 4

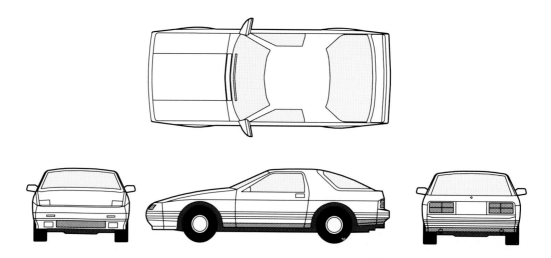

0 [   ] 4   MID-SIZE CAR AT 3/16" = 1'-0"

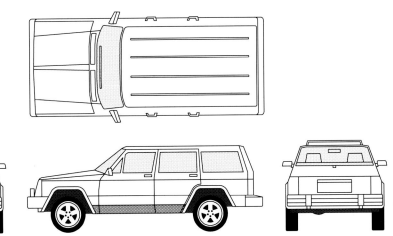

0 [   ] 4   FULL-SIZE CAR AT 3/16" = 1'-0"

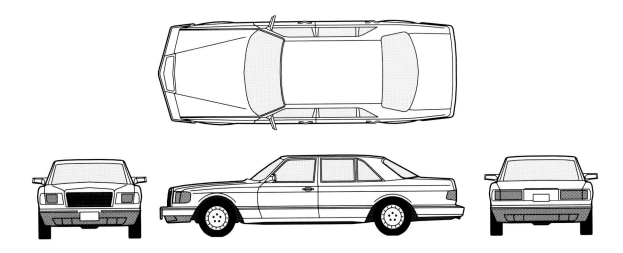

MINI VAN AT 3/16" = 1'-0"   0 [   ] 4

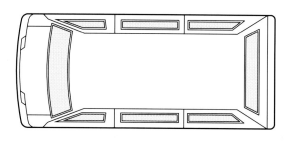

 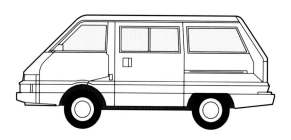 

COMPACT TRUCK AT 3/16" = 1'-0"   0 [   ] 4

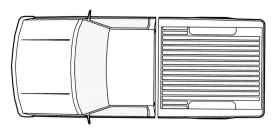

 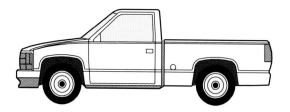 

0 [==========] 4

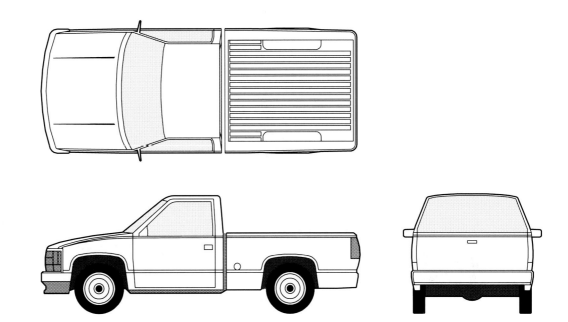

WD-35 TRUCK AT 3/16" = 1'-0"   0 ⬜⬜⬜ 4

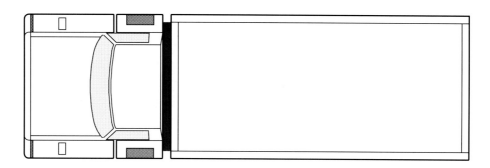

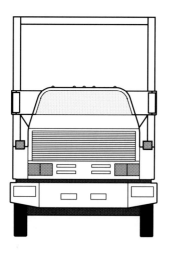

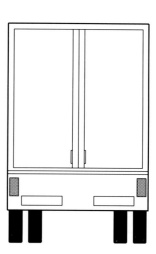

0 ▭ 4

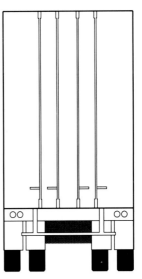

SCHOOL BUS AT 3/16" = 1'-0"   0 ▭ 4

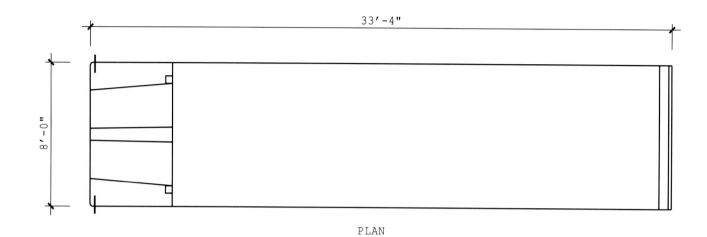

33'-4"

8'-0"

PLAN

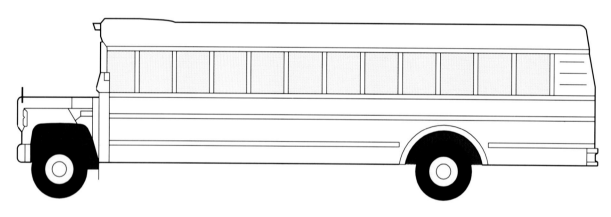

SIDE

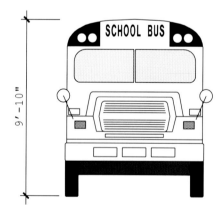

9'-10"

FRONT

BACK

0 ⬜ 8

COMPACT

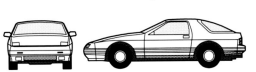

COMPACT SPORTS

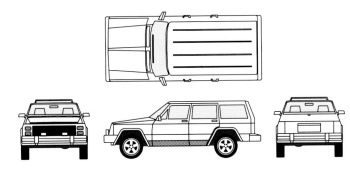

MID-SIZE

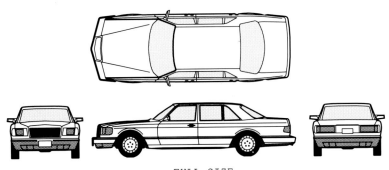

FULL-SIZE

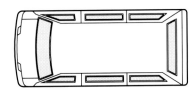

MINI-VAN

VEHICLES AT 1/8" = 1'-0"   0 ▭ 8

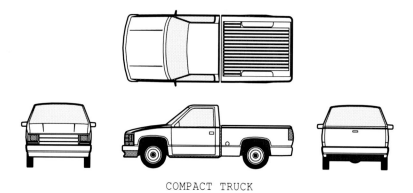

COMPACT TRUCK

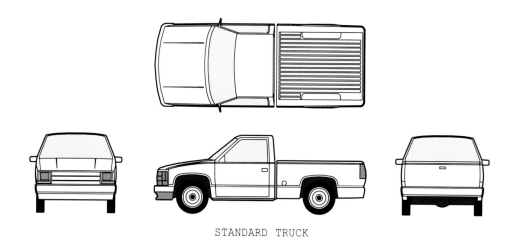

STANDARD TRUCK

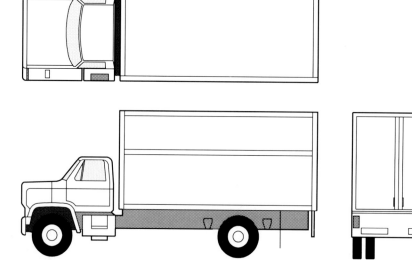

MEDIUM TRUCK

0 ☐ 8

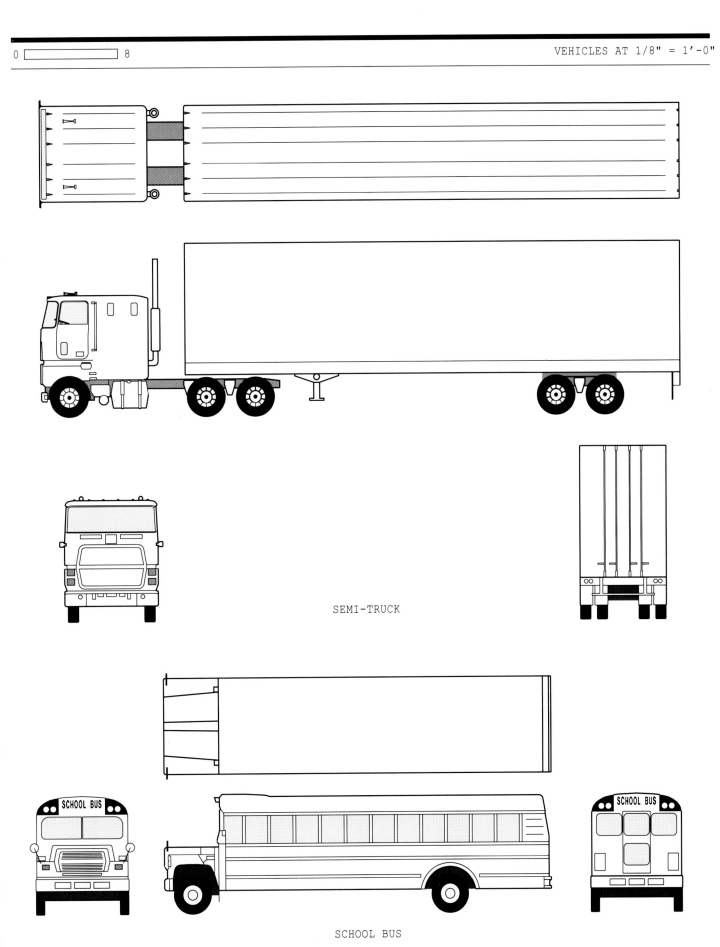

SEMI-TRUCK

SCHOOL BUS

VEHICLES AT 1" = 10'-0"

0 ▭ 10

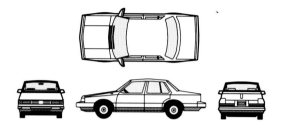

COMPACT

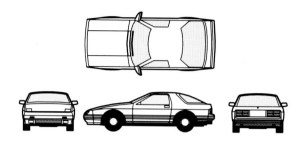

COMPACT SPORTS

MID-SIZE

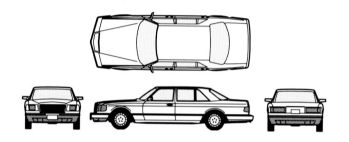

FULL-SIZE

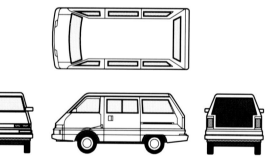

MINI-VAN

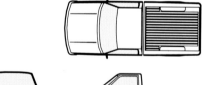

COMPACT TRUCK

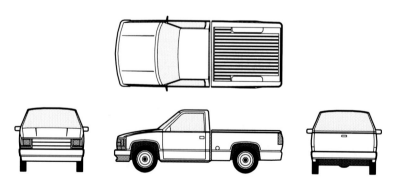

STANDARD TRUCK

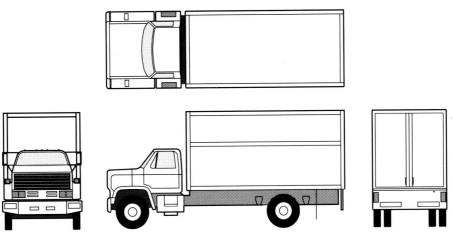

MEDIUM TRUCK

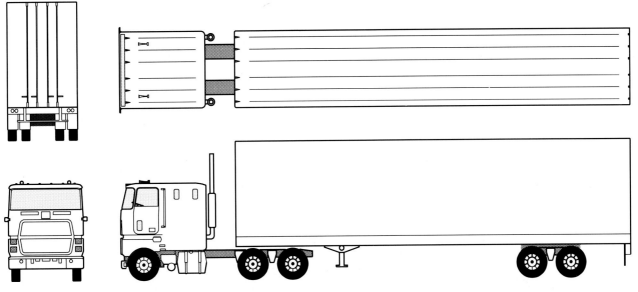

SEMI-TRUCK

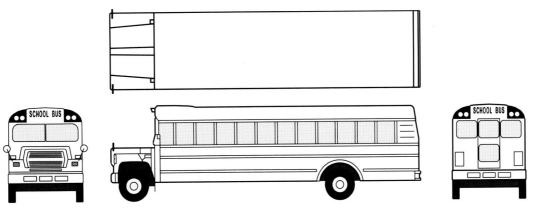

SCHOOL BUS

109

VEHICLES AT 3/32" = 1'-0"   0 ▭ 8

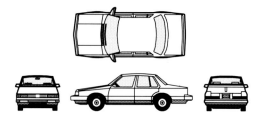

COMPACT

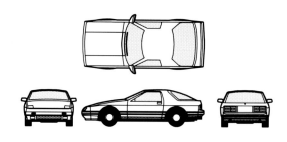

COMPACT SPORT

MID-SIZE

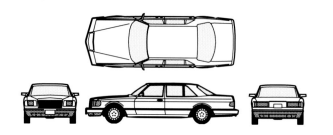

FULL-SIZE

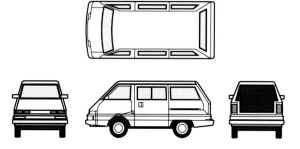

MINI-VAN

COMPACT TRUCK

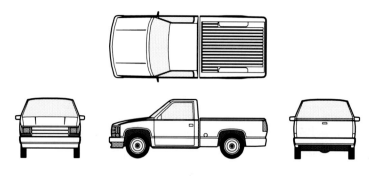

STANDARD TRUCK

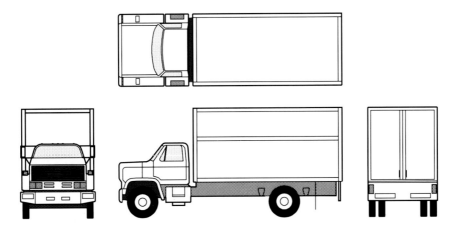

MEDIUM TRUCK

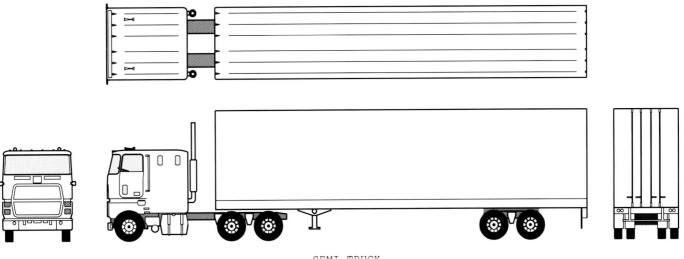

SEMI-TRUCK

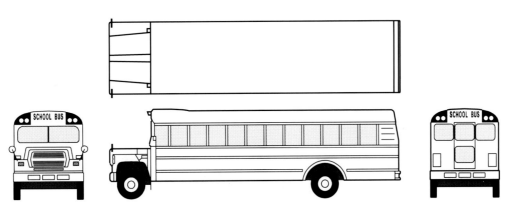

SCHOOL BUS

VEHICLES AT 1/16" = 1'-0"   0 ▭ 16

COMPACT

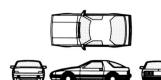

COMPACT

MID-SIZE

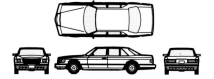

FULL-SIZE

MINI-VAN

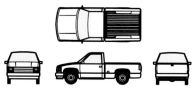

COMPACT TRUCK

STANDARD TRUCK

MEDIUM TRUCK

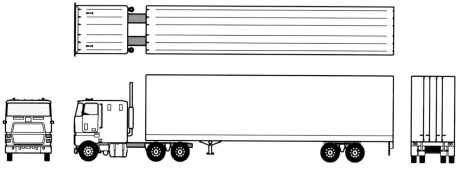

SEMI-TRUCK

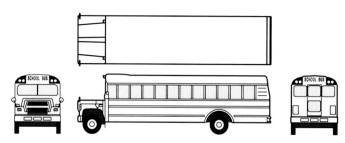

SCHOOL BUS

0 ▭ 20

COMPACT

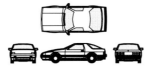

COMPACT

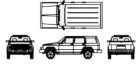

MID-SIZE

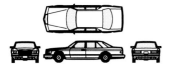

FULL-SIZE

MINI-VAN

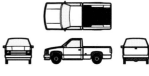

COMPACT TRUCK

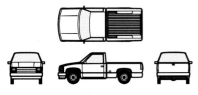

STANDARD TRUCK

MEDIUM TRUCK

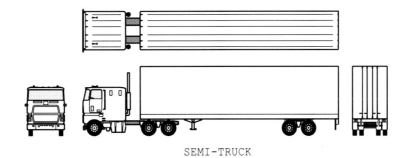

SEMI-TRUCK

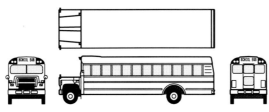

SCHOOL BUS

VEHICLES AT 1" = 30'-0"   0 ▭ 30

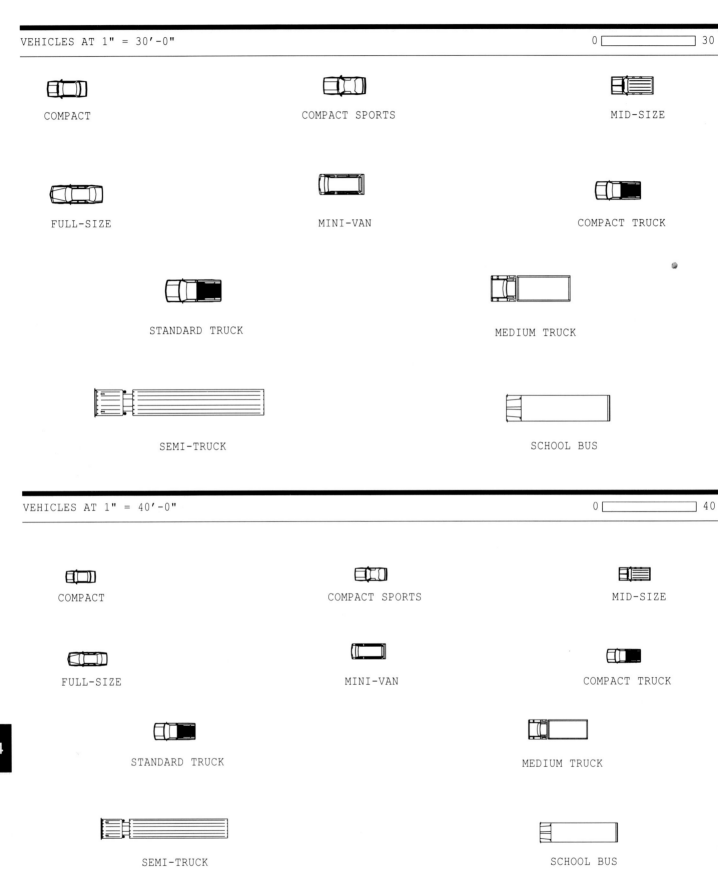

COMPACT   COMPACT SPORTS   MID-SIZE

FULL-SIZE   MINI-VAN   COMPACT TRUCK

STANDARD TRUCK   MEDIUM TRUCK

SEMI-TRUCK   SCHOOL BUS

VEHICLES AT 1" = 40'-0"   0 ▭ 40

COMPACT   COMPACT SPORTS   MID-SIZE

FULL-SIZE   MINI-VAN   COMPACT TRUCK

STANDARD TRUCK   MEDIUM TRUCK

SEMI-TRUCK   SCHOOL BUS

0 [   ] 2   4" x 8" BRICK RUNNING BOND AT 1/2" = 1'-0"

0 [   ] 2   4" x 8" BRICK STACKED BOND AT 1/2" = 1'-0"

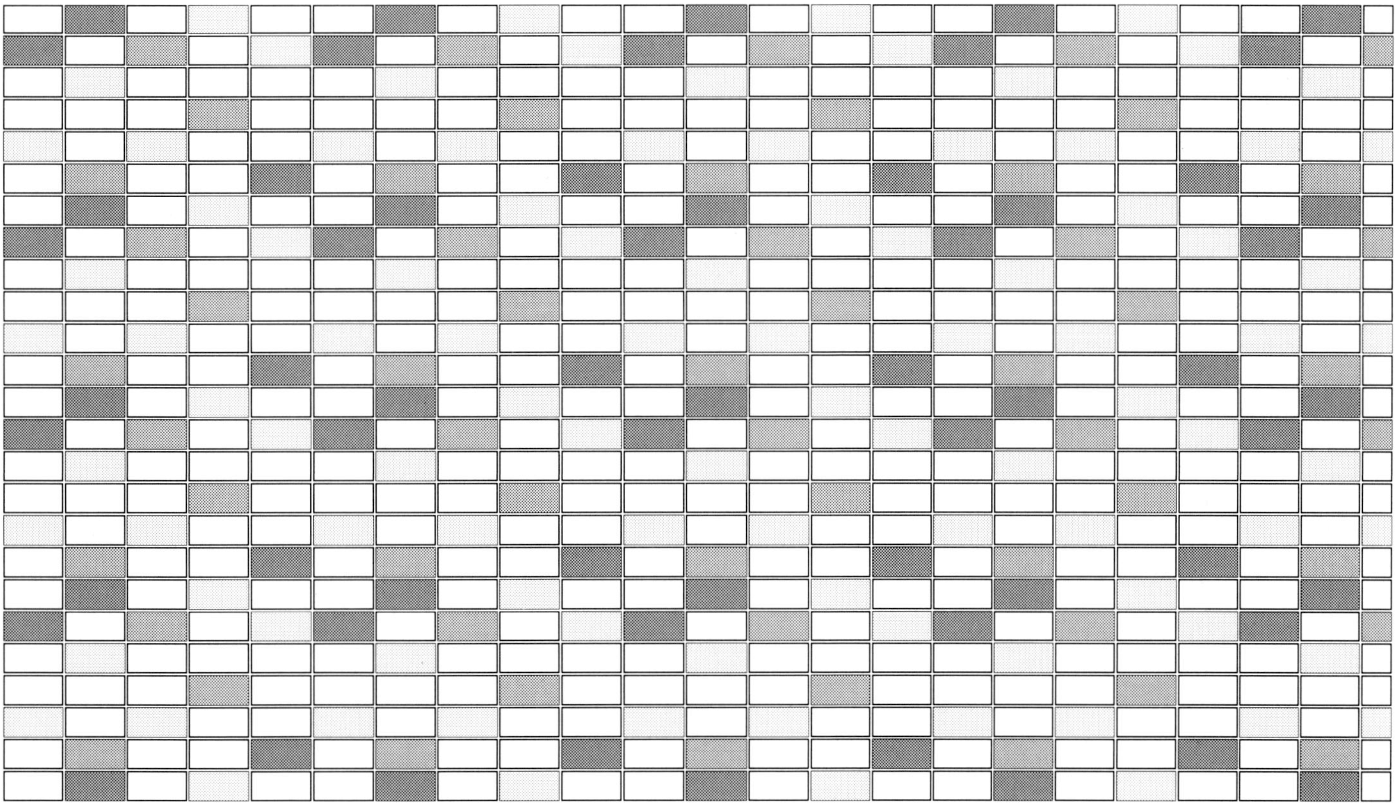

4" x 8" BRICK HERRINGBONE AT 1/2" = 1'-0"   0 ⬜ 2

4" x 8" BRICK BASKETWEAVE VERSION 1 AT 1/2" = 1'-0"   0 ⬜ 2

0 ⬚ 2   4" x 8" BRICK BASKETWEAVE VERSION 2 AT 1/2" = 1'-0"

0 ⬚ 2   4" x 8" BRICK BASKETWEAVE VERSION 3 AT 1/2" = 1'-0"

4" x 8" BRICK BASKETWEAVE VERSION 4 AT 1/2" = 1'-0"   0 [========] 2

PRECAST UNI-STONE AT 1/2" = 1'-0"   0 [========] 2

0 [========] 2   8" HEXAGONAL PRECAST AT 1/2" = 1'-0"

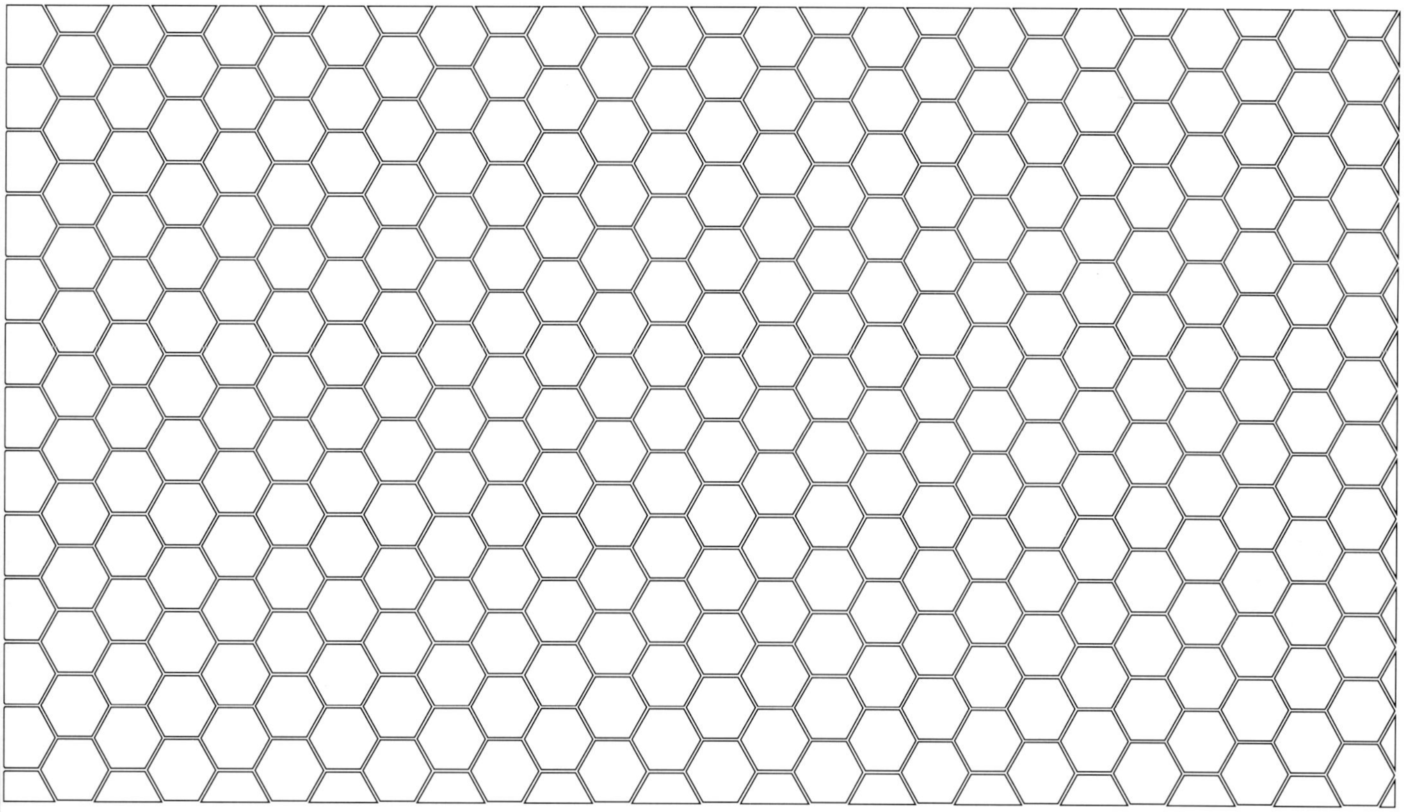

0 [========] 2   8" x 8" PRECAST AT 1/2" = 1'-0"

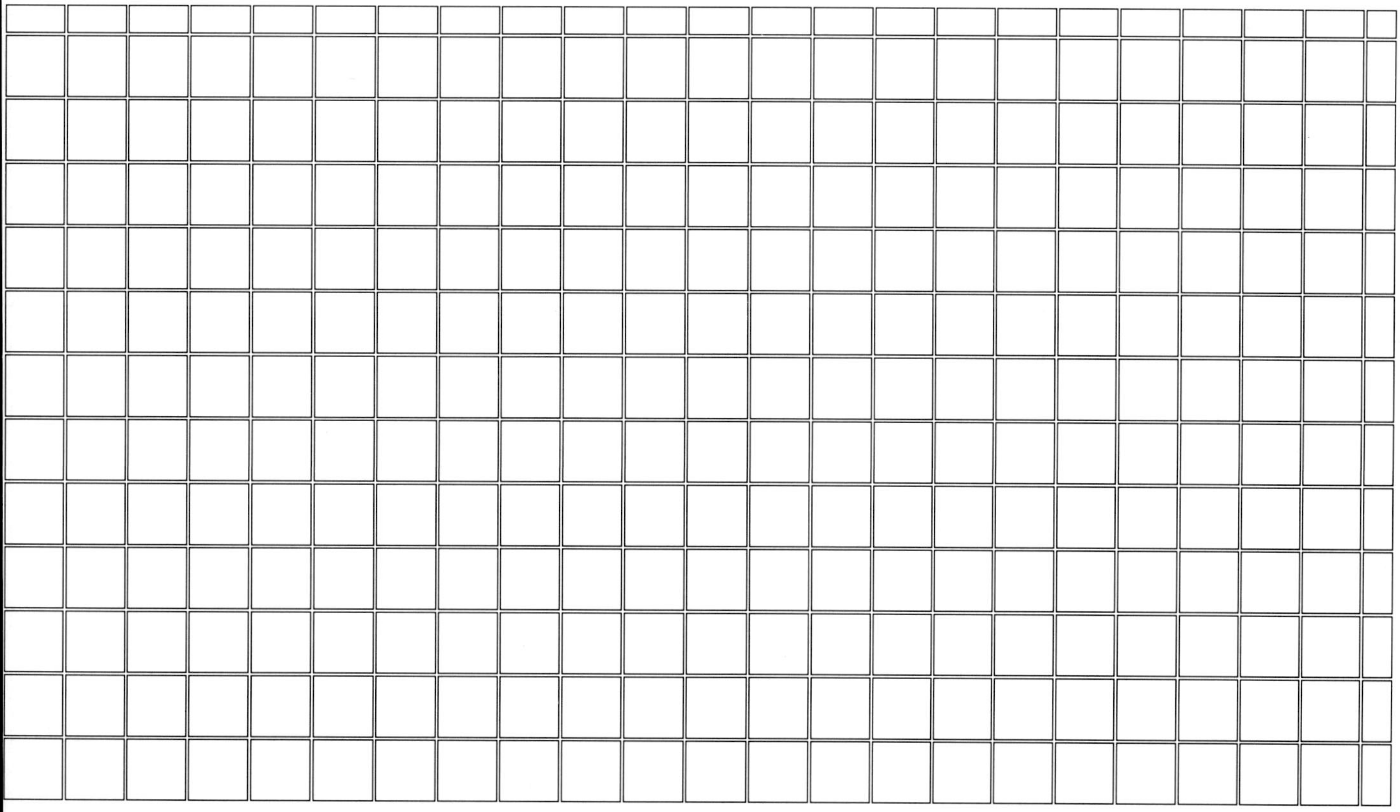

12" x 12" PRECAST AT 1/2" = 1'-0"   0 ⬜⬜⬜⬜⬜ 2

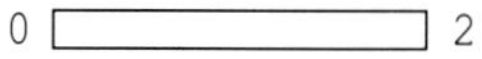

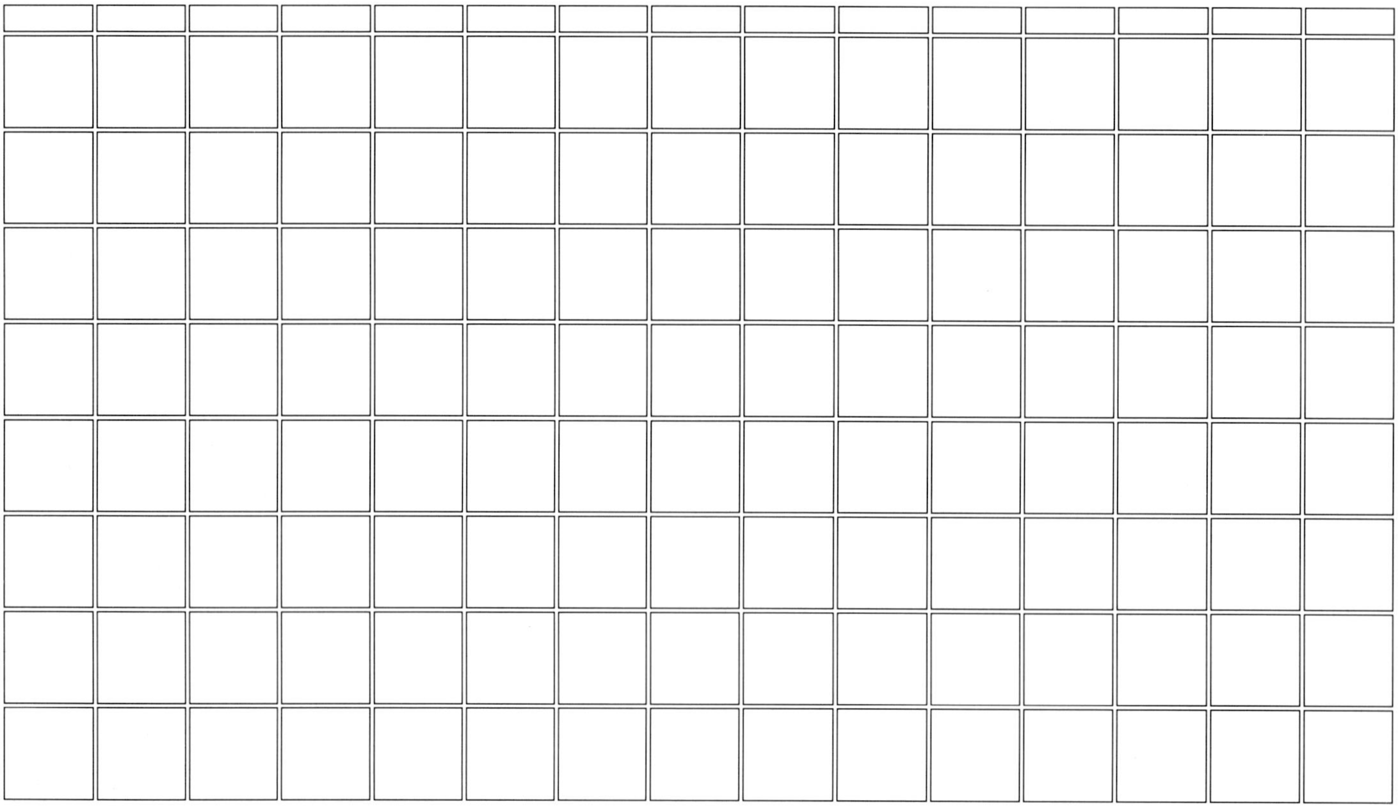

GRASSCRETE AT 1/2" = 1'-0"   0 ⬜⬜⬜⬜⬜ 2

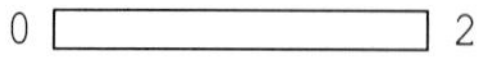

0 ▭ 2   4" x 4" STONE   RADIAL AT 1/2" = 1'-0"

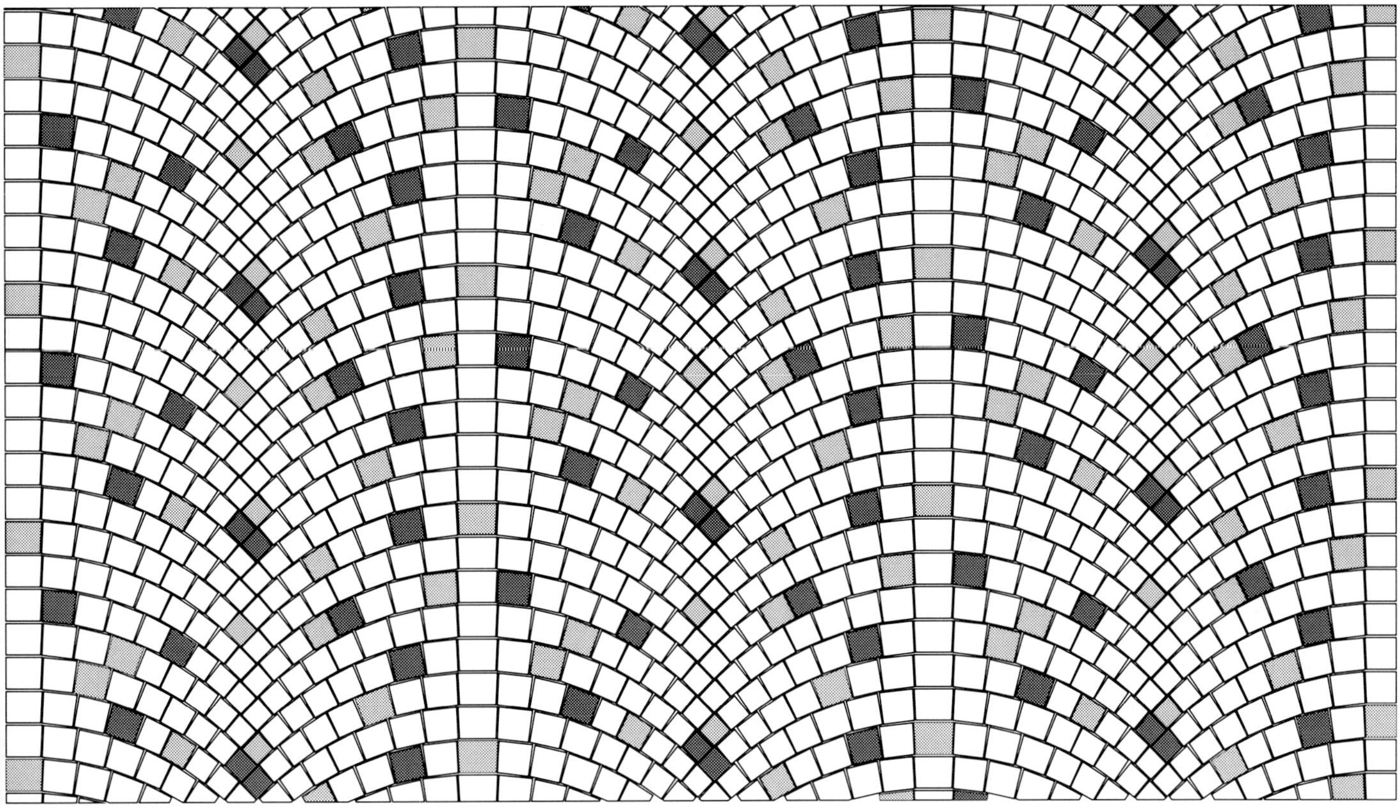

0 ▭ 2   4" x 4" STONE   FISHSCALE AT 1/2" = 1'-0"

UNCOURSED RANDOM STONE AT 1/2" = 1'-0"   0 ⬜ 2

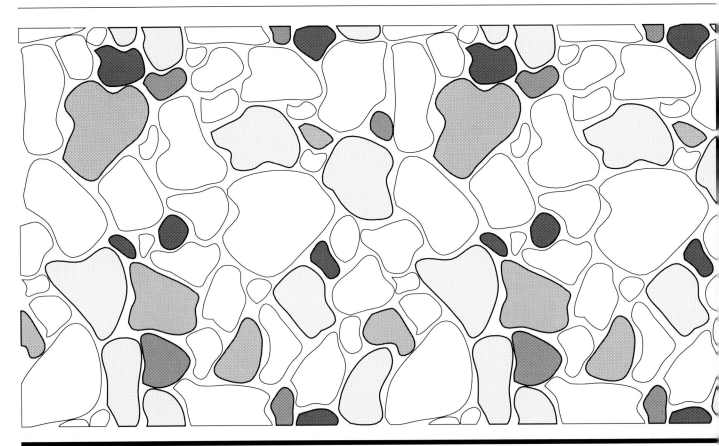

COURSED RANDOM STONE AT 1/2" = 1'-0"   0 ⬜ 2

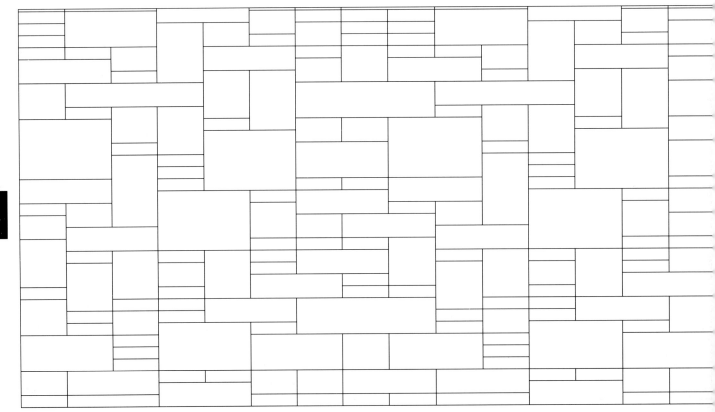

0 [____] 2   4" x 8" RUNNING BOND AT 3/8" = 1'-0"

0 [____] 2   4" x 8" STACKED BOND AT 3/8" = 1'-0"

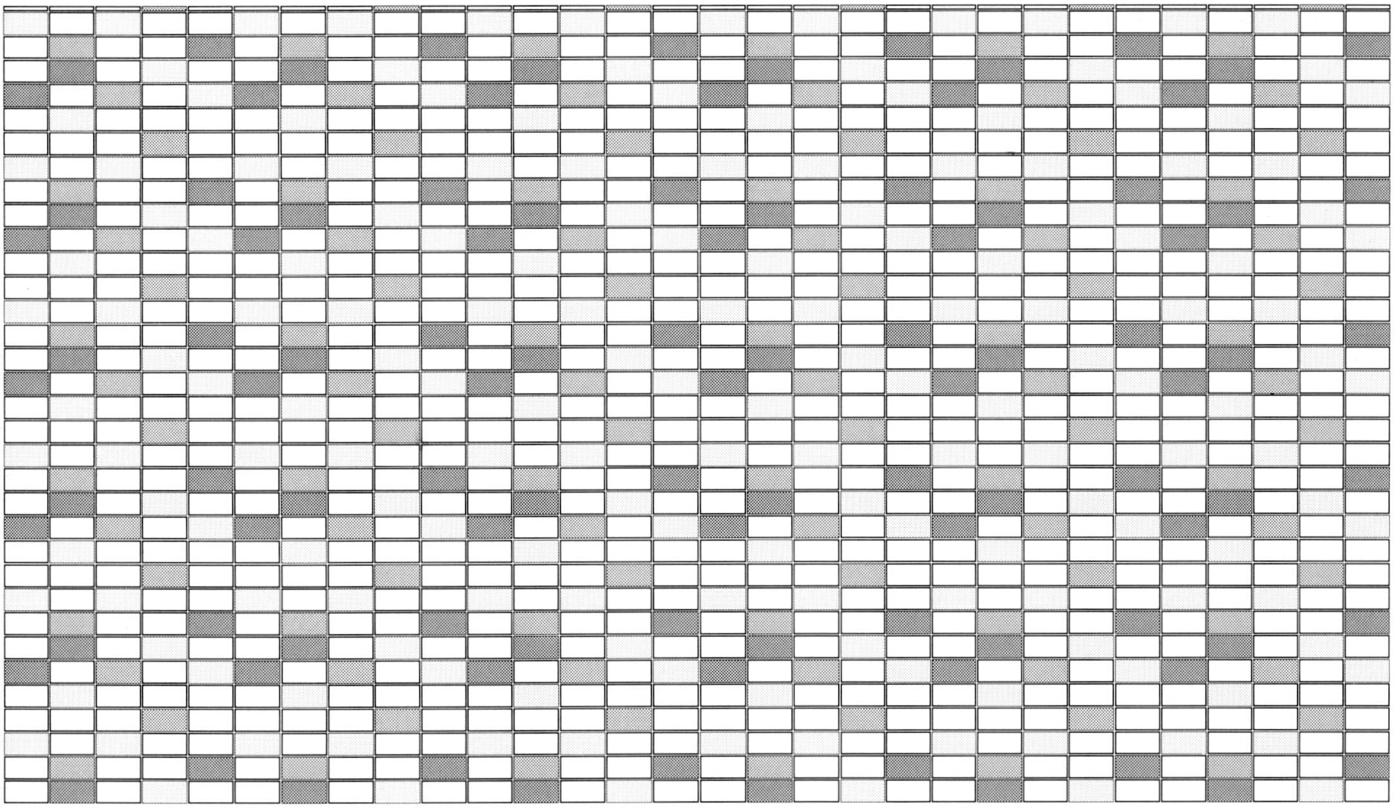

123

4" x 8" HERRINGBONE AT 3/8" = 1'-0"   0 ⬚ 2

4" x 8" BASKETWEAVE VERSION 1 AT 3/8" = 1'-0"   0 ⬚ 2

0 ⬜ 2   4" x 8" BASKETWEAVE VERSION 2 AT 3/8" = 1'-0"

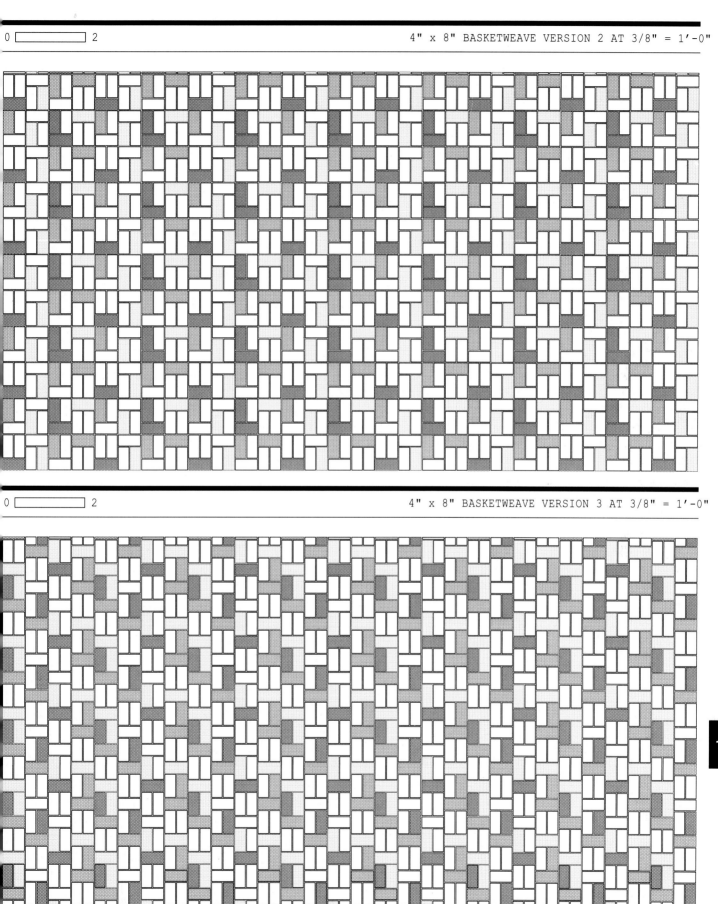

0 ⬜ 2   4" x 8" BASKETWEAVE VERSION 3 AT 3/8" = 1'-0"

4" x 8" BASKETWEAVE VERSION 4 AT 3/8" = 1'-0"   0 ☐ 2

UNI-STONE AT 3/8" = 1'-0"   0 ☐ 2

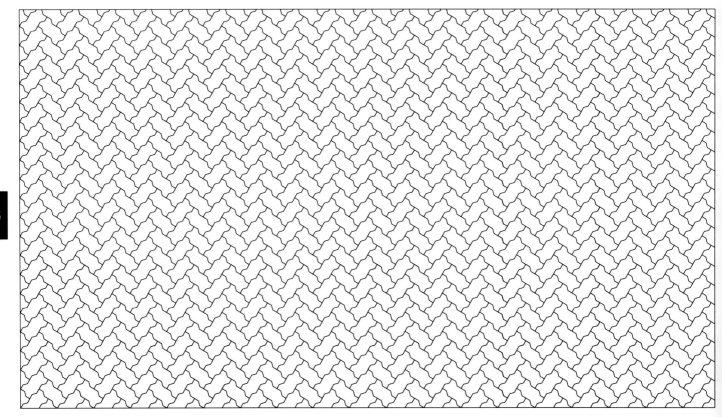

0 ⬜⬜⬜ 2   8" HEXAGONAL AT 3/8" = 1'-0"

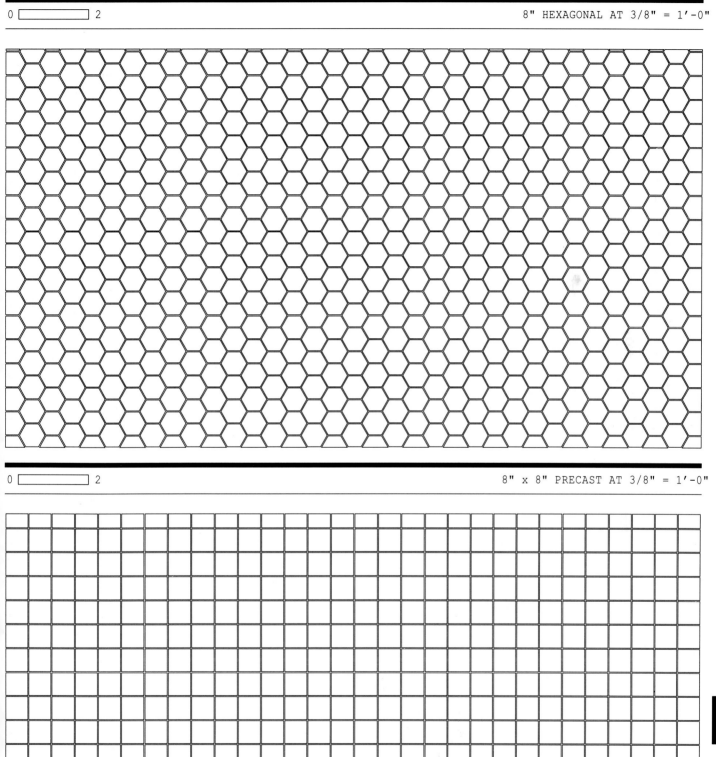

0 ⬜⬜⬜ 2   8" x 8" PRECAST AT 3/8" = 1'-0"

12" x 12" PRECAST AT 3/8" = 1'-0"   0 ▭ 2

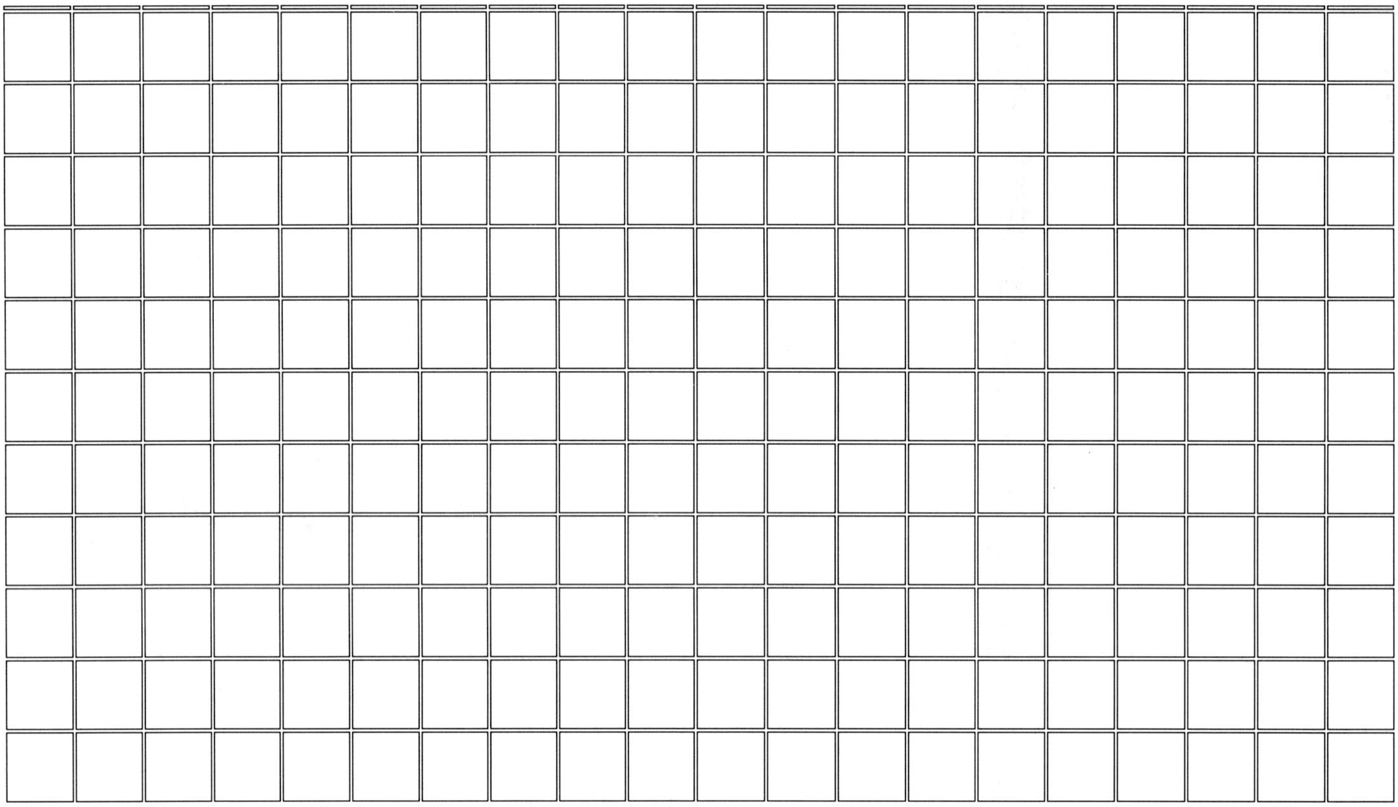

GRASSCRETE   AT 3/8" = 1'-0"   0 ▭ 2

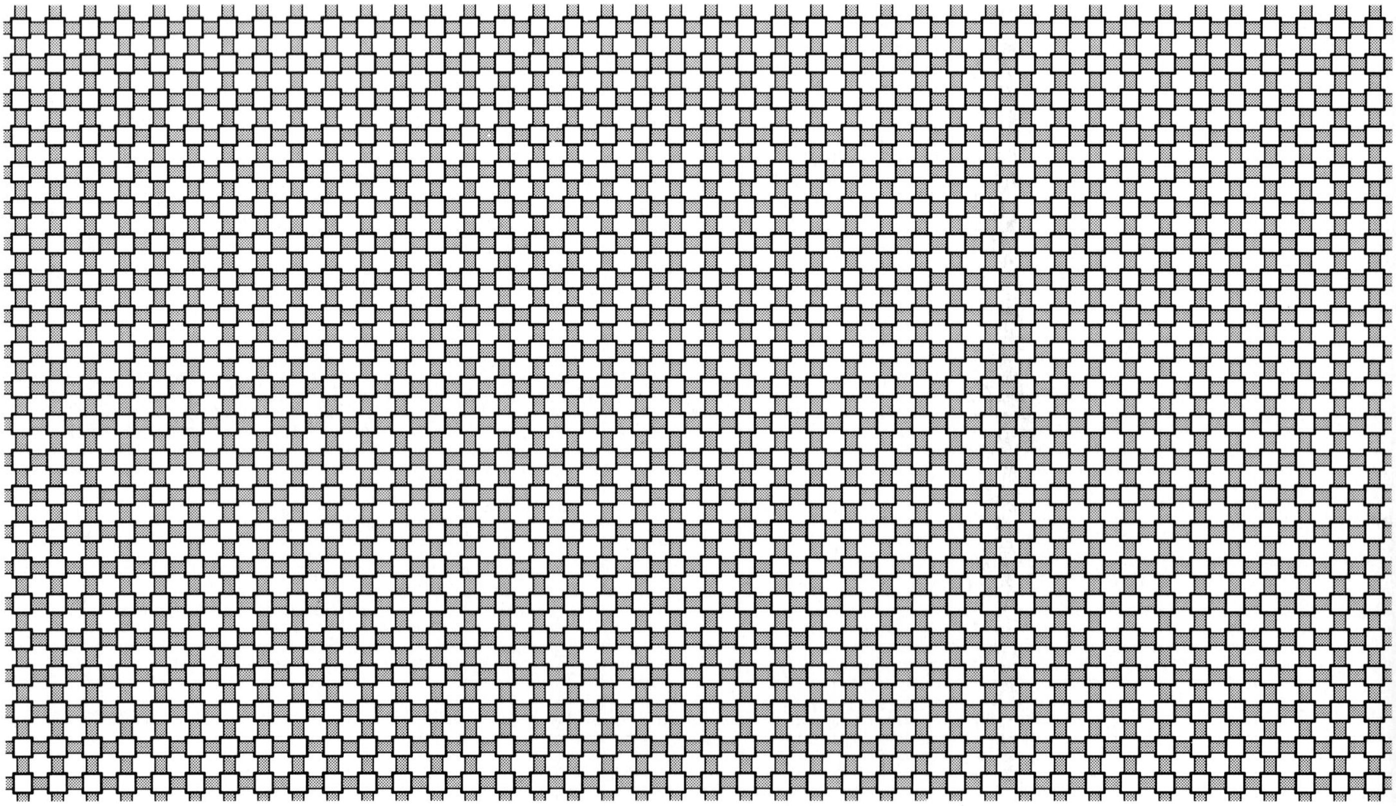

0 [   ] 2   4" x 4" RADIAL AT 3/8" = 1'-0"

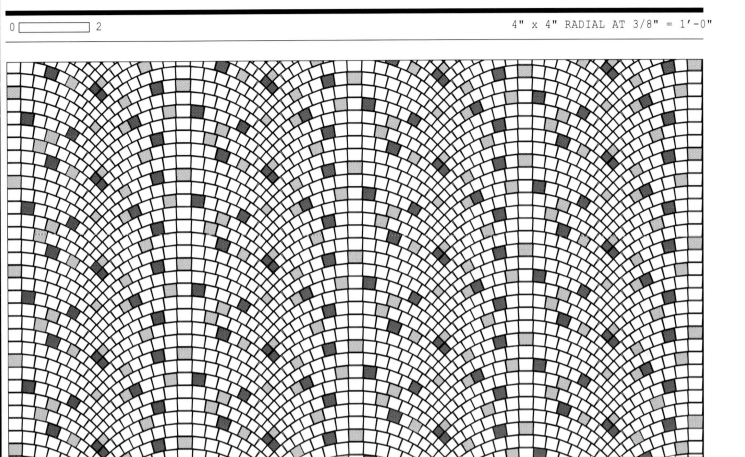

0 [   ] 2   4" x 4" FISHSCALE AT 3/8" = 1'-0"

UNCOURSED RANDOM AT 3/8" = 1'-0"   0 ▭ 2

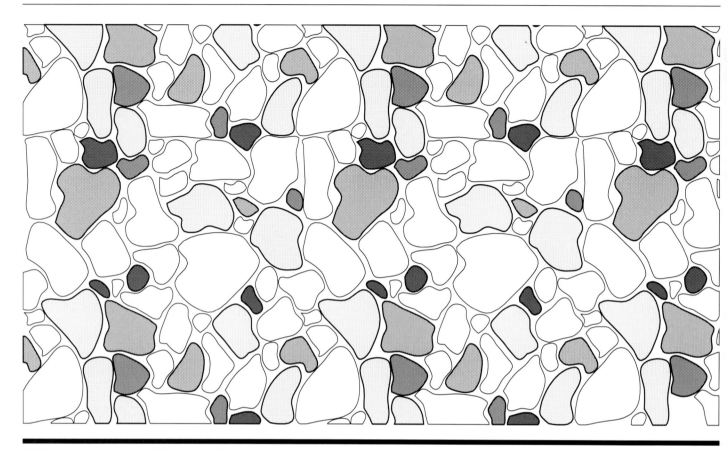

COURSED RANDOM AT 3/8" = 1'-0"   0 ▭ 2

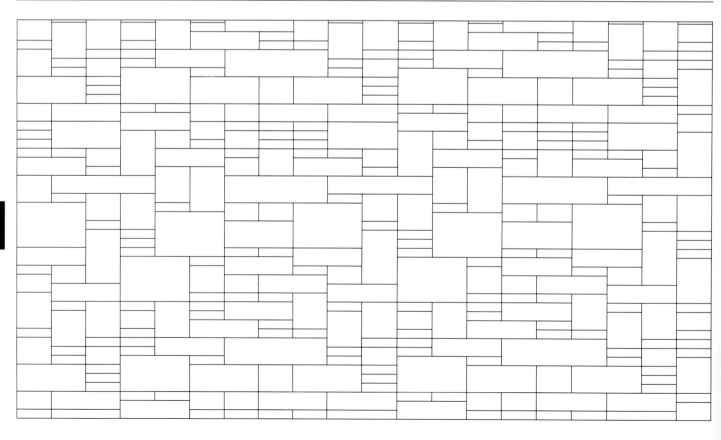

0 [====] 4   RUNNING BOND AT 1/4"=1'

0 [====] 4   STACKED BOND AT 1/4"=1'

0 [====] 4   HERRINGBONE AT 1/4"=1'

0 [====] 4   BASKETWEAVE AT 1/4"=1'

BASKETWEAVE AT 1/4" = 1'-0"   0 [========] 4

BASKETWEAVE AT 1/4" = 1'-0"   0 [========] 4

UNI-STONE AT 1/4" = 1'-0"   0 [========] 4

BASKETWEAVE AT 1/4" = 1'-0"   0 [========] 4

0 [   ] 4   8" HEXAGONAL AT 1/4" = 1'-0"

0 [   ] 4   8" PRECAST AT 1/4" = 1'-0"

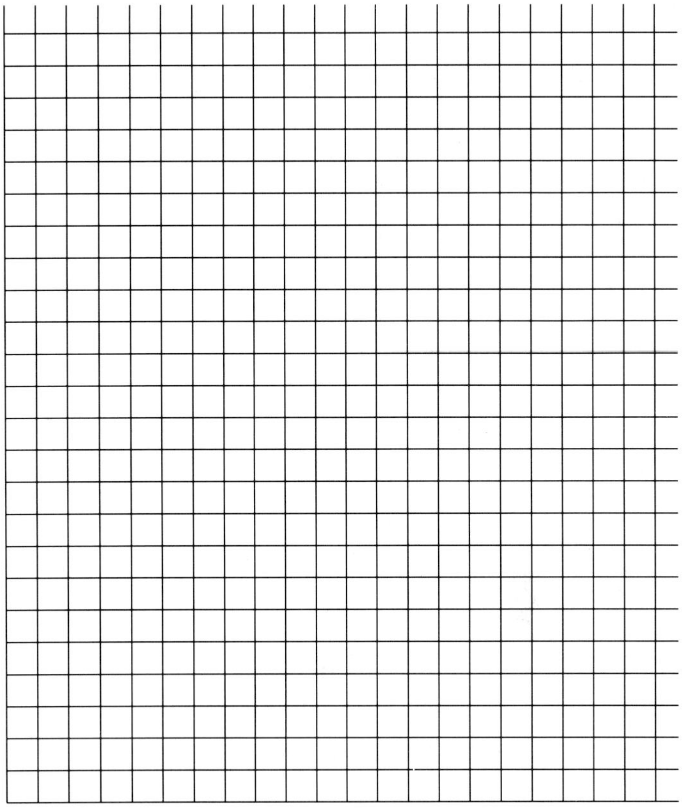

0 [   ] 4   12" PRECAST AT 1/4" = 1'-0"

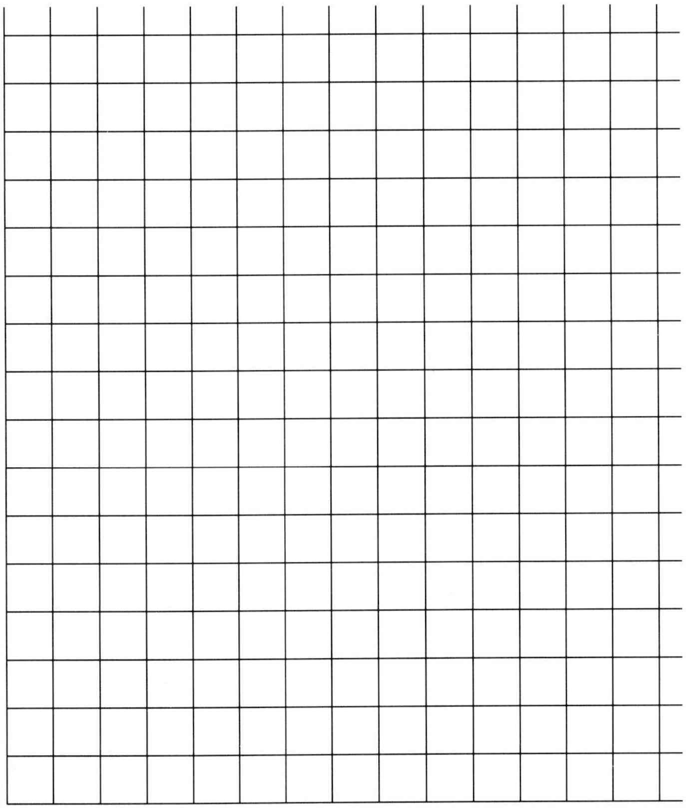

0 [   ] 4   GRASSCRETE AT 1/4" = 1'-0"

133

RADIAL AT 1/4" = 1'-0"   0 [_____] 4

FISHSCALE AT 1/4" = 1'-0"   0 [_____] 4

UNCOURSED RANDOM AT 1/4" = 1'-0" 0 [_____] 4

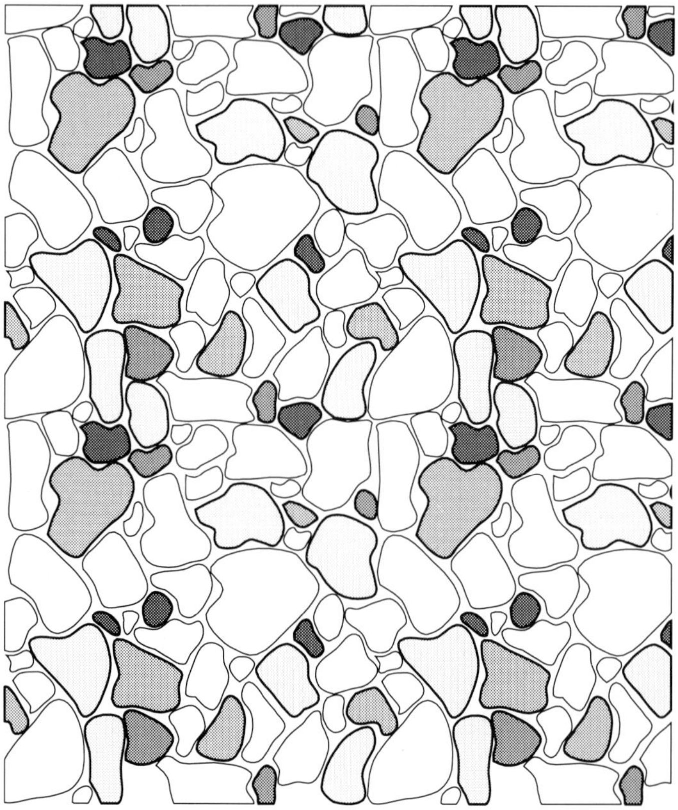

COURSED RANDOM AT 1/4" = 1'-0"   0 [_____] 4

0 [＿＿＿＿] 4 RUNNING BOND AT 3/16" = 1'-0"

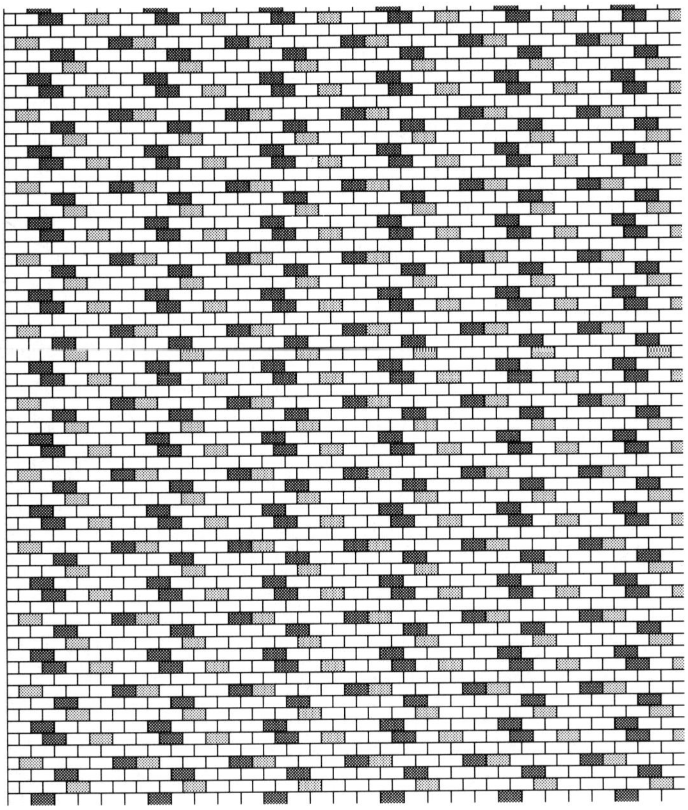

0 [＿＿＿＿] 4 STACKED BOND AT 3/16" = 1'-0"

0 [＿＿＿＿] 4 HERRINGBONE AT 3/16" = 1'-0"

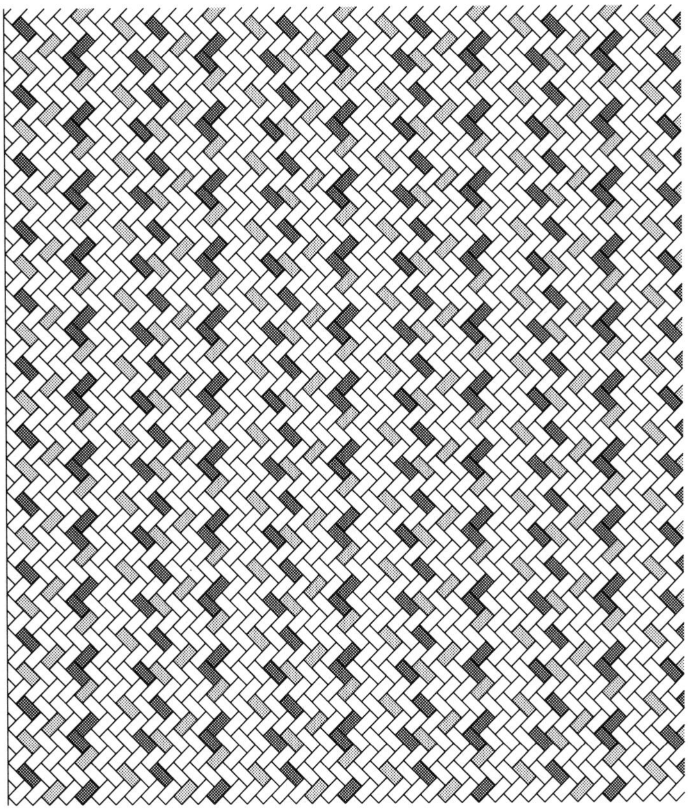

0 [＿＿＿＿] 4 BASKETWEAVE AT 3/16" = 1'-0"

BASKETWEAVE AT 3/16" = 1'-0" 0 ▭ 4

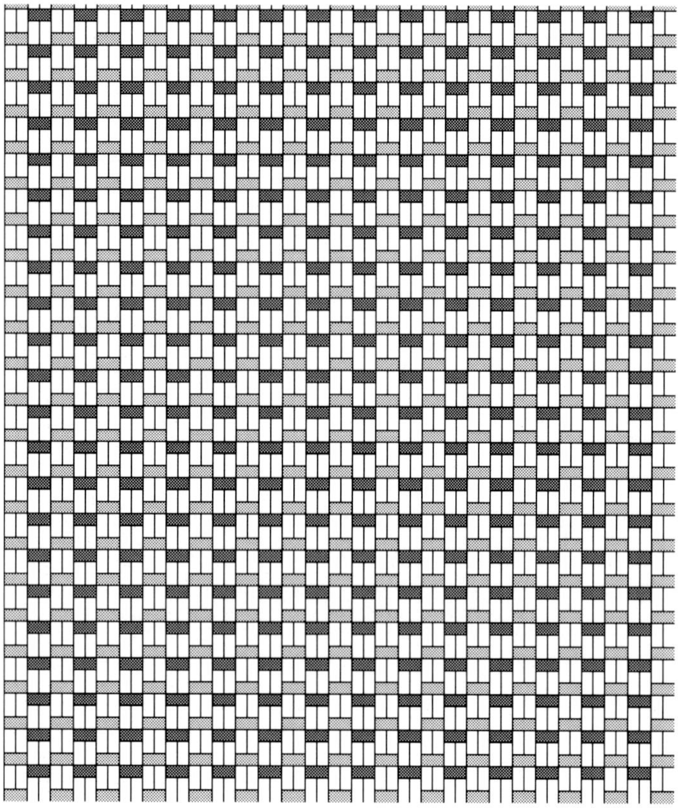

BASKETWEAVE AT 3/16" = 1'-0" 0 ▭ 4

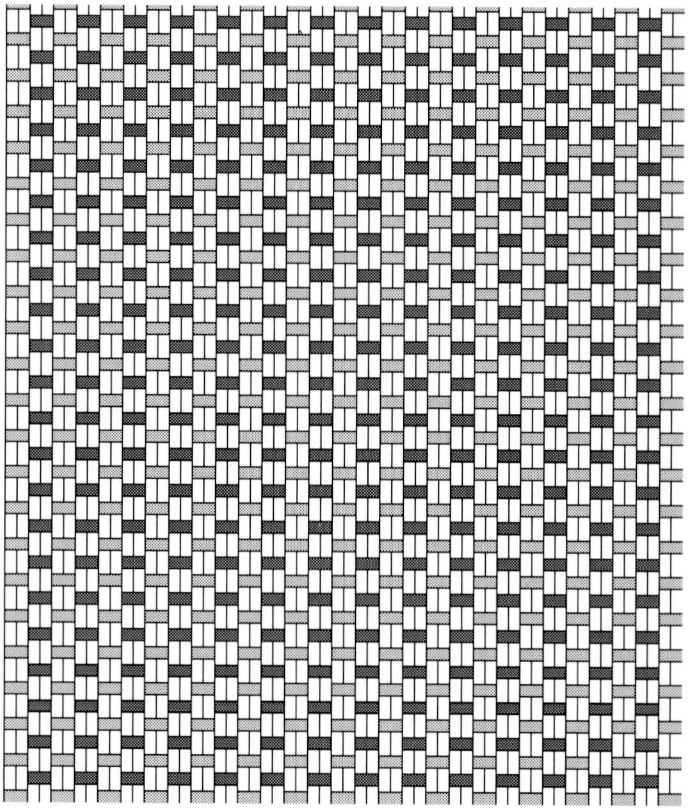

UNI AT STONE AT 3/16" = 1'-0" 0 ▭ 4

BASKETWEAVE AT 3/16" = 1'-0" 0 ▭ 4

0 [＝＝＝] 4   8" HEXAGONAL AT 3/16" = 1'-0"

0 [＝＝＝] 4   8" PRECAST AT 3/16" = 1'-0"

0 [＝＝＝] 4   12" PRECAST AT 3/16" = 1'-0"

0 [＝＝＝] 4   GRASSCRETE AT 3/16" = 1'-0"

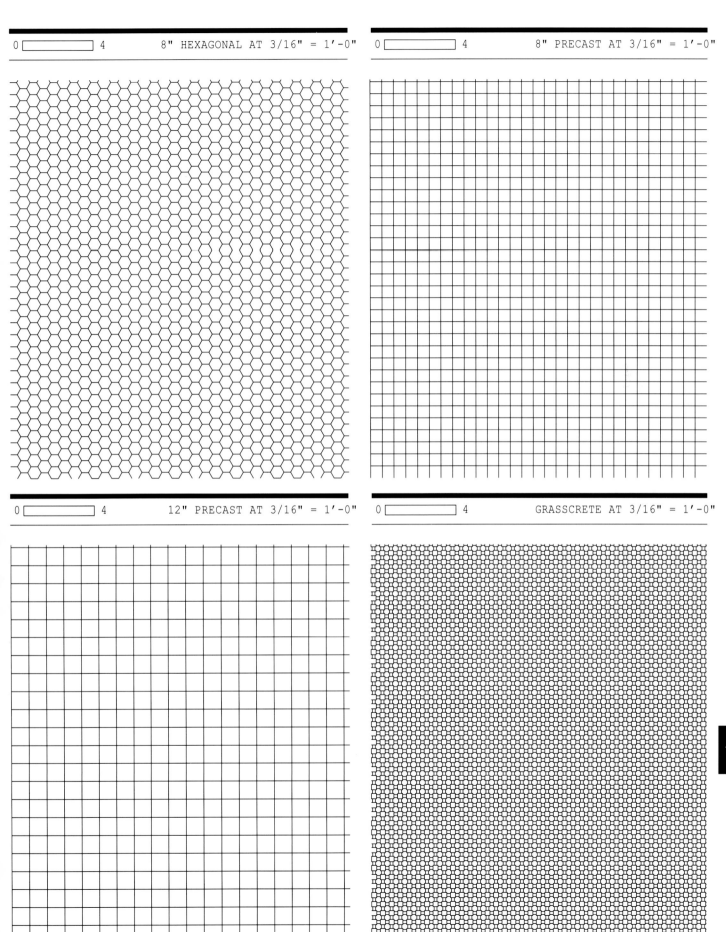

RADIAL AT 3/16" = 1'-0" 0 ▭ 4

FISHSCALE AT 3/16" = 1'-0" 0 ▭ 4

UNCOURSED RANDOM AT 3/16" = 1'-0" 0 ▭ 4

COURSED RANDOM AT 3/16" = 1'-0" 0 ▭ 4

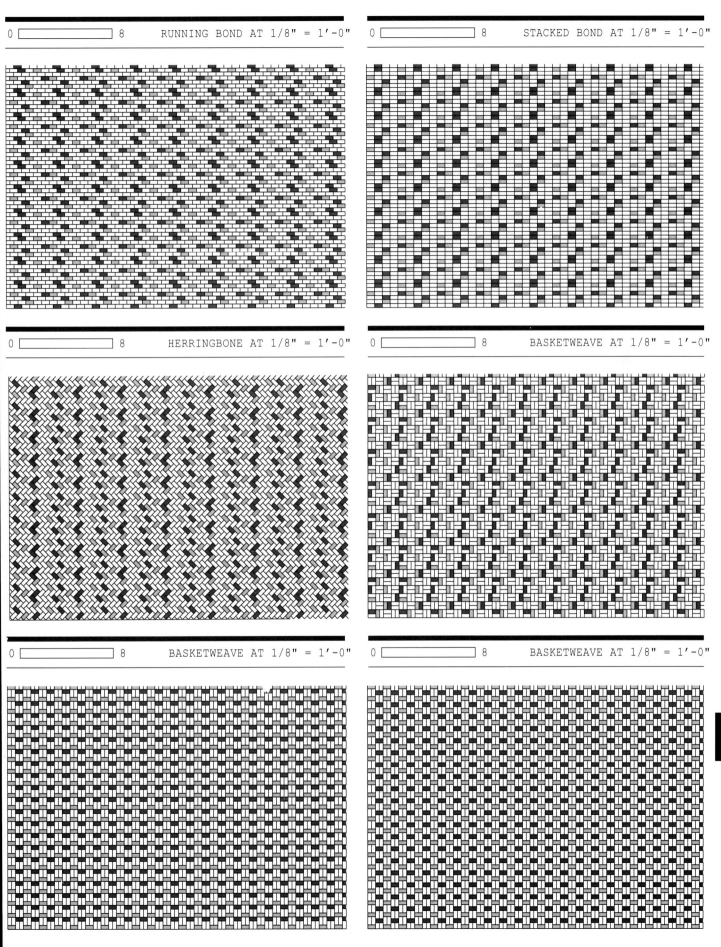

0 ⬚ 8   RUNNING BOND AT 1/8" = 1'-0"

0 ⬚ 8   STACKED BOND AT 1/8" = 1'-0"

0 ⬚ 8   HERRINGBONE AT 1/8" = 1'-0"

0 ⬚ 8   BASKETWEAVE AT 1/8" = 1'-0"

0 ⬚ 8   BASKETWEAVE AT 1/8" = 1'-0"

0 ⬚ 8   BASKETWEAVE AT 1/8" = 1'-0"

BASKETWEAVE AT 1/8" = 1'-0"   0 [========] 8

UNI AT STONE-1/8" = 1'-0"   0 [========] 8

8" HEXAGONAL AT 1/8" = 1'-0"   0 [========] 8

8" PRECAST AT 1/8" = 1'-0"   0 [========] 8

12" PRECAST AT 1/8" = 1'-0"   0 [========] 8

GRASSCRETE AT 1/8" = 1'-0"   0 [========] 8

0 ▭ 8   FISHSCALE AT 1/8" = 1'-0"

0 ▭ 8   RADIAL AT 1/8" = 1'-0"

0 ▭ 8   COURSED RANDOM AT 1/8' = 1'-0"

0 ▭ 8   UNCOURSED RANDOM AT 1/8" = 1'-0"

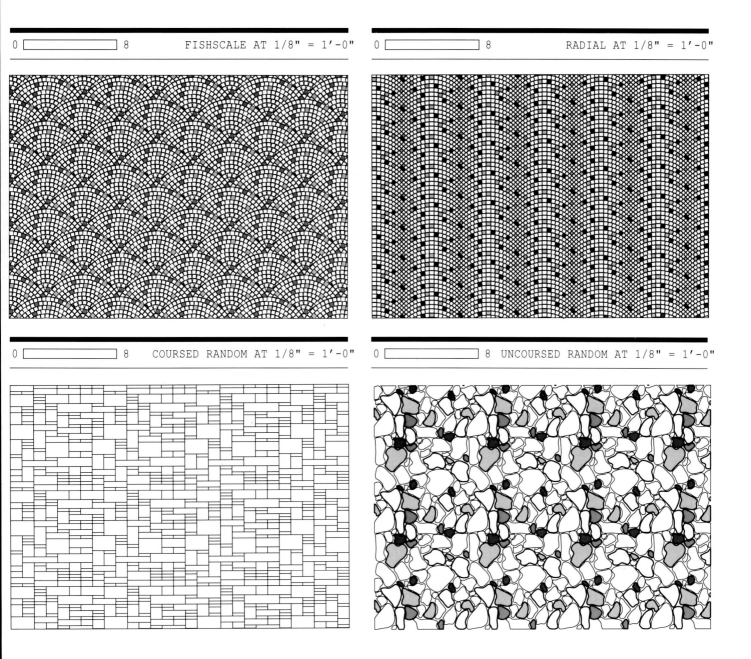

2" X 6" WOOD DECKING AT 1/2" = 1'-0"   0 ▭ 2

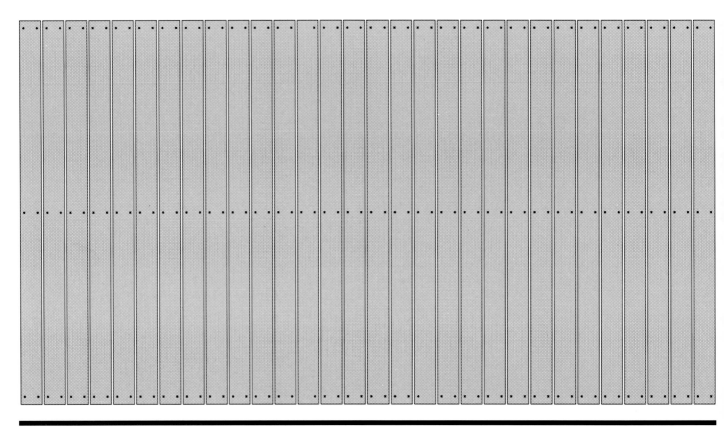

2" X 6" AND 2" X 4" WOOD DECKING AT 1/2" = 1'-0"   0 ▭ 2

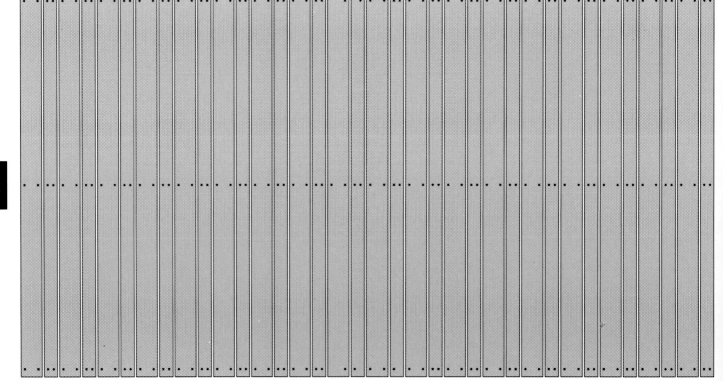

0 ⬛⬜⬜ 2   2" X 6" WOOD DECKING AT 3/8" = 1'-0"

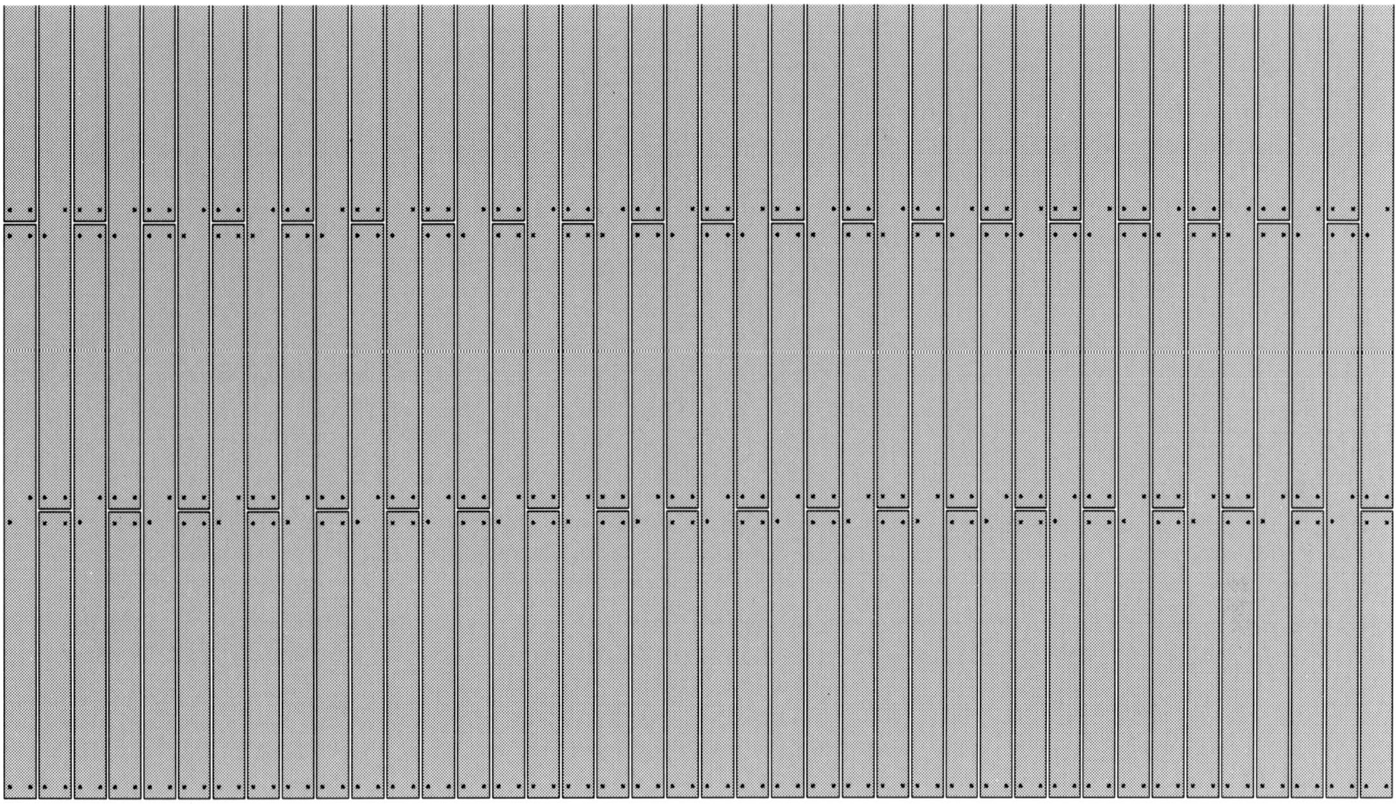

0 ⬛⬜⬜ 2   2" X 6" AND 2" X 4" WOOD DECKING AT 3/8" = 1'-0"

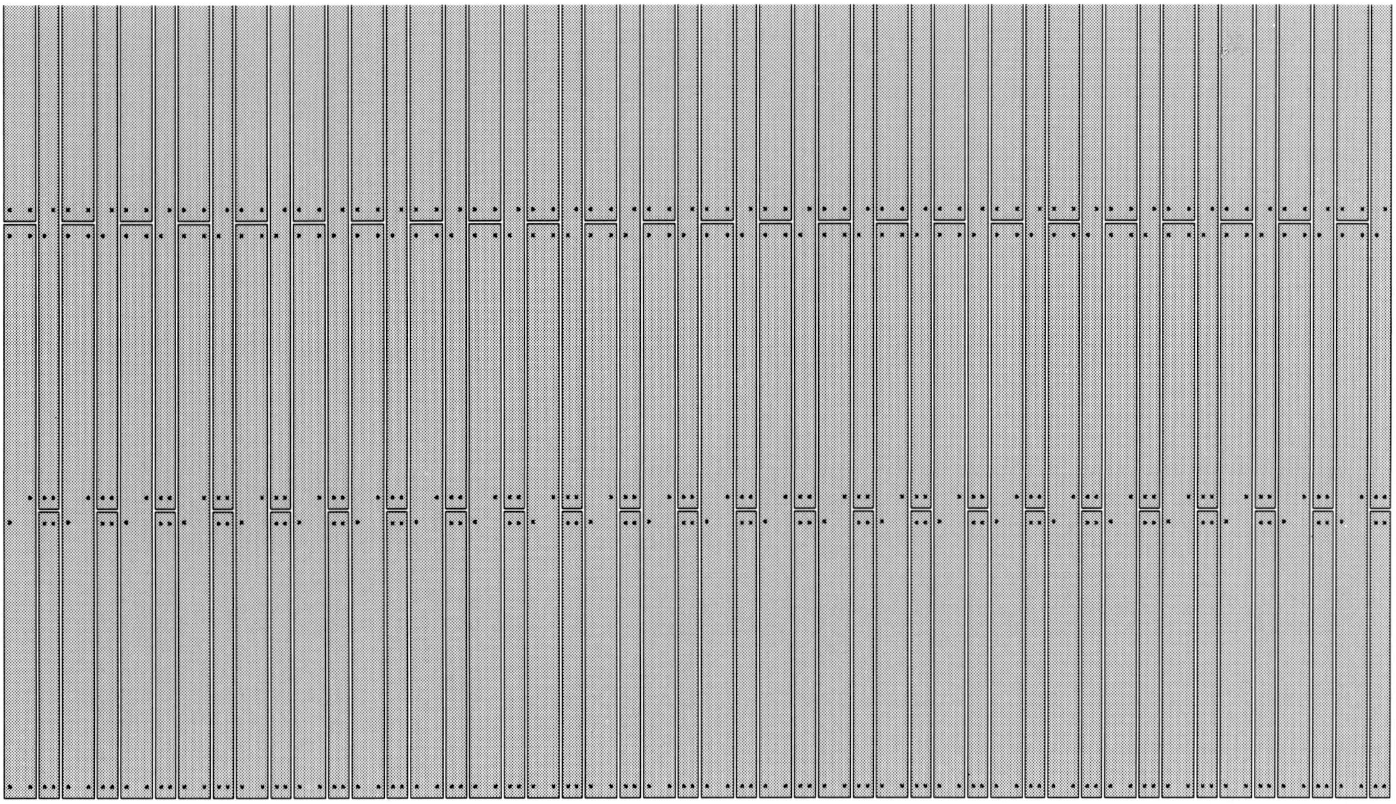

DECKING AT 1/4"=1'-0"   0 ▭ 4

DECKING AT 1/4"=1'-0"   0 ▭ 4

DECKING AT 3/16"=1'-0"   0 ▭ 4

DECKING AT 3/16"=1'-0"   0 ▭ 4

DECKING AT 1/8"=1'-0"   0 ▭ 8

DECKING AT 1/8"=1'-0"   0 ▭ 8

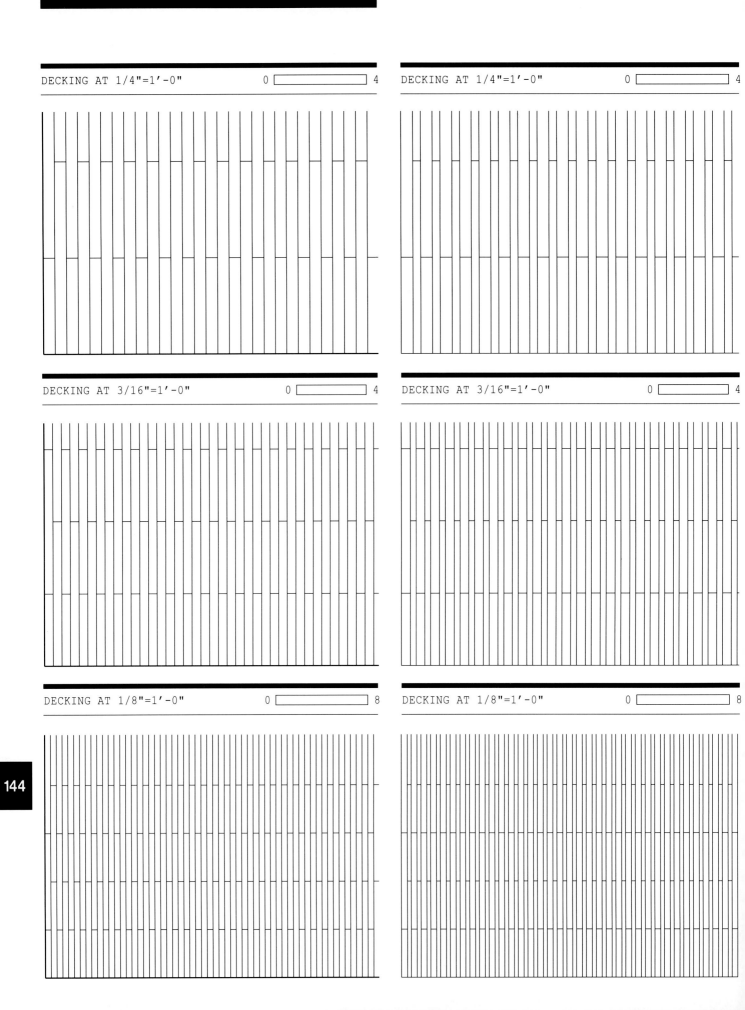

0 [   ] 2

11"

1'-2"

32.47 DEGREES   STEPS AT 7:11

7"

23.19 DEGREES   STEPS AT 6:14

1'-4"

6"

17.38 DEGREES   STEPS AT 5:16

1'-6"

5"

12.52 DEGREES   STEPS AT 4:18

4"

1'-8"

8.5 DEGREES   STEPS AT 3:21

3"

145

STEPS IN SECTION AT 3/8" = 1'-0"   0 ☐☐☐☐ 2

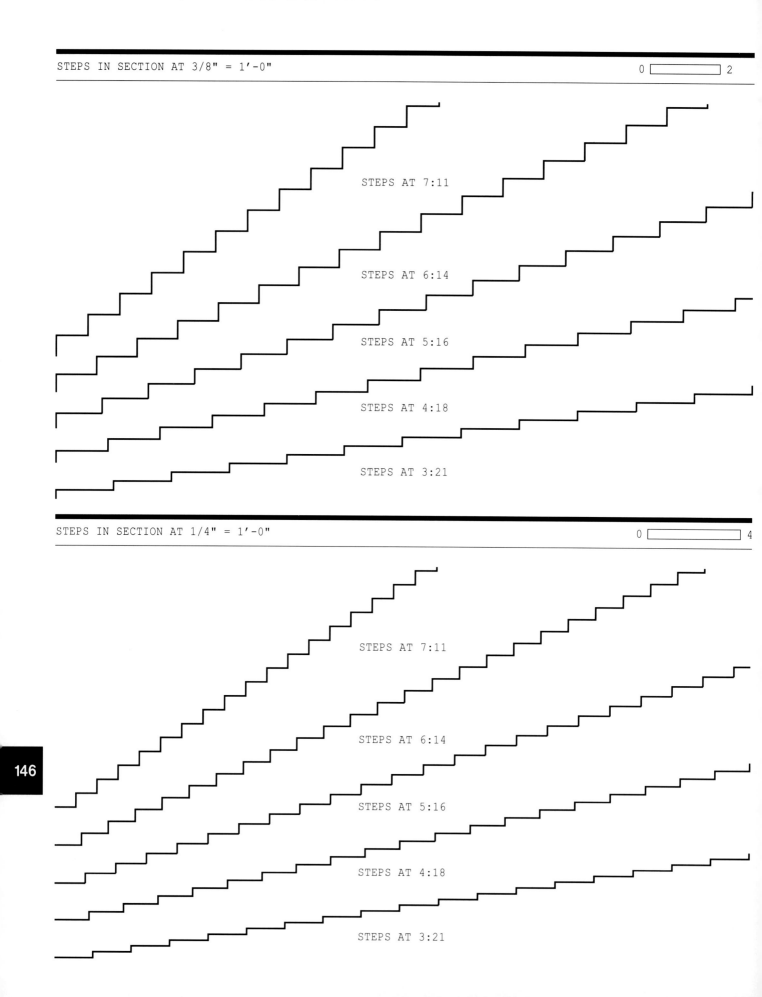

STEPS AT 7:11

STEPS AT 6:14

STEPS AT 5:16

STEPS AT 4:18

STEPS AT 3:21

STEPS IN SECTION AT 1/4" = 1'-0"   0 ☐☐☐☐ 4

STEPS AT 7:11

STEPS AT 6:14

STEPS AT 5:16

STEPS AT 4:18

STEPS AT 3:21

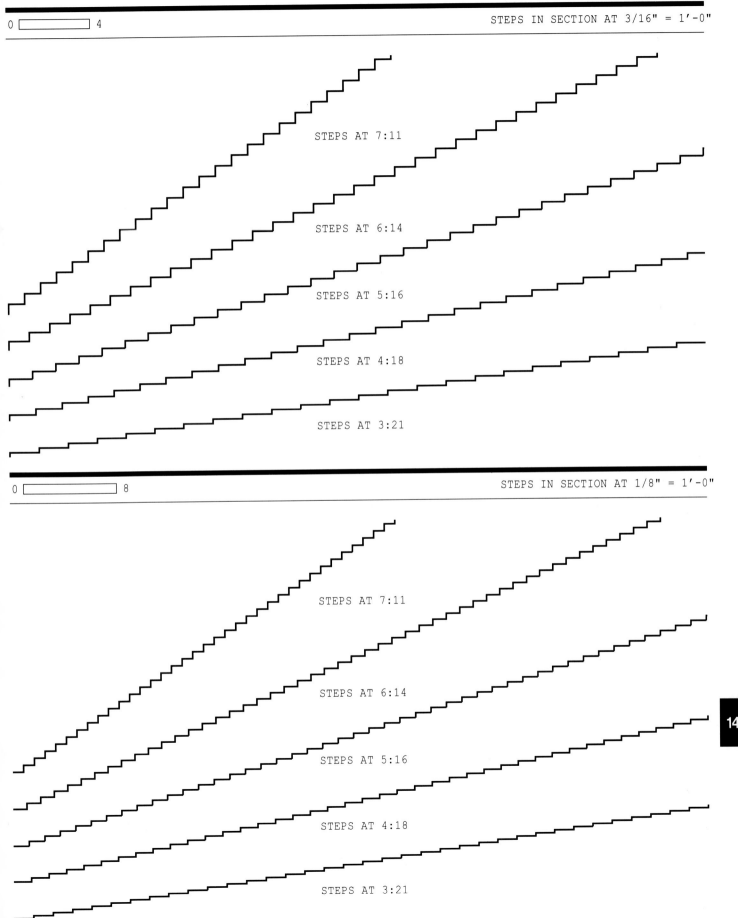

0 ▭ 4   STEPS IN SECTION AT 3/16" = 1'-0"

STEPS AT 7:11

STEPS AT 6:14

STEPS AT 5:16

STEPS AT 4:18

STEPS AT 3:21

0 ▭ 8   STEPS IN SECTION AT 1/8" = 1'-0"

STEPS AT 7:11

STEPS AT 6:14

STEPS AT 5:16

STEPS AT 4:18

STEPS AT 3:21

STEPS IN SECTION AT 1" = 10'-0" 0 ▭ 10

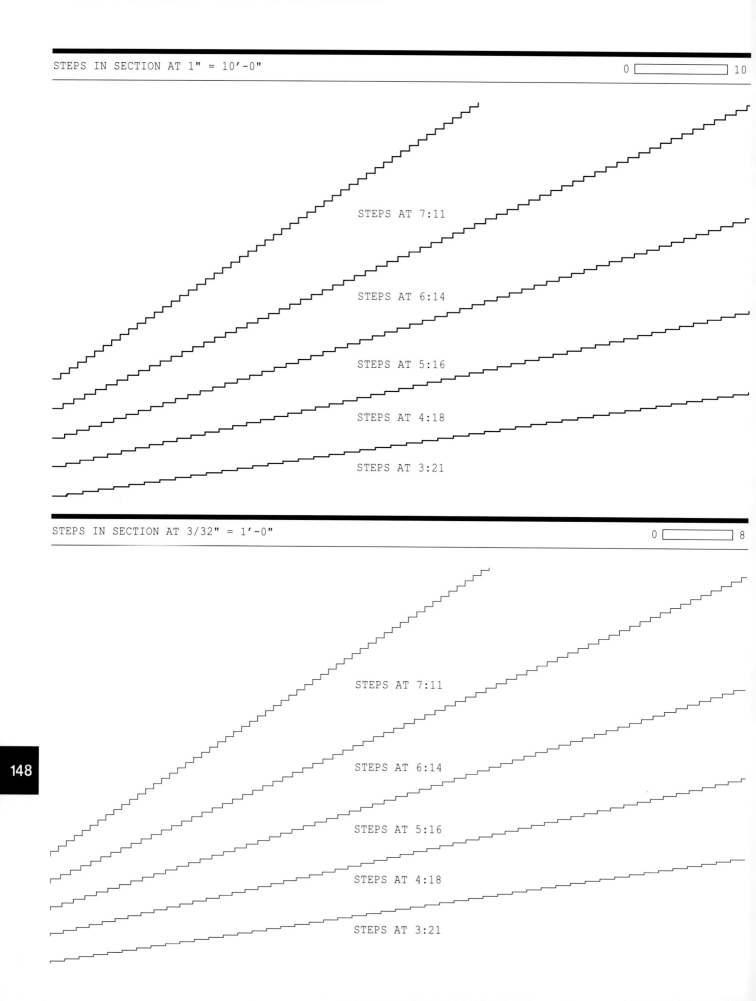

STEPS AT 7:11

STEPS AT 6:14

STEPS AT 5:16

STEPS AT 4:18

STEPS AT 3:21

STEPS IN SECTION AT 3/32" = 1'-0" 0 ▭ 8

STEPS AT 7:11

STEPS AT 6:14

STEPS AT 5:16

STEPS AT 4:18

STEPS AT 3:21

0 ▭ 16   STEPS IN SECTION AT 1/8" = 1'-0"

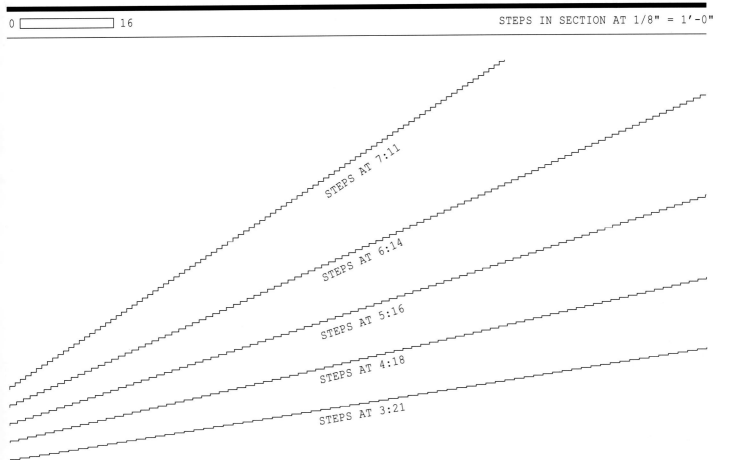

STEPS AT 7:11

STEPS AT 6:14

STEPS AT 5:16

STEPS AT 4:18

STEPS AT 3:21

TREE GRATES

ROUND TREE GRATES AT 1/2" = 1'-0"   0 ⬜ 2

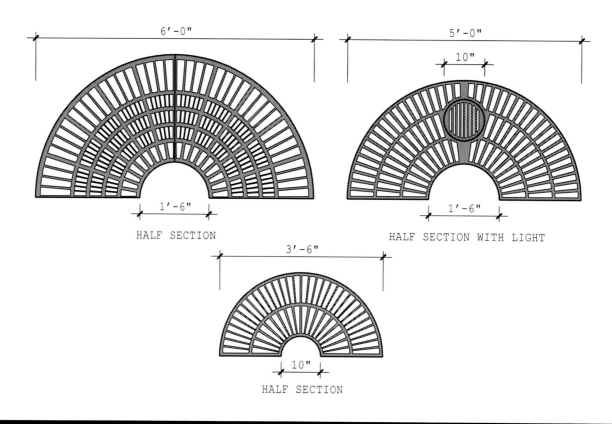

6'-0"

1'-6"

HALF SECTION

5'-0"

10"

1'-6"

HALF SECTION WITH LIGHT

3'-6"

10"

HALF SECTION

SQUARE TREE GRATES AT 1/2" = 1'-0"   0 ⬜ 2

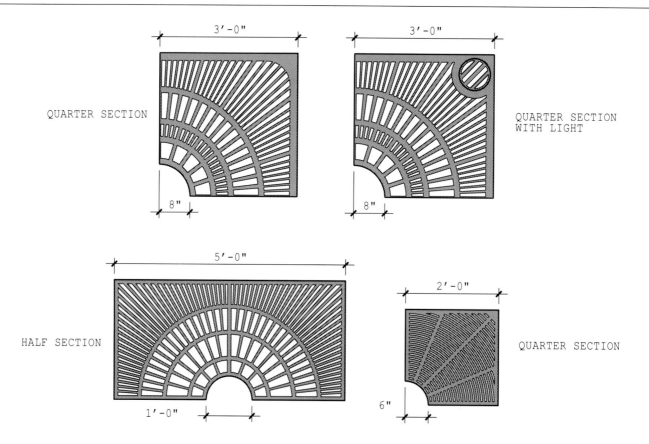

3'-0"

QUARTER SECTION

8"

3'-0"

QUARTER SECTION
WITH LIGHT

8"

5'-0"

HALF SECTION

1'-0"

2'-0"

QUARTER SECTION

6"

0 ▭ 2

TREE GRATES AT 3/8" = 1'-0"

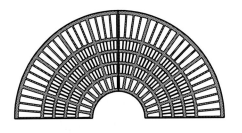 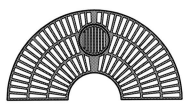 

 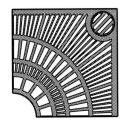 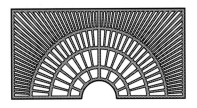

0 ▭ 4

TREE GRATES AT 1/4" = 1'-0"

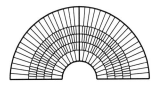 

  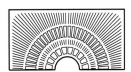

0 ▭ 4

TREE GRATES AT 3/16" = 1'-0"

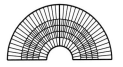

0 ▭ 8

TREE GRATES AT 1/8" = 1'-0"

BOLLARDS

BOLLARDS AT 3/4" = 1'-0"　　　　　　　　　　　　　　　　　　　0 ▭ 1

LIGHT BOLLARD

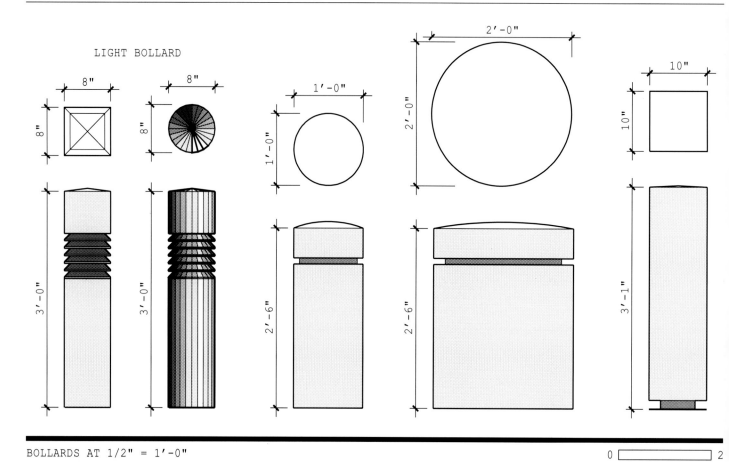

BOLLARDS AT 1/2" = 1'-0"　　　　　　　　　　　　　　　　　　　0 ▭ 2

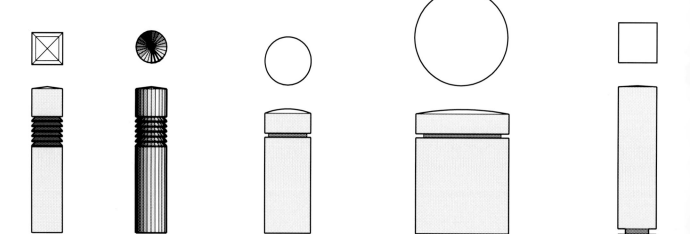

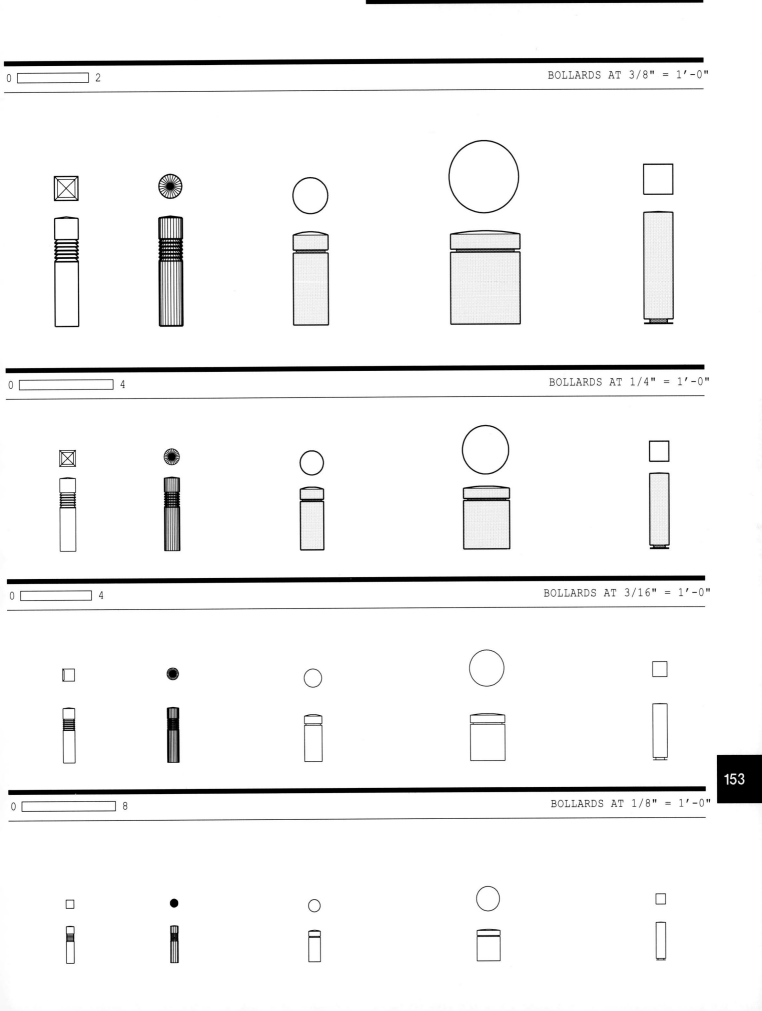

0 ▭ 2   BOLLARDS AT 3/8" = 1'-0"

0 ▭ 4   BOLLARDS AT 1/4" = 1'-0"

0 ▭ 4   BOLLARDS AT 3/16" = 1'-0"

153

0 ▭ 8   BOLLARDS AT 1/8" = 1'-0"

DRINKING FOUNTAINS AT 1/2" = 1'-0   0 ⬚━━━━━ 2

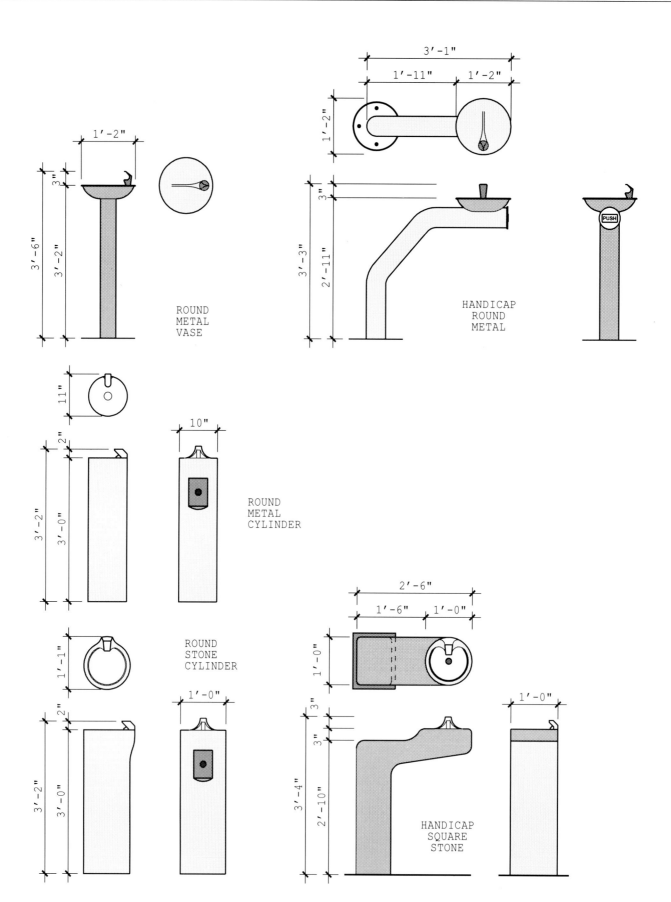

ROUND
METAL
VASE

HANDICAP
ROUND
METAL

ROUND
METAL
CYLINDER

ROUND
STONE
CYLINDER

HANDICAP
SQUARE
STONE

154

0 ▭ 2   DRINKING FOUNTAINS AT 3/8" = 1'-0"

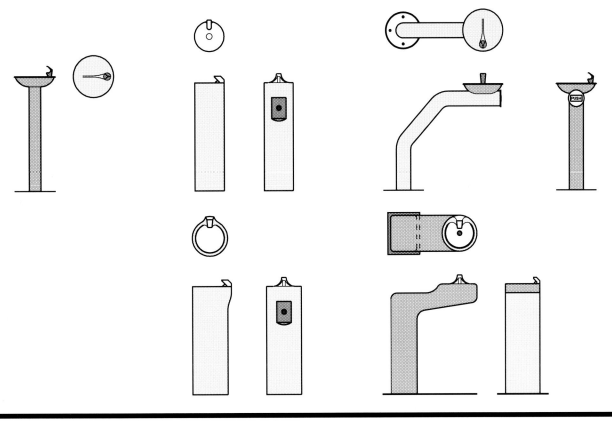

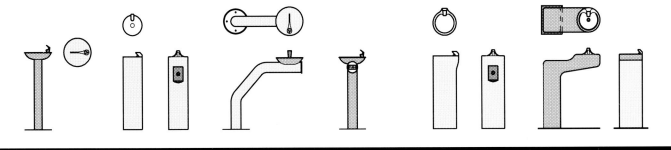

0 ▭ 4   DRINKING FOUNTAINS AT 1/4" = 1'-0"

0 ▭ 4   DRINKING FOUNTAINS AT 3/16" = 1'-0"

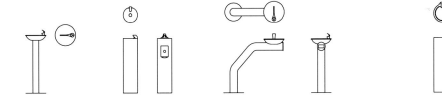

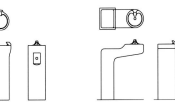

DRINKING FOUNTAINS AT 1/8" = 1'-0"   0 ▭ 8

  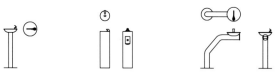

DRINKING FOUNTAINS AT 1" = 10'-0"   0 ▭ 10

  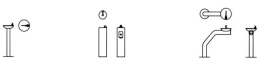

DRINKING FOUNTAINS AT 3/32" = 1'-0"   0 ▭ 8

0 ▭ 2

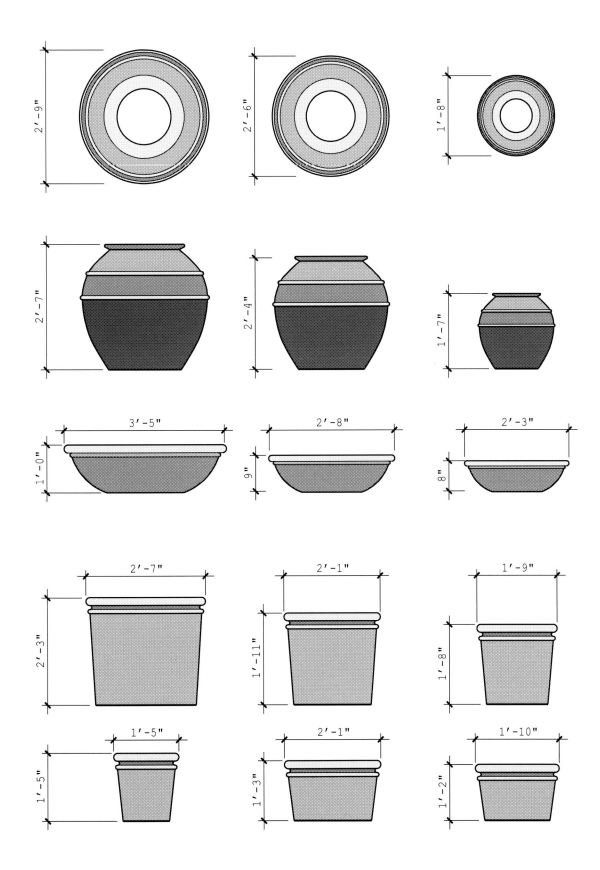

CYLINDERS OR SQUARES AT 1/2" = 1'-0"

0 ▭ 2

6'-0"

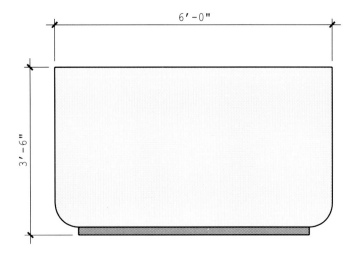

5'-0"

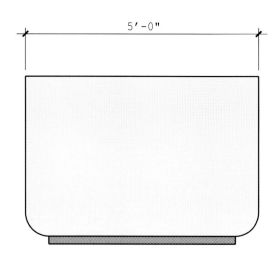

3'-6"

3'-0"

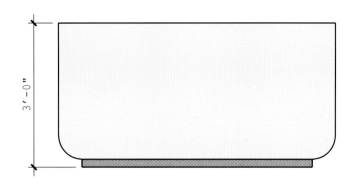

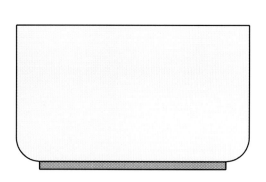

2'-6"

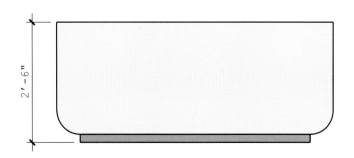

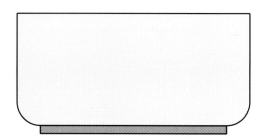

0 ▭ 2   CYLINDERS OR SQUARES AT 1/2" = 1'-0"

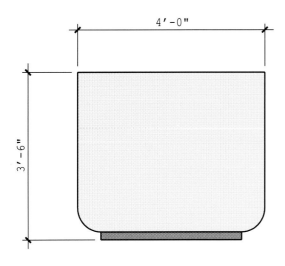

4'-0"

3'-6"

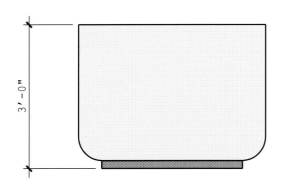

3'-0"

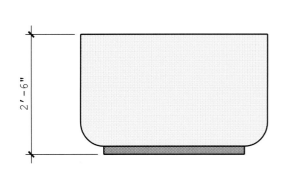

2'-6"

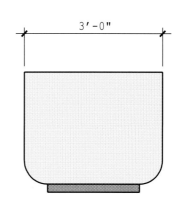

3'-0"

PLANTERS

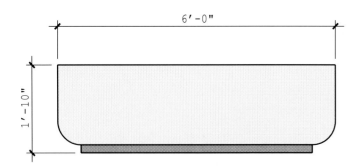

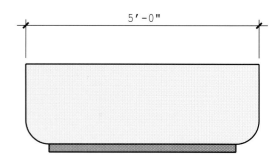

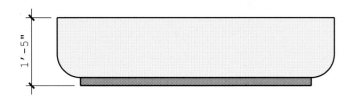

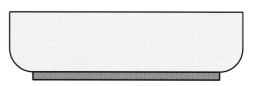

160

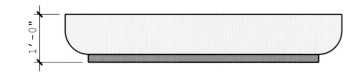

0 ▭ 2

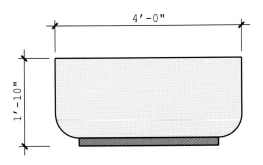

4'-0"

1'-10"

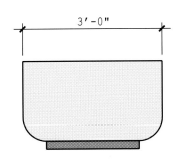

3'-0"

2'-0"

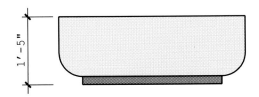

1'-5"

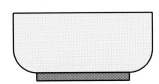

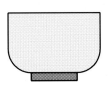

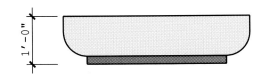

1'-0"

PLANTERS AT 3/8" = 1'-0"   0 ▭ 2

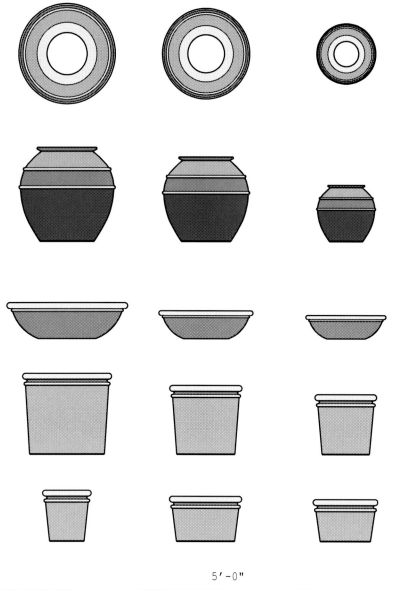

6'-0"   5'-0"   4'-0"

3'-6"

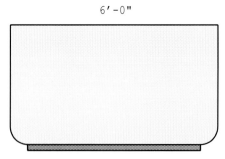
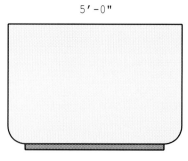
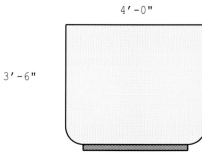

3'-0"

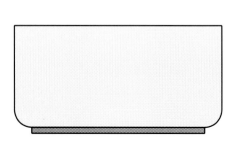

0 ⬜ 2

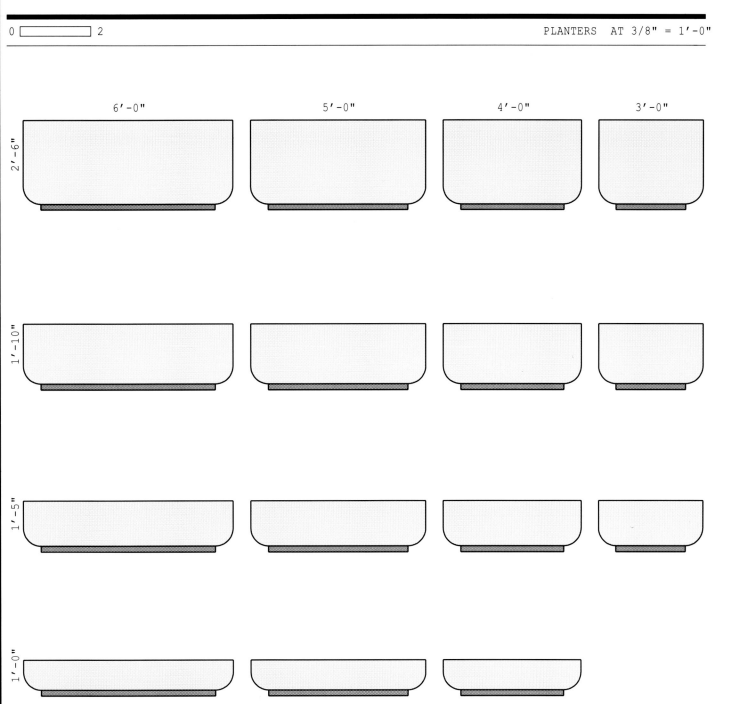

6'-0"   5'-0"   4'-0"   3'-0"

2'-6"

1'-10"

1'-5"

1'-0"

2'-2"   2'-0"

2'-2"   2'-0"

PLANTERS

0 ▭ 4

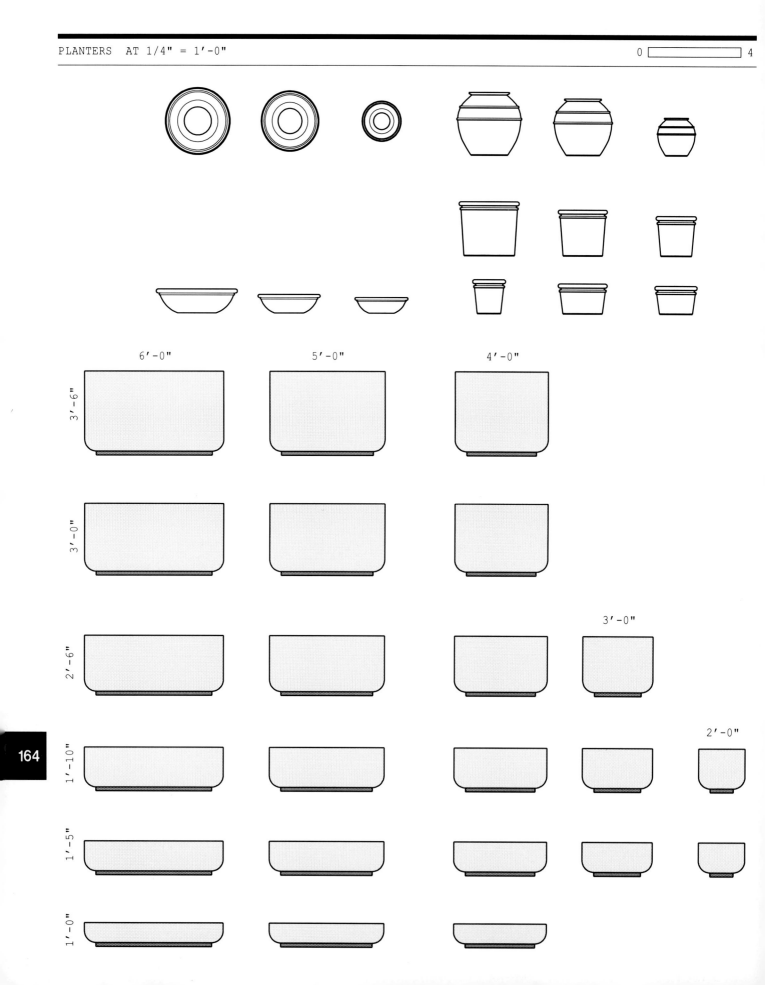

6'-0"   5'-0"   4'-0"

3'-6"

3'-0"

3'-0"

2'-6"

2'-0"

1'-10"

1'-5"

1'-0"

164

0 [━━━━] 4

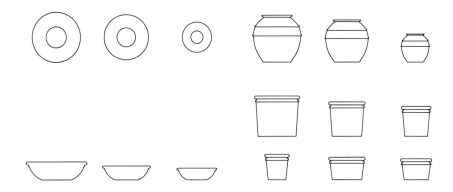

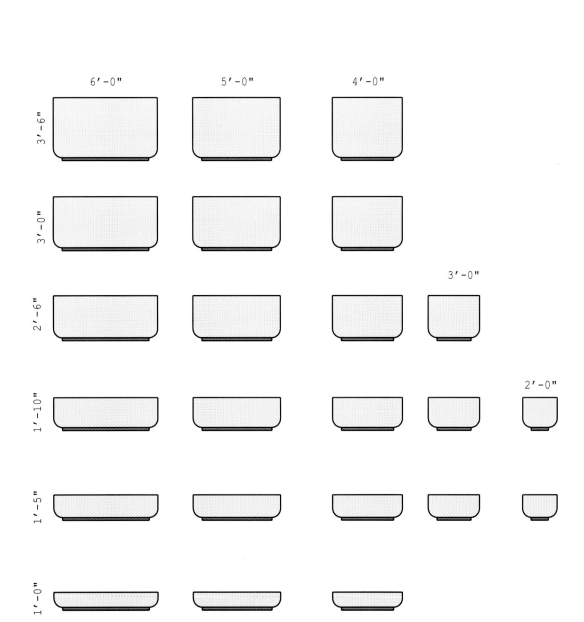

PLANTERS AT 1/8" = 1'-0"   0 ⬛━━━━━━━ 8

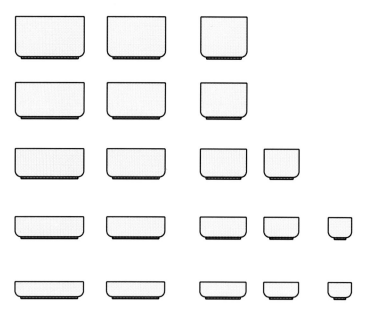

0 ▭ 1

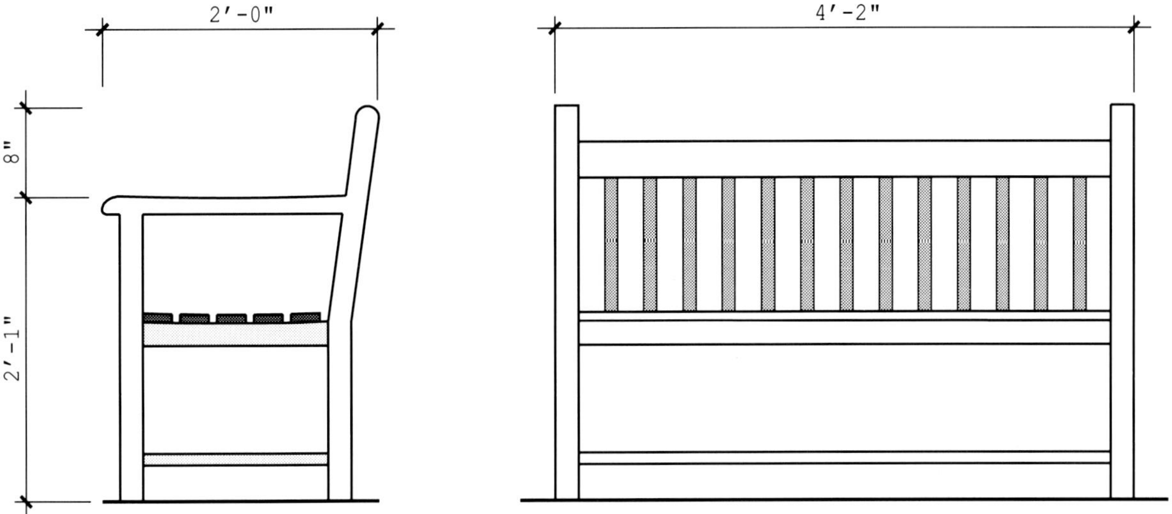

2'-0"

8"

2'-1"

4'-2"

TRADITIONAL

1'-9"

1'-4"

1'-6"

6'-0"

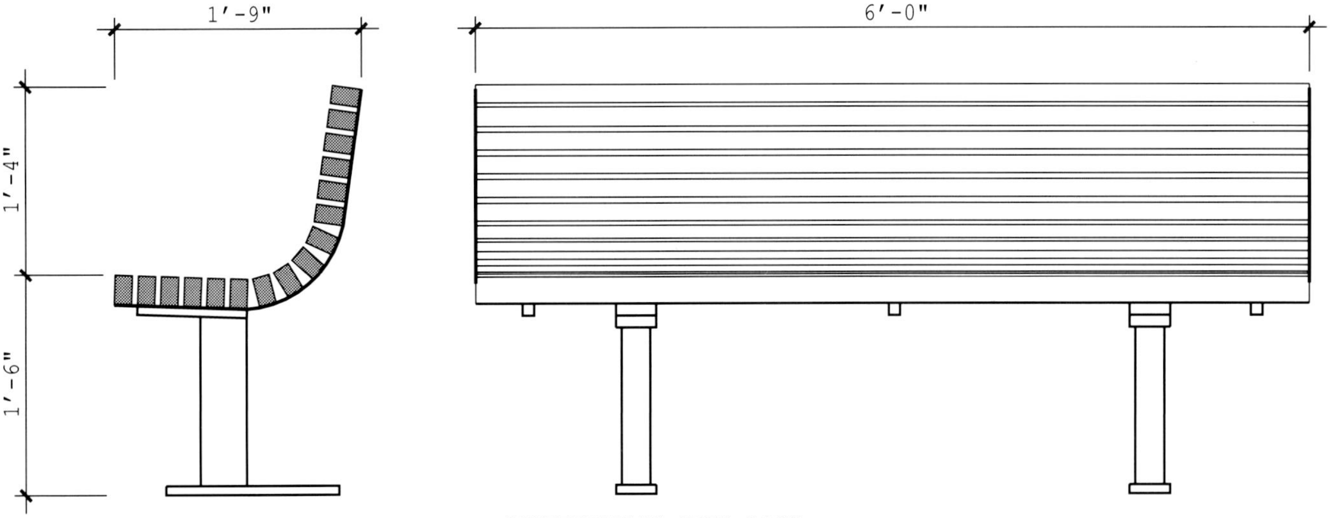

CONTEMPORARY WITH BACK

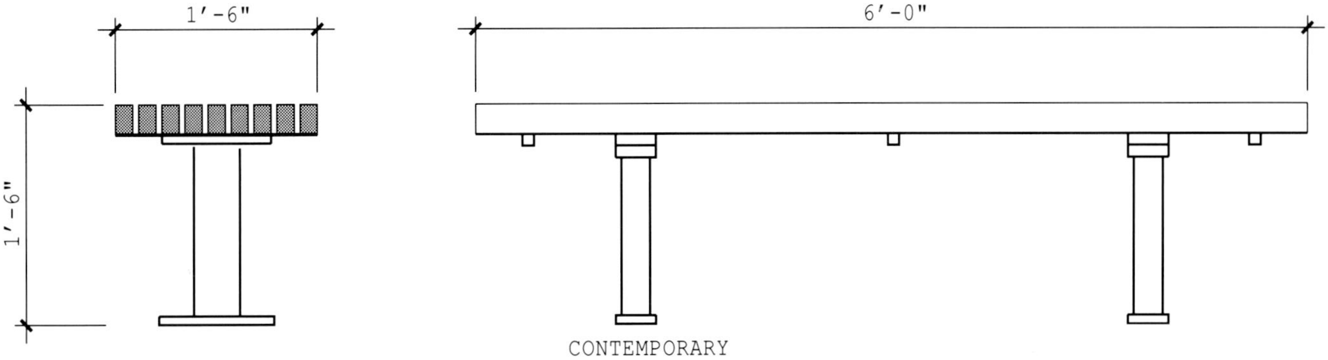

1'-6"

1'-6"

6'-0"

CONTEMPORARY

BENCHES

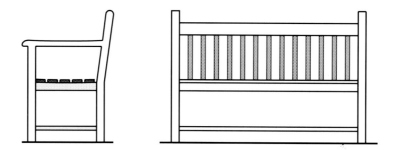

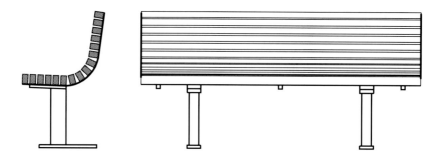

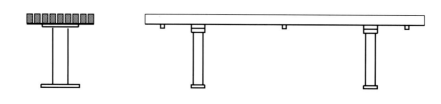

0 [   ] 2   BENCHES AT 3/8" = 1'-0"

0 [   ] 4   BENCHES AT 1/4" = 1'-0"

0 [   ] 4   BENCHES AT 3/16" = 1'-0"

0 [   ] 8   BENCHES AT 1/8" = 1'-0"

STANDARD TRAFFIC SIGNALS AT 1/4" = 1'-0"

0 ⬜ 4

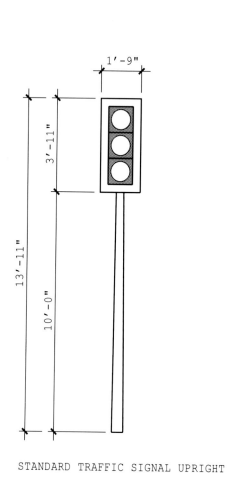

STANDARD TRAFFIC SIGNAL UPRIGHT

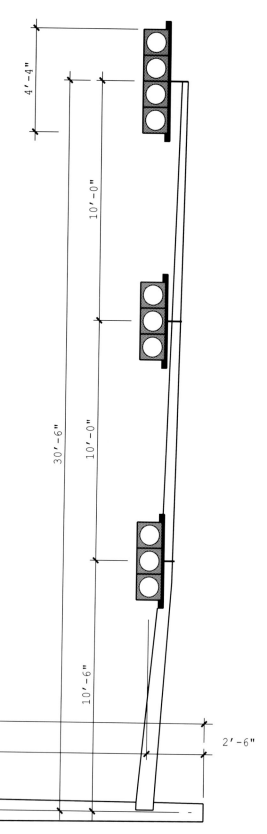

STANDARD TRAFFIC SIGNAL CANTILEVER

170

CONTEMPORARY TRAFFIC SIGNALS AT 1/4" = 1'-0"

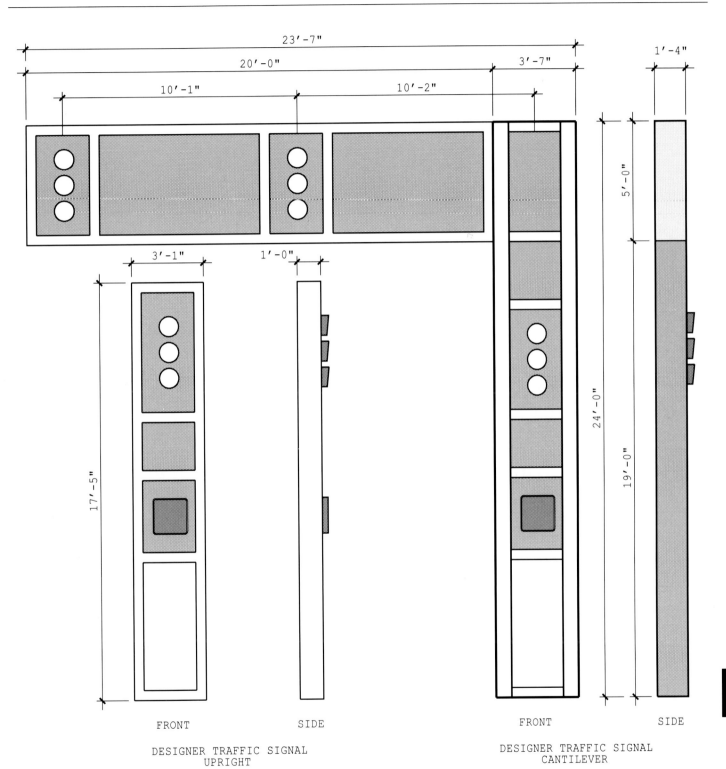

DESIGNER TRAFFIC SIGNAL
UPRIGHT

DESIGNER TRAFFIC SIGNAL
CANTILEVER

TRAFFIC SIGNALS AT 3/8" = 1'-0"

0 ▭ 4

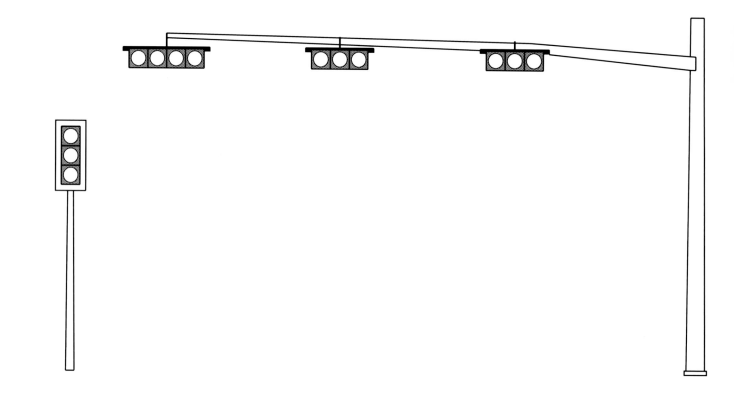

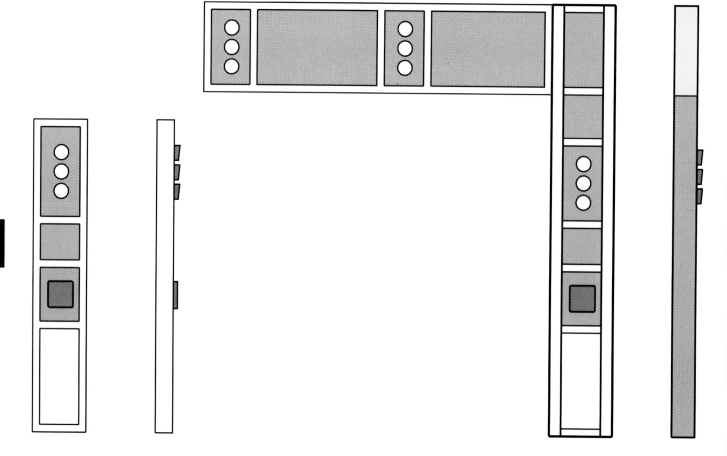

0 ⬚━━━━━ 8

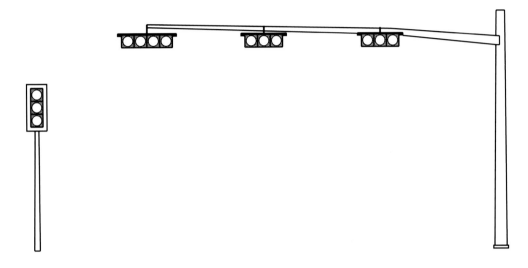

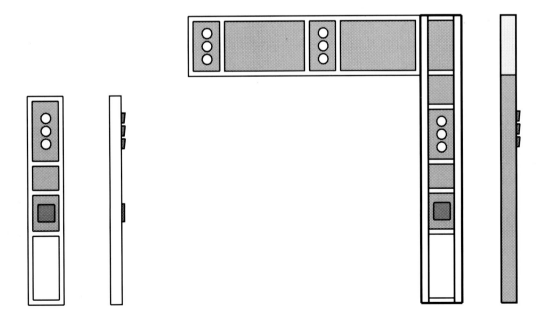

TRAFFIC SIGNALS

TRAFFIC SIGNALS AT 1" = 10'-0" 0 ⬜ 10

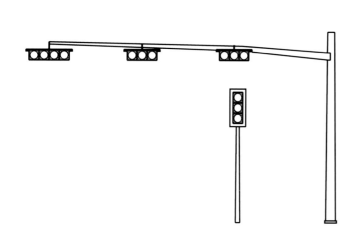 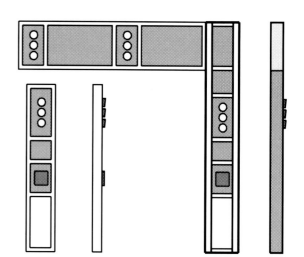

TRAFFIC SIGNALS AT 3/32" = 1'-0" 0 ⬜ 8

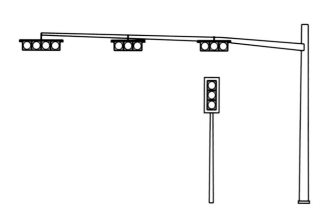 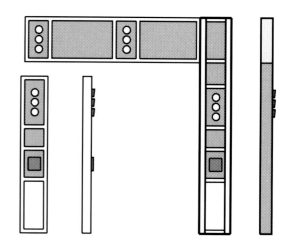

174

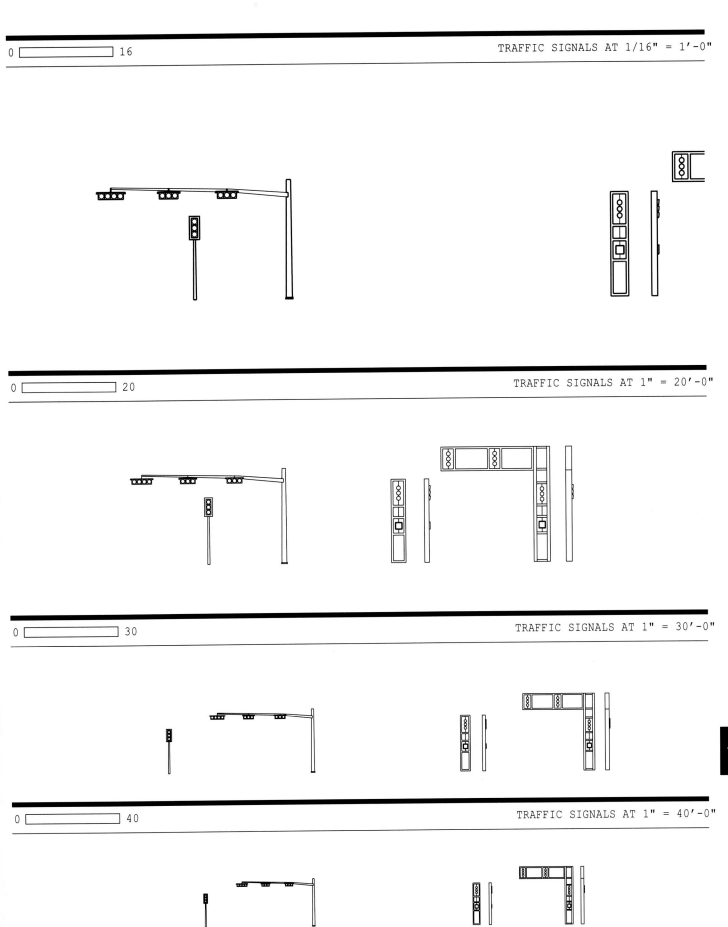

0 [▭] 16   TRAFFIC SIGNALS AT 1/16" = 1'-0"

0 [▭] 20   TRAFFIC SIGNALS AT 1" = 20'-0"

0 [▭] 30   TRAFFIC SIGNALS AT 1" = 30'-0"

175

0 [▭] 40   TRAFFIC SIGNALS AT 1" = 40'-0"

LIGHT POLES

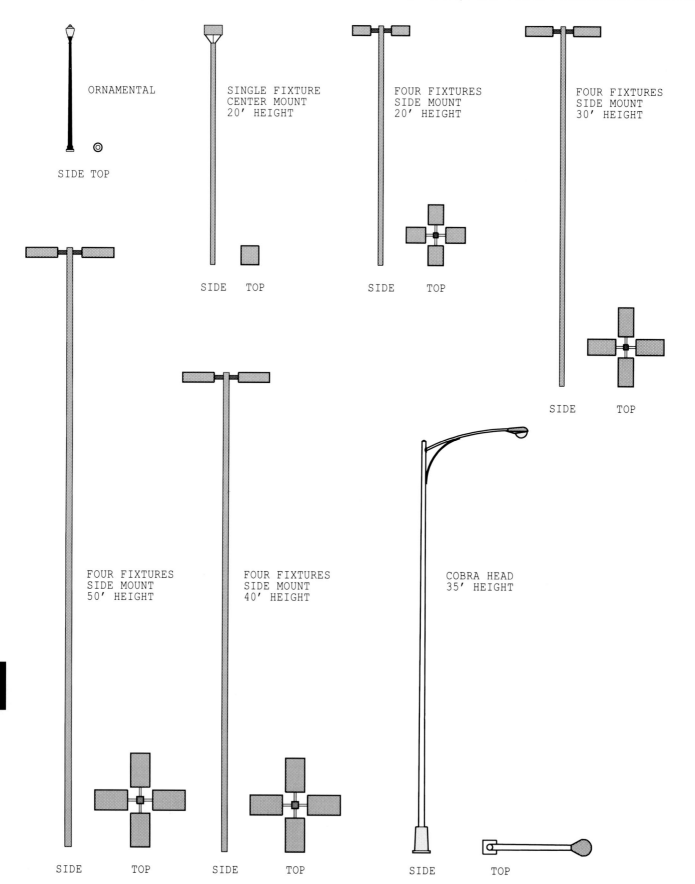

ORNAMENTAL

SIDE TOP

SINGLE FIXTURE
CENTER MOUNT
20' HEIGHT

SIDE   TOP

FOUR FIXTURES
SIDE MOUNT
20' HEIGHT

SIDE   TOP

FOUR FIXTURES
SIDE MOUNT
30' HEIGHT

SIDE   TOP

FOUR FIXTURES
SIDE MOUNT
50' HEIGHT

SIDE   TOP

FOUR FIXTURES
SIDE MOUNT
40' HEIGHT

SIDE   TOP

COBRA HEAD
35' HEIGHT

SIDE   TOP

176

0 10 LIGHT POLES AT 1" = 10'- 0"

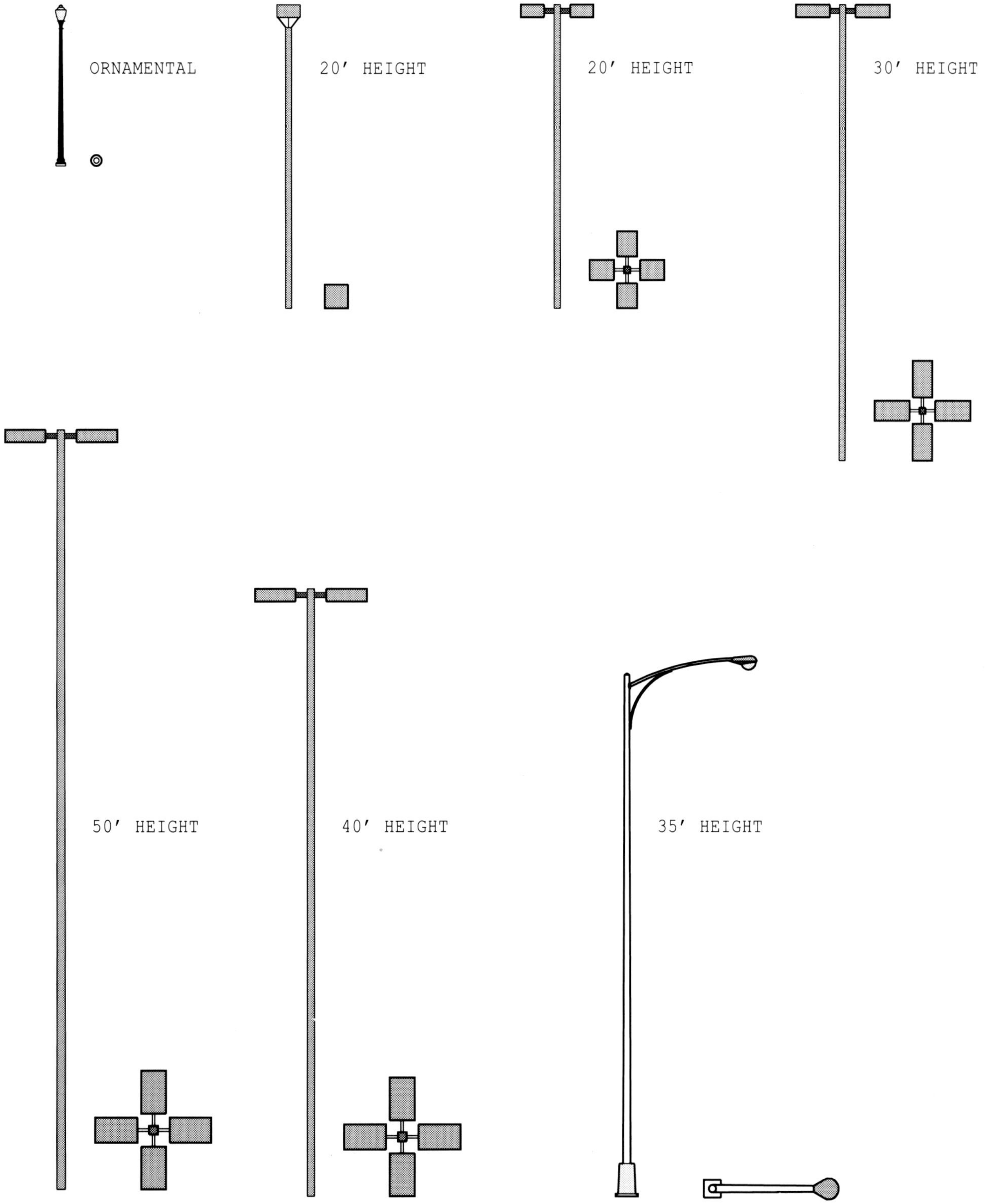
ORNAMENTAL
20' HEIGHT
20' HEIGHT
30' HEIGHT
50' HEIGHT
40' HEIGHT
35' HEIGHT

LIGHT POLES

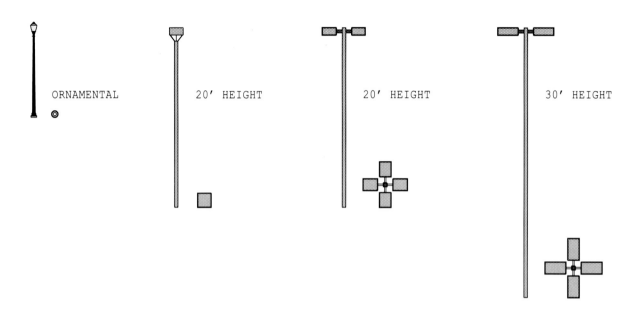

ORNAMENTAL   20' HEIGHT   20' HEIGHT   30' HEIGHT

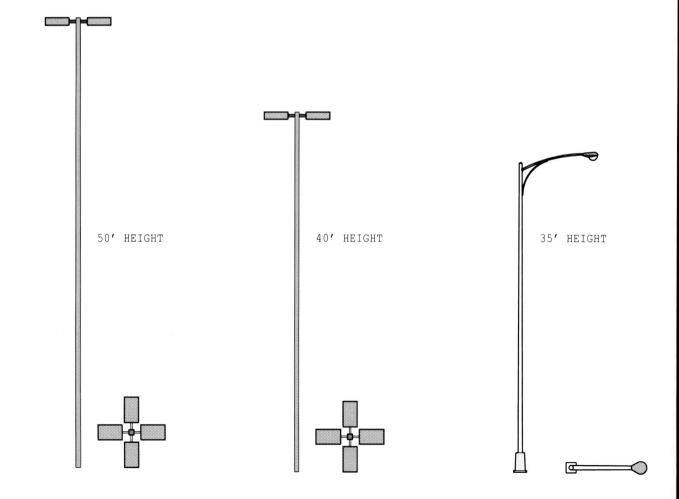

50' HEIGHT   40' HEIGHT   35' HEIGHT

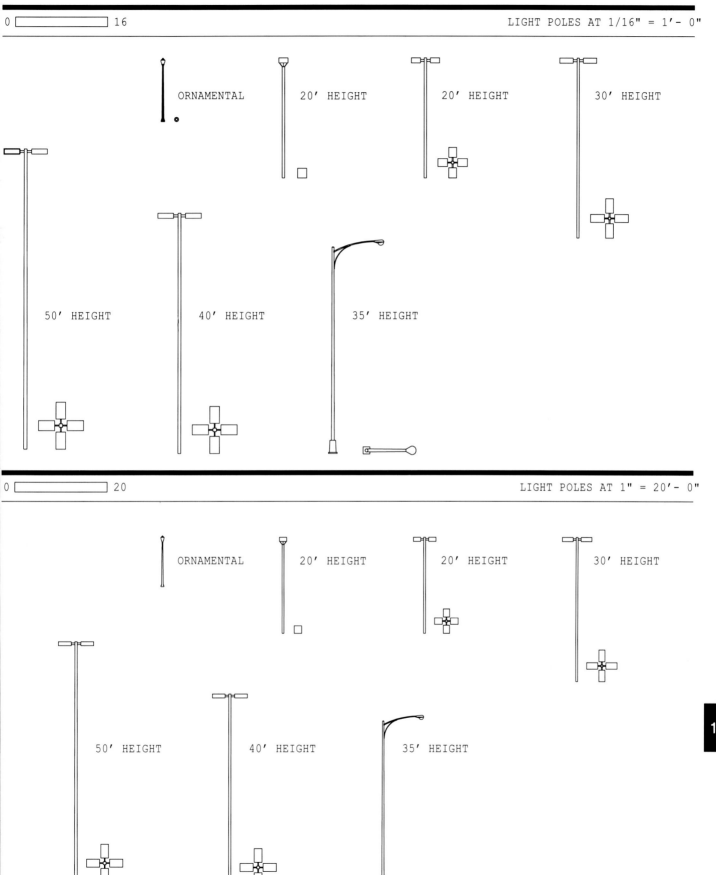

0 [_____] 16   LIGHT POLES AT 1/16" = 1'- 0"

ORNAMENTAL   20' HEIGHT   20' HEIGHT   30' HEIGHT

50' HEIGHT   40' HEIGHT   35' HEIGHT

0 [_____] 20   LIGHT POLES AT 1" = 20'- 0"

ORNAMENTAL   20' HEIGHT   20' HEIGHT   30' HEIGHT

50' HEIGHT   40' HEIGHT   35' HEIGHT

LIGHT POLES

LIGHT POLES AT 1" = 30'- 0"   0 [＿＿＿＿＿] 30

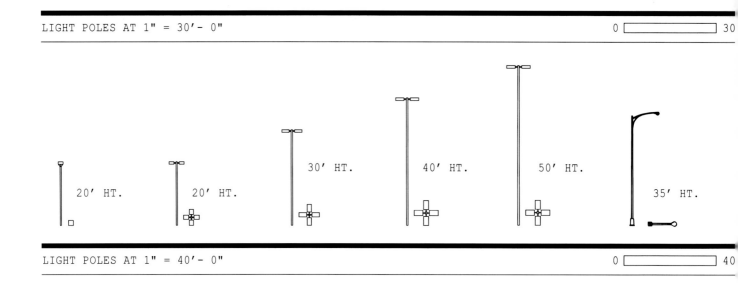

20' HT.   20' HT.   30' HT.   40' HT.   50' HT.   35' HT.

LIGHT POLES AT 1" = 40'- 0"   0 [＿＿＿＿＿] 40

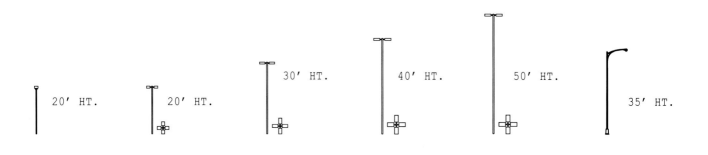

20' HT.   20' HT.   30' HT.   40' HT.   50' HT.   35' HT.

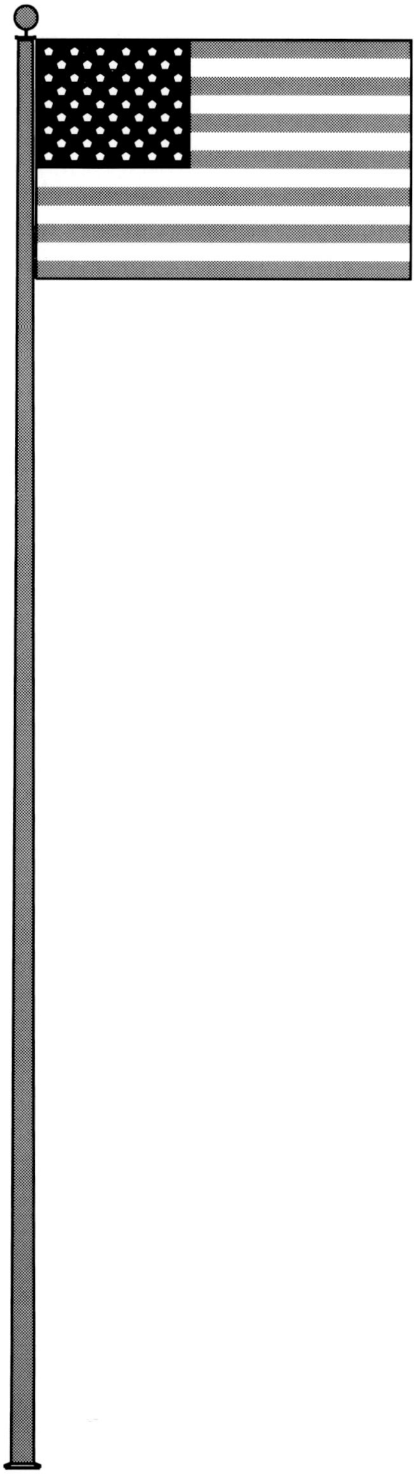

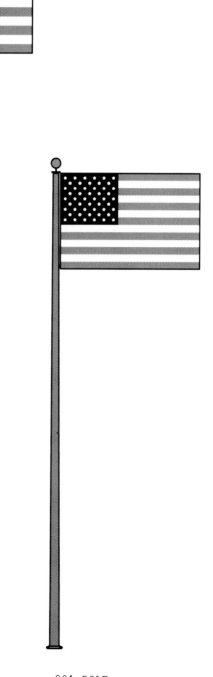

30' POLE
5'x8' FLAG

20' POLE
4'x6' FLAG

FLAGPOLES AT 3/8" = 1'-0"   0 ▭ 4

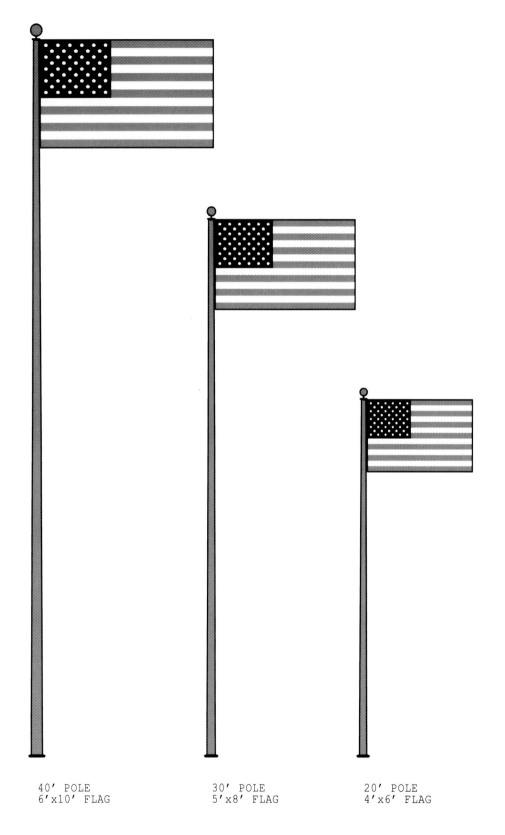

40' POLE
6'x10' FLAG

30' POLE
5'x8' FLAG

20' POLE
4'x6' FLAG

0 [   ] 8

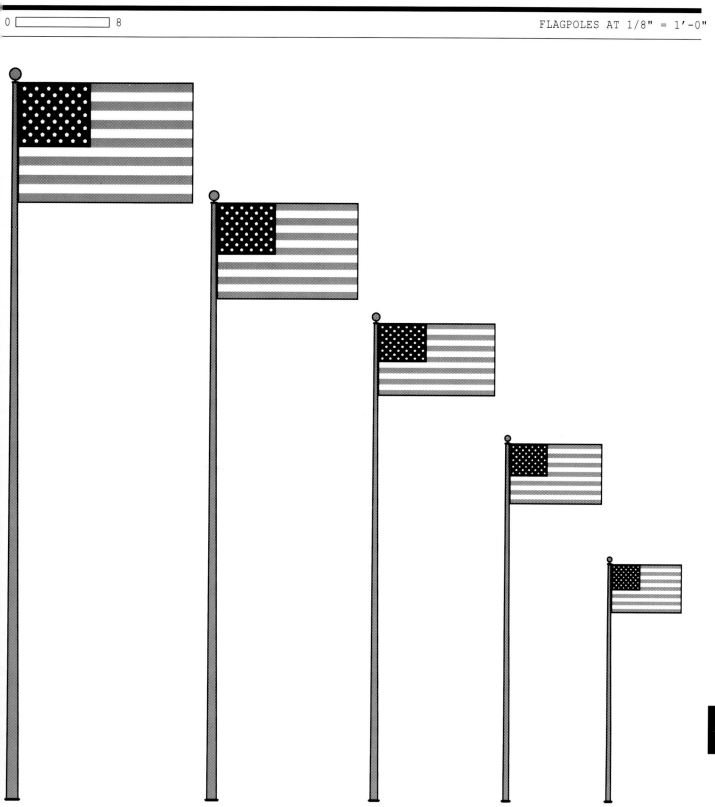

60' POLE
10'x15' FLAG

50' POLE
8'x12' FLAG

40' POLE
6'x10' FLAG

30' POLE
5'x8' FLAG

20' POLE
4'x6' FLAG

FLAGPOLES

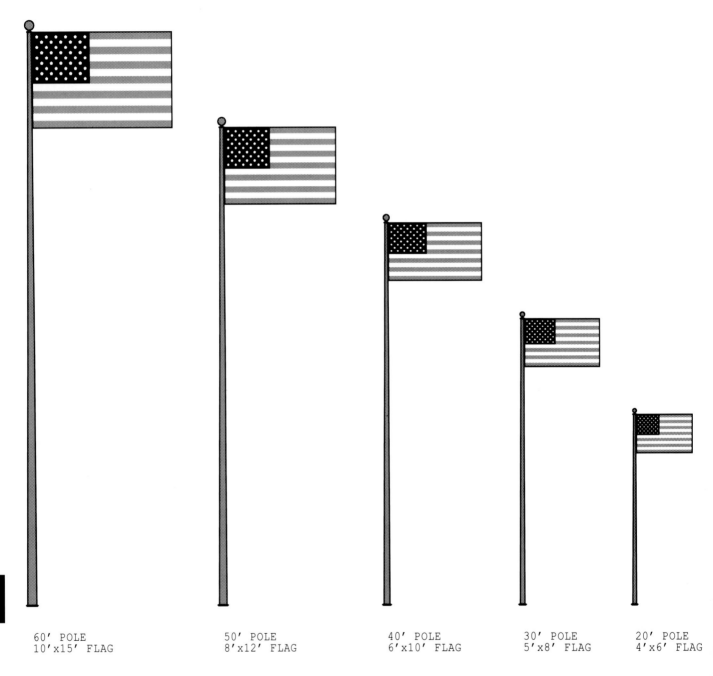

60' POLE
10'x15' FLAG

50' POLE
8'x12' FLAG

40' POLE
6'x10' FLAG

30' POLE
5'x8' FLAG

20' POLE
4'x6' FLAG

0 ⬚ 8

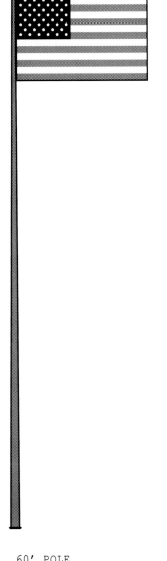

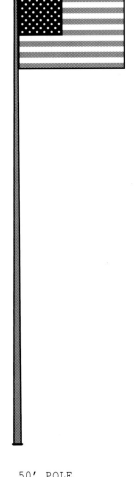

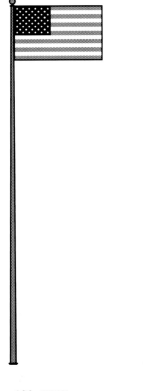

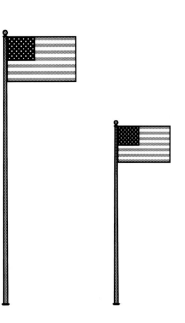

60' POLE
10'x15' FLAG

50' POLE
8'x12' FLAG

40' POLE
6'x10' FLAG

30' POLE
5'x8' FLAG

20' POLE
4'x6' FLAG

FLAGPOLES

FLAGPOLES AT 1/16" = 1'-0"   0 ▭ 16

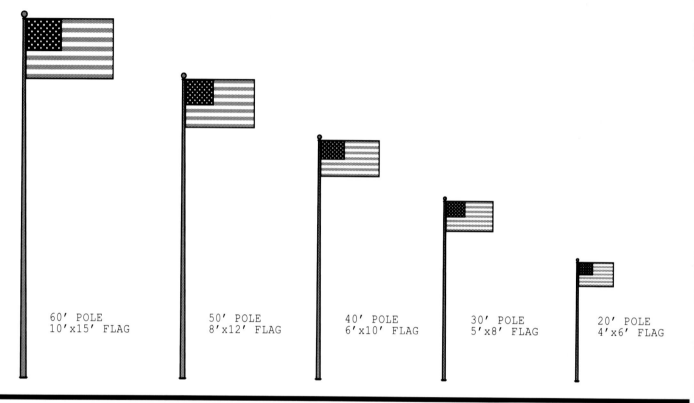

60' POLE   50' POLE   40' POLE   30' POLE   20' POLE
10'x15' FLAG   8'x12' FLAG   6'x10' FLAG   5'x8' FLAG   4'x6' FLAG

FLAGPOLES AT 1" = 20'-0"   0 ▭ 20

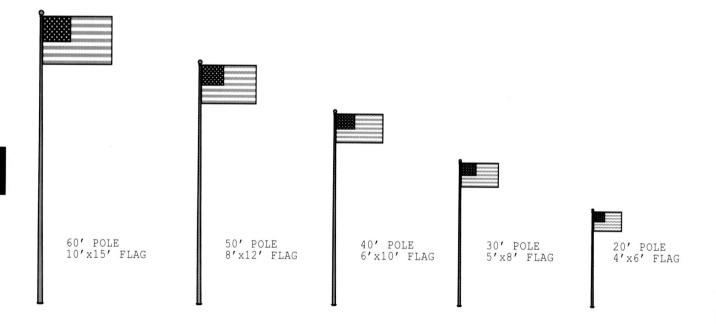

60' POLE   50' POLE   40' POLE   30' POLE   20' POLE
10'x15' FLAG   8'x12' FLAG   6'x10' FLAG   5'x8' FLAG   4'x6' FLAG

0 ☐ 30

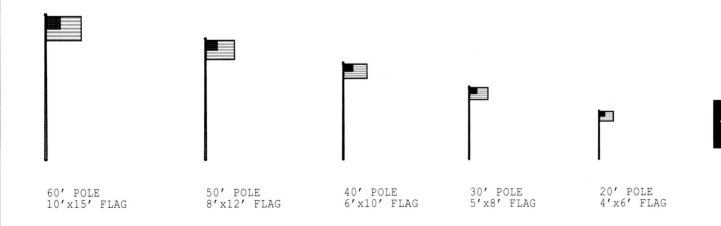

| 60' POLE | 50' POLE | 40' POLE | 30' POLE | 20' POLE |
| 10'x15' FLAG | 8'x12' FLAG | 6'x10' FLAG | 5'x8' FLAG | 4'x6' FLAG |

0 ☐ 40

FLAGPOLES AT 1" = 40'-0"

| 60' POLE | 50' POLE | 40' POLE | 30' POLE | 20' POLE |
| 10'x15' FLAG | 8'x12' FLAG | 6'x10' FLAG | 5'x8' FLAG | 4'x6' FLAG |

6' CHAIN LINK AT 1/2" = 1'-0"   0 [   ] 2

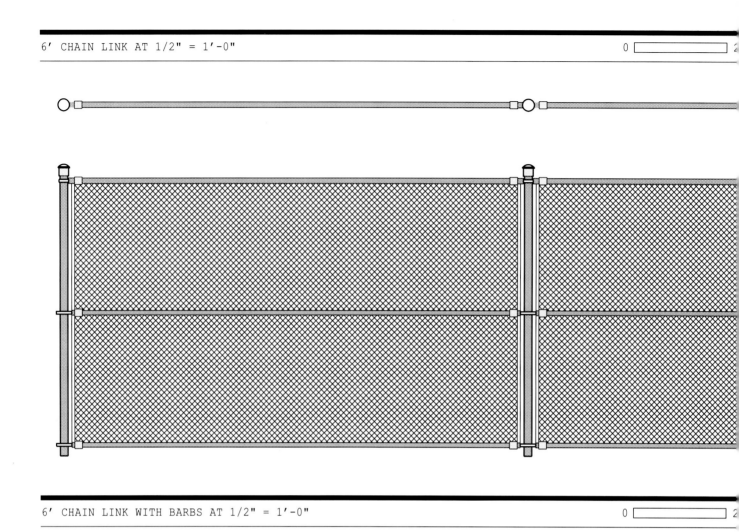

6' CHAIN LINK WITH BARBS AT 1/2" = 1'-0"   0 [   ] 2

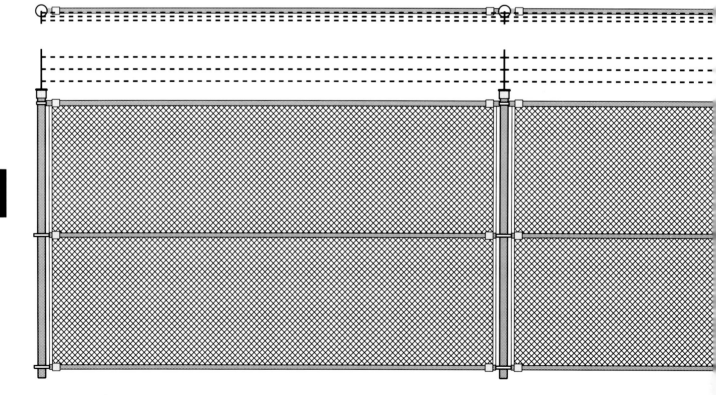

0 ⬜ 2　　　　　　　　　　6' ORNAMENTAL IRON AT 1/2" = 1'-0"

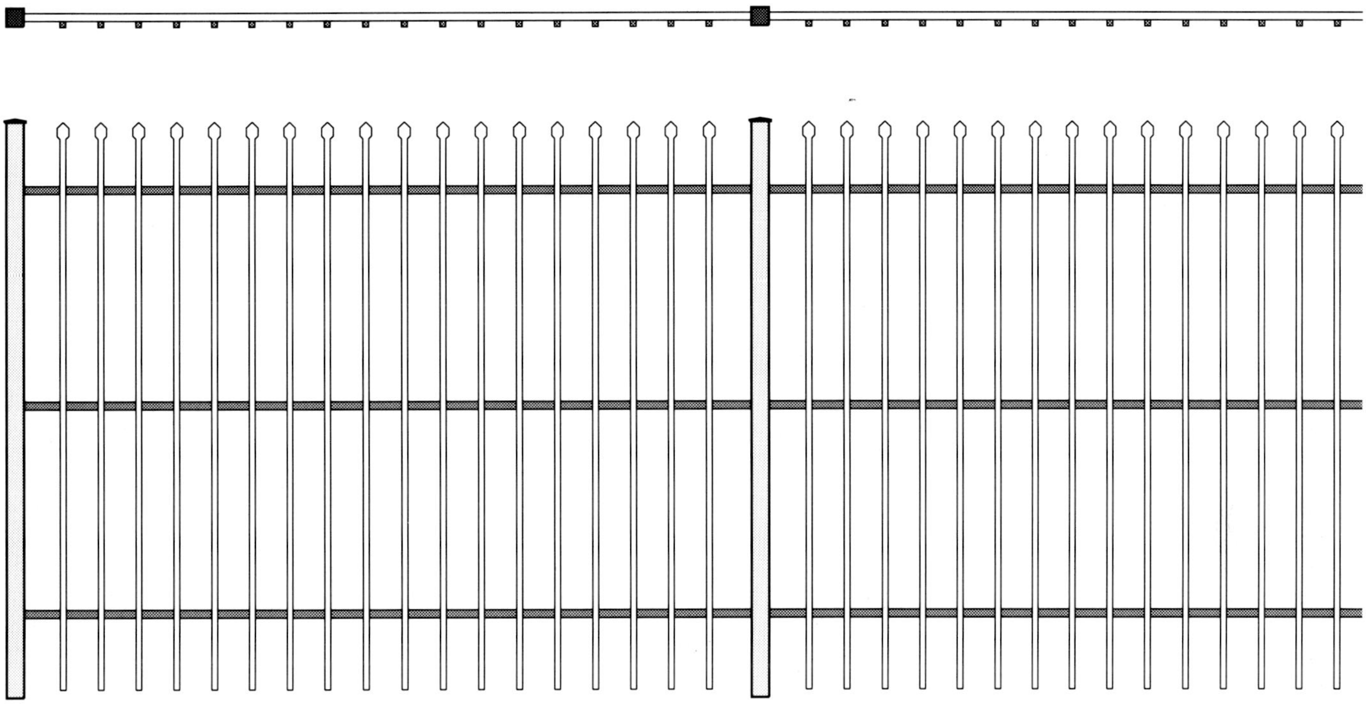

0 ⬜ 2　　　　　　　　　　6' ORNAMENTAL IRON AT 1/2" = 1'-0"

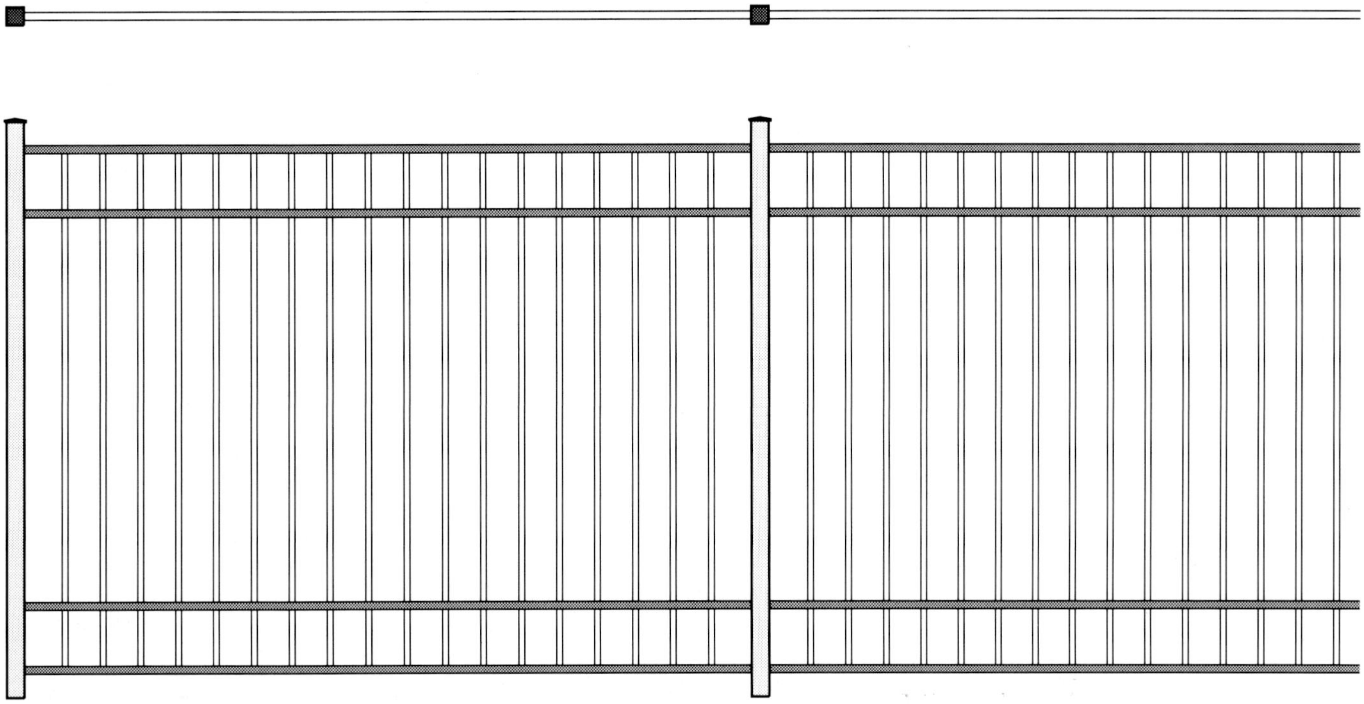

4' ORNAMENTAL IRON AT 1/2" = 1'-0"   0 [========] 2

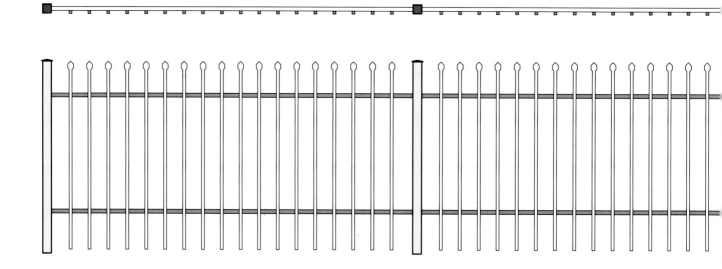

6' HEIGHT WOOD BOARD ON BOARD AT 1/2" = 1'-0"   0 [========] 2

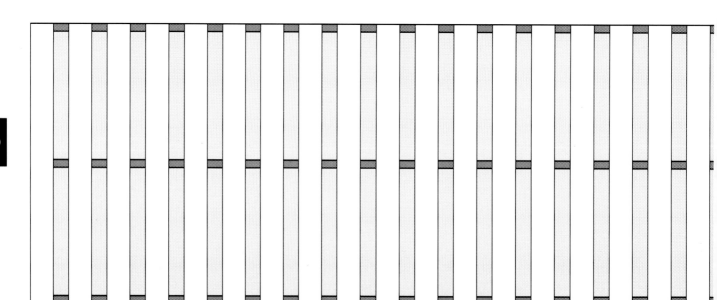

0 ⊏⟺⟹ 2   6' WOOD SOLID AT 1/2" = 1'-0"

0 ⊏⟺⟹ 2   6' WOOD SHADOW BOX AT 1/2" = 1'-0"

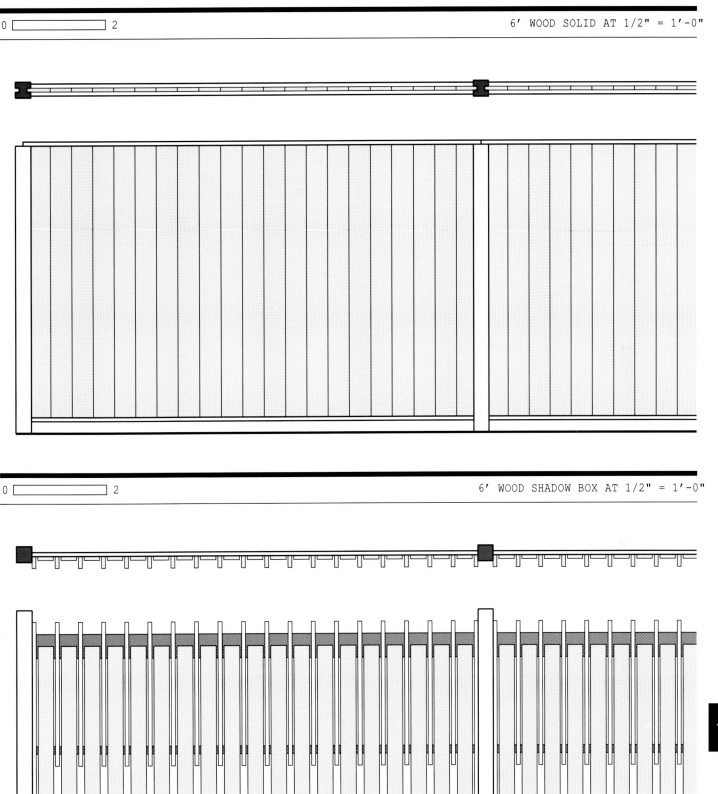

4' WOOD PICKET AT 1/2" = 1'-0"   0 ▭ 2

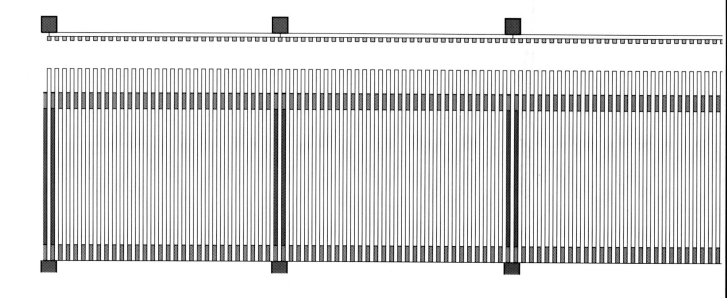

SPLIT RAIL AT 1/2" = 1'-0"   0 ▭ 2

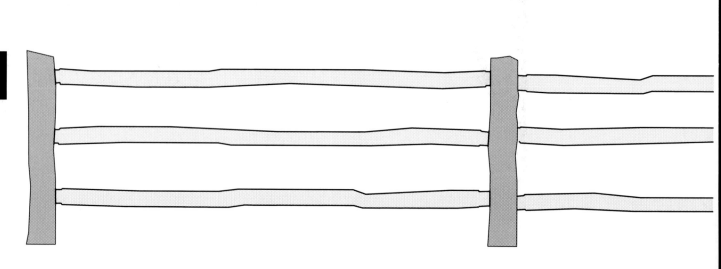

0 [========] 2   6' CHAIN LINK AT 3/8" = 1'-0"

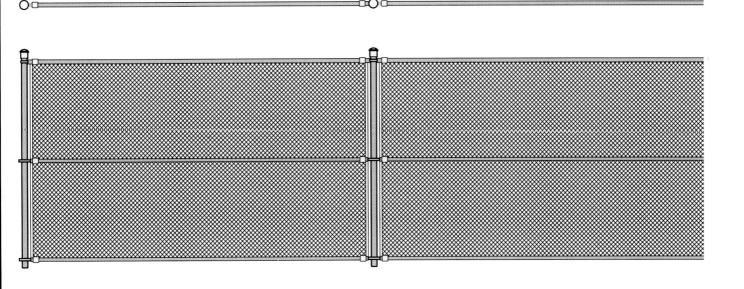

0 [========] 2   6' CHAIN LINK WITH BARBS AT 3/8" = 1'-0"

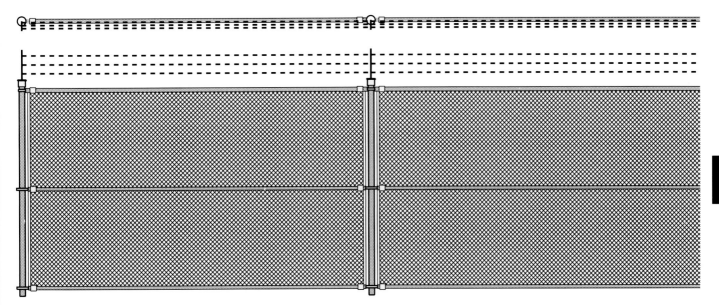

6' ORNAMENTAL IRON AT 3/8" = 1'-0"   0 [_____] 2

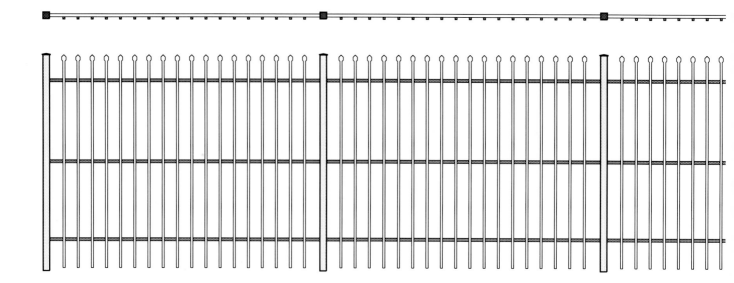

6' ORNAMENTAL IRON AT 3/8" = 1'-0"   0 [_____] 2

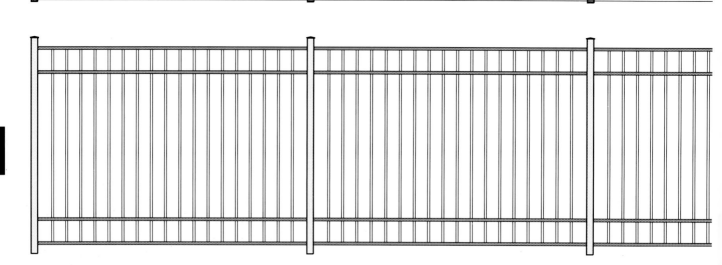

0 ⬜ 2   4' ORNAMENTAL IRON AT 3/8" = 1'-0"

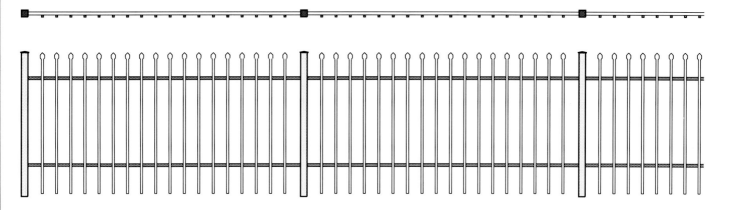

0 ⬜ 2   6' WOOD BOARD ON BOARD AT 3/8" = 1'-0"

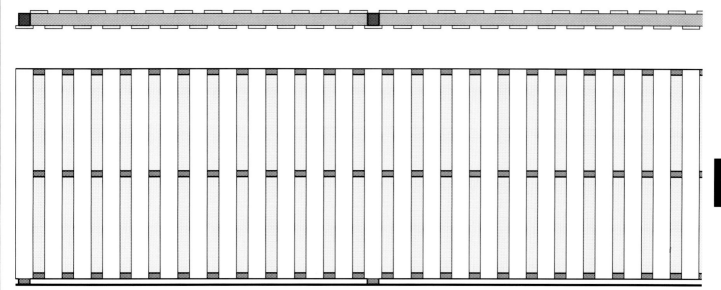

6' WOOD SOLID AT 3/8" = 1'-0"   0 ▭ 2

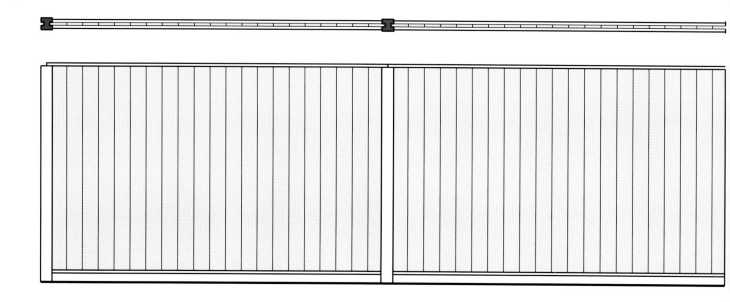

6' WOOD SHADOW BOX AT 3/8" = 1'-0"   0 ▭ 2

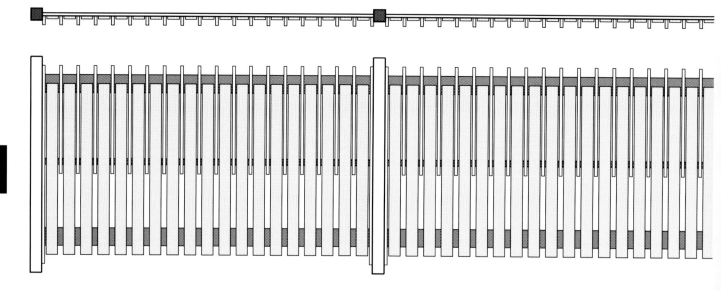

0 [▭] 2   6' WOOD PICKET AT 3/8" = 1'-0"

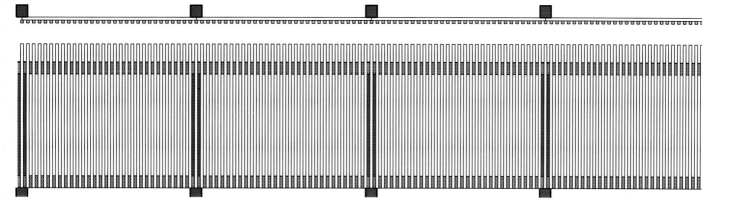

0 [▭] 2   SPLIT RAIL AT 3/8" = 1'-0"

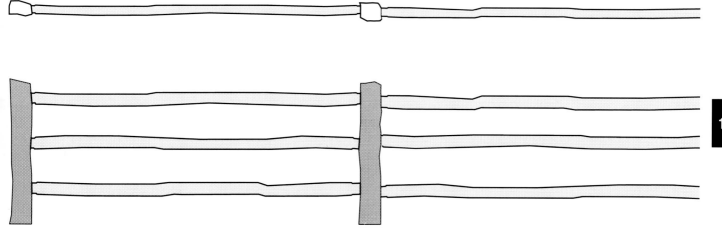

6' CHAIN LINK AT 1/4" = 1'-0"   0 ▭ 4

6' CHAIN LINK WITH BARBS AT 1/4" = 1'-0"   0 ▭ 4

6' ORNAMENTAL IRON AT 1/4" = 1'-0"   0 ▭ 4

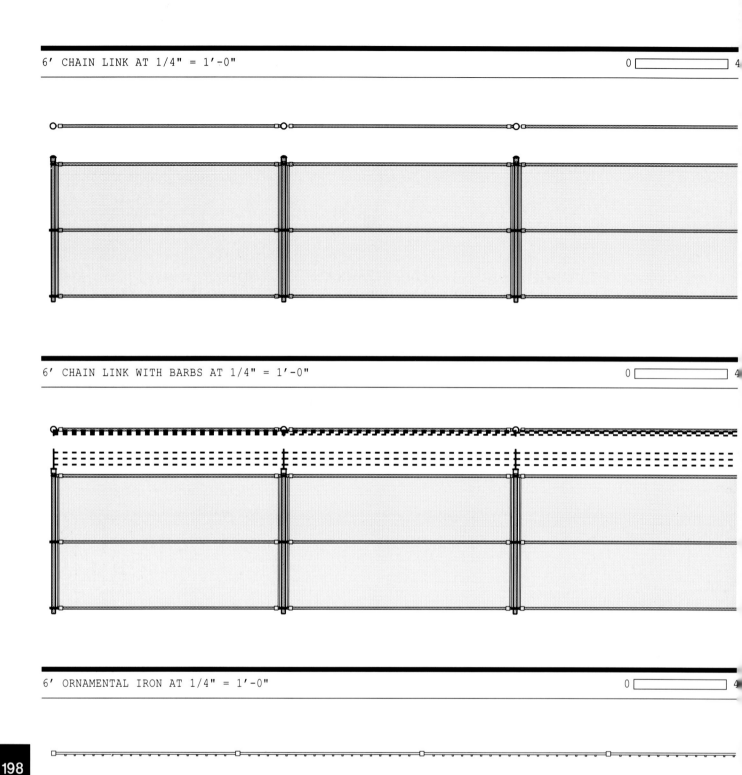

6' ORNAMENTAL IRON AT 1/4" = 1'-0"   0 [   ] 4

4' ORNAMENTAL IRON AT 1/4" = 1'-0"   0 [   ] 4

6' WOOD BOARD ON BOARD AT 1/4" = 1'-0"   0 [   ] 4

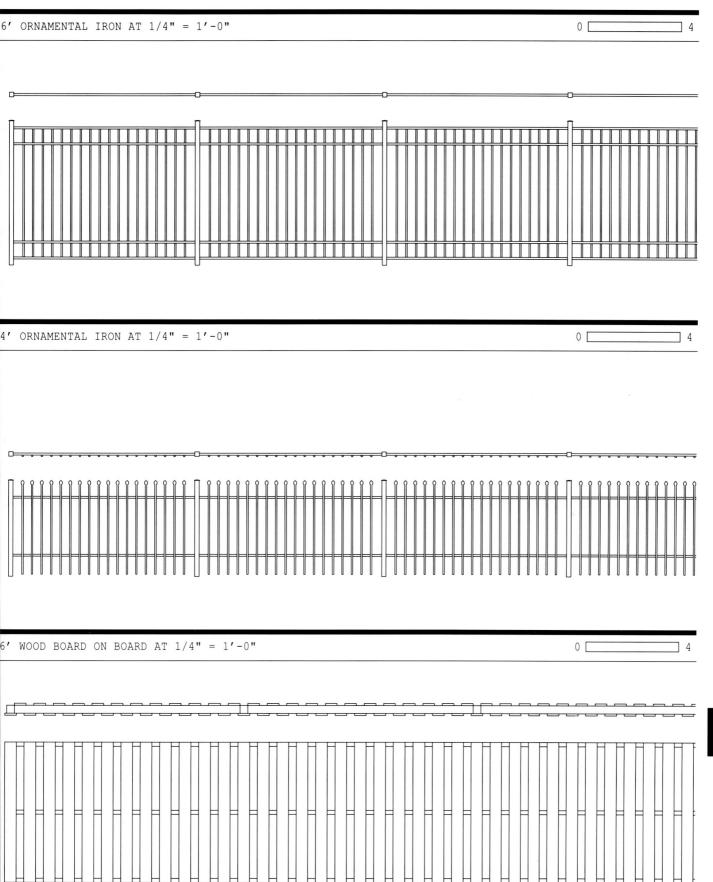

6' WOO SOLID AT 1/4" = 1'-0"   0 ▭ 4

6' WOOD SHADOW BOX AT 1/4" = 1'-0"   0 ▭ 4

WOOD PICKET AT 1/4" = 1'-0"   0 ▭ 4

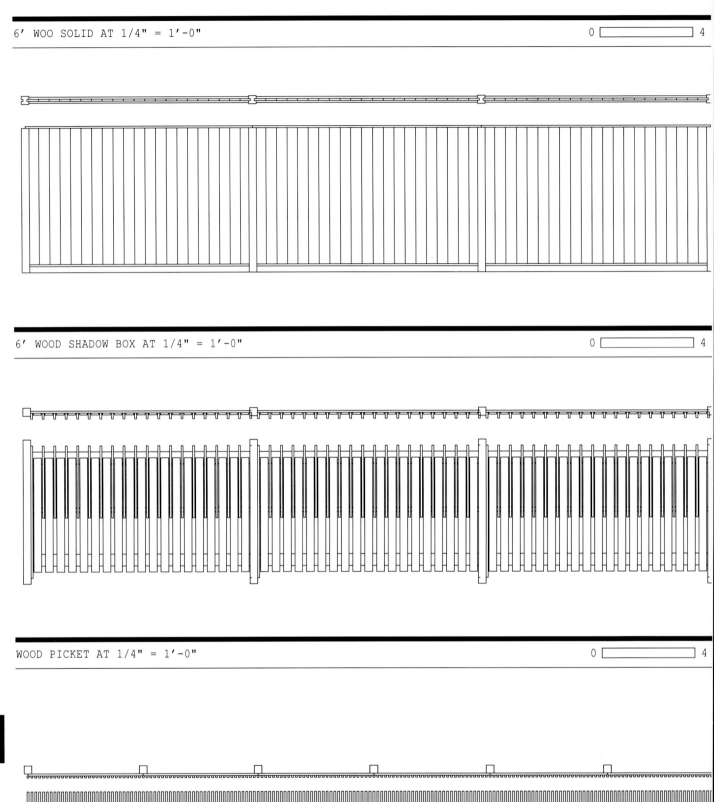

0 [====] 4   6' CHAIN LINK AT 3/16" = 1'-0"

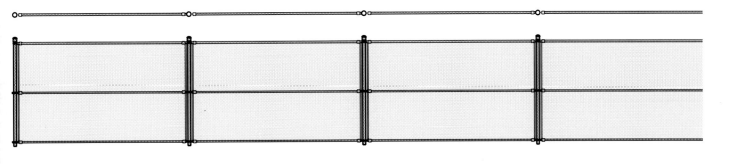

0 [====] 4   6' CHAIN LINK WITH BARBS AT 3/16" = 1'-0"

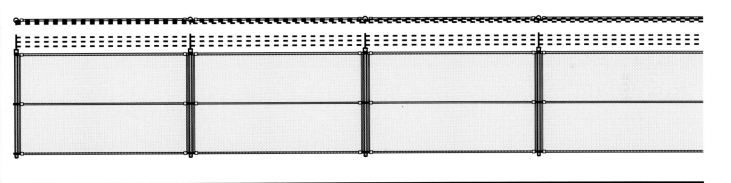

0 [====] 4   6' ORNAMENTAL IRON AT 3/16" = 1'-0"

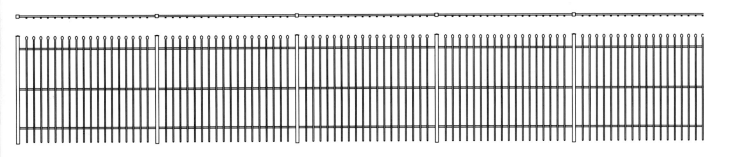

6' ORNAMENTAL IRON AT 3/16" = 1'-0" 0 ▭ 4

4' ORNAMENTAL IRON AT 3/16" = 1'-0" 0 ▭ 4

6' WOOD BOARD ON BOARD AT 3/16" = 1'-0" 0 ▭ 4

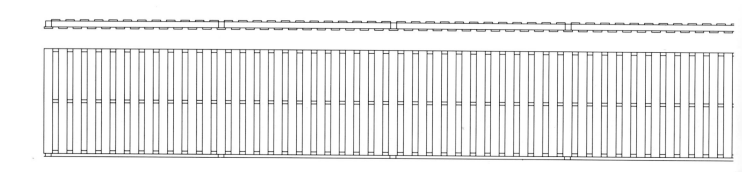

6' WOOD SOLID AT 3/16" = 1'-0"   0 [   ] 4

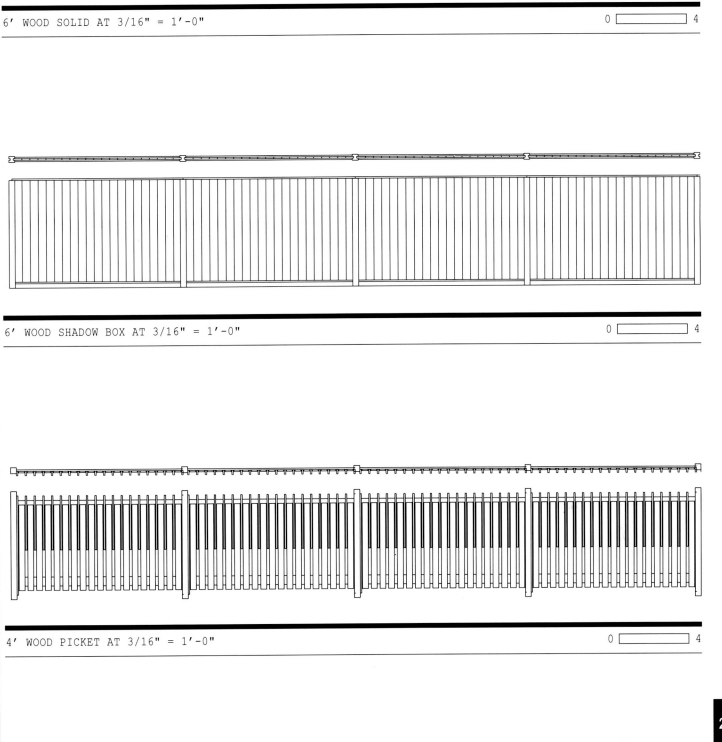

6' WOOD SHADOW BOX AT 3/16" = 1'-0"   0 [   ] 4

4' WOOD PICKET AT 3/16" = 1'-0"   0 [   ] 4

6' CHAIN LINK AT 1/8" = 1'-0"   0 [   ] 8

6' CHAIN LINK WITH BARBS AT 1/8" = 1'-0"   0 [   ] 8

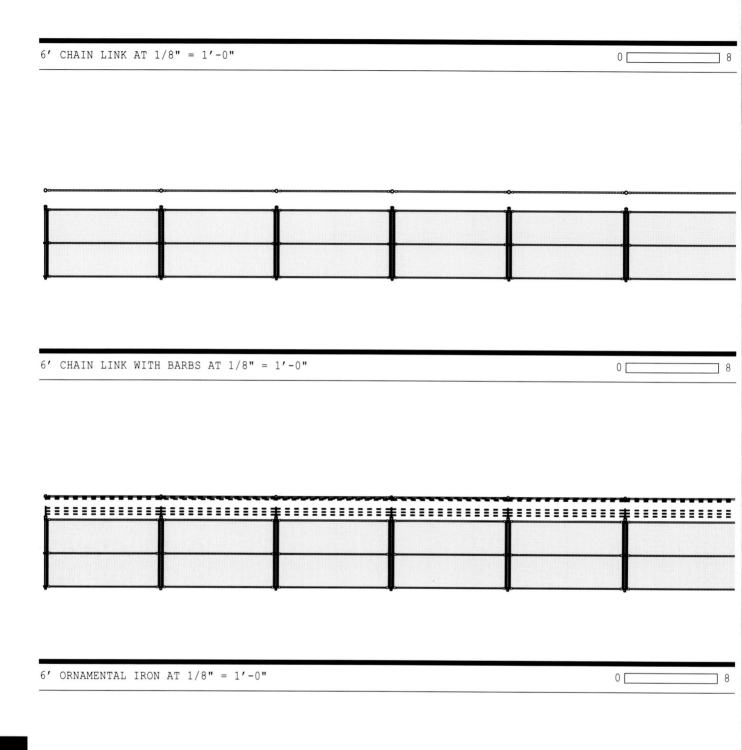

6' ORNAMENTAL IRON AT 1/8" = 1'-0"   0 [   ] 8

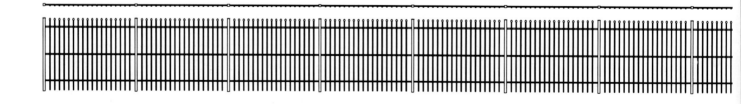

0 [　　　　　] 8   6' ORNAMENTAL IRON AT 1/8" = 1'-0"

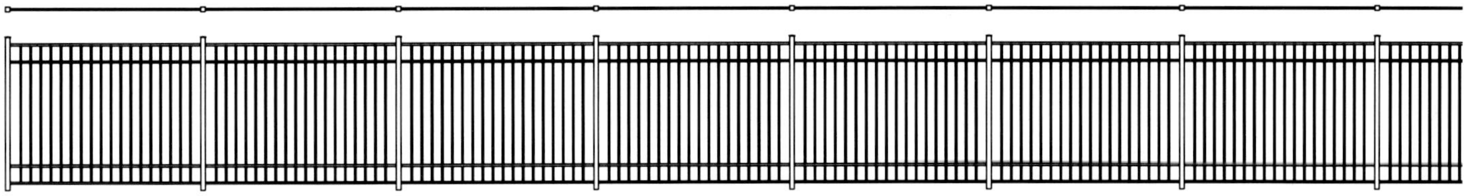

0 [　　　　　] 8   4' ORNAMENTAL IRON AT 1/8" = 1'-0"

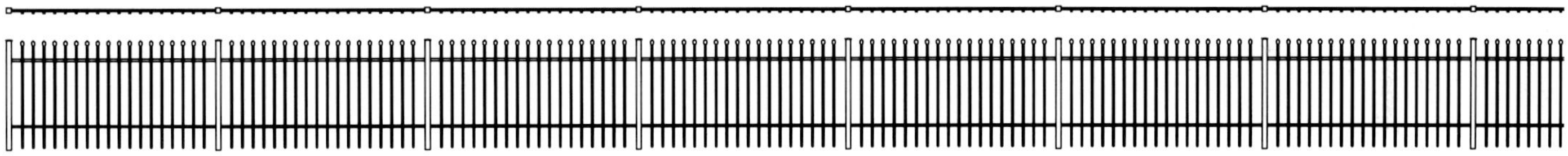

0 [　　　　　] 8   6' WOOD BOARD ON BOARD AT 1/8" = 1'-0"

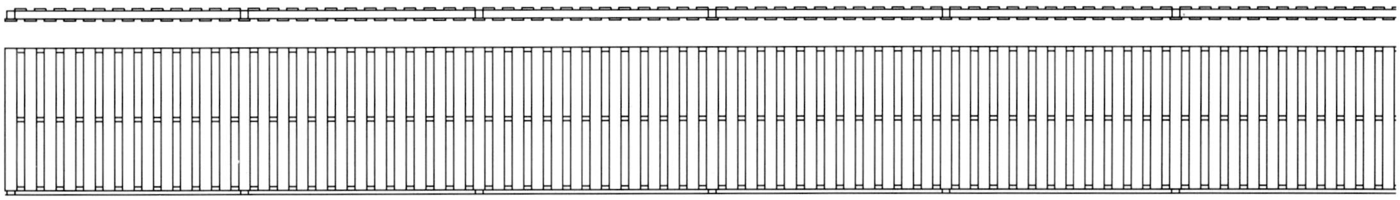

205

6' WOOD SOLID AT 1/8" = 1'-0"   0 ⬜⬜⬜⬜ 8

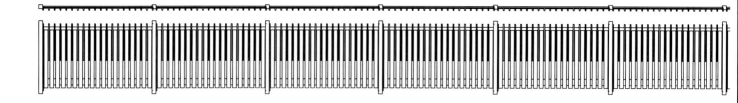

6' WOOD SHADOW BOX AT 1/8" = 1'-0"   0 ⬜⬜⬜⬜ 8

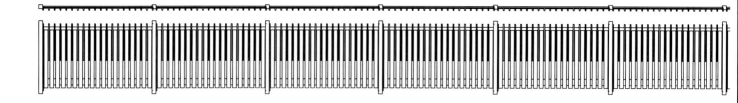

4' WOOD PICKET AT 1/8" = 1'-0"   0 ⬜⬜⬜⬜ 8

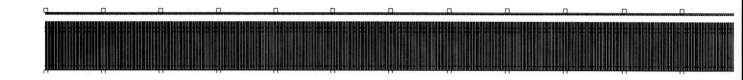

0 2 2 2/3" x 8" RUNNING BOND AT 1/2 = 1'-0"

0 2 2 2/3" x 8" COMMON BOND AT 1/2 = 1'-0"

0 2 2 2/3" x 8" GARDEN AT 1/2 = 1'-0"

0 2 2 2/3" x 8" ENGLISH AT 1/2 = 1'-0"

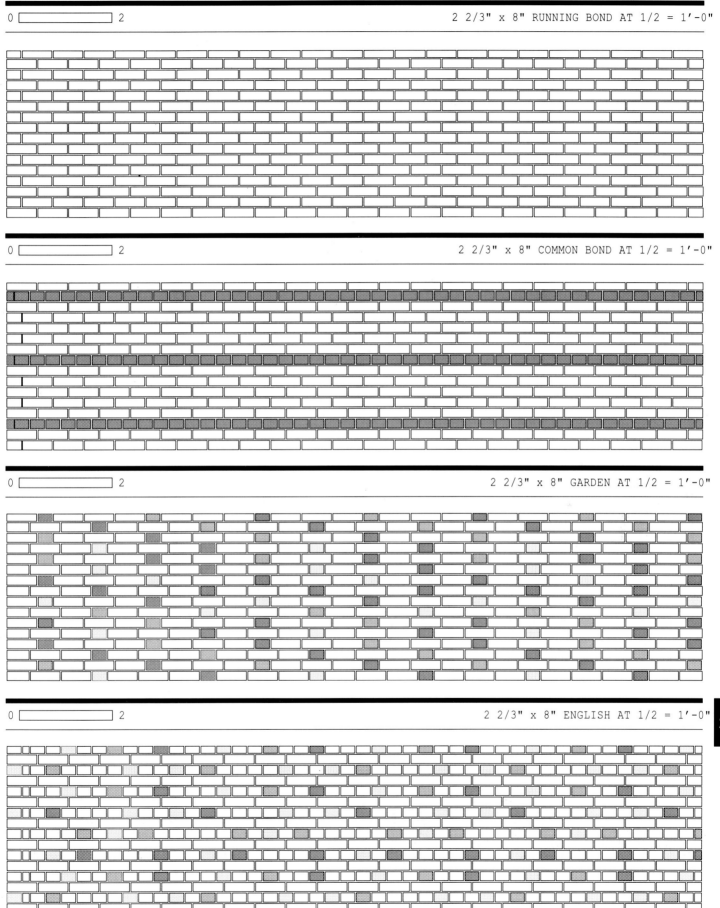

2 2/3" x 8" STACK BOND AT 1/2 = 1'-0"   0 ▭ 2

2 2/3" x 8" FLEMISH AT 1/2 = 1'-0"   0 ▭ 2

RANDOM STONE AT 1/2" = 1'-0"   0 ▭ 2

8" x 16" CMU AT 1/2 = 1'-0"   0 ▭ 2

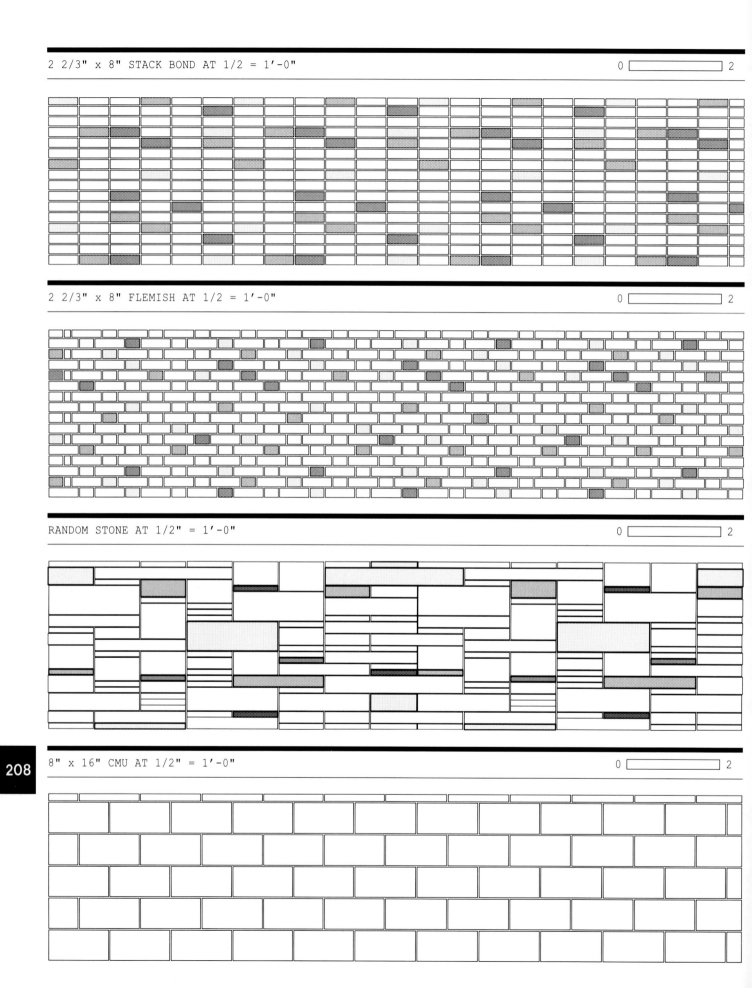

0 ⬜ 2   2 2/3" x 8" RUNNING BOND AT 3/8 = 1'-0"

0 ⬜ 2   2 2/3" x 8" COMMON BOND AT 3/8 = 1'-0"

0 ⬜ 2   2 2/3" x 8" GARDEN AT 3/8 = 1'-0"

0 ⬜ 2   2 2/3" x 8" ENGLISH AT 3/8 = 1'-0"

2 2/3" x 8" STACK BOND AT 3/8 = 1'-0"   0 ▭ 2

2 2/3" x 8" FLEMISH AT 3/8 = 1'-0"   0 ▭ 2

RANDOM STONE AT 3/8" = 1'-0"   0 ▭ 2

8" x 16" CMU AT 3/8" = 1'-0"   0 ▭ 2

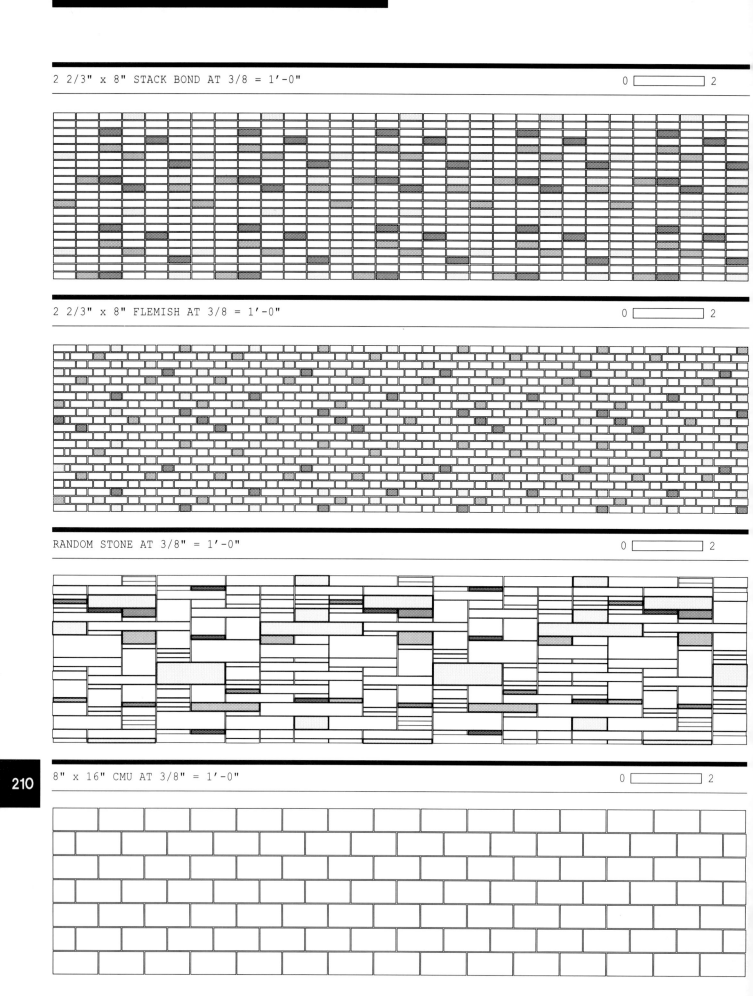

0 [_____] 4   2 2/3" x 8" RUNNING BOND AT 1/4 = 1'-0"

0 [_____] 4   2 2/3" x 8" COMMON BOND AT 1/4 = 1'-0"

0 [_____] 4   2 2/3" x 8" GARDEN AT 1/4 = 1'-0"

0 [_____] 4   2 2/3" x 8" ENGLISH AT 1/4 = 1'-0"

2 2/3" x 8" STACK BOND AT 1/4 = 1'-0"   0 ▭ 4

2 2/3" x 8" FLEMISH AT 1/4 = 1'-0"   0 ▭ 4

RANDOM STONE AT 1/4" = 1'-0"   0 ▭ 4

8" x 16" CMU AT 1/4" = 1'-0"   0 ▭ 4

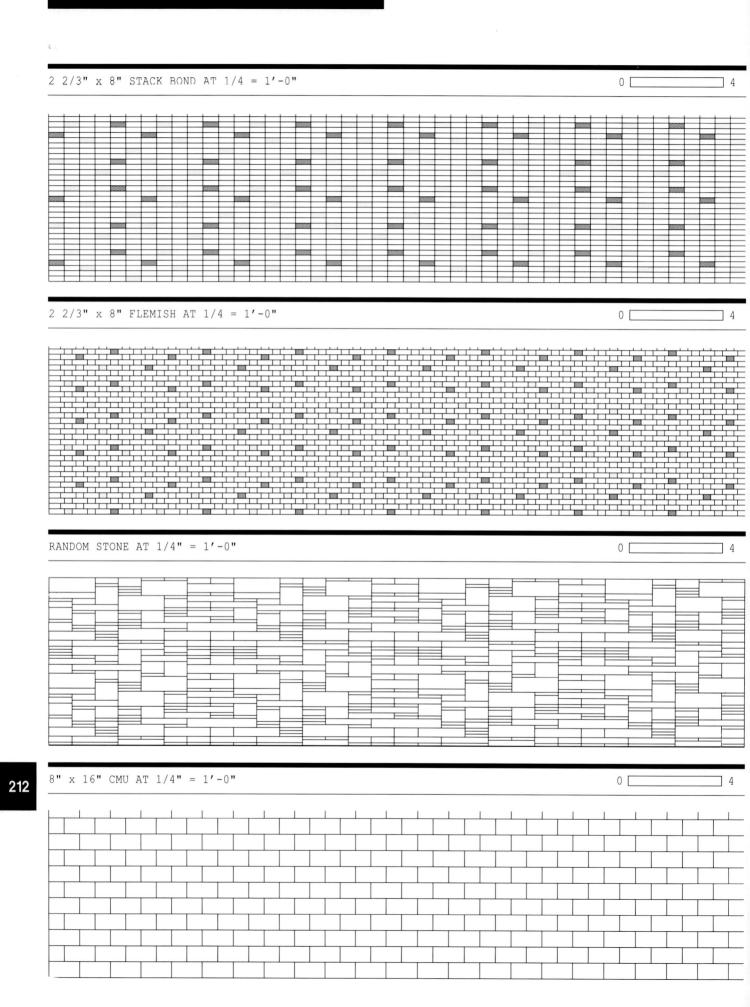

0 [   ] 4   2 2/3" x 8" RUNNING BOND AT 3/16 = 1'-0"

0 [   ] 4   2 2/3" x 8" COMMON BOND AT 3/16 = 1'-0"

0 [   ] 4   2 2/3" x 8" GARDEN AT 3/16 = 1'-0"

0 [   ] 4   2 2/3" x 8" ENGLISH AT 3/16 = 1'-0"

2 2/3" x 8" STACK BOND AT 3/16 - 1'-0"   0 ▭ 4

2 2/3" x 8" FLEMISH AT 3/16 = 1'-0"   0 ▭ 4

RANDOM STONE AT 3/16" = 1'-0"   0 ▭ 4

8" x 16" CMU AT 3/16" = 1'-0"   0 ▭ 4

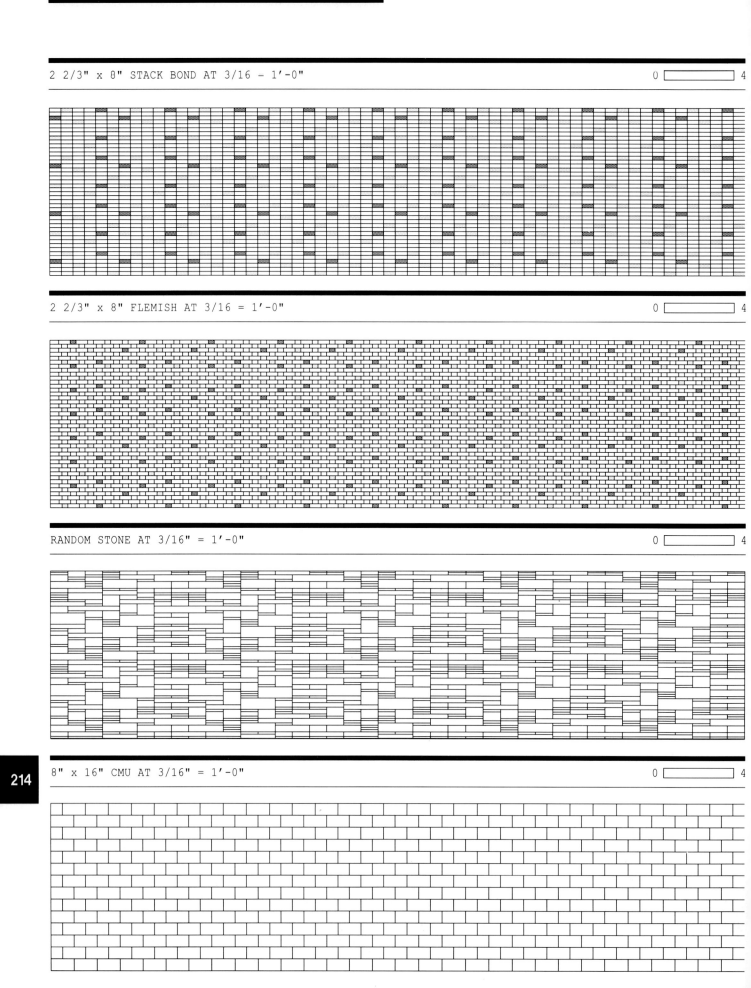

0 [   ] 8   2 2/3" .x 8" RUNNING BOND AT 1/8 = 1'-0"

0 [   ] 8   2 2/3" x 8" COMMON BOND AT 1/8 = 1'-0"

0 [   ] 8   2 2/3" x 8" GARDEN AT 1/8 = 1'-0"

0 [   ] 8   2 2/3" x 8" ENGLISH AT 1/8 = 1'-0"

2 2/3" x 8" STACK BOND AT 1/8 = 1'-0"   0 ⬛️ 8

2 2/3" x 8" FLEMISH AT 1/8 = 1'-0"   0 ⬛️ 8

RANDOM STONE AT 1/8" = 1'-0"   0 ⬛️ 8

8" x 16" CMU AT 1/8" = 1'-0"   0 ⬛️ 8

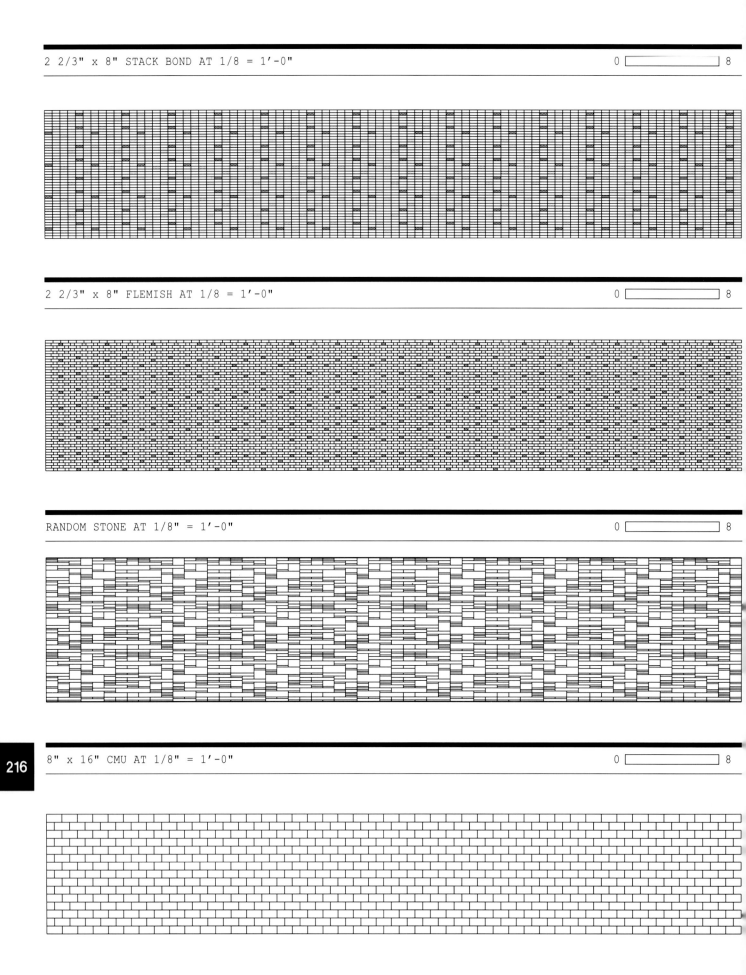

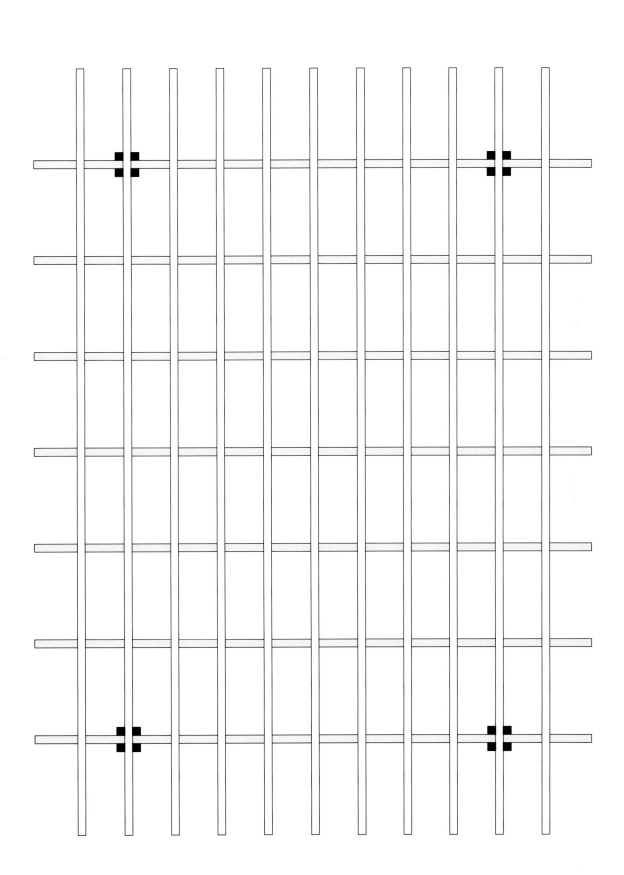

ARBOR OVER 6' WALK AT 1/2" = 1'-0"   0 ▭ 2

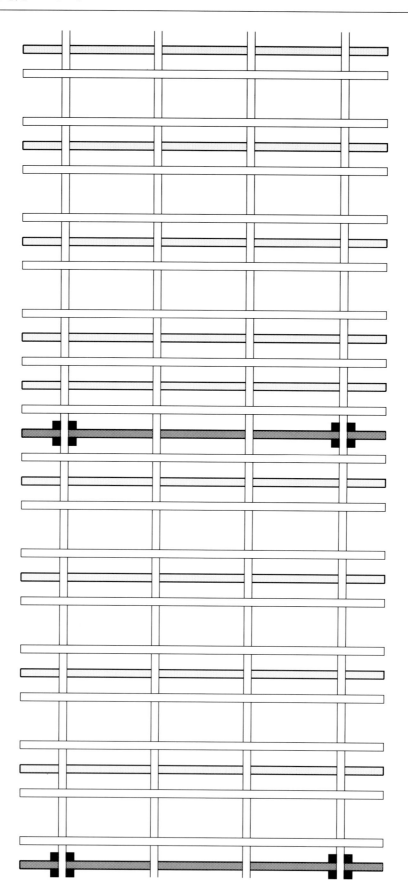

0 ▭ 2   ARBORS AT 3/8" = 1'-0"

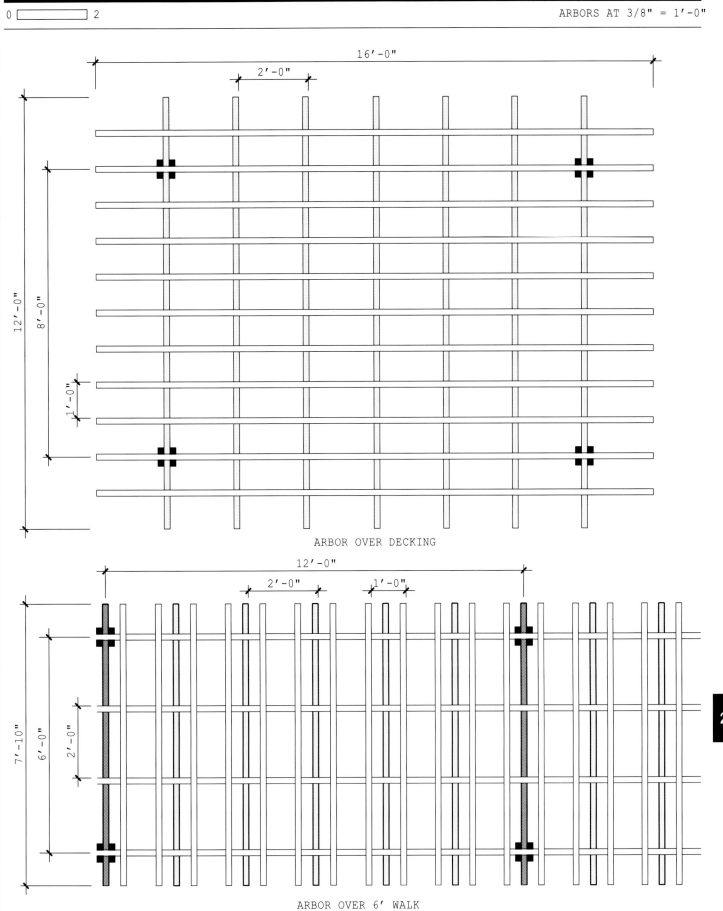

16'-0"

2'-0"

12'-0"

8'-0"

1'-0"

ARBOR OVER DECKING

12'-0"

2'-0"   1'-0"

7'-10"

6'-0"

2'-0"

ARBOR OVER 6' WALK

ARBORS AT 1/4" = 1'-0"   0 ▭ 4

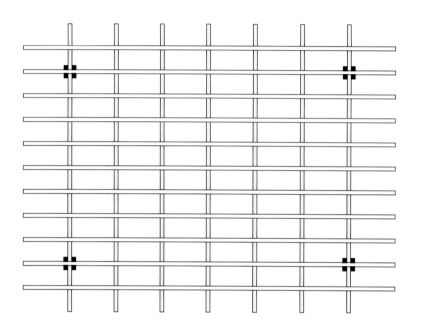

ARBOR OVER DECKING

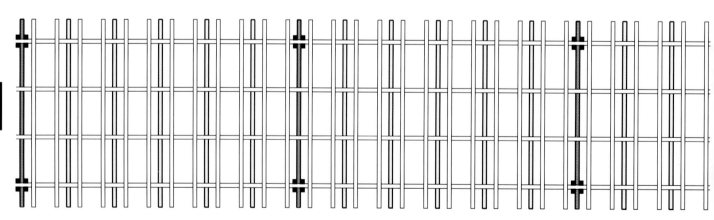

ARBOR OVER 6' WALK

0 ⬛ 4

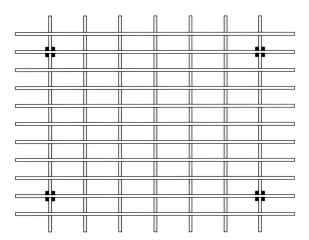

ARBOR OVER DECKING

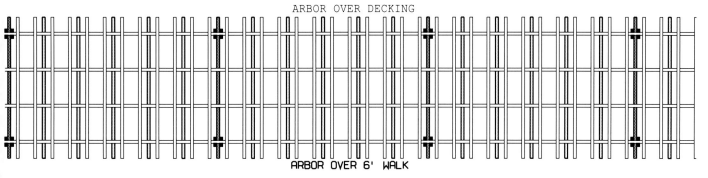

ARBOR OVER 6' WALK

0 ⬛ 8   ARBORS AT 1/8" = 1'-0"

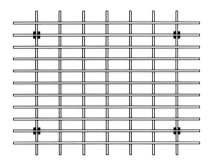

ARBOR OVER DECKING

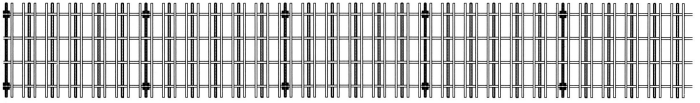

ARBOR OVER 6' WALK

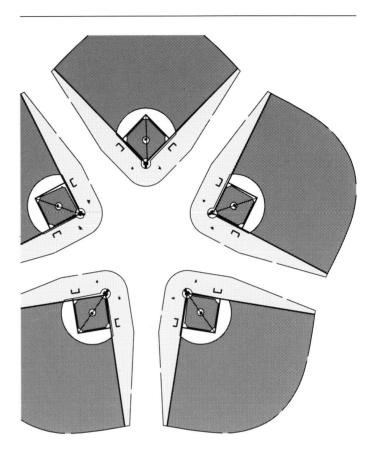

BASEBALL/SOFTBALL	VIEW	PLAN	SCALE	240	360	480	600	720	1,200	2,400	4,800	12,000
OFFICAL BASEBALL		●		229	235	241	247	253	257	259	260	260
BRONCO BASEBALL		●		230	236	242	248	254	257	259	260	260
PONY BASEBALL		●		231	237	243	249	254	257	259	260	260
LITTLE LEAGUE BASEBALL		●		232	238	244	250	255	257	259	260	260
12" SOFTBALL		●		233	239	245	251	255	258	259	260	260
16" SOFTBALL		●		234	240	246	252	256	258	259	260	260

FIELDS	VIEW	PLAN	FRONT	SIDE	SCALE	480	600	720	1,200	2,400	4,800
FOOTBALL		●				261	267	273	277	280	281
TOUCH OR FLAG FOOTBALL		●				262	268	274	277	280	281
LACROSSE		●				263	269	274	277	280	281
SOCCER		●				264	270	275	277	280	281
TEAM HANDBALL		●				265	271	274	278	280	281
RUGBY		●				266	272	276	278	280	281
POLO		●							279	280	281

GOLF	VIEW	PLAN	FRONT	SIDE	SCALE	1,200	2,400	4,800
DRIVING RANGE		●				282	284	286
PAR 3 HOLE		●				283	285	286
PAR 4 HOLE		●					285	286
PAR 5 HOLE		●						286

HARD COURTS	VIEW	PLAN	SCALE	96	120	128	192	240	360	480	600	720
BADMINTON		●		287	299	309	321	326	329	331	333	333
BASKETBALL AAU		●		288	300	310	318	325	329	331	333	333
BASKETBALL NCAA		●		289	301	311	319	325	329	331	333	333
BASKETBALL HIGH SCHOOL		●		290	302	312	320	326	329	331	333	333
ONE WALL HANDBALL		●		291	303	313	321	326	329	331	333	333
THREE WALL HANDBALL		●		292	303	313	321	326	329	331	333	333
FOUR WALL HANDBALL		●		292	304	314	321	326	329	331	333	333
TETHERBALL		●		293	304	314	323	328	106	332	333	333
HOPSCOTCH		●		293	304	314	321	326	329	331	333	333
SHUFFLEBOARD		●		294	304	314	321	327	329	331	333	333

HARD COURTS	VIEW	PLAN	SCALE	96	120	128	192	240	360	480	600	720
TENNIS		●		295	305	315	322	327	330	332	333	333
DECK TENNIS		●		296	306	316	323	327	330	332	333	333
PADDLE TENNIS		●		297	307	316	323	327	330	332	333	333
VOLLEYBALL		●		298	308	316	324	328	330	332	333	333

SOFT COURTS	VIEW	PLAN	FRONT	SIDE	SCALE	96	120	128	192	240	360	480
CROQUET		●				334	337	339	341	342	344	346
HORSESHOES		●				335	338	340	341	342	344	346
ROQUE		●				336	338	340	341	342	344	346
LAWN BOWLING		●								343	345	346

TRACK	VIEW	PLAN	FRONT	SIDE	SCALE	240	360	480	600	720	1,200	2,400
1/4 MILE TRACK		●						357	362	366	369	371
SHOT PUT		●				347	353	358	363	367	370	371
HAMMER THROW		●				348	354	359	364	368	370	371
DISCUS THROW		●				349	355	360	365	367	370	371
JAVELIN		●				350	356	361	363	367	370	371
LONG JUMP		●				351	353	358	363	367	370	371
TRIPLE JUMP		●				351	353	358	363	367	370	371
POLE VAULT		●				351	353	358	363	367	370	371
HIGH JUMP		●				352	353	358	363	367	370	371

RANGE	VIEW	PLAN	SCALE	240	360	480	600	720	1,200	2,400	4,800	12,000
ARCHERY		●		372	377	380	382	384	385	389	392	394
AUTOMATIC TRAP		●		373	378	381	383	384	385	389	392	394
SKEET		●		374	378	381	383	384	386	390	392	394
TRAP		●		375	378	381	383	384	387	391	392	394
COMBINATION		●		376	379	381	383	384	388	392	393	394

COMBINATIONS	VIEW	PLAN	FRONT	SIDE	SCALE	240	360	480	600	720	1,200	2,400	4,800
BASKETBALL/VOLLEYBALL		●				395	398	400	402	403	404		
TENN/VOLL/BSKT/BADM/SHUFF		●				396	398	400	402	403	404		
2 TENNIS COURTS		●				397	399	400	402	403	404		
4 TENNIS COURTS		●					399	401	402	403	404		
1/4 MILE RUNNING TRACK		●									404	408	410
BASEBALL/SOFTBALL/FOOTBALL		●									405	408	410
4 BASEBALL		●									406	408	410
5 BASEBALL		●									407	409	410

COMMERCIAL POOLS	VIEW	PLAN	FRONT	SIDE	SCALE	192	240	360	480	600	720	1,200
50 METER POOL		●				411	416	420	424	426	427	428
25 METER POOL		●				412	417	421	424	426	427	428
DIVING POOL		●				413	418	422	425	426	427	428
WATER POLO		●				414	417	421	424	426	427	428
HOCKEY		●				415	419	423	425	426	427	428

RESIDENTIAL POOLS	VIEW	PLAN	FRONT	SIDE	SCALE	96	120	128	192	240	360	480
KIDNEY SHAPED 600 SF. FT.		●				429	434	437	439	440	441	442
KIDNEY SHAPED 800 SF. FT.		●				429	434	437	439	440	441	442
KIDNEY SHAPED 1,000 SF. FT.		●				430	434	437	439	440	441	442
KIDNEY SHAPED 1,200 SF. FT.		●				430	434	437	439	440	441	442
RECTANGULAR		●				431	435	438	439	440	441	442
CORNER CUT		●				432	435	438	439	440	441	442
CORNER RADIUS CUT		●				433	435	438	439	440	441	442
1/2 LAP POOL		●					435	438	439	440	441	442
LAP POOL		●					436	438	439	440	441	442

227

PLAYGROUNDS	VIEW	PLAN	FRONT	SIDE	SCALE	48	64	96	120	128	192	240
SLIDE		●				443	449	452	456	459	462	462
4 SEAT SWING		●				444	449	452	456	459	462	462
HORIZONTAL BARS		●				445	450	452	456	459	462	462
SPIN AROUND		●				446	450	452	456	459	462	462
SPRING TOYS		●				445	450	452	456	459	462	462

PLAYGROUNDS	VIEW	PLAN	FRONT	SIDE	SCALE	48	64	96	120	128	192	240
CLIMBING BARS		●				446	450	452	457	460	463	463
SMALL PLAYSTRUCTURE		●				448	451	453	458	461	463	463
MEDIUM PLAYSTRUCTURE		●				448	451	454	458	461	463	463
LARGE PLAYSTRUCTURE		●				448	451	456	234	462	463	463

0 [   ] 20

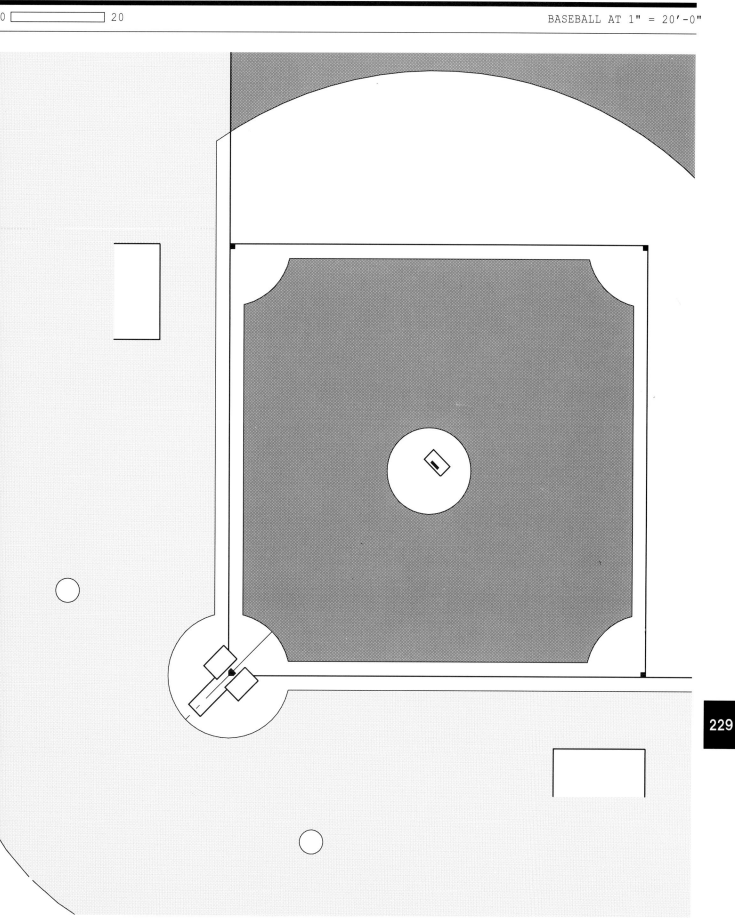

BRONCO LEAGUE BASEBALL AT 1" = 20'-0"

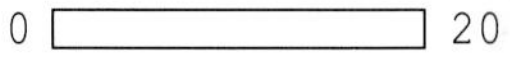

0 ▭ 20

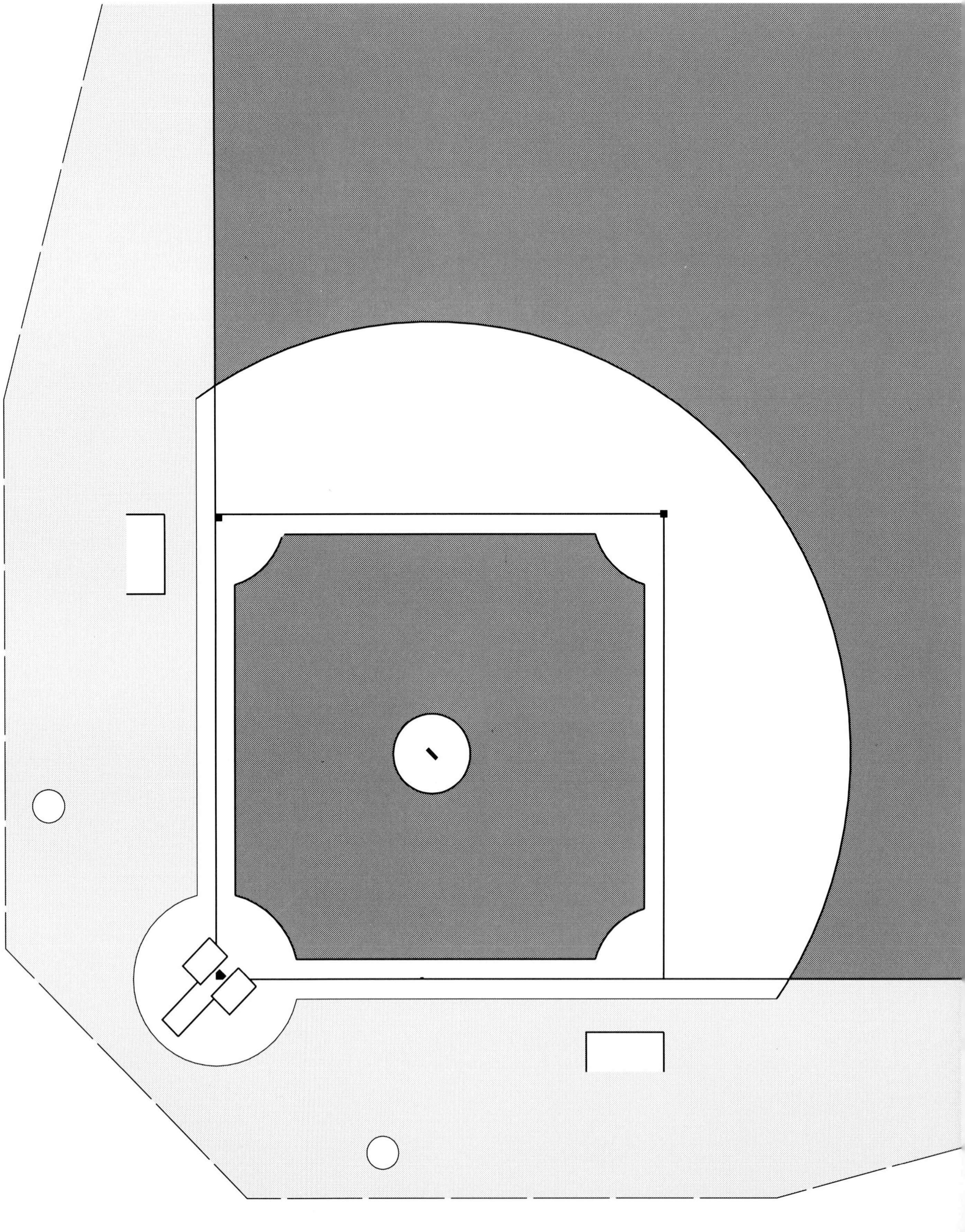

0 ⬚ 20

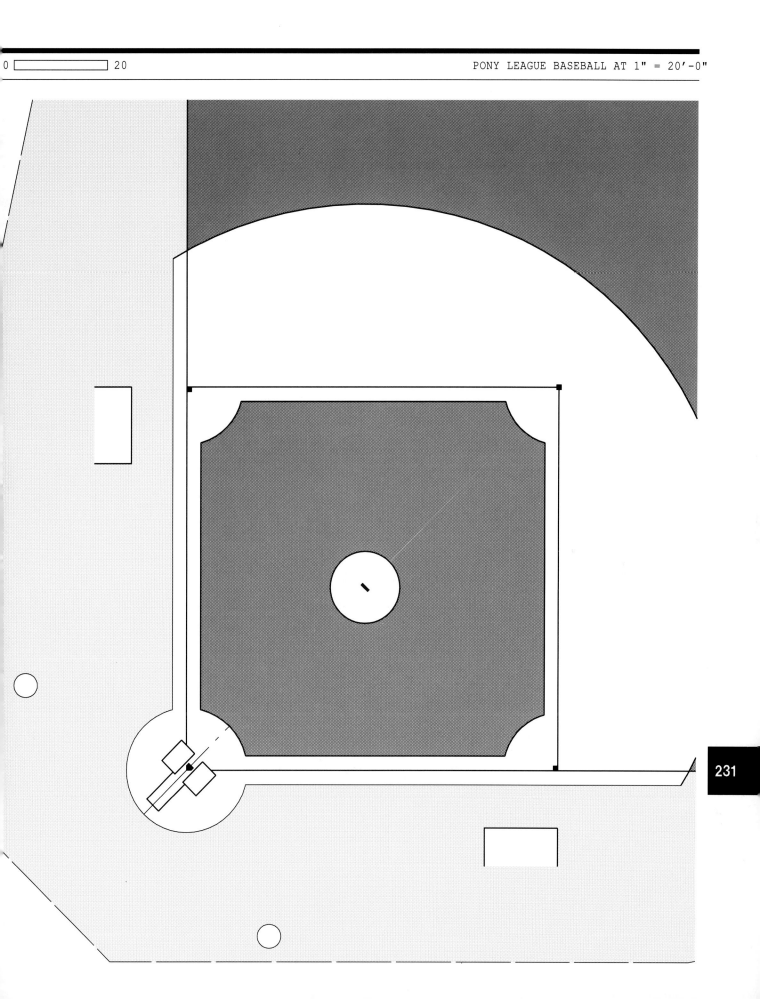

LITTLE LEAGUE BASEBALL AT 1" = 20'-0"   0 ▭ 20

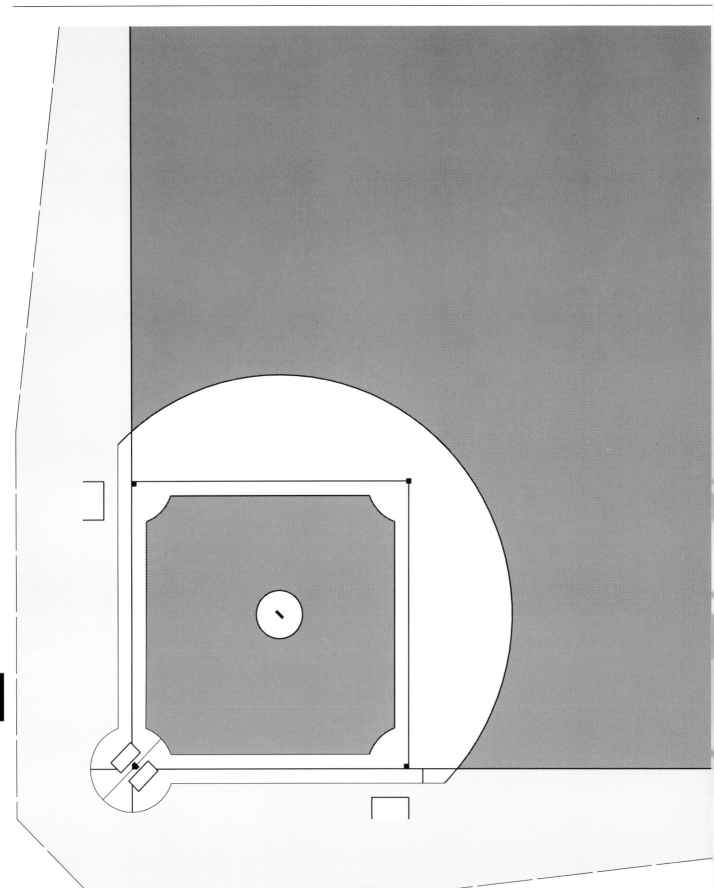

12" SOFTBALL AT 1" = 20'-0"

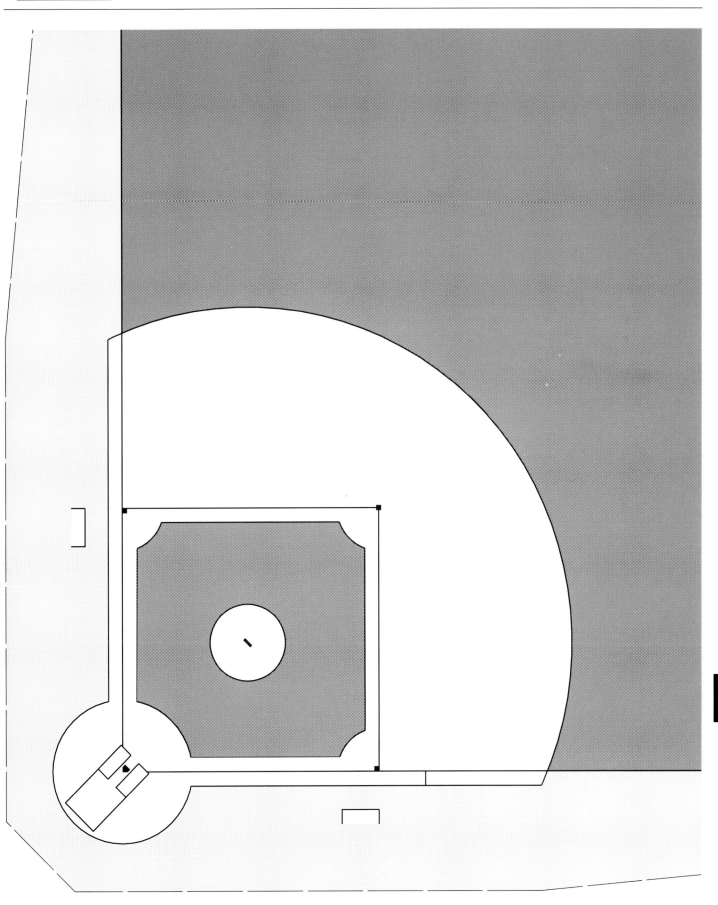

16" SOFTBALL AT 1" = 20'-0"

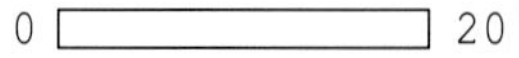

0 [   ] 20

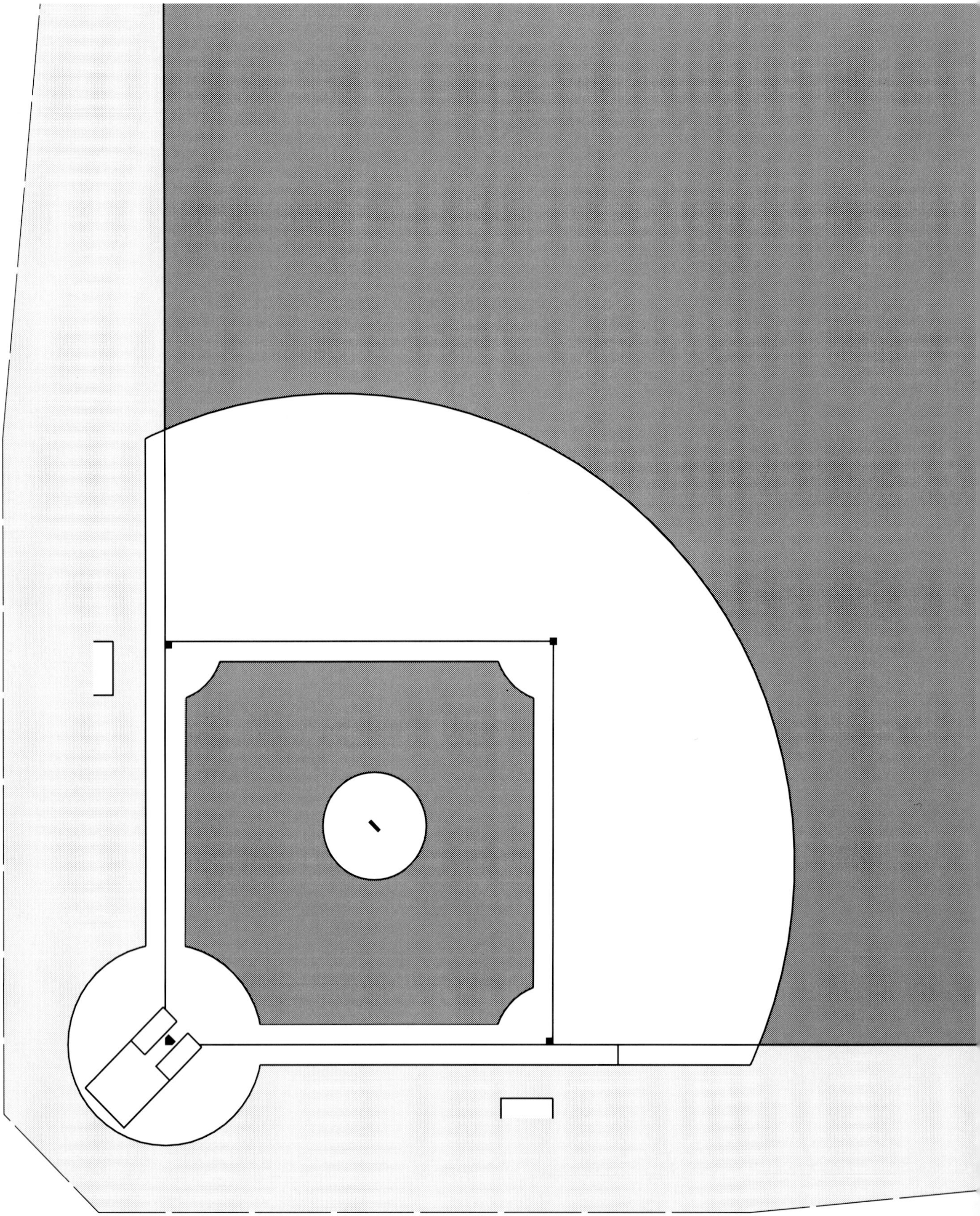

0 ▭ 30

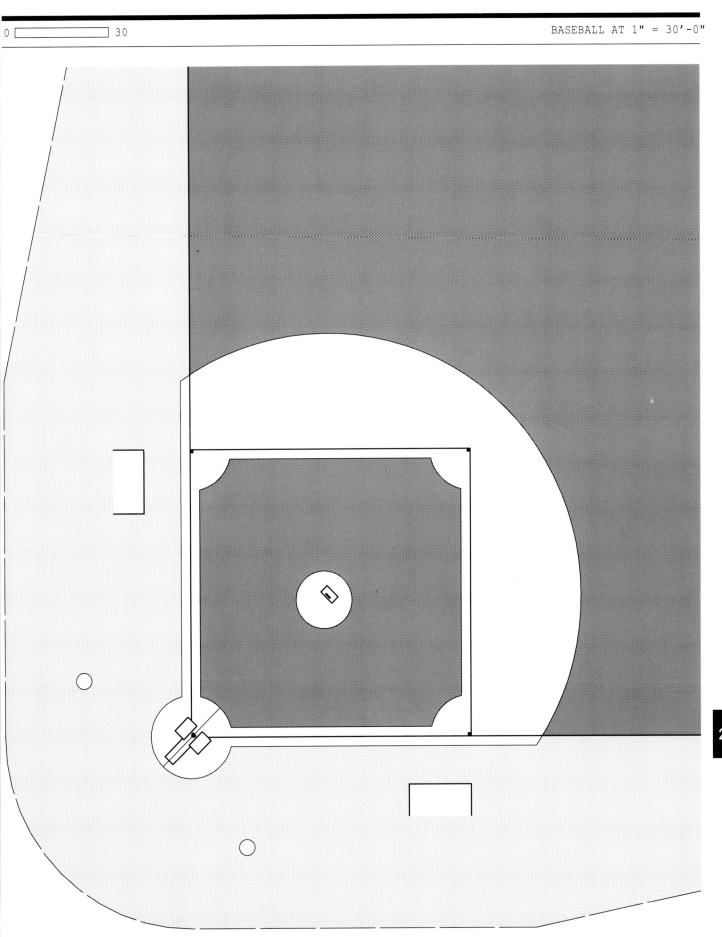

BRONCO LEAGUE BASEBALL AT 1" = 30'-0"   0 ▭ 30

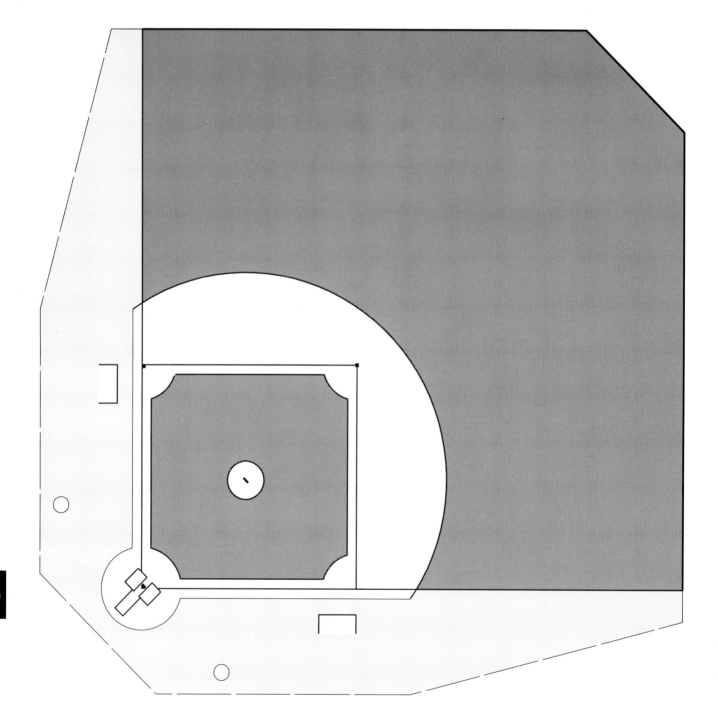

0 ⬚ 30

PONY LEAGUE BASEBALL AT 1" = 30'-0"

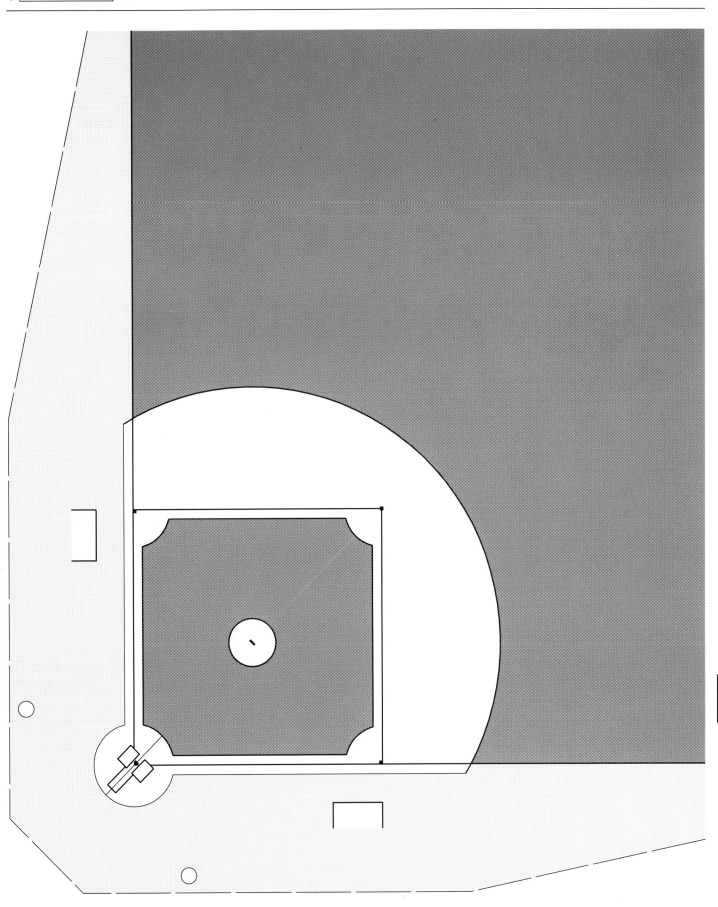

LITTLE LEAGUE BASEBALL AT 1" = 30'-0"

0 ⊏━━━━━⊐ 30

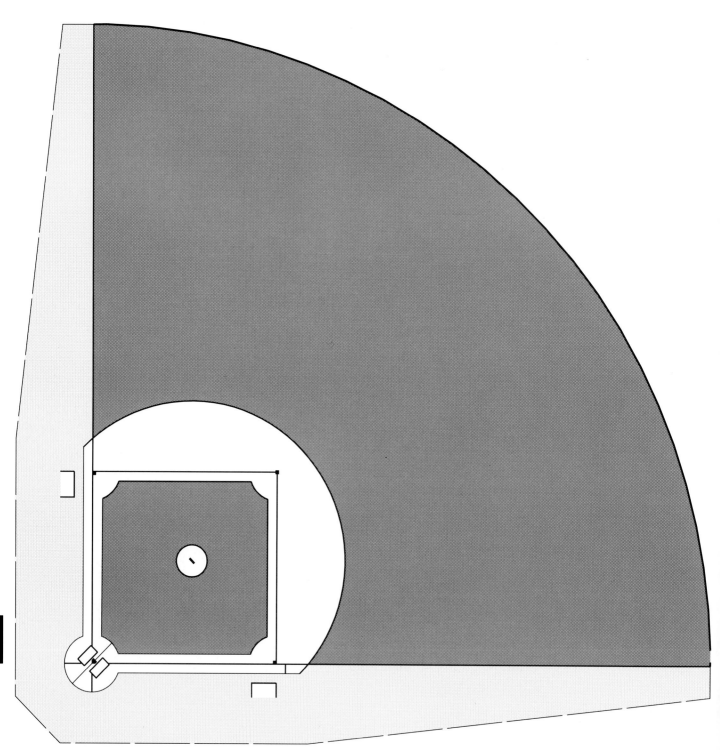

0 30

12" SOFTBALL AT 1" = 30'-0"

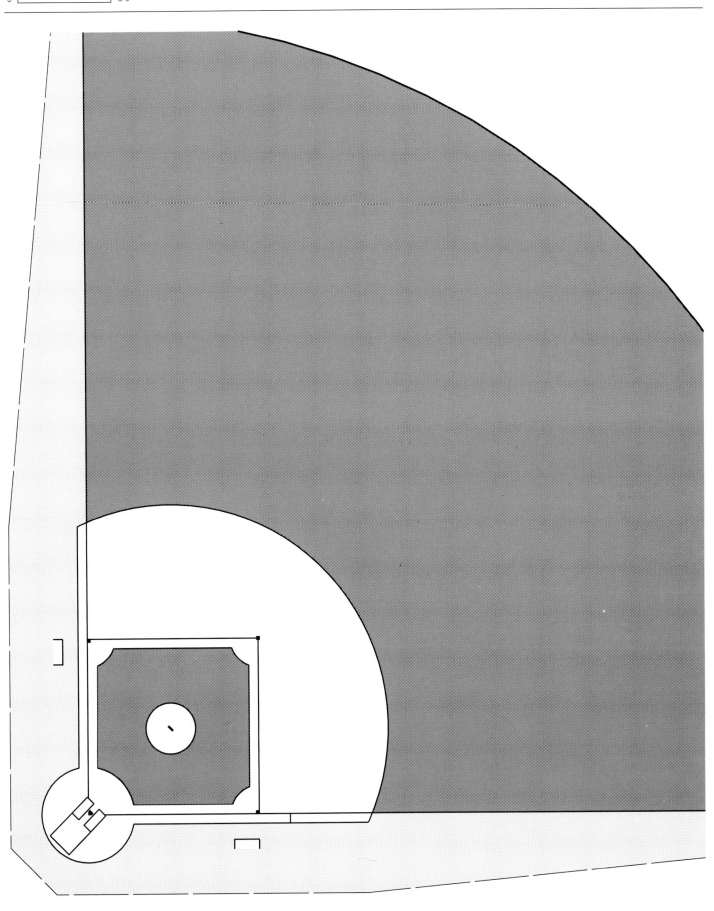

16" SOFTBALL AT 1" = 30'-0"

0 ⌷━━━━━━━⌷ 30

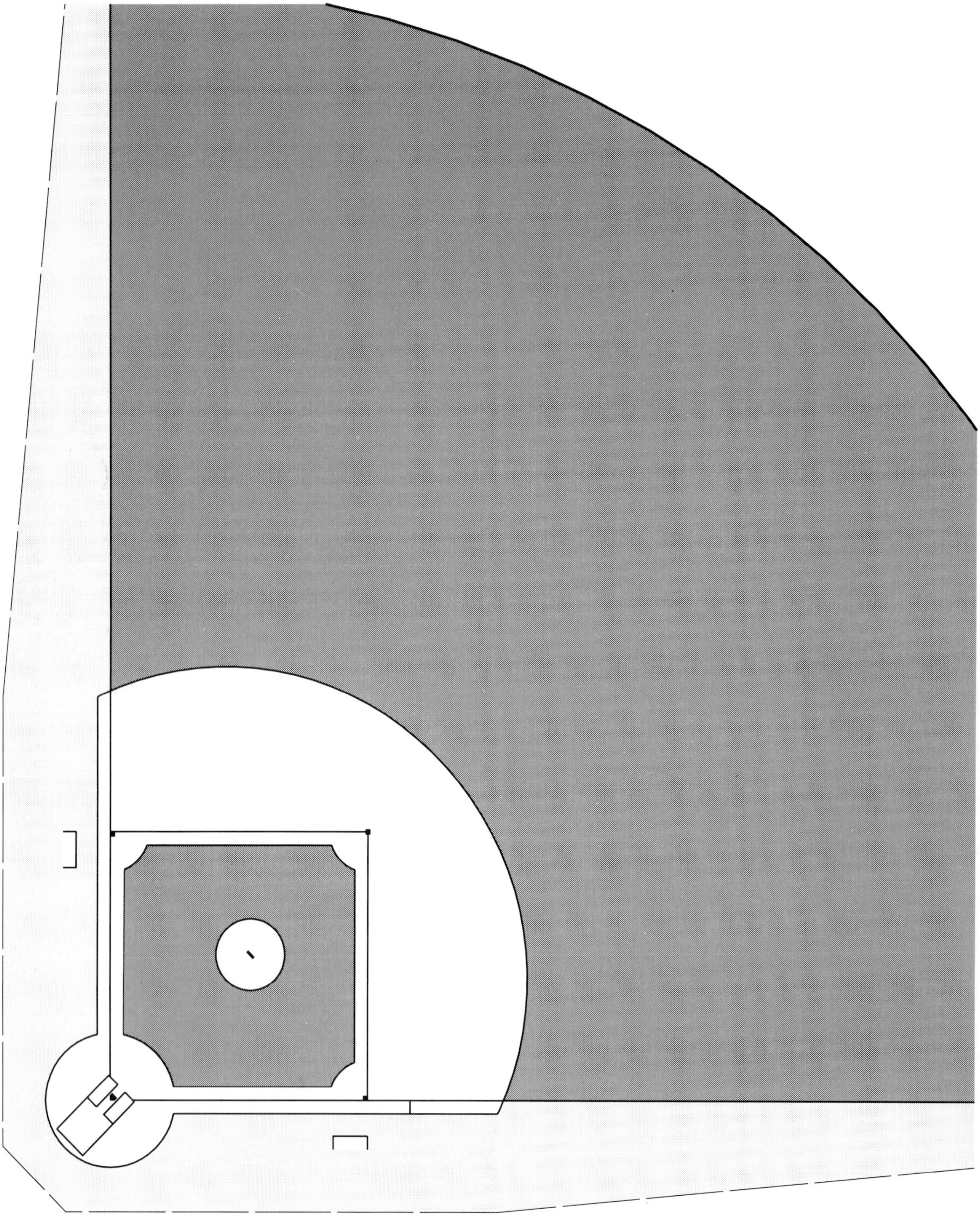

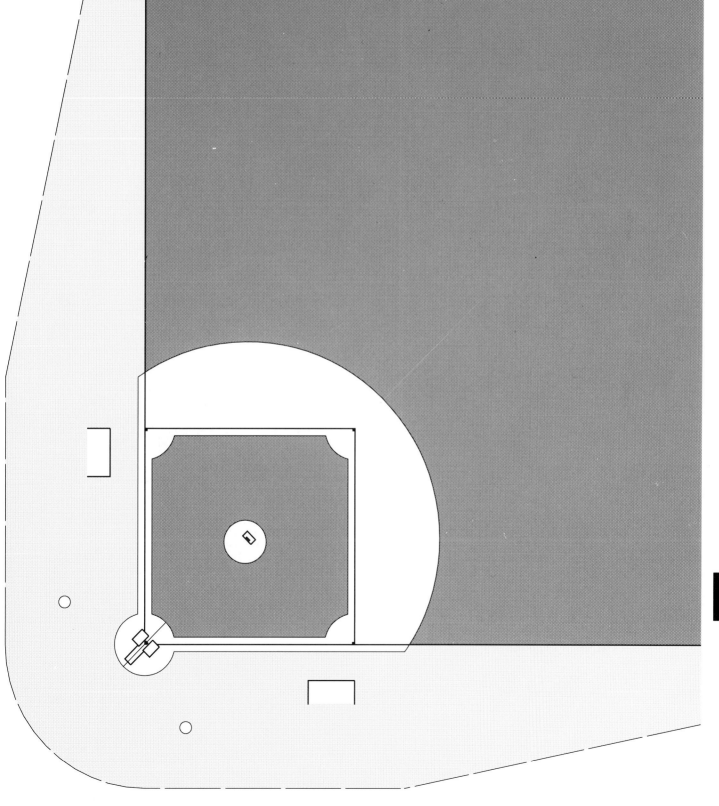

BRONCO LEAGUE BASEBALL AT 1" = 40'-0"

0 ▭ 40

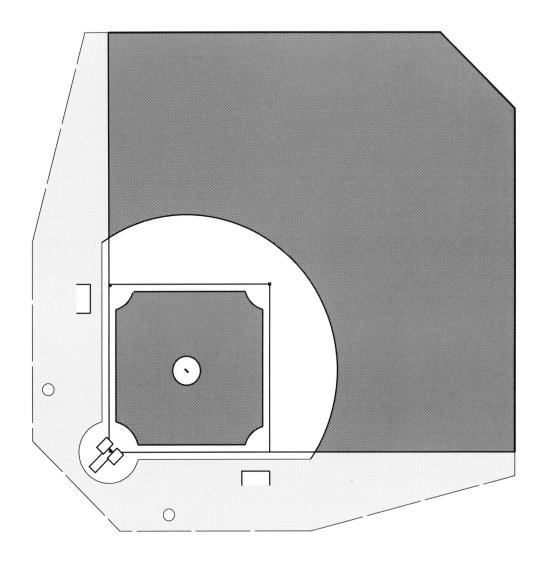

0 40

PONY LEAGUE BASEBALL AT 1" = 40'-0"

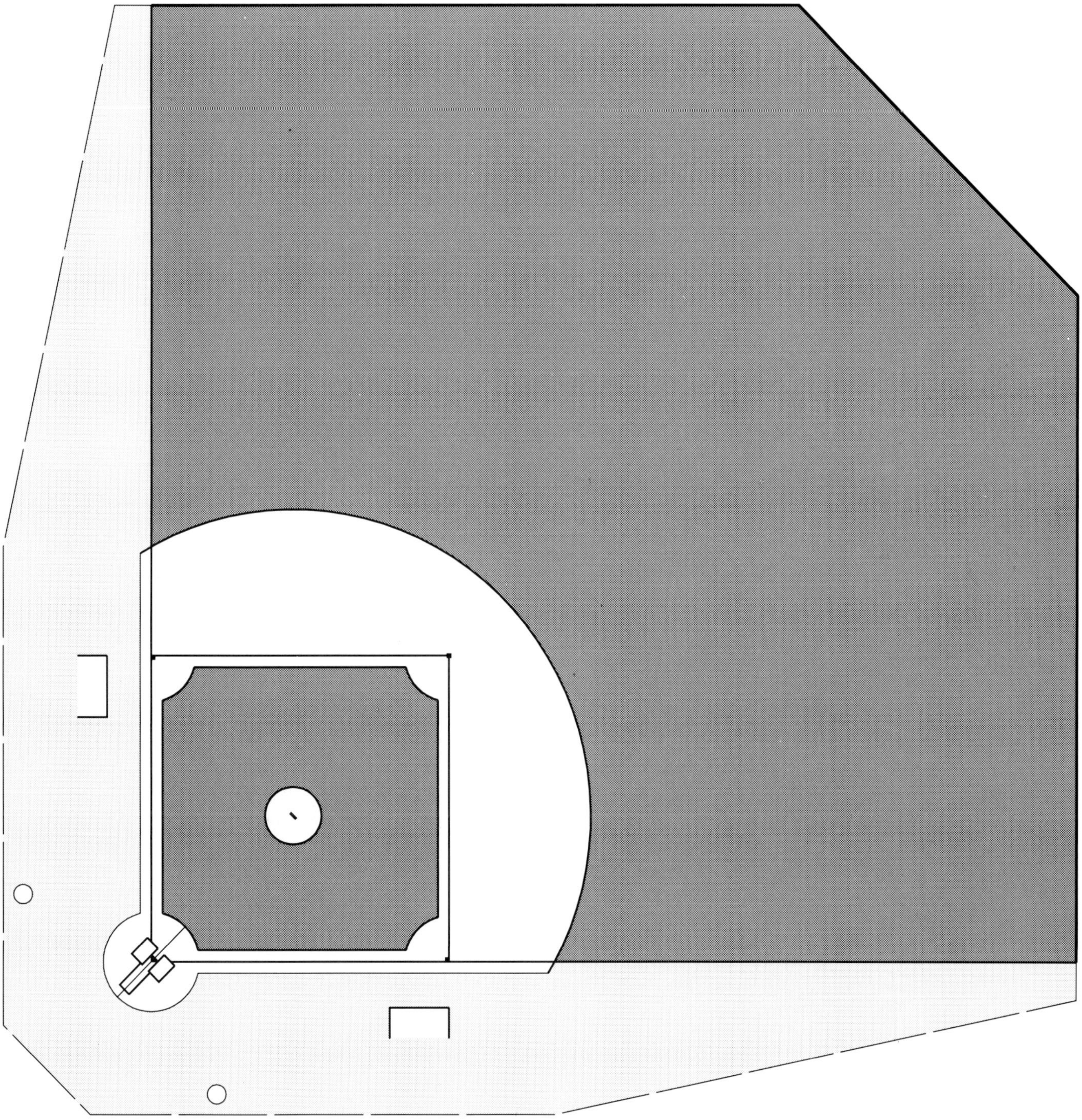

BASEBALL/SOFTBALL

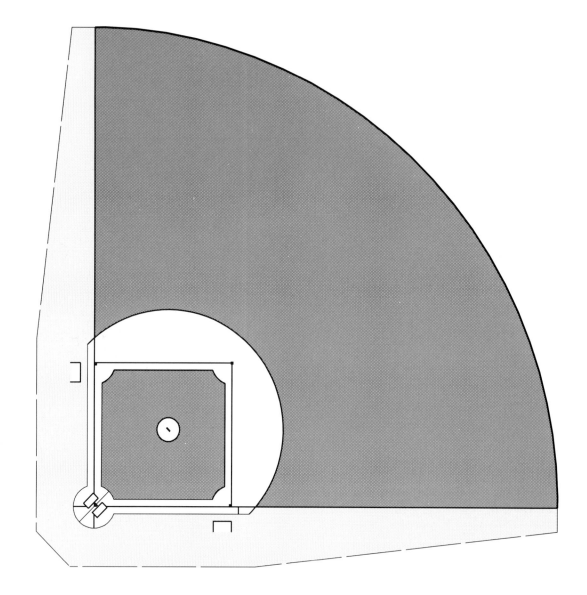

244

0 [========] 40

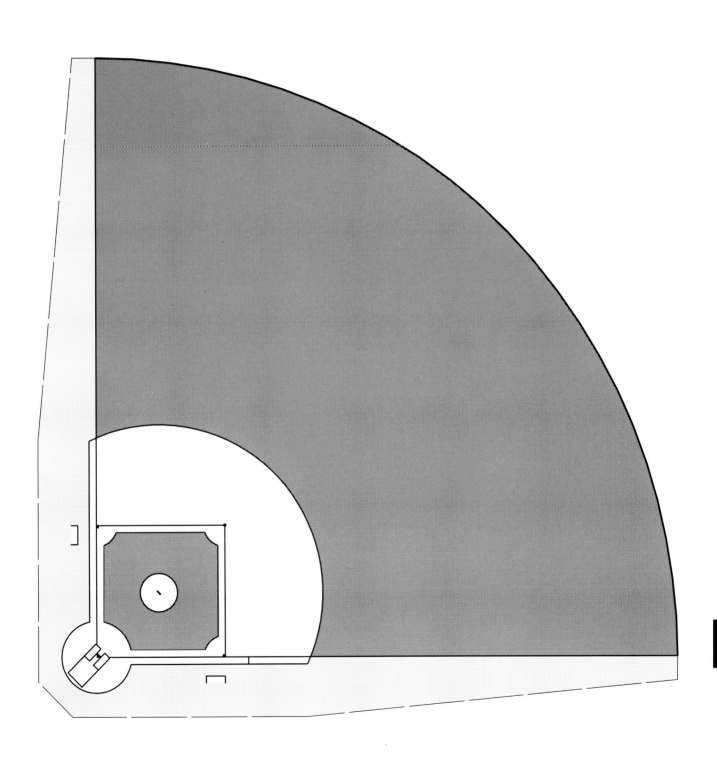

16" SOFTBALL AT 1" = 40'-0"

0 ▭ 40

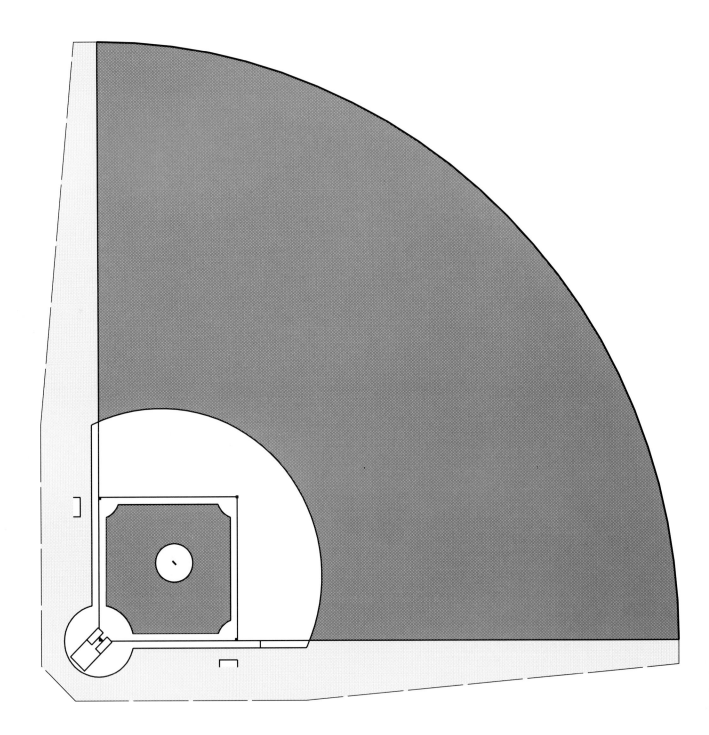

0 [   ] 50

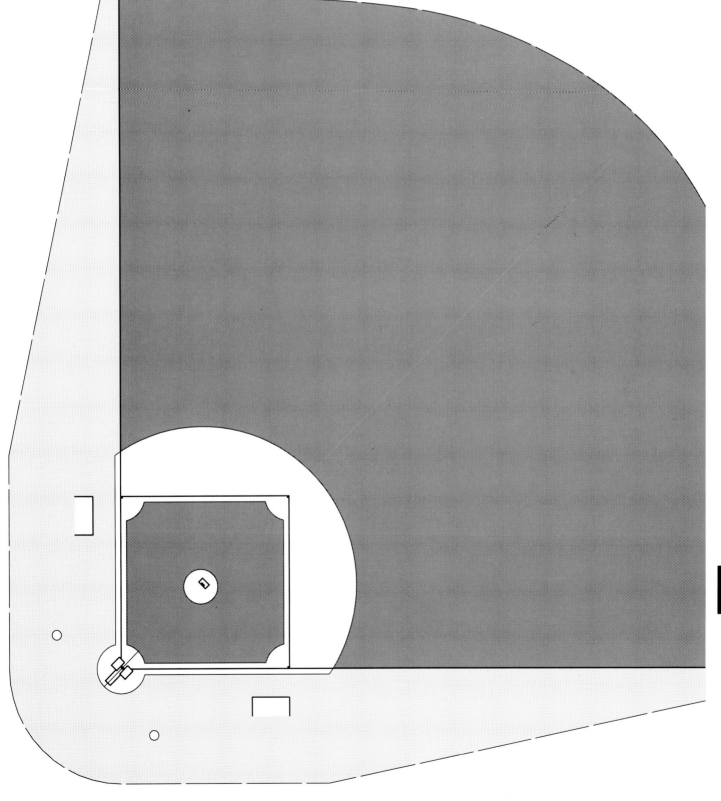

BRONCO LEAGUE BASEBALL AT 1" = 50'-0"   0 ▭ 50

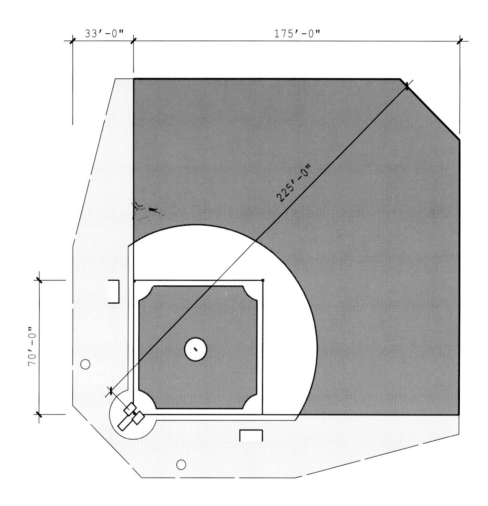

33'-0"   175'-0"

225'-0"

70'-0"

PLAYING AREA
30,119 SQUARE FEET
.691 ACRES

SAFETY AREA
9,912 SQUARE FEET
.228 ACRES

TOTAL AREA REQUIRED
40,031 SQUARE FEET
.919 ACRES

0 ▭ 50

PONY LEAGUE BASEBALL AT 1" = 50'-0"

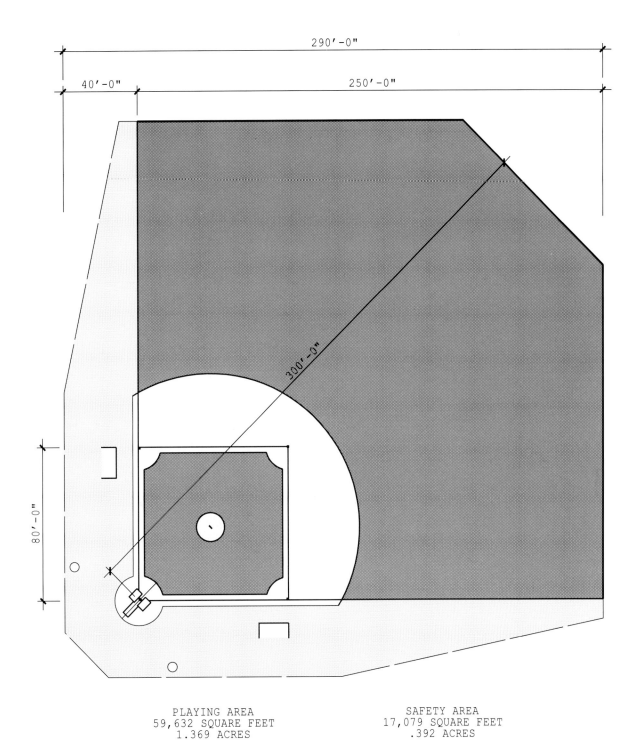

290'-0"

40'-0"   250'-0"

300'-0"

80'-0"

PLAYING AREA
59,632 SQUARE FEET
1.369 ACRES

SAFETY AREA
17,079 SQUARE FEET
.392 ACRES

TOTAL AREA REQUIRED
76,711 SQUARE FEET
1.761 ACRES

LITTLE LEAGUE BASEBALL AT 1" = 50'-0"   0 ▭ 50

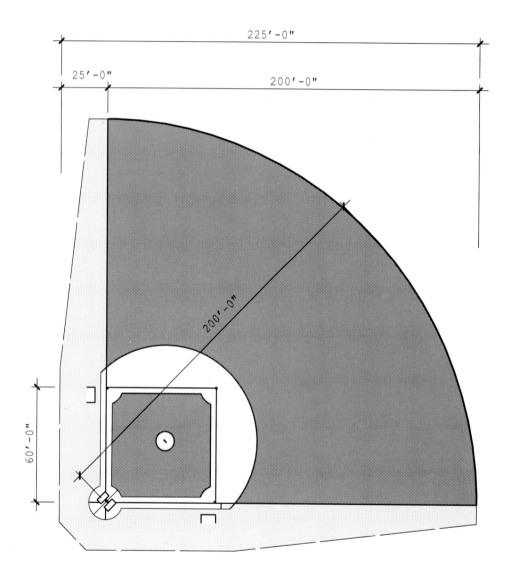

225'-0"

25'-0"   200'-0"

200'-0"

60'-0"

PLAYING AREA
31,315 SQUARE FEET
.719 ACRES

SAFETY AREA
8.570 SQUARE FEET
.197 ACRES

TOTAL AREA REQUIRED
39,885 SQUARE FEET
.916 ACRES

0 [▭▭▭▭] 50

12" SOFTBALL AT 1" = 50'-0"

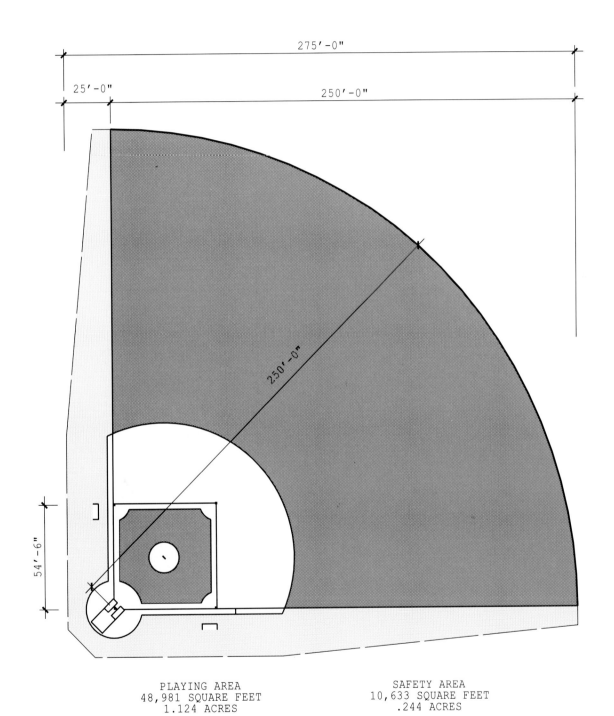

275'-0"

25'-0"

250'-0"

250'-0"

54'-6"

PLAYING AREA
48,981 SQUARE FEET
1.124 ACRES

SAFETY AREA
10,633 SQUARE FEET
.244 ACRES

TOTAL AREA REQUIRED
59,615 SQUARE FEET
1.369 ACRES

16" SOFTBALL AT 1" = 50'-0"

0 ▭ 50

275'-0"

25'-0"

250'-0"

250'-0"

60'-0"

PLAYING AREA
49,003 SQUARE FEET
1.125 ACRES

SAFETY AREA
10,633 SQUARE FEET
.244 ACRES

TOTAL AREA REQUIRED
59,637 SQUARE FEET
1.369 ACRES

0 ▭ 60

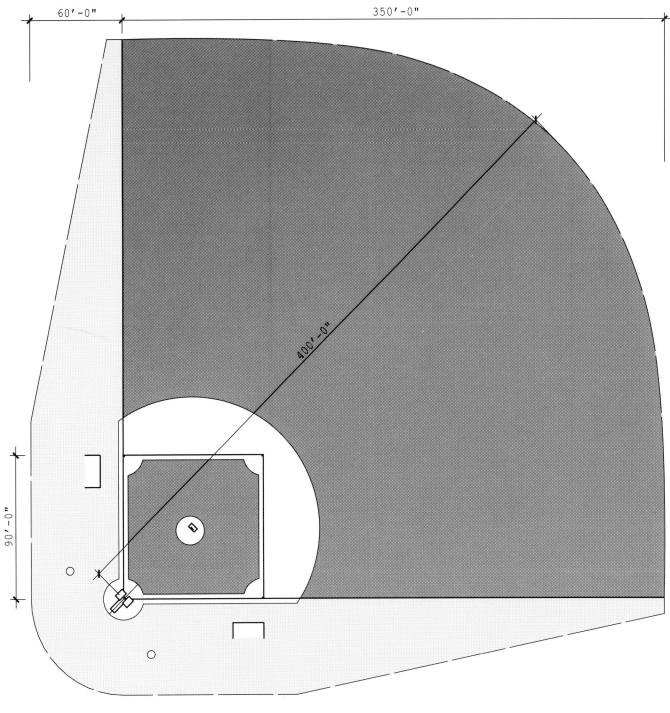

60'-0"   350'-0"

400'-0"

90'-0"

PLAYING AREA
110,320 SQUARE FEET
2.533 ACRES

SAFETY AREA
32,870 SQUARE FEET
.755 ACRES

TOTAL AREA REQUIRED
143,190 SQUARE FEET
3.287 ACRES

BASEBALL AT 1" = 60'-0"   0 [====] 60

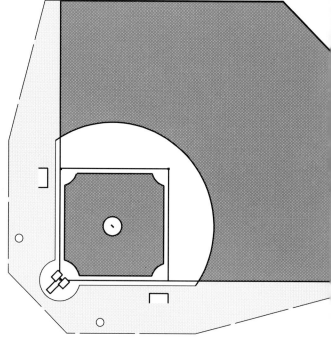

BRONCO LEAGUE

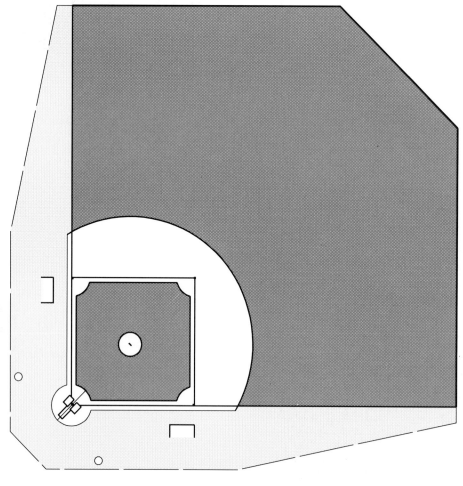

PONY LEAGUE

0 60

BASEBALL AT 1" = 60′-0"

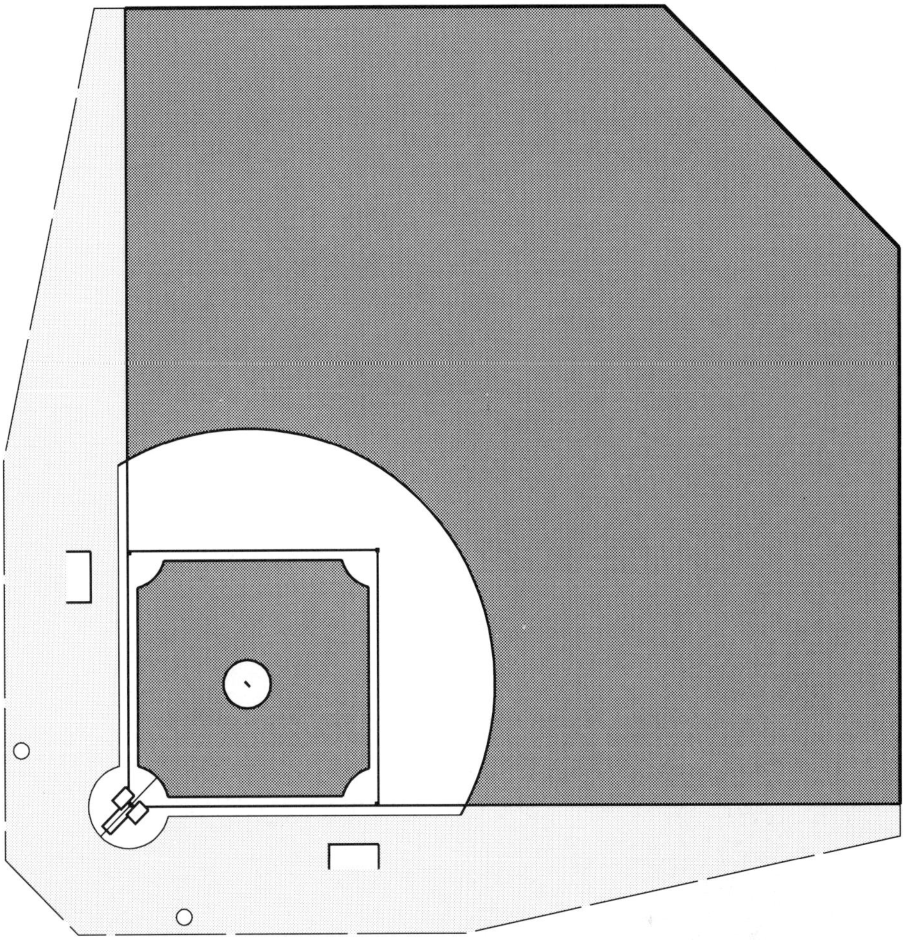

LITTLE LEAGUE

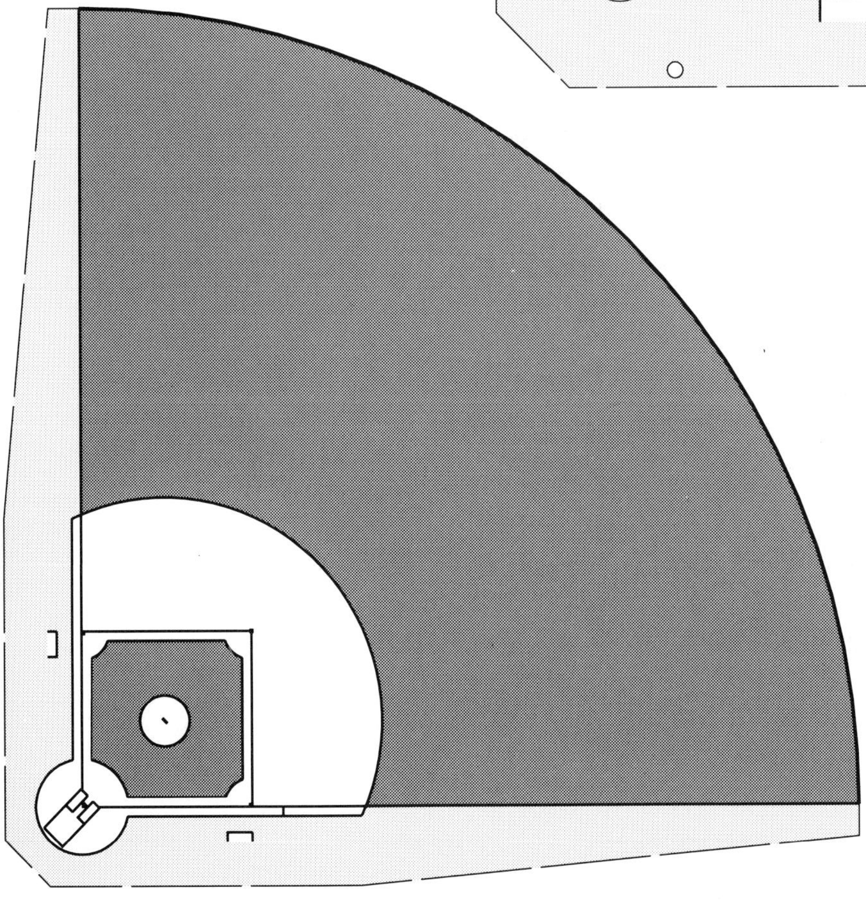

12" SOFTBALL

SOFTBALL AT 1" = 60'-0"

0 [========] 60

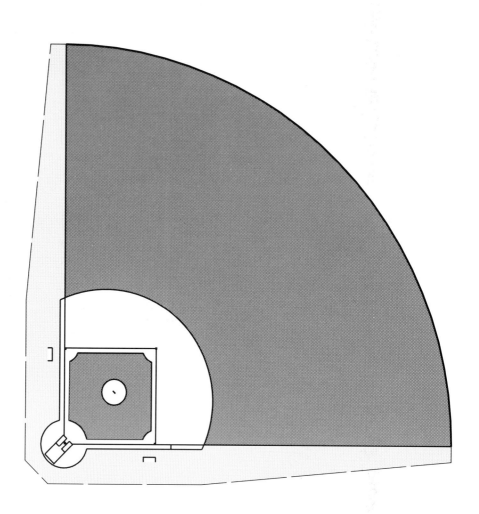

16" SOFTBALL

0 ▭ 100

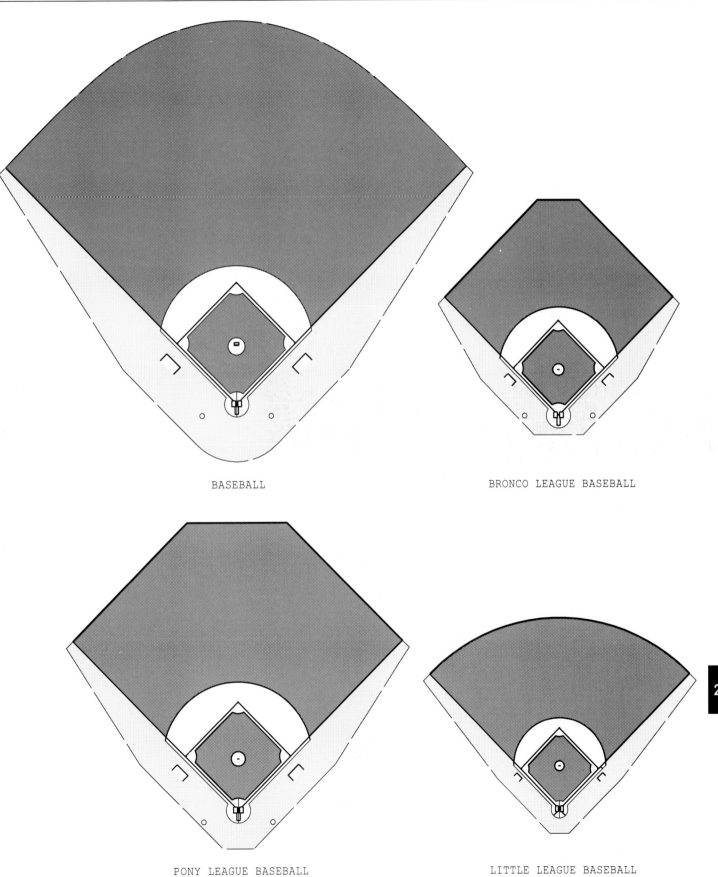

BASEBALL

BRONCO LEAGUE BASEBALL

PONY LEAGUE BASEBALL

LITTLE LEAGUE BASEBALL

SOFTBALL AT 1" = 100'-0"   0 ☐ 100

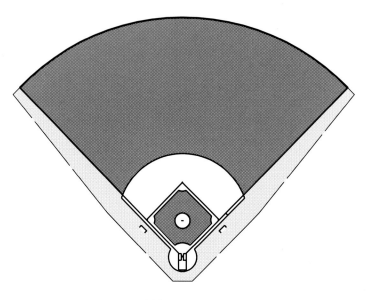

12" SOFTBALL

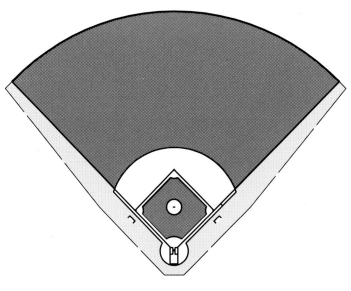

16" SOFTBALL

0 ☐☐☐ 200   BASEBALL AT 1" = 200'-0"

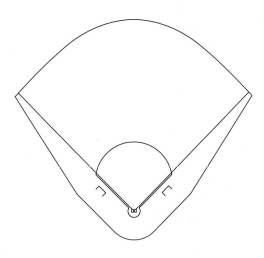

BASEBALL

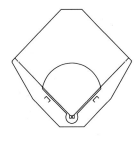

BRONCO LEAGUE BASEBALL

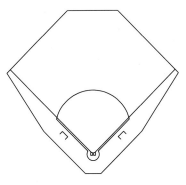

PONY LEAGUE BASEBALL

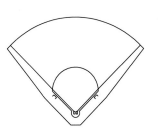

LITTLE LEAGUE BASEBALL

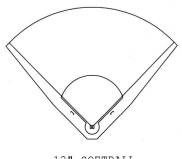

12" SOFTBALL

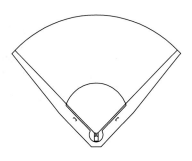

16" SOFTBALL

BASEBALL AT 1" = 400'-0"   0 ☐ 400

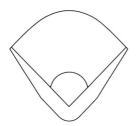

BASEBALL

BRONCO LEAGUE BASEBALL

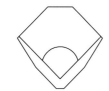

PONY LEAGUE BASEBALL

LITTLE LEAGUE BASEBALL

16" SOFTBALL

12" SOFTBALL

BASEBALL AT 1" = 1,000'-0"   0 ☐ 1000

BASEBALL

BRONCO LEAGUE BASEBALL

PONY LEAGUE BASEBALL

LITTLE LEAGUE BASEBALL

16" SOFTBALL

12" SOFTBALL

40

HALF
LINE

5 10 15 20 25 30 35 40 45 50 45 40 35 30 25 20 15 10 5
5 10 15 20 25 30 35 40 45 50 45 40 35 30 25 20 15 10 5

5 10 15 20 25 30 35 40 45 50 45 40 35 30 25 20 15 10 5
5 10 15 20 25 30 35 40 45 50 45 40 35 30 25 20 15 10 5

261

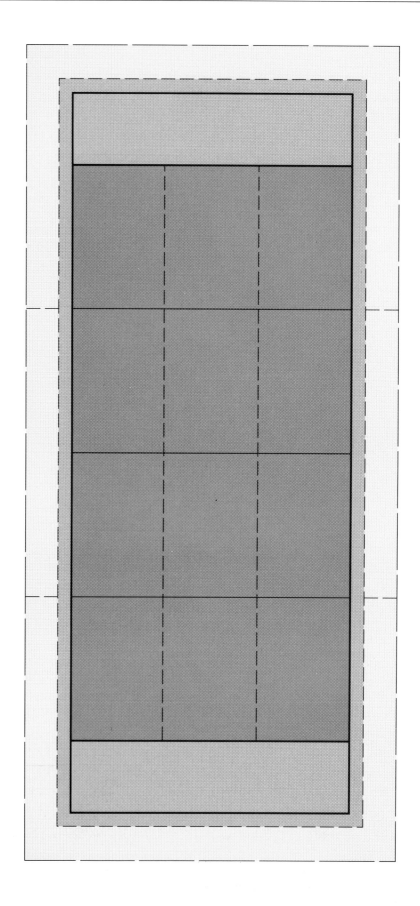

LACROSSE FIELD AT 1" = 40'-0"

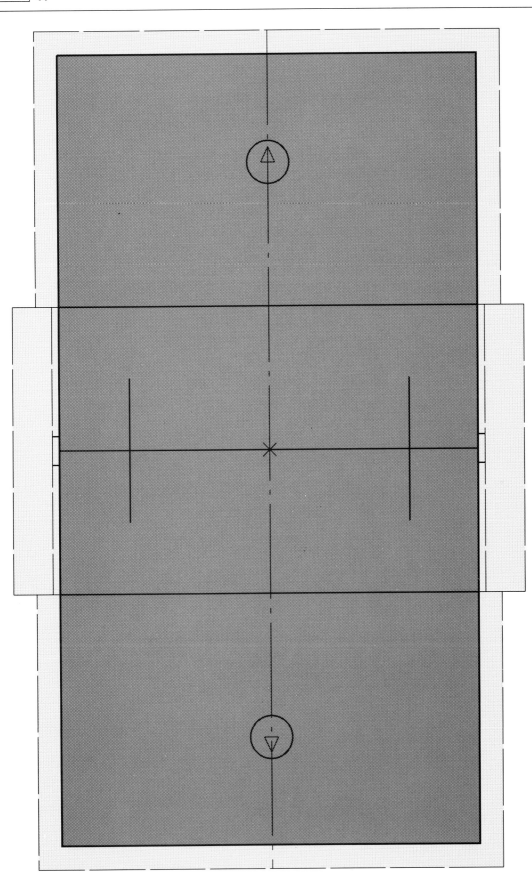

SOCCER FIELD AT 1" = 40'-0"

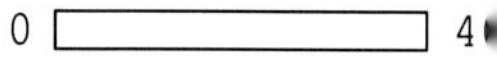

0 ⬜ 4

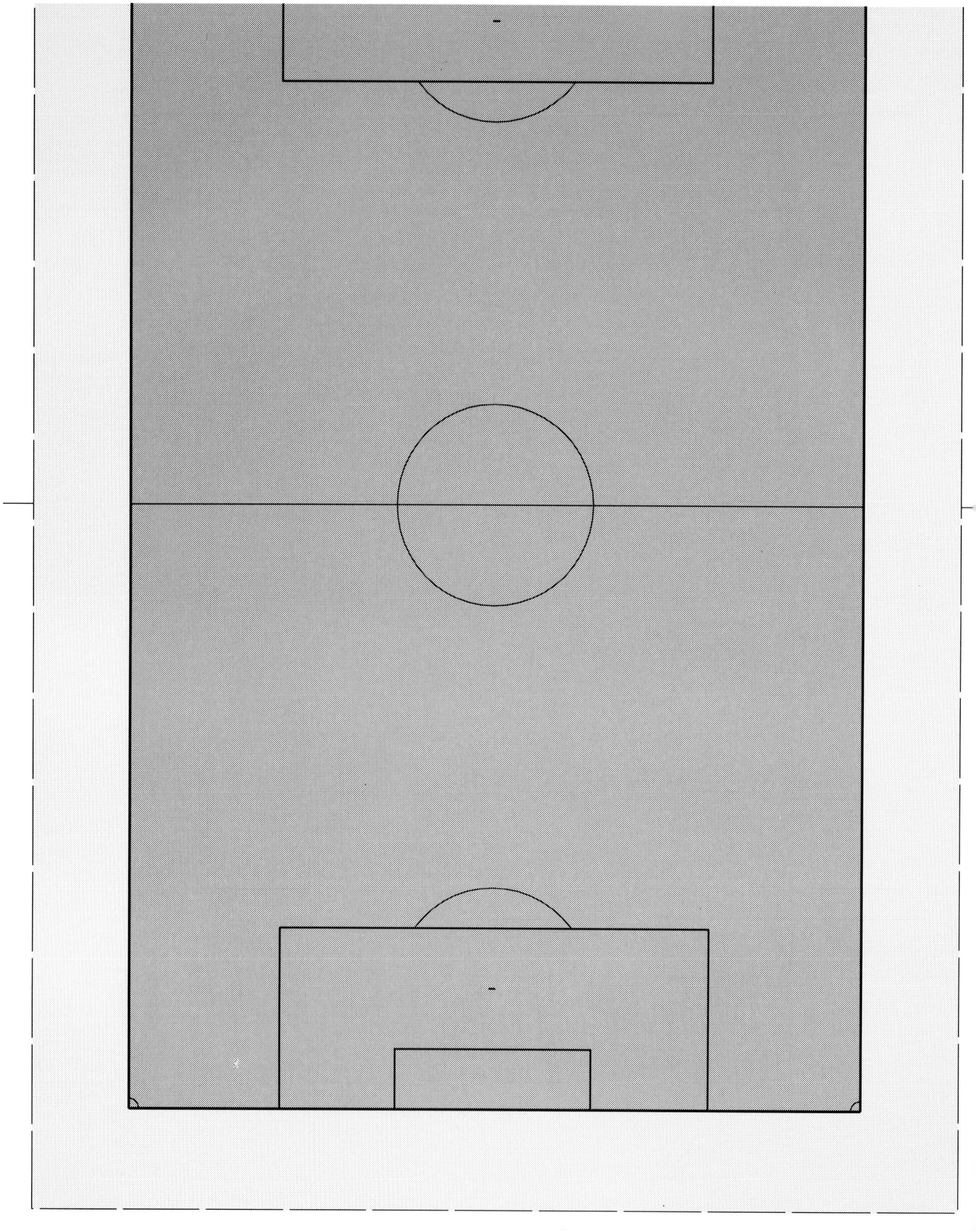

0 [   ] 40

105'-8"

20'-0"   65'-8"   20'-0"

20'-0"

171'-4"

131'-4"

20'-0"

PLAYING AREA
8,624 SQUARE FEET
.19 ACRES

SAFETY AREA
855 SQUARE FEET
.02 ACRES

TOTAL AREA REQUIRED
9,479 SQUARE FEET
.21 ACRES

RUGBY FIELD AT 1" = 40'-0"

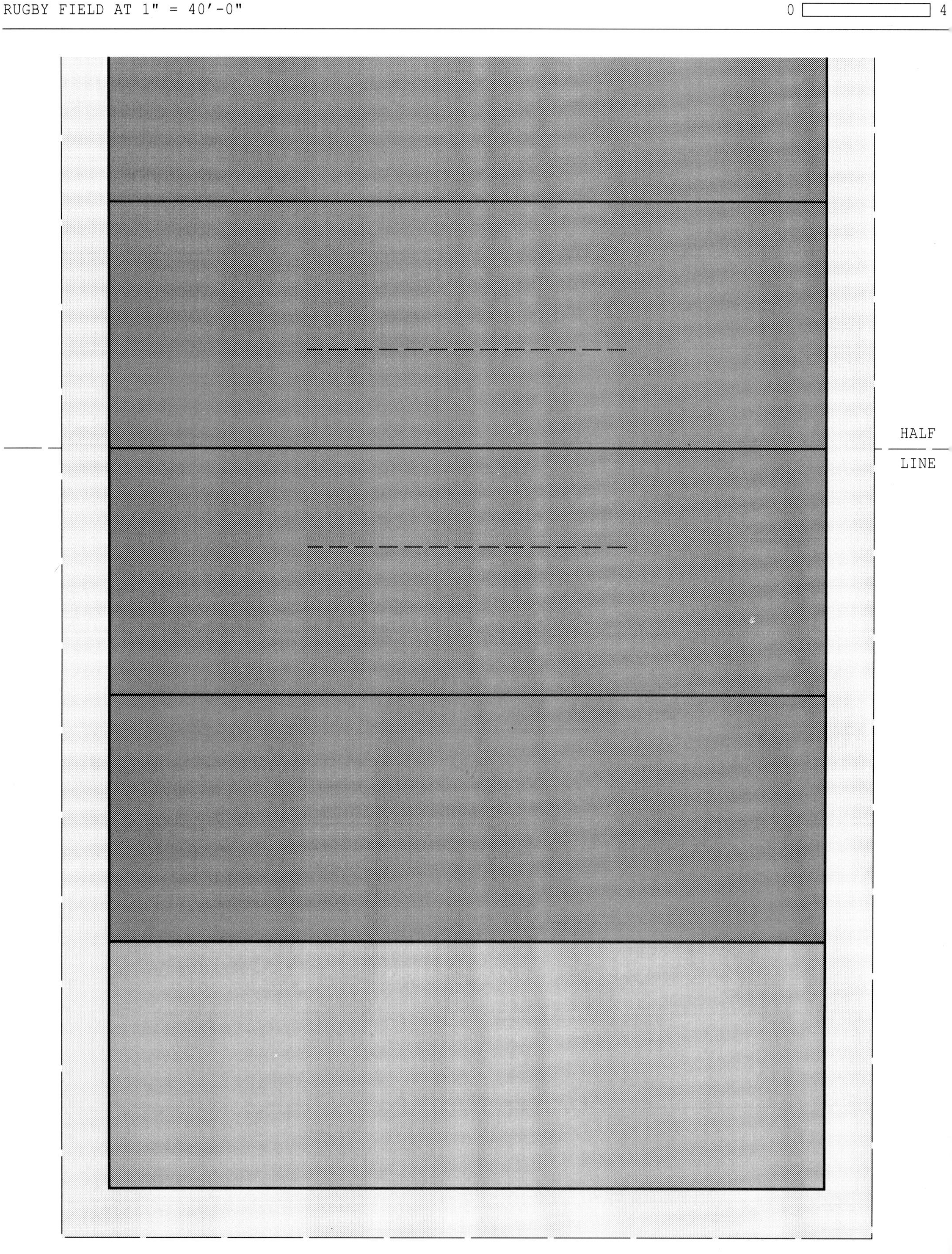

0 [=====] 4

HALF
LINE

50

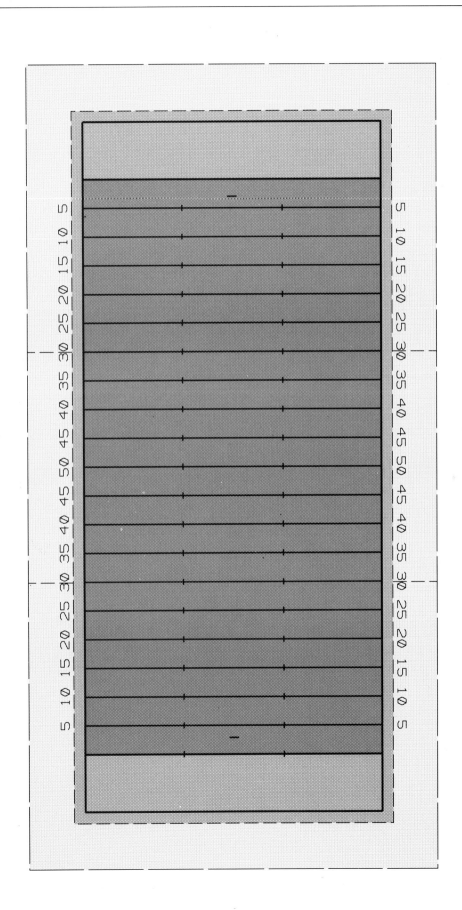

FLAG OR TOUCH FOOTBALL AT 1" = 50'-0"   0 ▭ 50

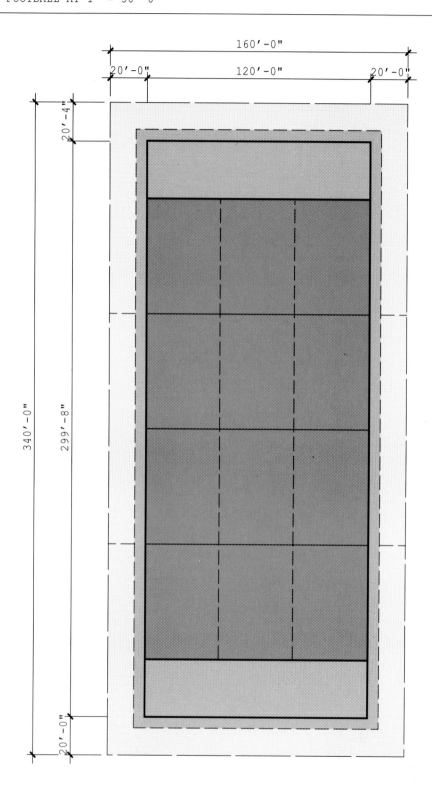

PLAYING AREA
39,903 SQUARE FEET
.82 ACRES

SAFETY AREA
18,387 SQUARE FEET
.42 ACRES

TOTAL AREA REQUIRED
54,291 SQUARE FEET
1.24 ACRES

0 ⬛▭▭ 50   LACROSSE FIELD AT 1" = 50'-0"

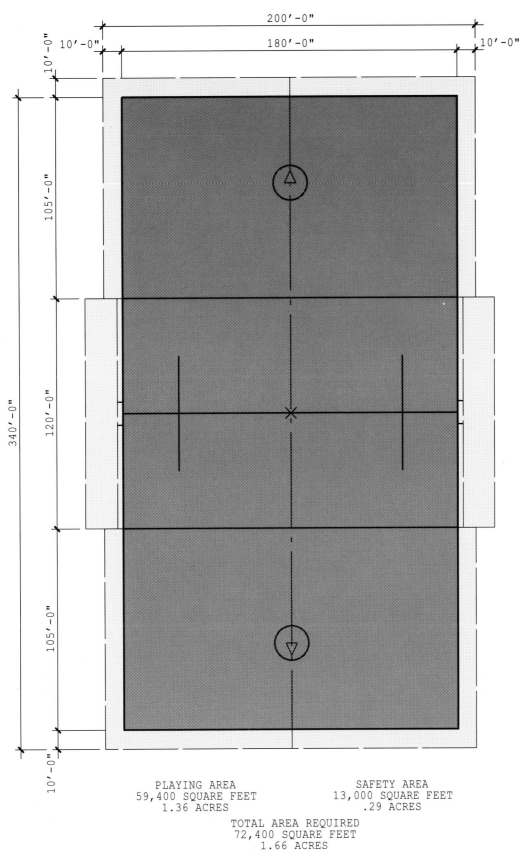

PLAYING AREA
59,400 SQUARE FEET
1.36 ACRES

SAFETY AREA
13,000 SQUARE FEET
.29 ACRES

TOTAL AREA REQUIRED
72,400 SQUARE FEET
1.66 ACRES

269

SOCCER FIELD AT 1" = 50'-0"

0 ⬛▭▭▭▭ 50

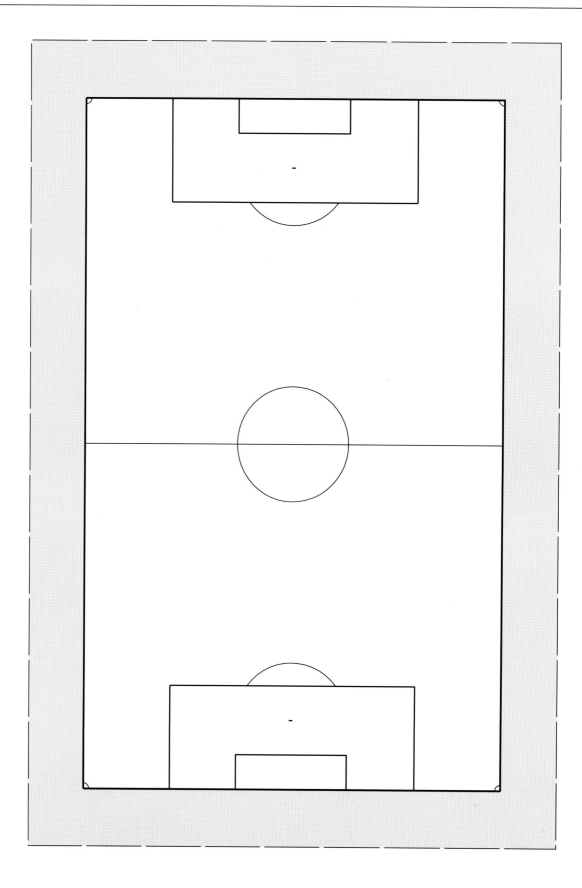

0 [⬜⬜⬜⬜] 50

TEAM HANDBALL FIELD AT 1" = 50'-0"

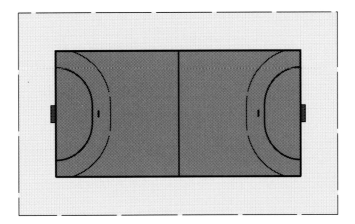

RUGBY FIELD AT 1" = 50'-0"

0 ▭ 50

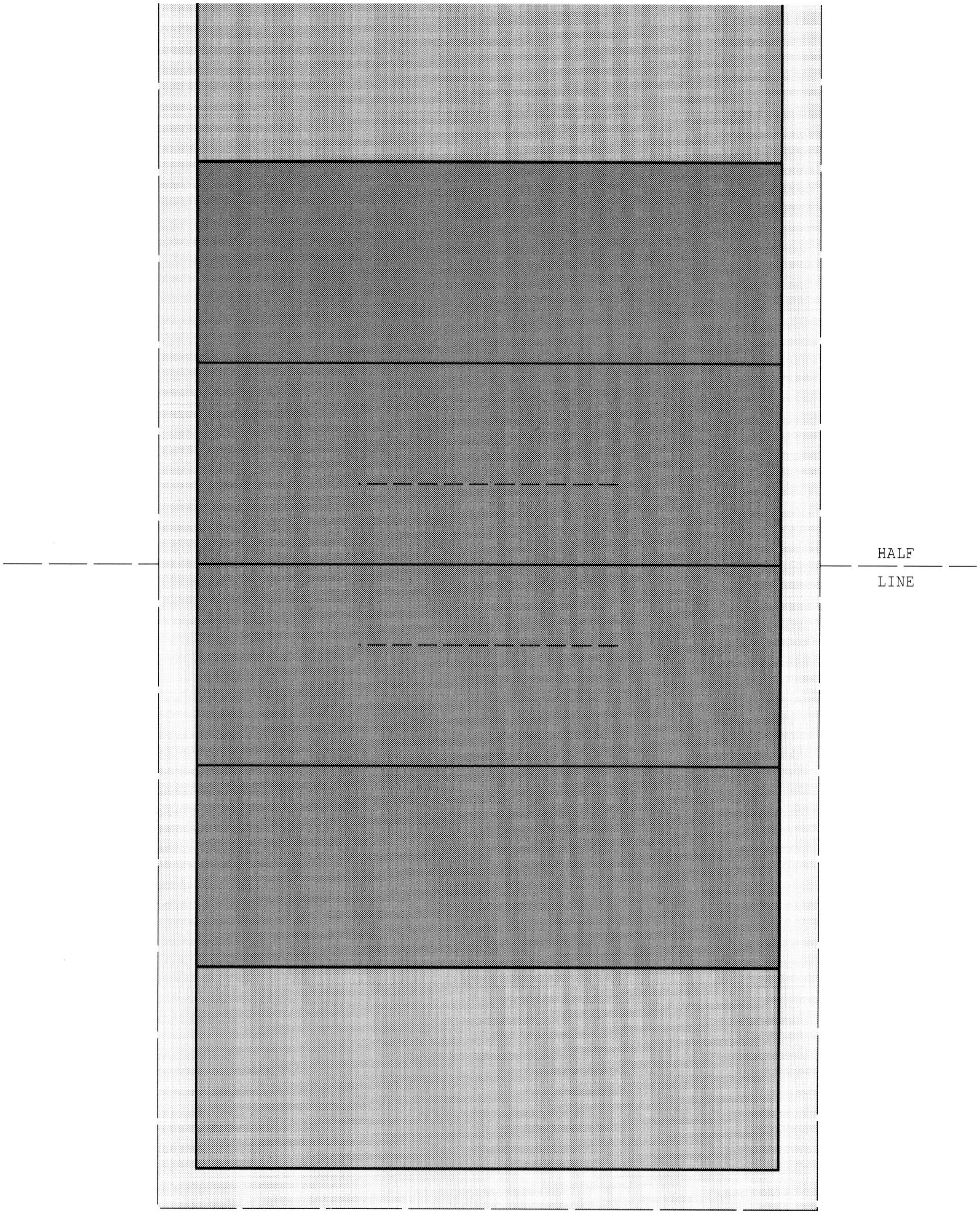

HALF
LINE

0 ▭ 60

FOOTBALL FIELD AT 1" = 60'-0"

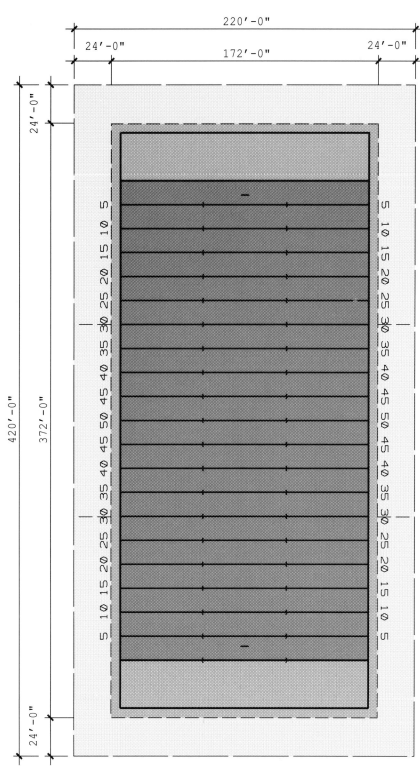

220'-0"

24'-0"   172'-0"   24'-0"

24'-0"

420'-0"   372'-0"

24'-0"

PLAYING AREA
57,600 SQUARE FEET
1.32 ACRES

SAFETY AREA
34,800 SQUARE FEET
.79 ACRES

TOTAL AREA REQUIRED
92,400 SQUARE FEET
2.12 ACRES

FIELDS AT 1" = 60'-0"

0 ▭ 60

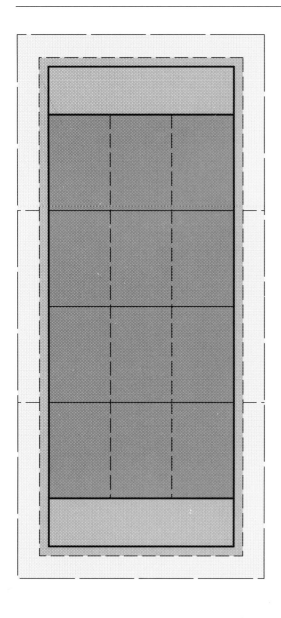

FLAG OR TOUCH FOOTBALL

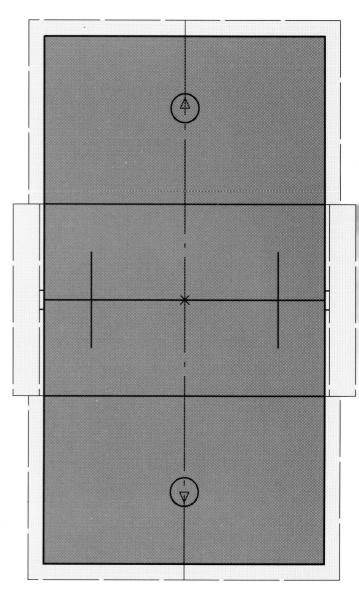

LACROSSE

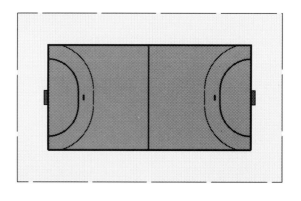

TEAM HANDBALL

0 ▭ 60

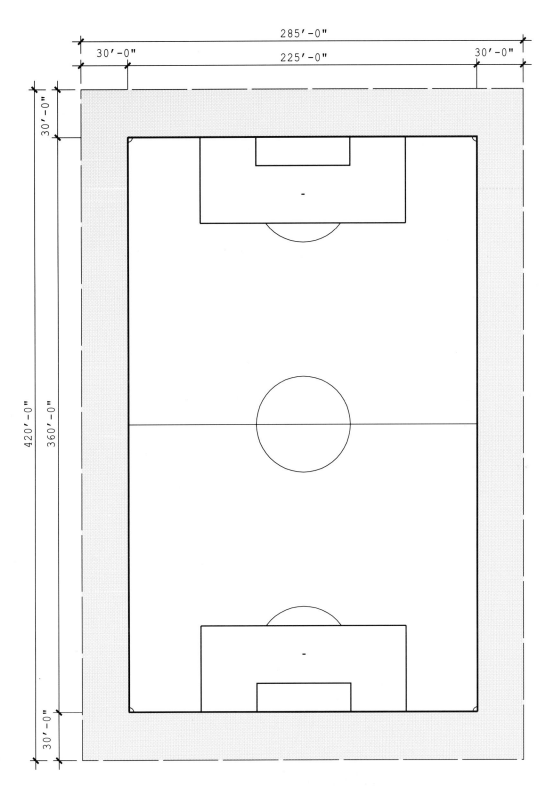

PLAYING AREA
81,103 SQUARE FEET
1.86 ACRES

SAFETY AREA
38,596 SQUARE FEET
.88 ACRES

TOTAL AREA REQUIRED
119,699 SQUARE FEET
2.74 ACRES

RUGBY FIELD AT 1" = 60'-0"   0 [_____] 60

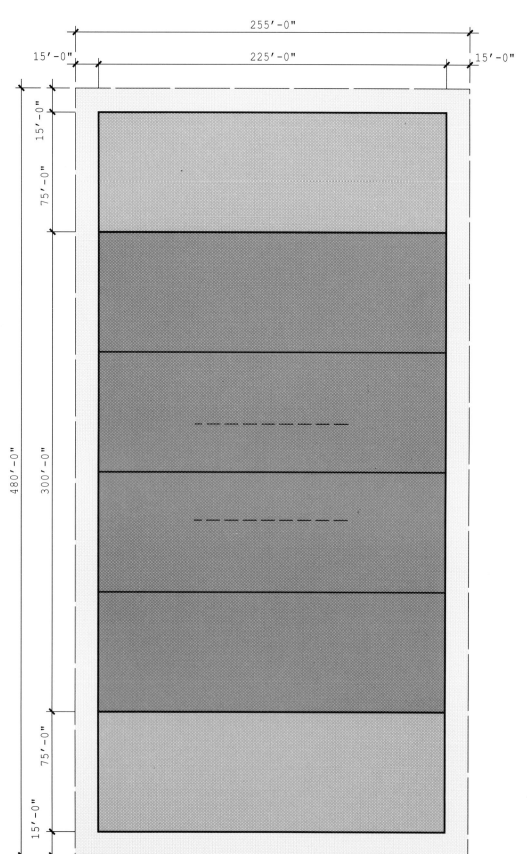

255'-0"

15'-0"   225'-0'   15'-0"

15'-0"

75'-0"

480'-0"   300'-0"

75'-0"

15'-0"

PLAYING AREA
101,250 SQUARE FEET
2.32 ACRES

SAFETY AREA
21,150 SQUARE FEET
.48 ACRES

TOTAL AREA REQUIRED
122,400 SQUARE FEET
2.81 ACRES

0 ▭ 100

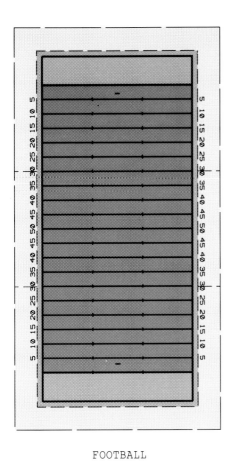

FOOTBALL

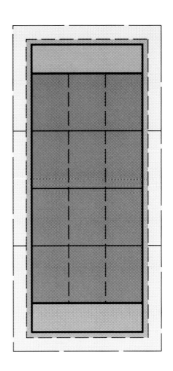

FLAG OF TOUCH FOOTBALL

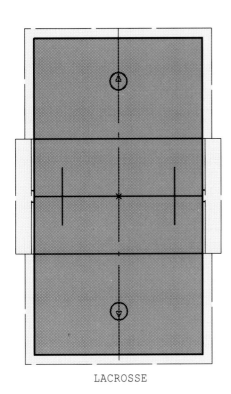

LACROSSE

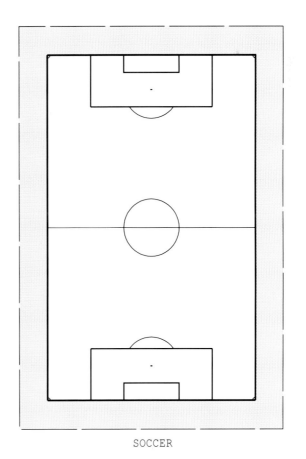

SOCCER

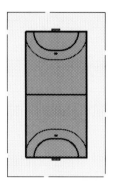

TEAM HANDBALL

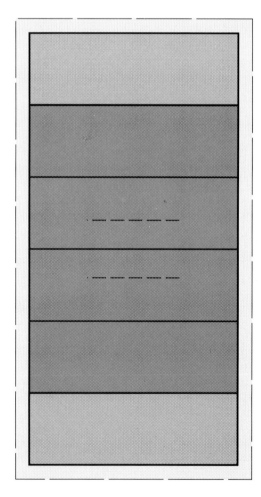

RUGBY

0 ▭ 100

HALF
LINE

FIELDS AT 1" = 200'-0"   0 [========] 200

FOOTBALL

FLAG OR TOUCH FOOTBALL

LACROSSE

SOCCER

TEAM HANDBALL

RUGBY

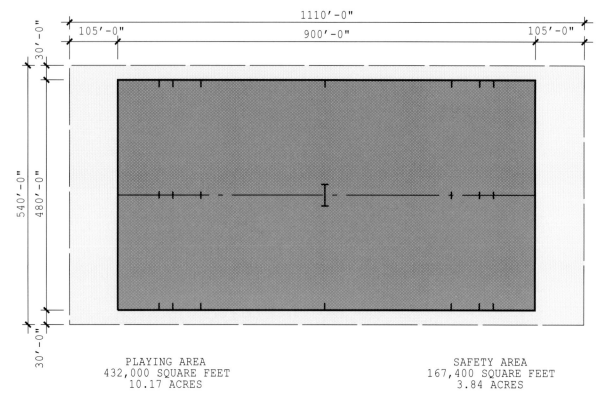

PLAYING AREA
432,000 SQUARE FEET
10.17 ACRES

SAFETY AREA
167,400 SQUARE FEET
3.84 ACRES

TOTAL AREA REQUIRED
599,400 SQUARE FEET
14.01 ACRES

0 ☐ 400

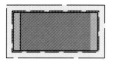

FOOTBALL

FLAG OR TOUCH FOOTBALL

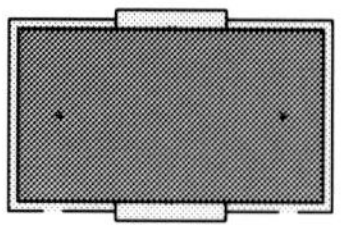

LACROSSE

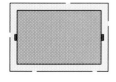

SOCCER

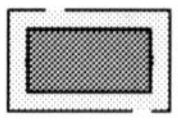

TEAM HANDBALL

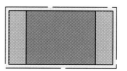

RUGBY

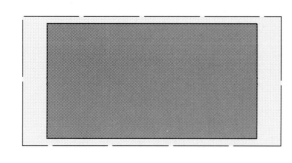

POLO

GOLF DRIVING RANGE AT 1" = 100'-0"   0 ▭ 100

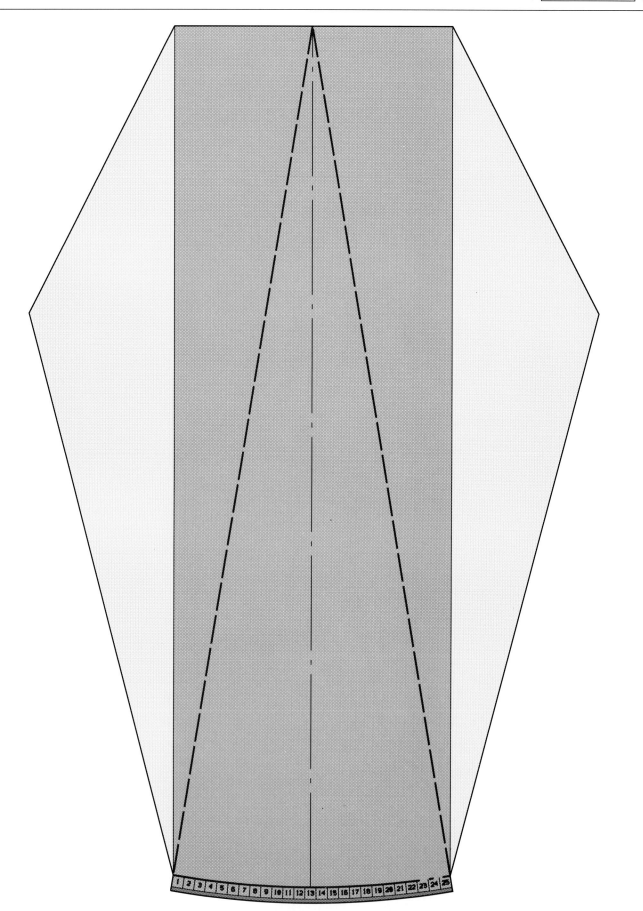

0 ▭ 100

TYPICAL GOLF HOLE - PAR 3 AT 1" = 100'-0"

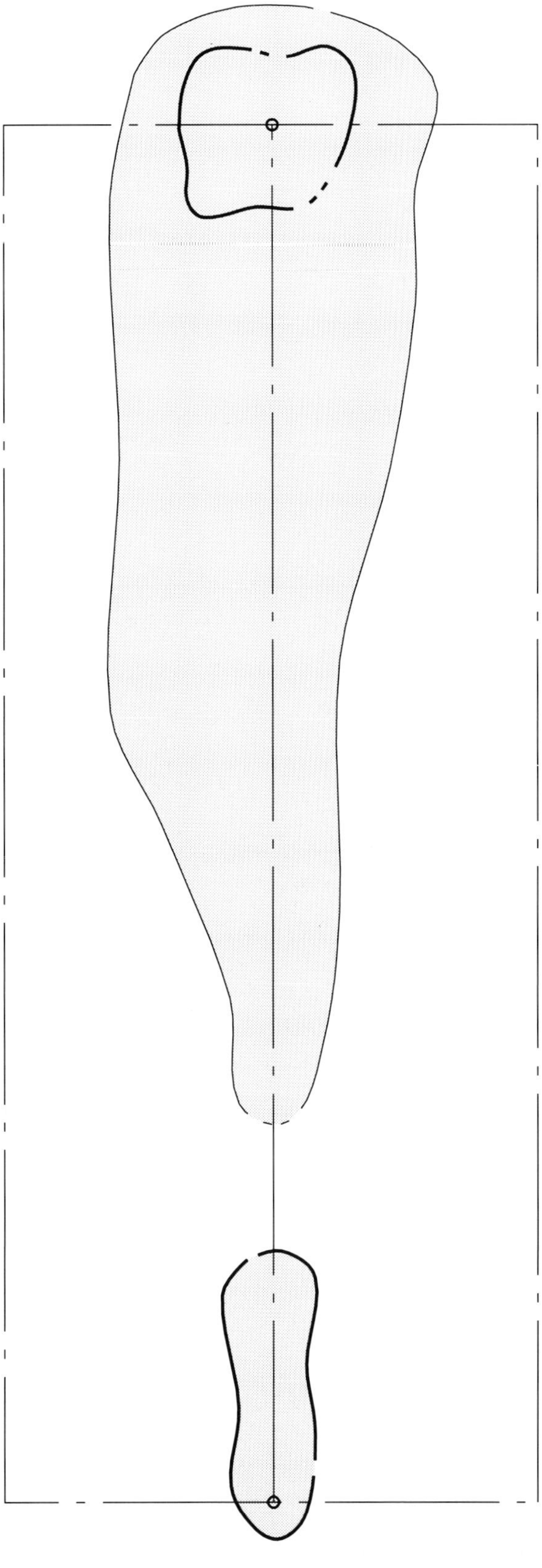

GOLF DRIVING RANGE AT 1" = 200'-0"   0 ⬚ 200

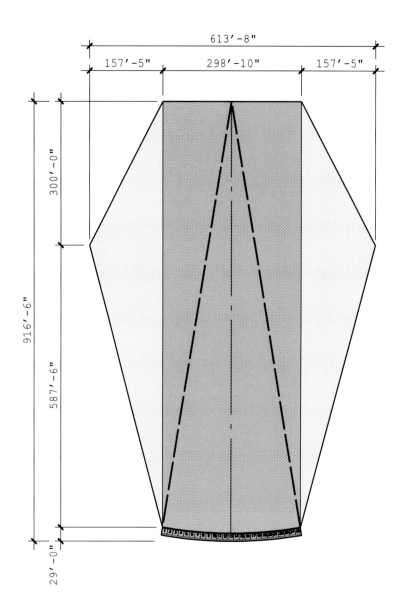

TOTAL AREA REQUIRED
412,337 SQUARE FEET
9.46 ACRES

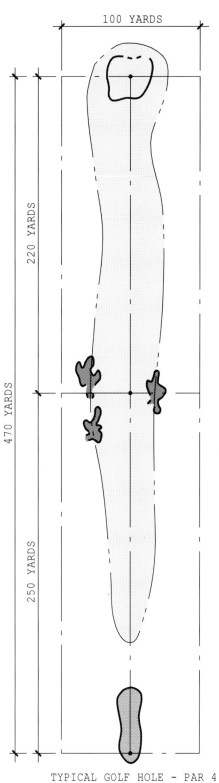

100 YARDS

220 YARDS

470 YARDS

250 YARDS

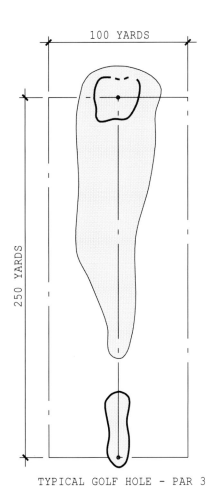

100 YARDS

250 YARDS

TYPICAL GOLF HOLE - PAR 3

TEES, FAIRWAYS AND GREENS
90,000 SQUARE FEET + -
2 ACRES

TYPICAL GOLF HOLE - PAR 4

TEES, FAIRWAYS AND GREENS
175,000 SQUARE FEET + -
4 ACRES

GOLF

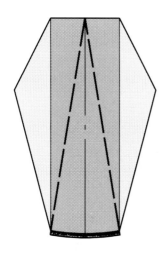

GOLF DRIVING RANGE

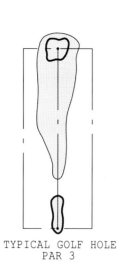

TYPICAL GOLF HOLE
PAR 3

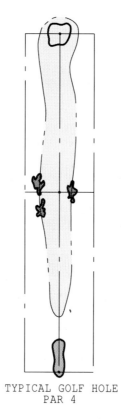

TYPICAL GOLF HOLE
PAR 4

100 YARDS

200 YARDS

200 YARDS

750 YARDS

250 YARDS

TYPICAL GOLF HOLE
PAR 5

TEES, FAIRWAYS AND GREENS
275,000 SQUARE FEET + -
6.3 ACRES

0 | 8

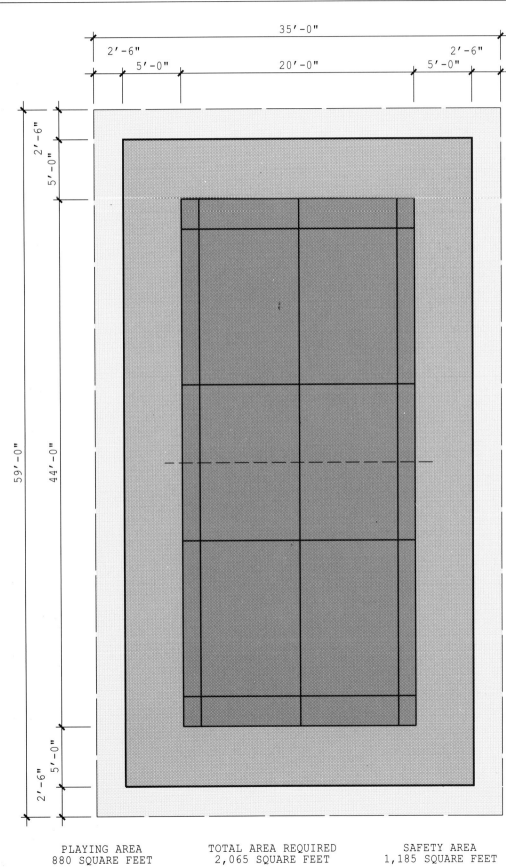

35'-0"

2'-6"   5'-0"   20'-0"   5'-0"   2'-6"

2'-6"   5'-0"

59'-0"   44'-0"

2'-6"   5'-0"

PLAYING AREA
880 SQUARE FEET

TOTAL AREA REQUIRED
2,065 SQUARE FEET

SAFETY AREA
1,185 SQUARE FEET

BASKETBALL COURT - AAU AT 1/8" = 1'-0"

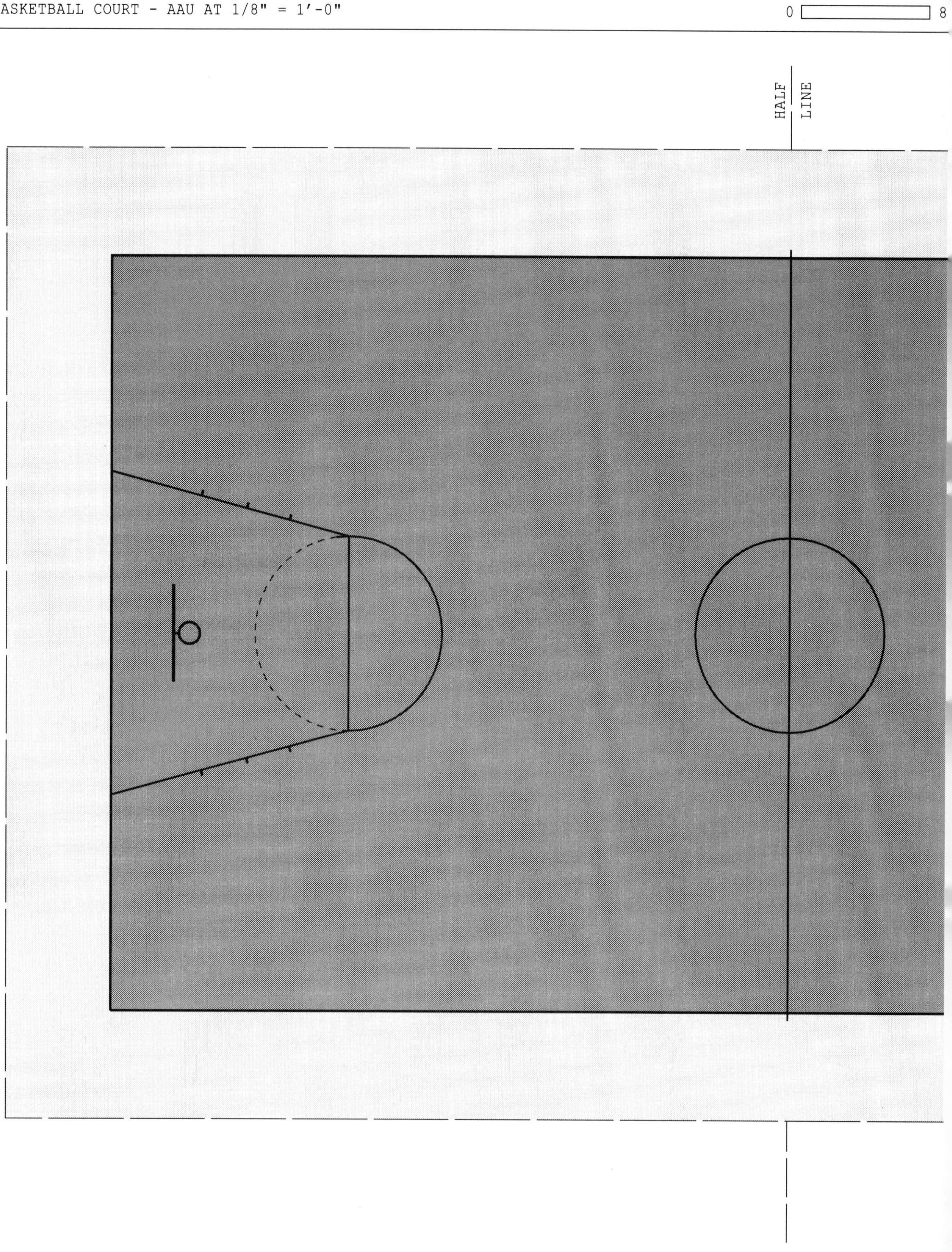

0 [   ] 8

HALF
LINE

0 [▭▭▭▭▭] 8

BASKETBALL COURT NCAA AT 1/8" = 1'-0"

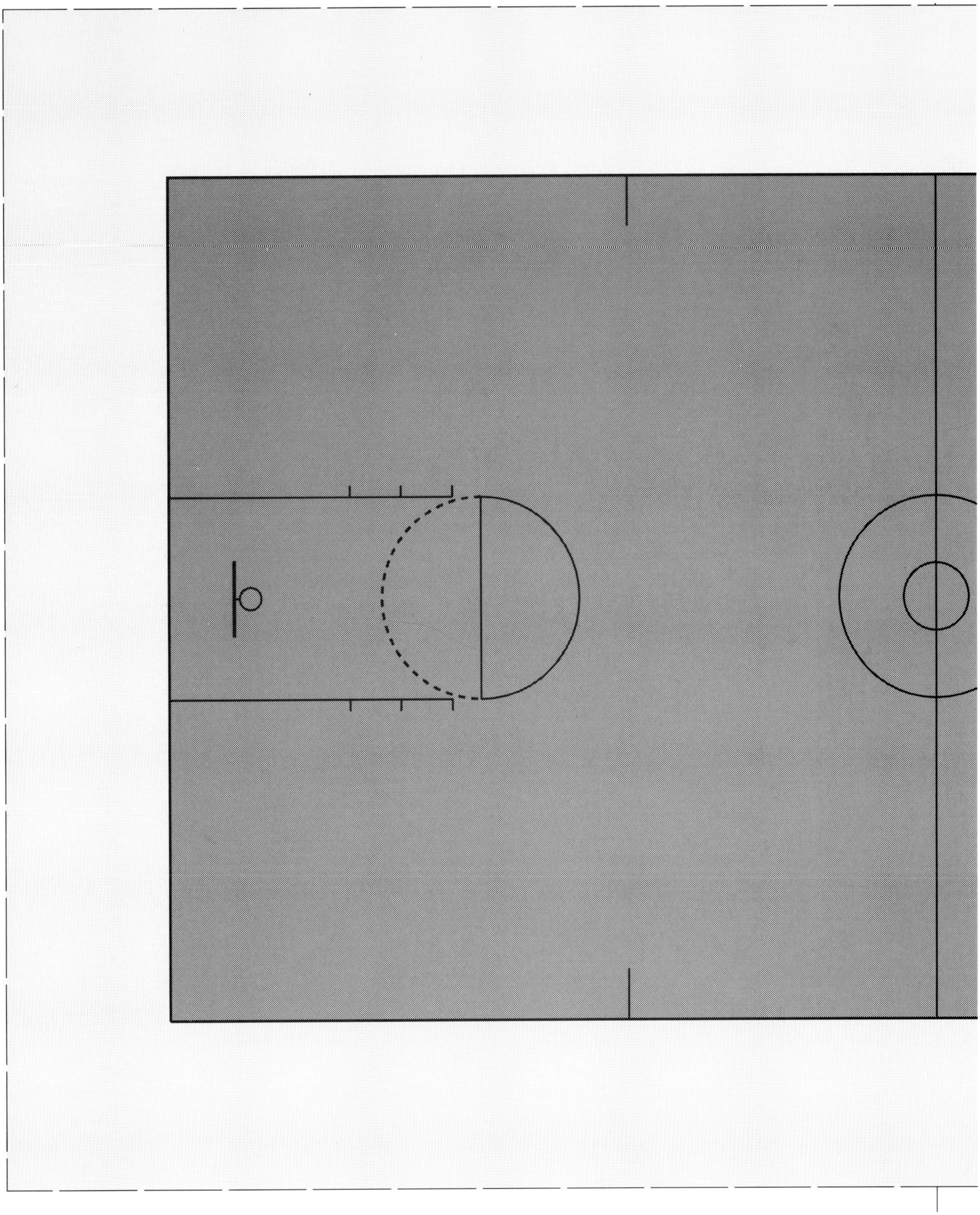

BASKETBALL COURT - HIGH SCHOOL AT 1/8" = 1'-0"   0 ▭ 8

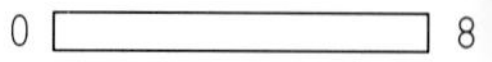

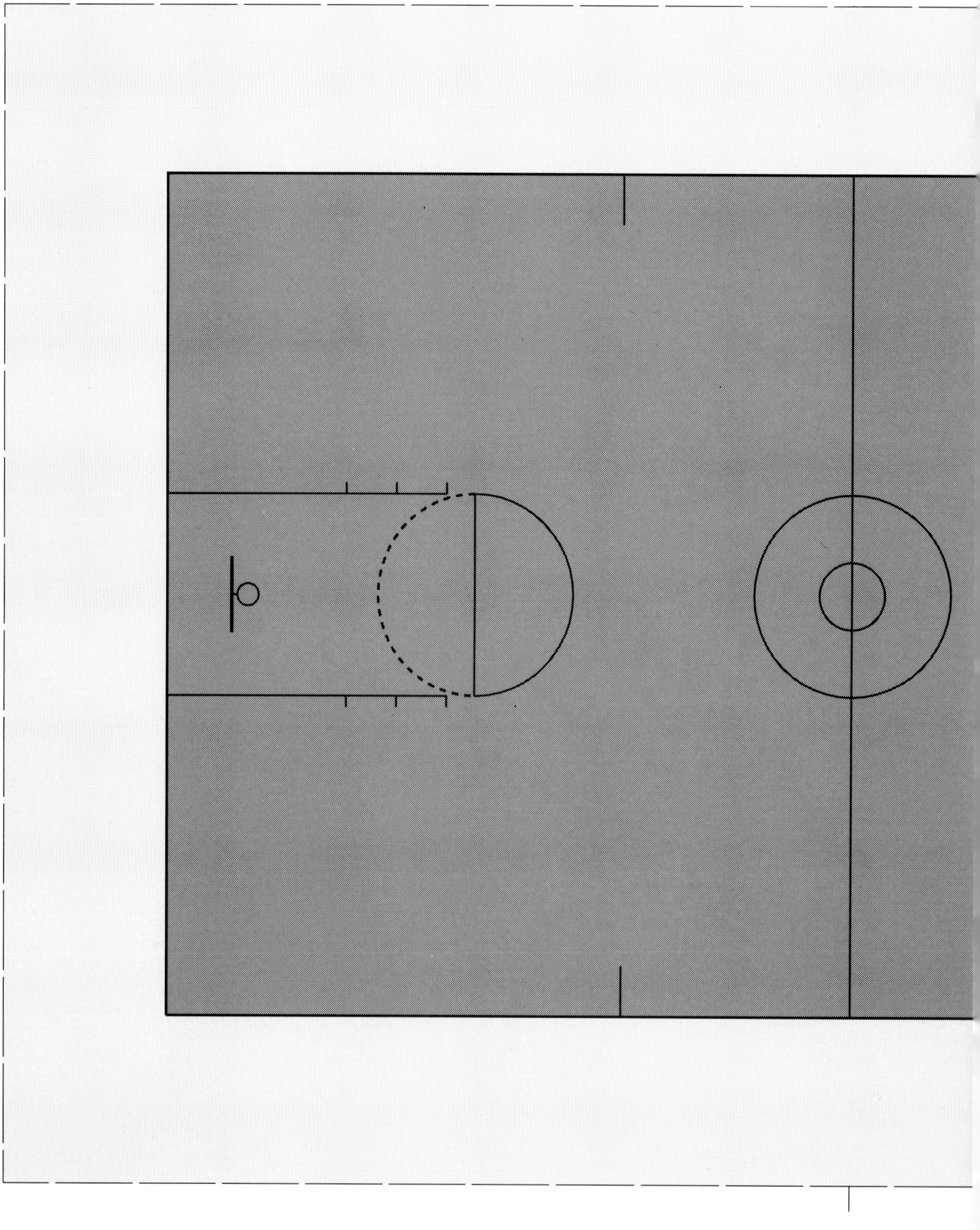

0 ⬜ 8

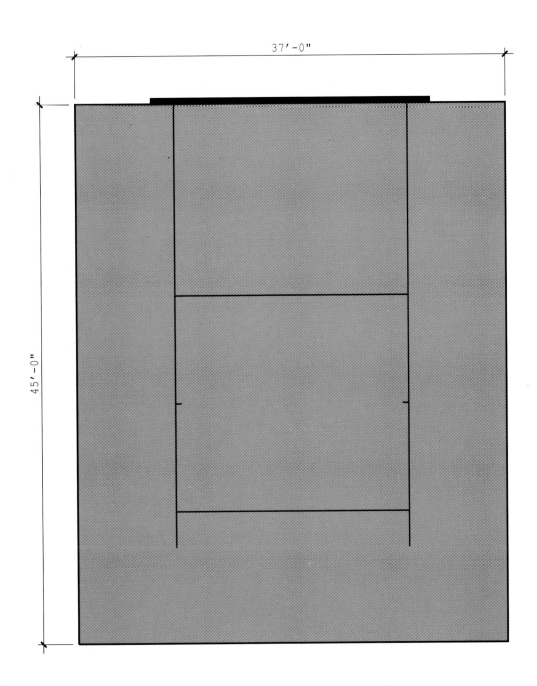

37'-0"

45'-0"

PLAYING AREA
1,665 SQUARE FEET

TWO AND THREE WALL HANDBALL COURT AT 1/8" = 1'-0"   0 ▭ 8

20'-0"

50'-0"

40'-0"

10'-0"

20'-0"

40'-0"

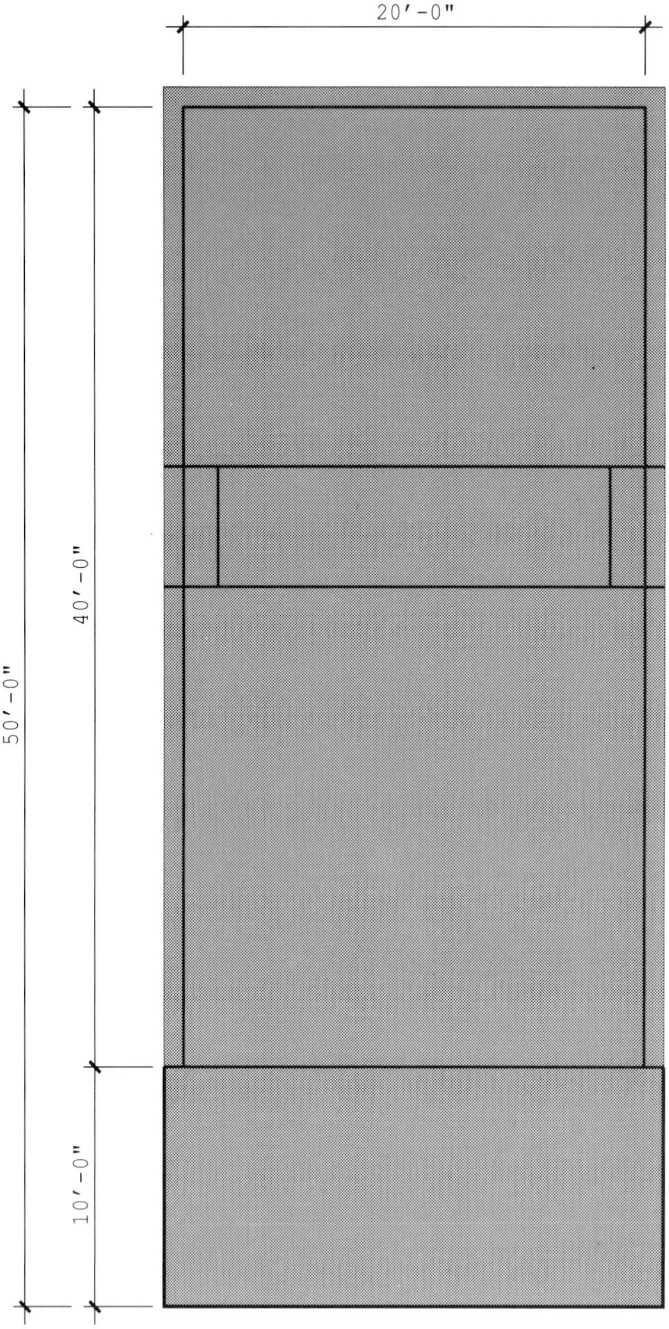

3 WALL HANDBALL

PLAYING AREA
1,000 SQUARE FEET

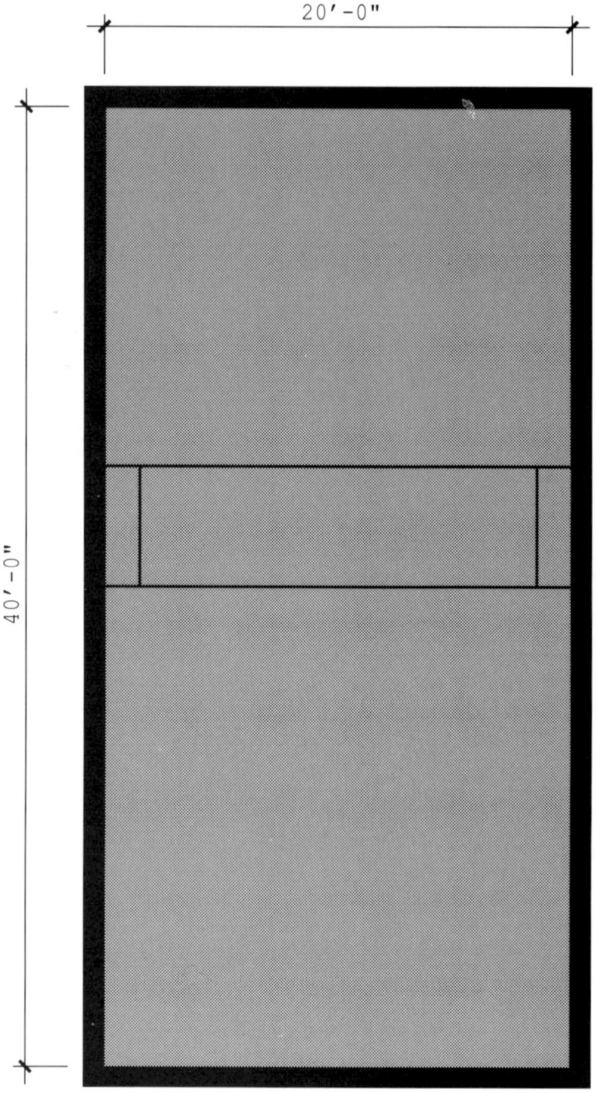

4 WALL HANDBALL

PLAYING AREA
800 SQUARE FEET

40'-0"
10'-0"
20'-0"
10'-0"

TETHERBALL

PLAYING AREA   SAFETY AREA
310 SQUARE FEET   1,290 SQUARE FEET

TOTAL AREA REQUIRED
1,600 SQUARE FEET

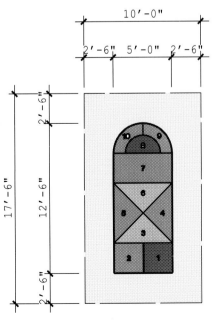

10'-0"
2'-6"   5'-0"   2'-6"
2'-6"
17'-6"
12'-6"
2'-6"

HOPSCOTCH

PLAYING AREA   SAFETY AREA
60 SQUARE FEET   115 SQUARE FEET

TOTAL AREA REQUIRED
175 SQUARE FEET

SHUFFLEBOARD COURT AT 1/8" = 1'-0"

0 ⬛▭▭▭ 8

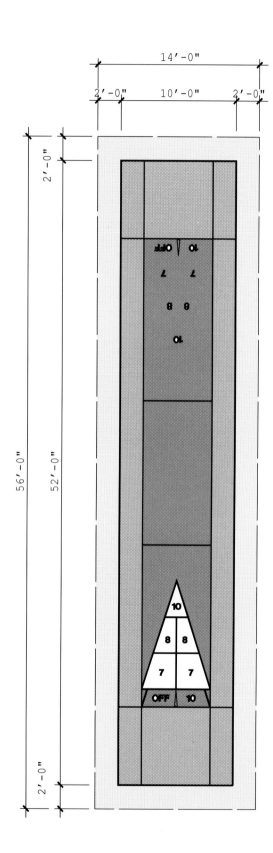

PLAYING AREA
520 SQUARE FEET

SAFETY AREA
264 SQUARE FEET

TOTAL AREA REQUIRED
784 SQUARE FEET

TENNIS COURT AT 1/8" = 1'-0"

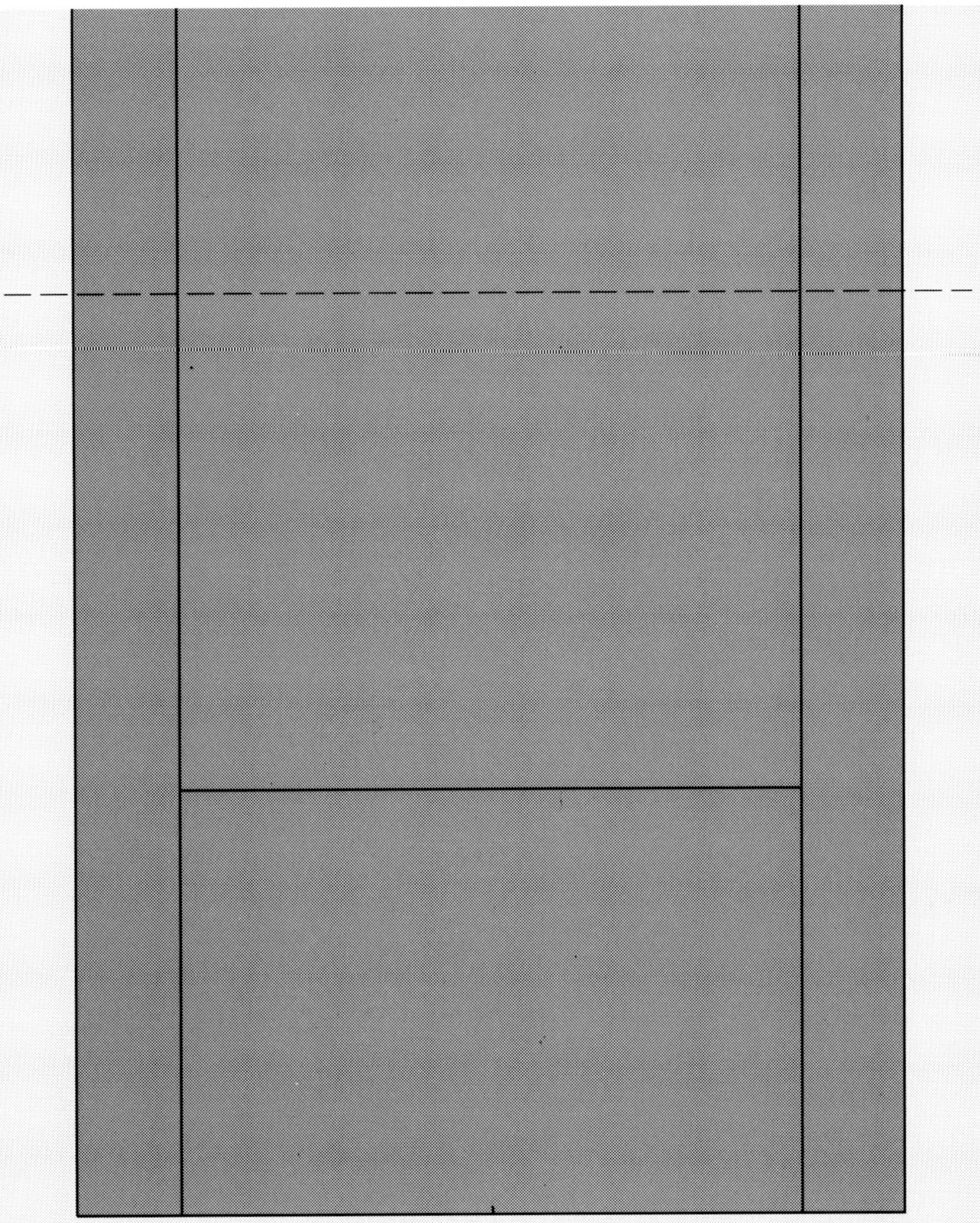

DECK TENNIS COURT AT 1/8" = 1'-0"   0 [   ] 8

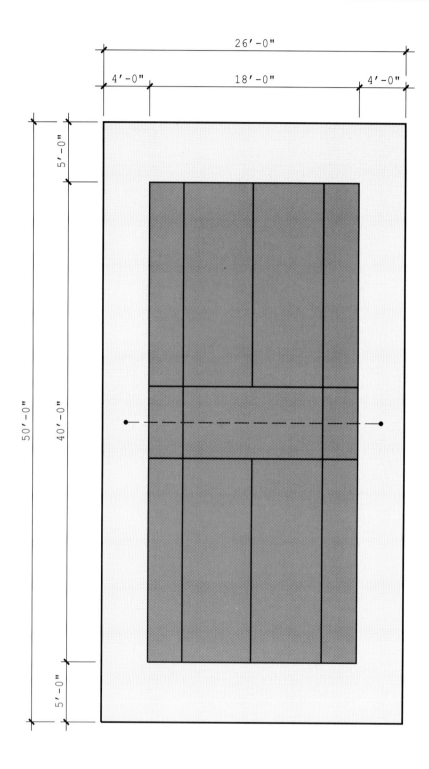

PLAYING AREA
720 SQUARE FEET

SAFETY AREA
580 SQUARE FEET

TOTAL AREA REQUIRED
1,300 SQUARE FEET

0 ☐ 8   PADDLE TENNIS COURT AT 1/8" = 1'-0"

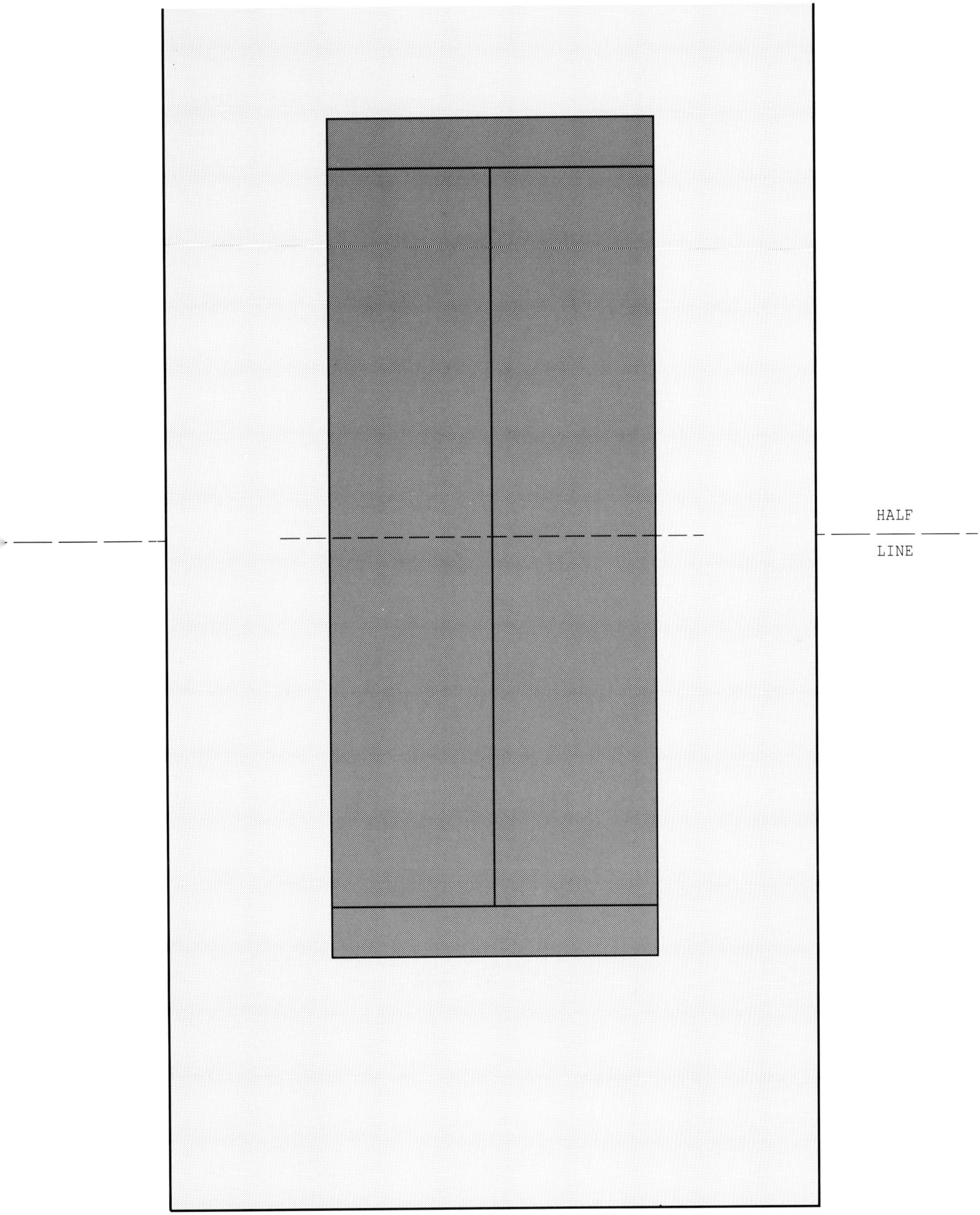

HALF

LINE

VOLLEYBALL COURT AT 1/8" = 1'-0"

0 [   ] 8

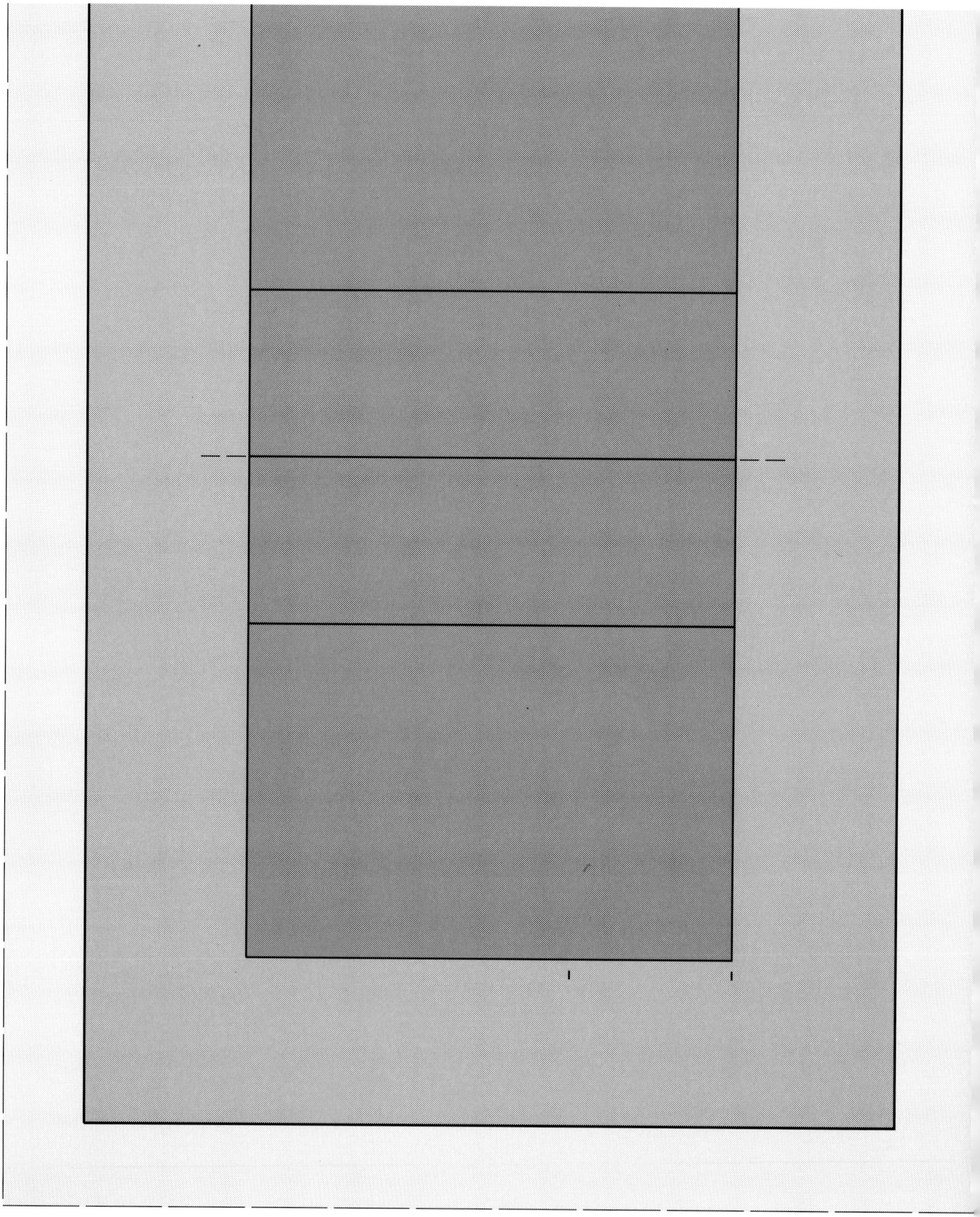

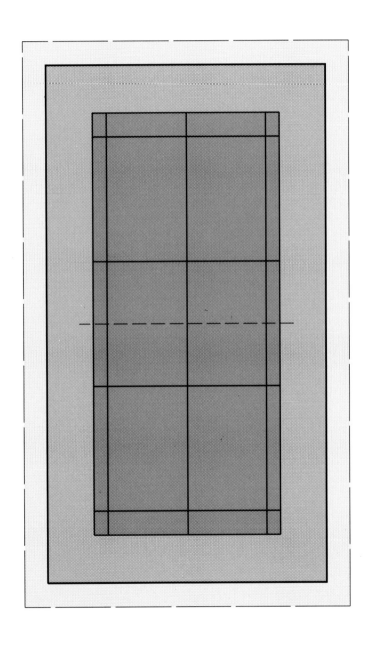

BASKETBALL COURT - AAU AT 1" = 10'-0"

0 ▭ 1

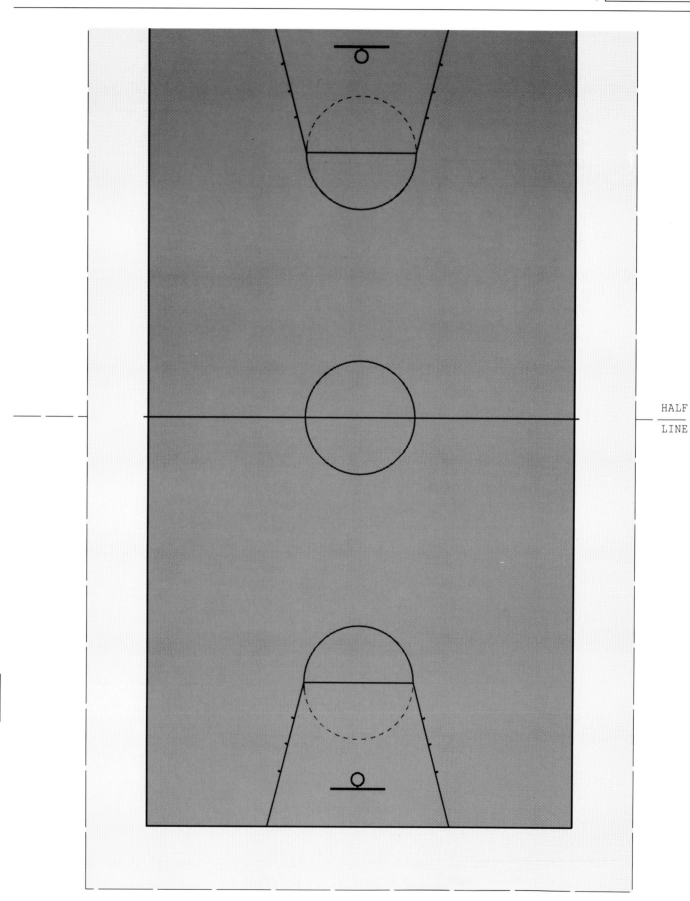

HALF
LINE

0 ▭ 10

BASKETBALL COURT NCAA AT 1" = 10'-0"

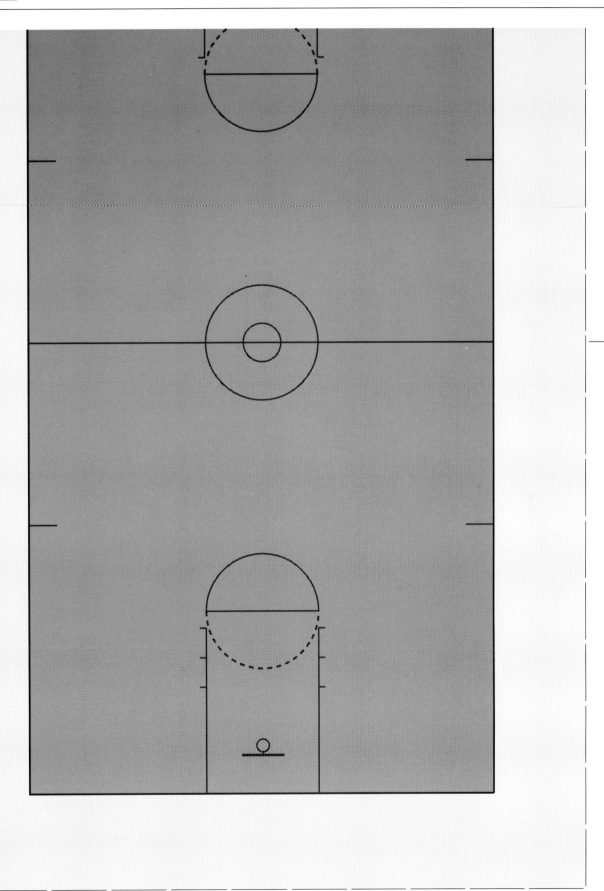

BASKETBALL COURT - HIGH SCHOOL AT 1" = 10'-0"

0 [_____] 10

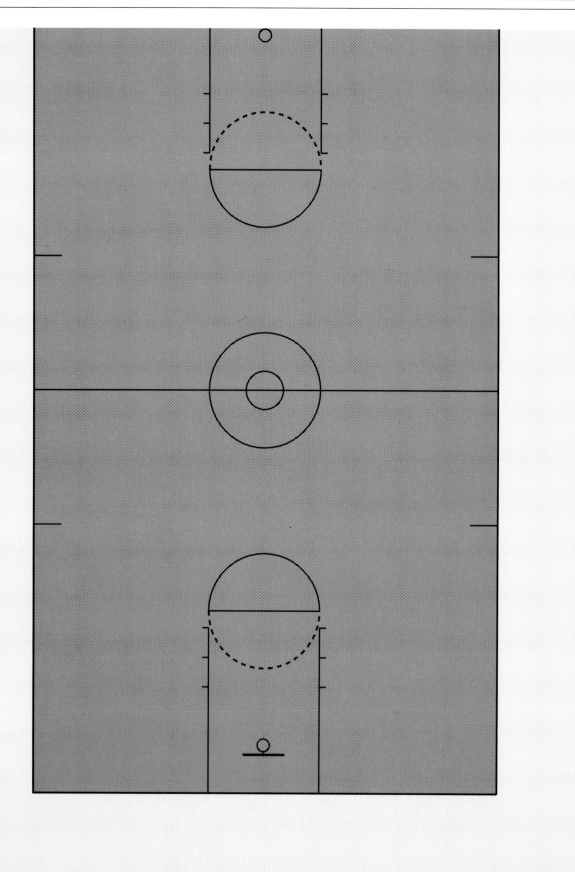

0 10 HANDBALL COURTS AT 1" = 10'-0"

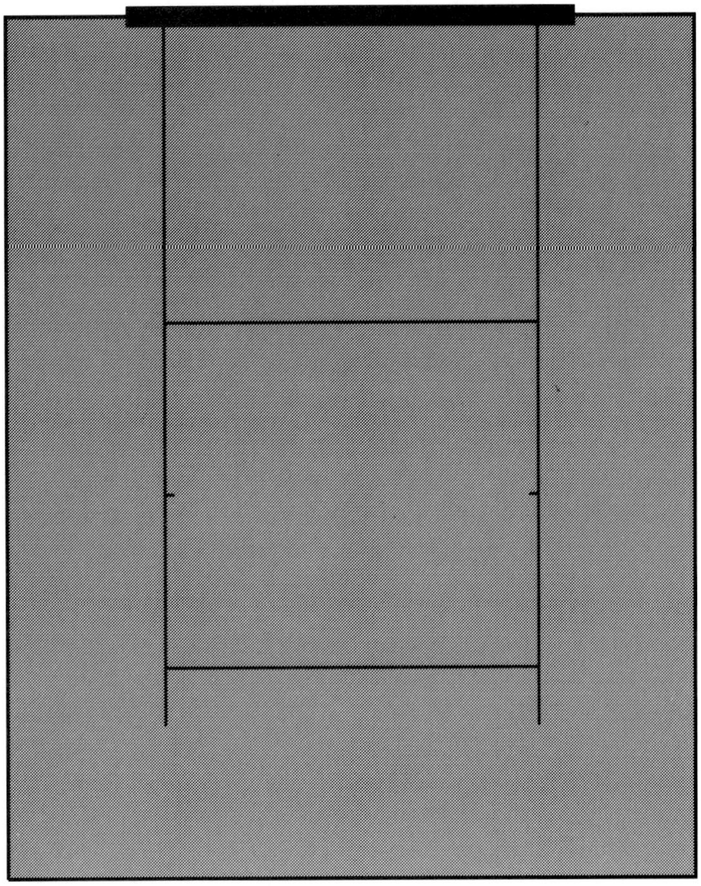

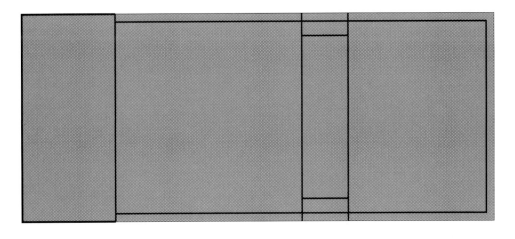

ONE WALL HANDBALL

THREE WALL HANDBALL

COURTS AT 1" = 10'-0"   0 ▭ 10

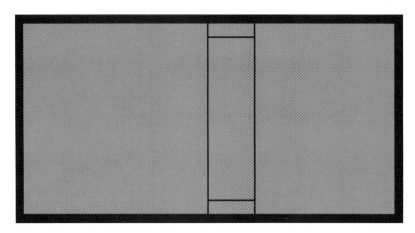

FOUR WALL HANDBALL

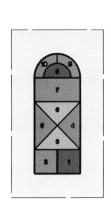

HOPSCOTCH

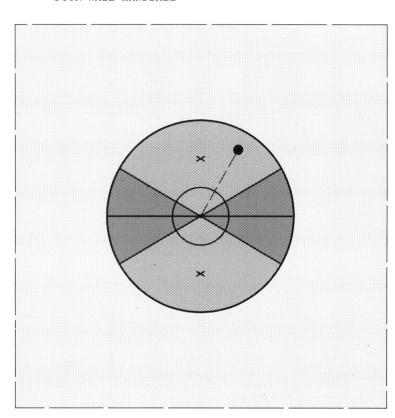

TETHERBALL

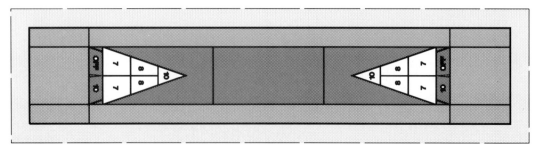

SHUFFLEBOARD

0 ▭ 10   TENNIS COURT AT 1/10" = 1'-0"

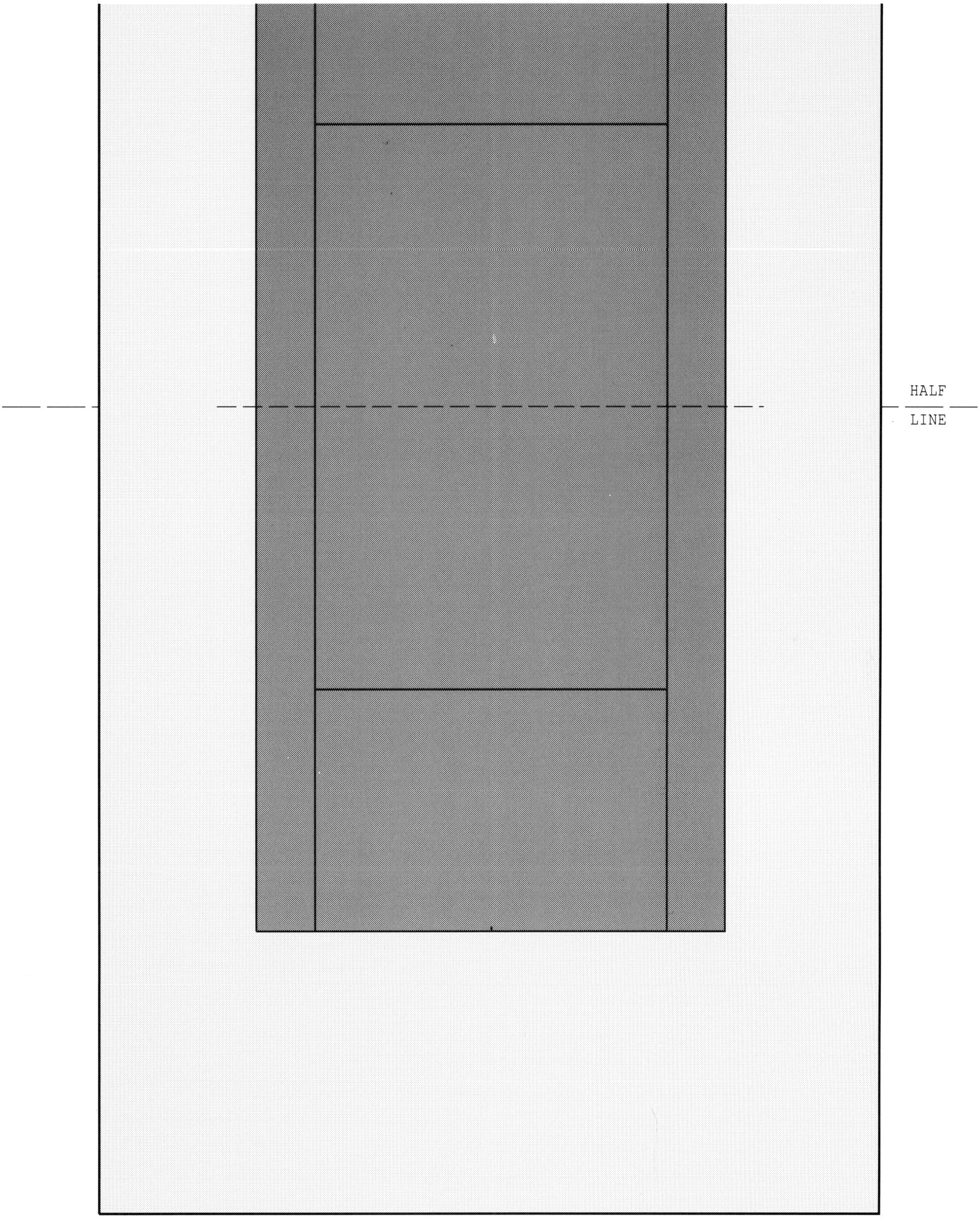

HALF
LINE

DECK TENNIS COURT AT 1/10" = 1'-0"   0 ☐☐☐☐☐ 10

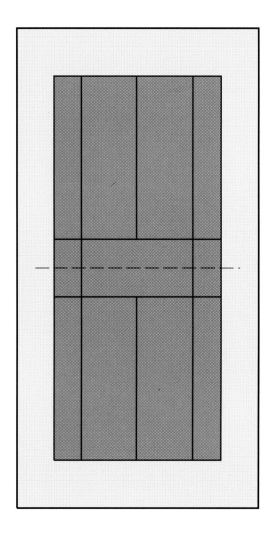

0 [   ] 10

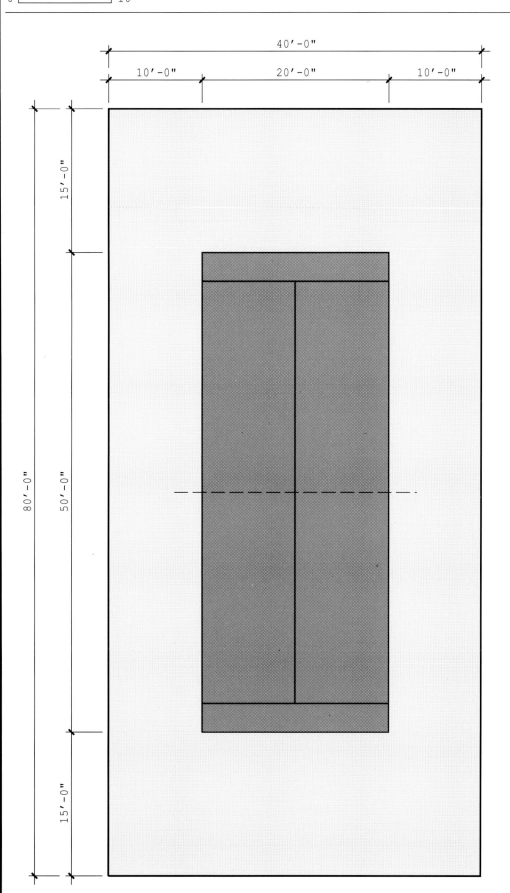

40'-0"

10'-0" 20'-0" 10'-0"

15'-0"

80'-0"

50'-0"

15'-0"

PLAYING AREA
1,000 SQUARE FEET

SAFETY AREA
2,200 SQUARE FEET

TOTAL AREA REQUIRED
3,200 SQUARE FEET

VOLLEYBALL COURT AT 1" = 10'-0"

0 ⊏━━━━━⊐ 10

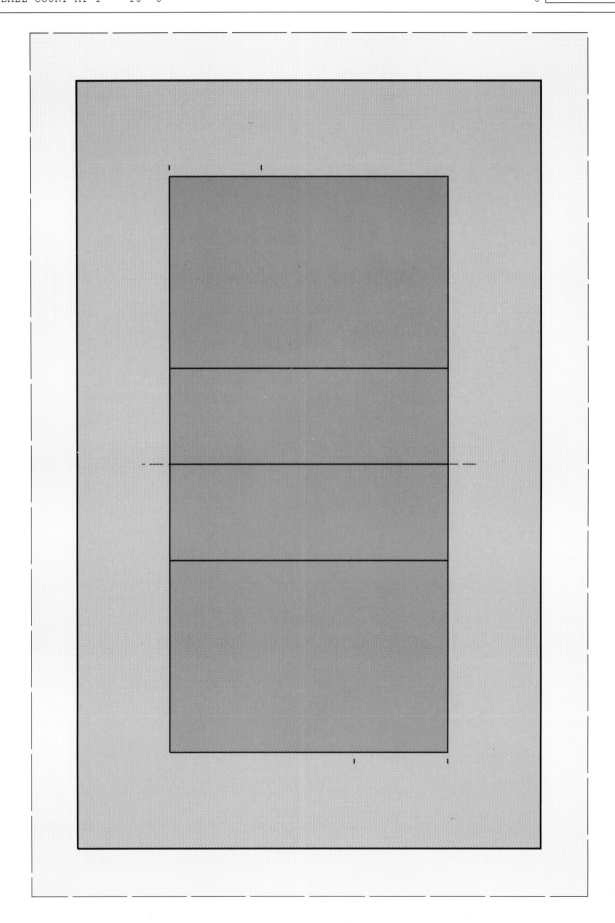

0 [========] 8

BADMINTON COURT AT 3/32" = 1'-0"

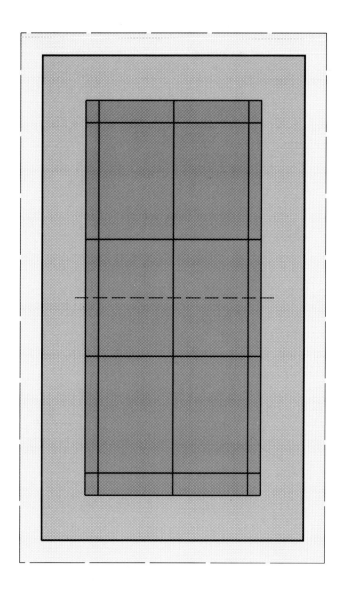

BASKETBALL COURT - AAU AT 3/32" = 1'-0"   0 ⬜ 8

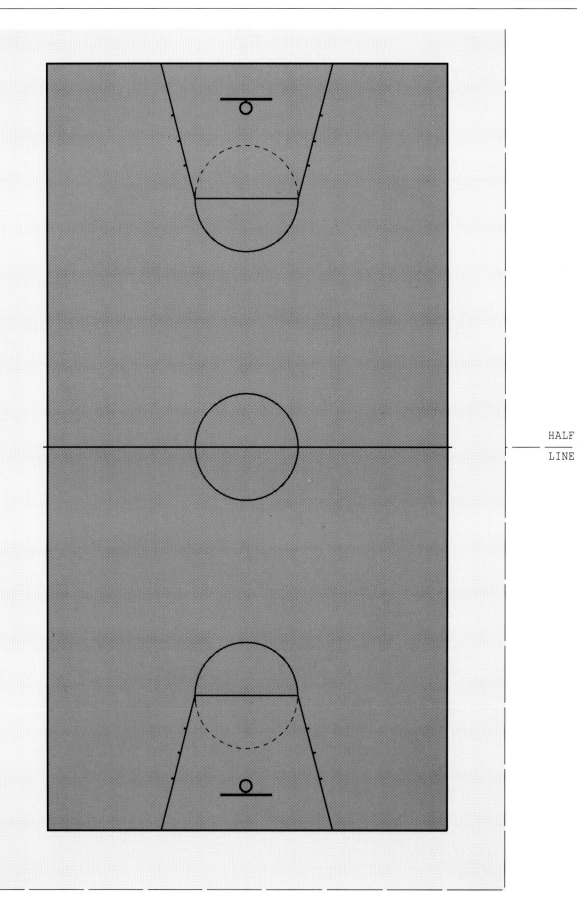

HALF
LINE

0 ⬚ 8

BASKETBALL COURT NCAA AT 3/32" = 1'-0"

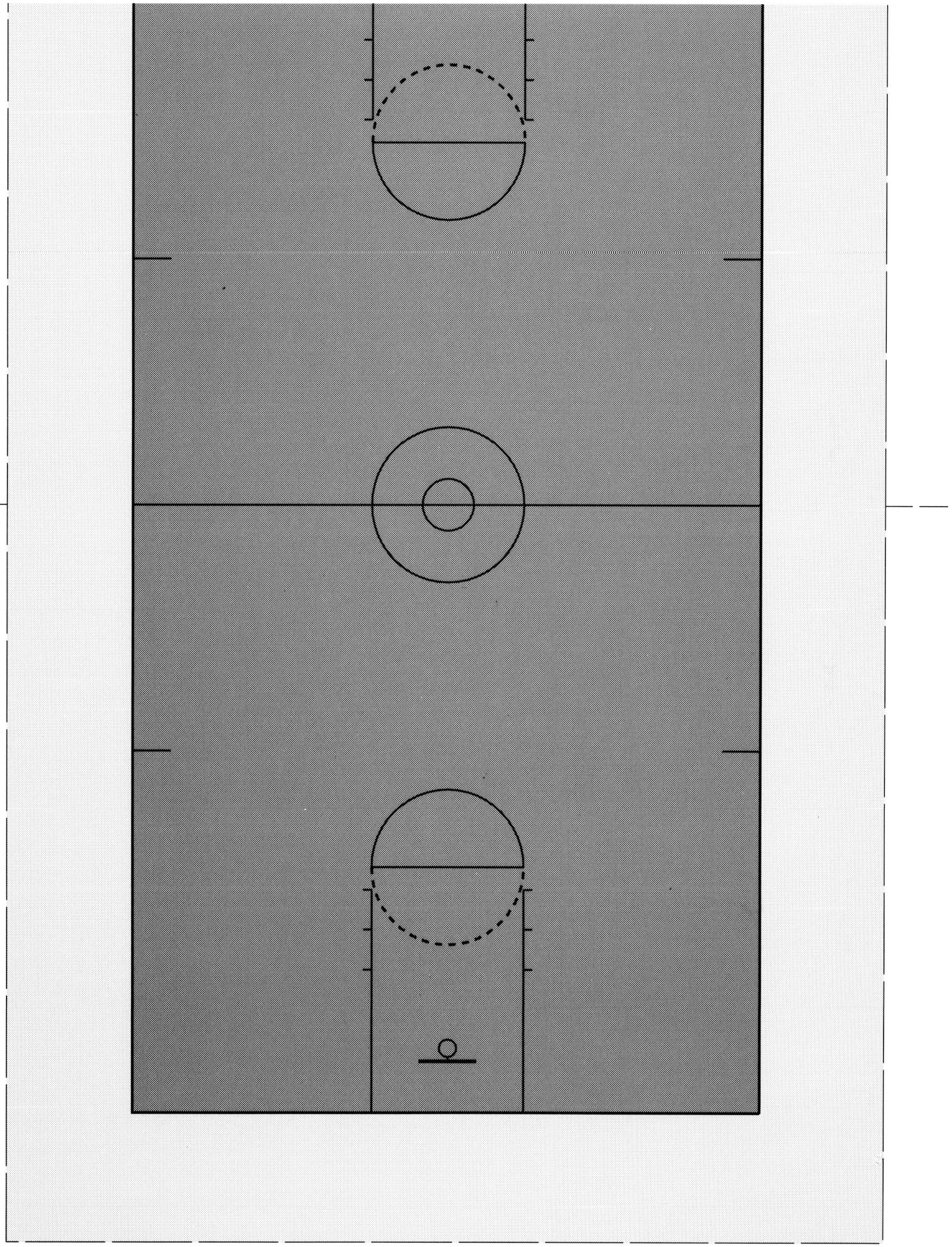

311

BASKETBALL COURT - HIGH SCHOOL AT 3/32" = 1'-0"   0 ▭ 8

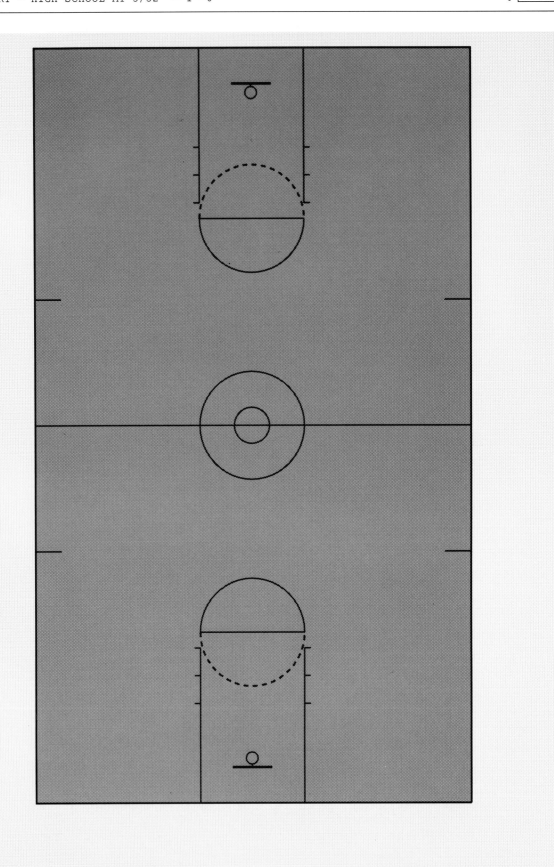

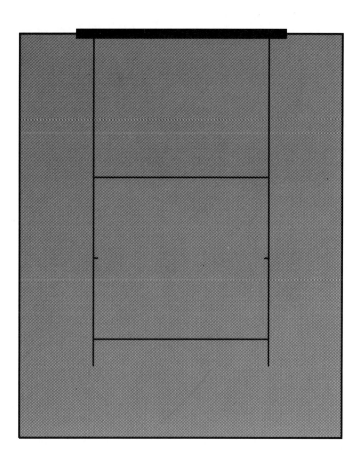

ONE WALL HANDBALL

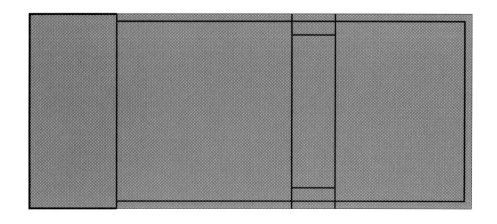

THREE WALL HANDBALL

COURTS AT 3/32" = 1'-0"

0 ⬜ 8

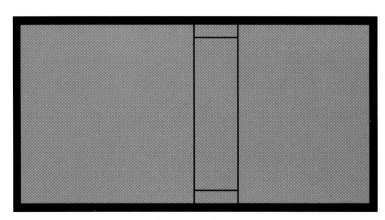

FOUR WALL HANDBALL

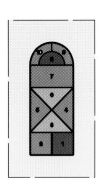

HOPSCOTCH

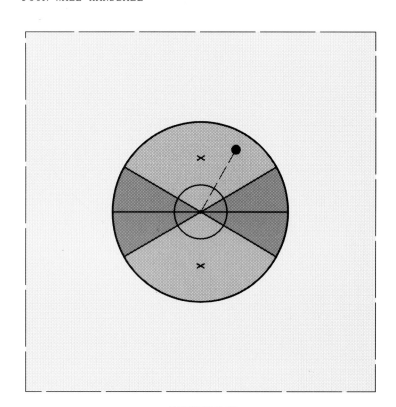

TETHERBALL

314

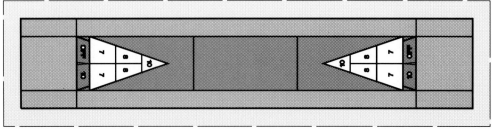

SHUFFLEBOARD

0 ⬜ 8

HALF
LINE

TENNIS COURTS AT 3/32" = 1'-0"   0 ⊏══════⊐ 8

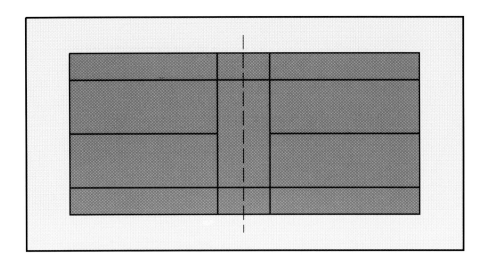

DECK TENNIS

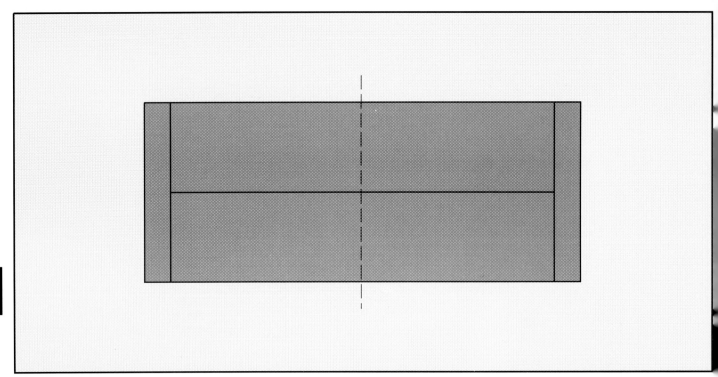

PADDLE TENNIS

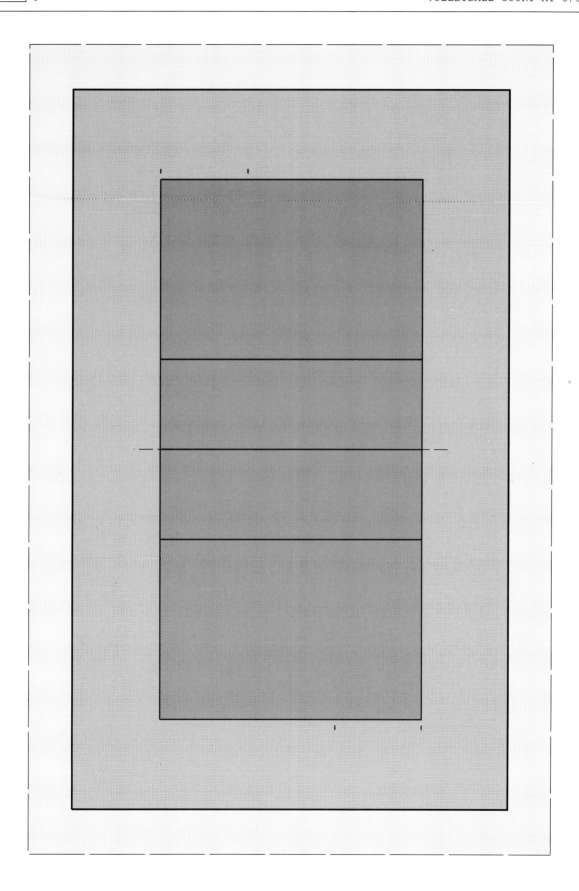

BASKETBALL COURT - AAU AT 1/16" = 1'-0"   0 ☐ 16

59'-1"
14 METERS

6'-7"   45'-11"   6'-7"
2 METERS   10 METERS   2 METERS

6'-7"

98'-6"   85'-4"
30 METERS   26 METERS

6'-7"

6'-7"

PLAYING AREA
3,918 SQUARE FEET

SAFETY AREA
1,901 SQUARE FEET

TOTAL AREA REQUIRED
5,819 SQUARE FEET

0 [========] 16   BASKETBALL COURT - NCAA AT 1/16" = 1'-0"

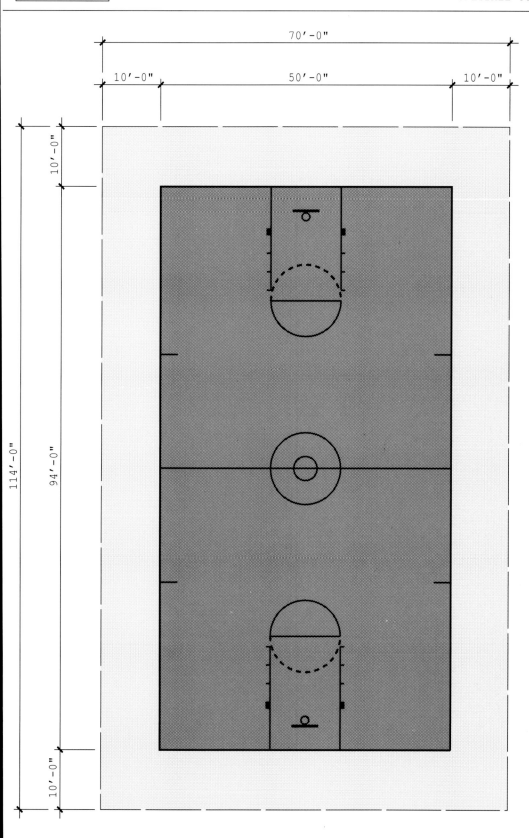

70'-0"

10'-0"   50'-0"   10'-0"

10'-0"

114'-0"

94'-0"

10'-0"

PLAYING AREA
4,700 SQUARE FEET

SAFETY AREA
3,280 SQUARE FEET

TOTAL AREA REQUIRED
7,980 SQUARE FEET

BASKETBALL COURT - HIGH SCHOOL AT 1/16" = 1'-0"   0 ▭▭▭▭▭ 16

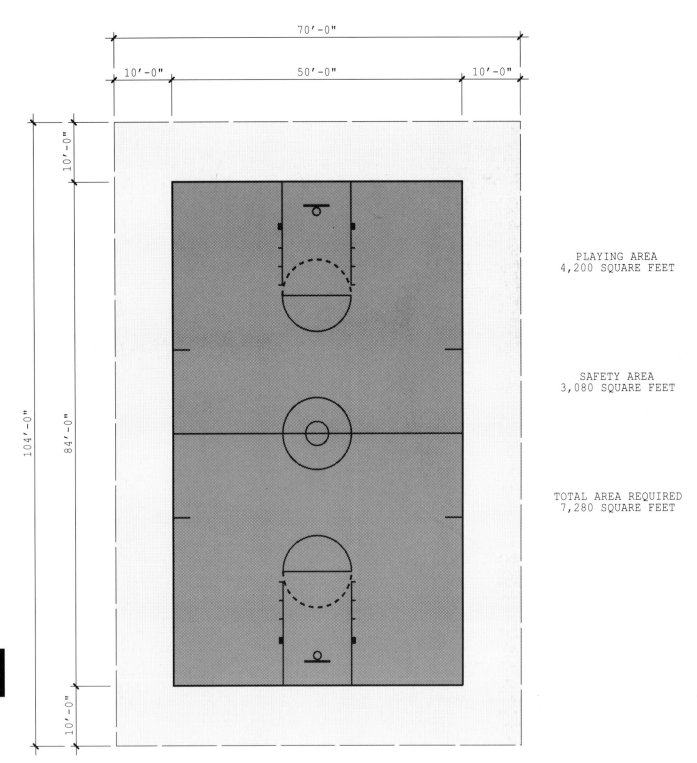

PLAYING AREA
4,200 SQUARE FEET

SAFETY AREA
3,080 SQUARE FEET

TOTAL AREA REQUIRED
7,280 SQUARE FEET

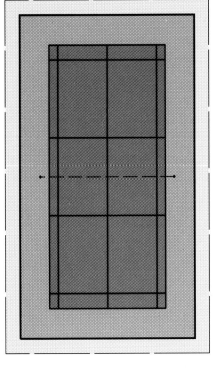

BADMINTON

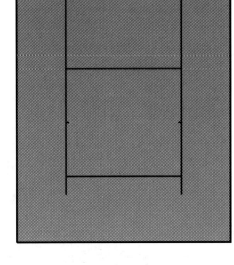

ONE WALL HANDBALL

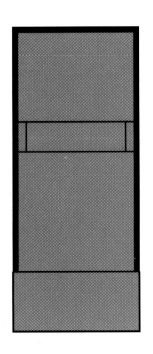

THREE WALL HANDBALL

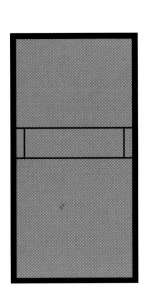

FOUR WALL HANDBALL

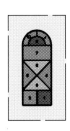

HOPSCOTCH

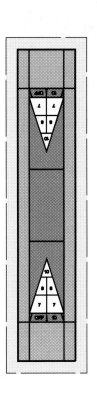

SHUFFLEBOARD

TENNIS COURT AT 1/16" = 1'-0"

0 ☐ 1

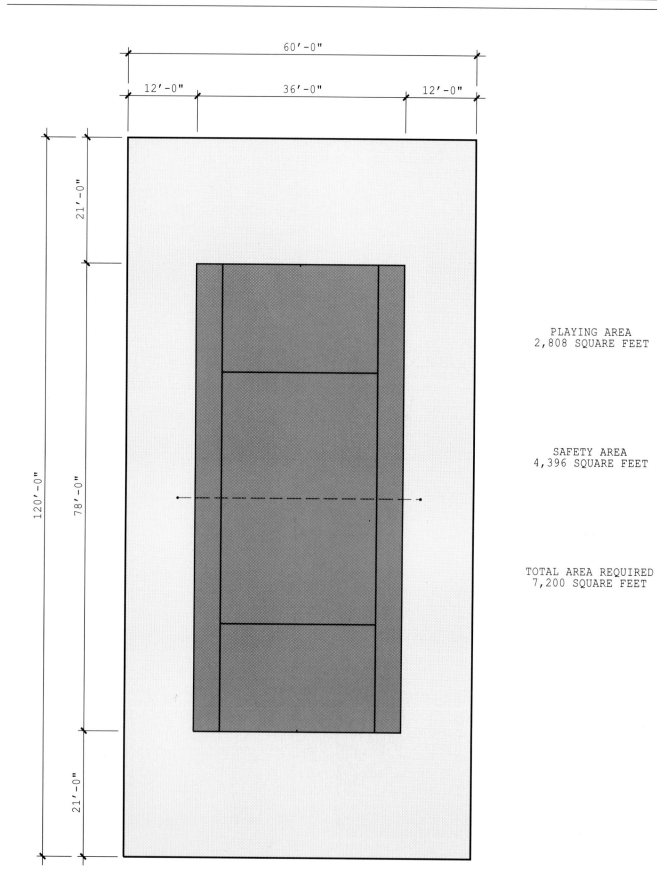

60'-0"

12'-0"   36'-0"   12'-0"

21'-0"

120'-0"

78'-0"

21'-0"

PLAYING AREA
2,808 SQUARE FEET

SAFETY AREA
4,396 SQUARE FEET

TOTAL AREA REQUIRED
7,200 SQUARE FEET

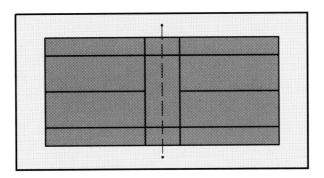

DECK TENNIS

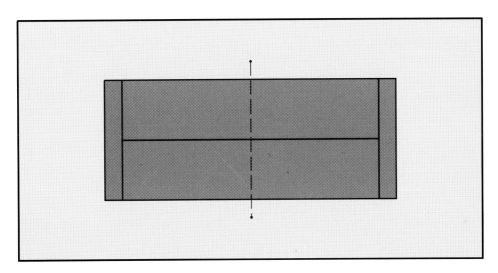

PADDLE TENNIS

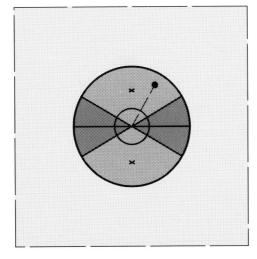

TETHERBALL

VOLLEYBALL COURT AT 1/16" = 1'-0"   0 ▭

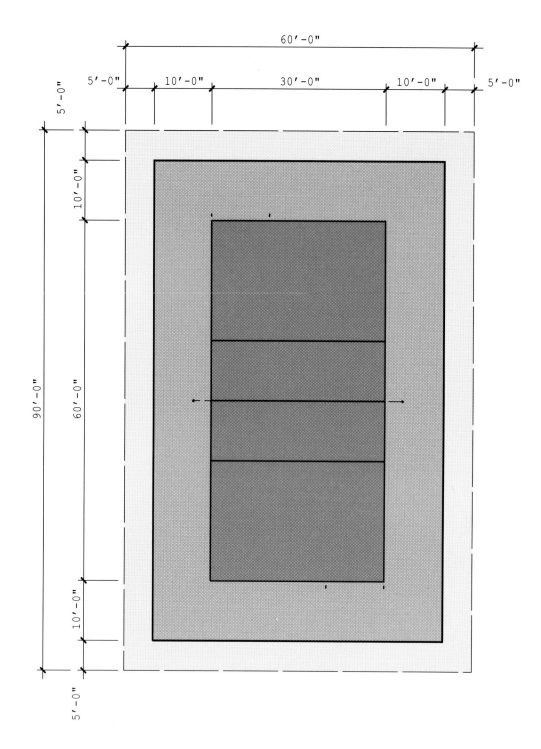

PLAYING AREA
1,800 SQUARE FEET

SAFETY AREA
3,600 SQUARE FEET

TOTAL AREA REQUIRED
5,400 SQUARE FEET

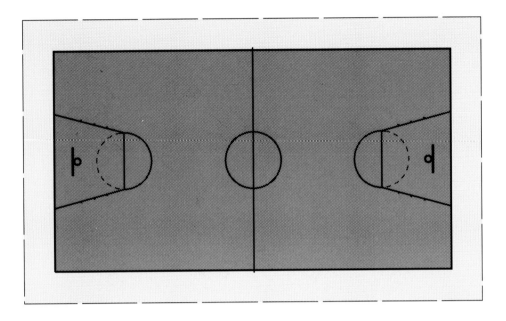

BASKETBALL - AAU

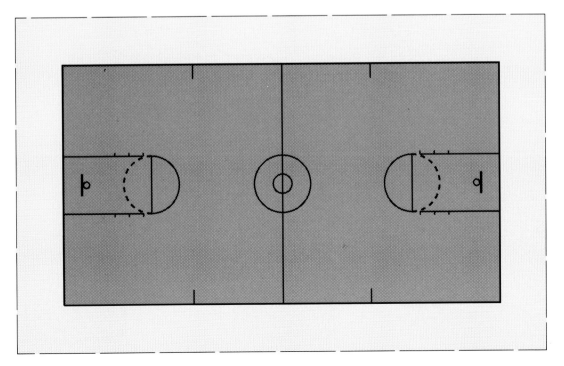

BASKETBALL - NCAA

COURTS AT 1" = 20'-0"

0 [   ] 20

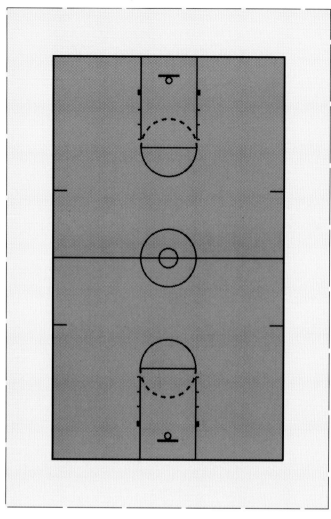

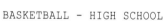

BASKETBALL - HIGH SCHOOL

HOPSCOTCH

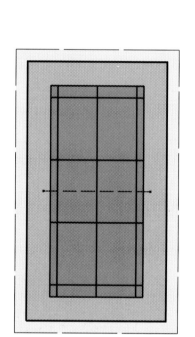

BADMINTON

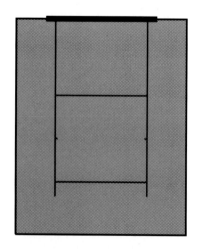

ONE WALL HANDBALL

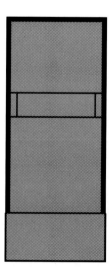

THREE WALL HANDBALL

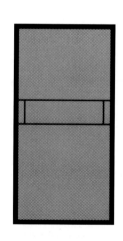

FOUR WALL HANDBALL

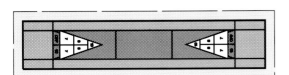

SHUFFLEBOARD

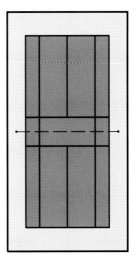

DECK TENNIS

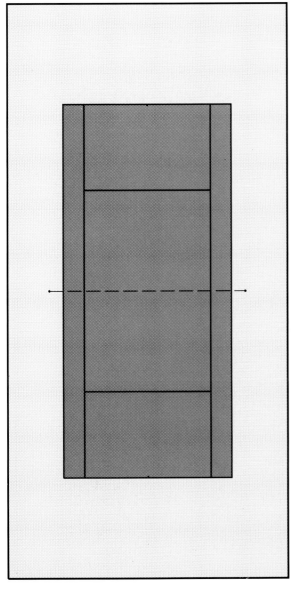

TENNIS

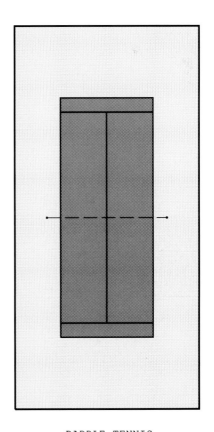

PADDLE TENNIS

COURTS AT 1" = 20'-0"

0 [========] 20

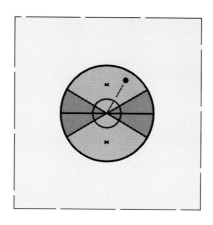

TETHERBALL

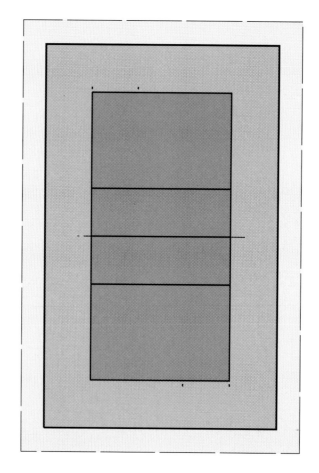

VOLLEYBALL

 30

COURTS AT 1" = 30'-0"

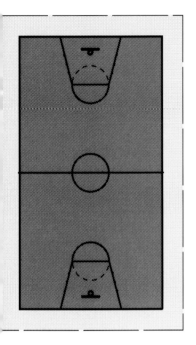

BASKETBALL - AAU

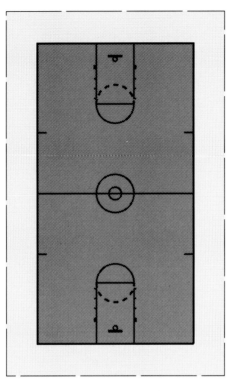

BASKETBALL - NCAA

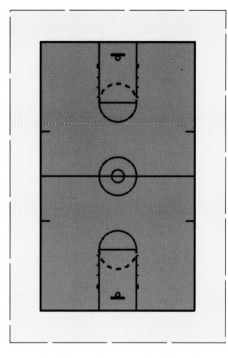

BASKETBALL - HIGH SCHOOL

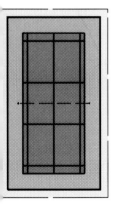

BADMINTON

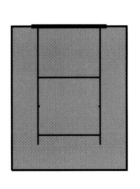

ONE WALL HANDBALL

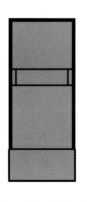

ONE WALL HANDBALL

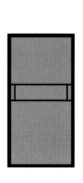

ONE WALL HANDBALL

HOPSCOTCH

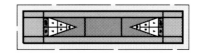

SHUFFLEBOARD

COURTS AT 1" = 30'-0"

0 ▭▭▭▭▭ 30

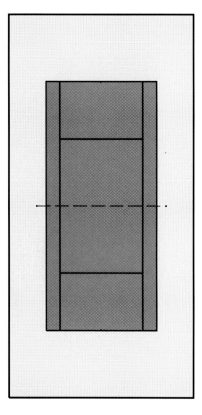

TENNIS

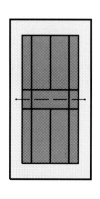

DECK TENNIS

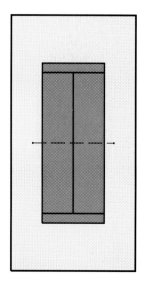

PADDLE TENNIS

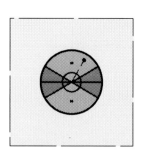

TETHERBALL

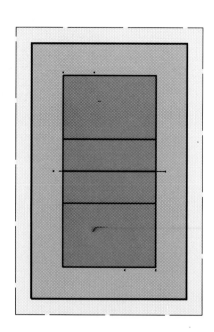

VOLLEYBALL

0 ▭ 40   COURTS AT 1" = 40'-0"

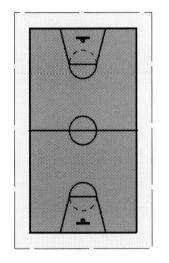

BASKETBALL - AAU

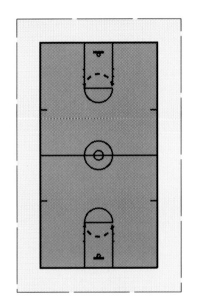

BASKETBALL - NCAA

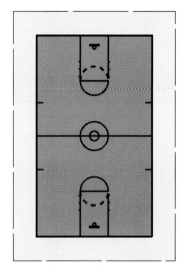

BASKETBALL - HIGH SCHOOL

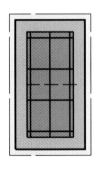

BADMINTON

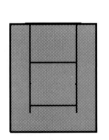

ONE WALL HANDBALL

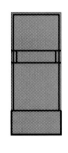

ONE WALL HANDBALL

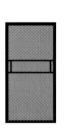

ONE WALL HANDBALL

HOPSCOTCH

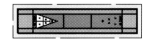

SHUFFLEBOARD

COURTS AT 1" = 40'-0"

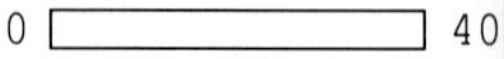

0   40

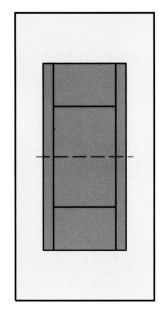

TENNIS

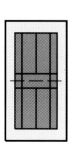

DECK TENNIS

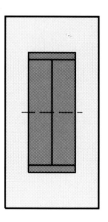

PADDLE TENNIS

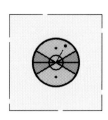

TETHERBALL

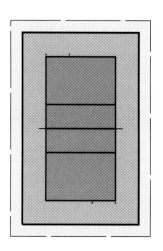

VOLLEYBALL

0 [====] 50   COURTS AT 1" = 50'-0"

BASKETBALL - AAU   BASKETBALL - NCAA   BASKETBALL - HIGH SCHOOL   TENNIS   VOLLEYBALL

ONE-WALL HANDBALLTHREE-WALL HANDBALL FOUR-WALL HANDBALL DECK TENNIS   PADDLE TENNIS

0 [====] 60   COURTS AT 1" = 60'-0"

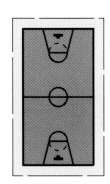

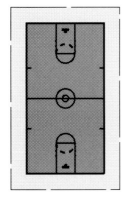
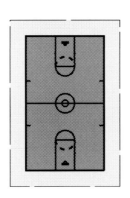
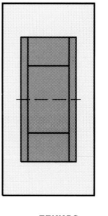
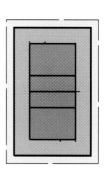

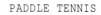

BASKETBALL - AAU   BASKETBALL - NCAA   BASKETBALL - HIGH SCHOOL   TENNIS   VOLLEYBALL

ONE-WALL HANDBALLTHREE-WALL HANDBALL FOUR-WALL HANDBALL DECK TENNIS   PADDLE TENNIS

CROQUET AT 1/8" = 1'-0"

0 ⬜ 8

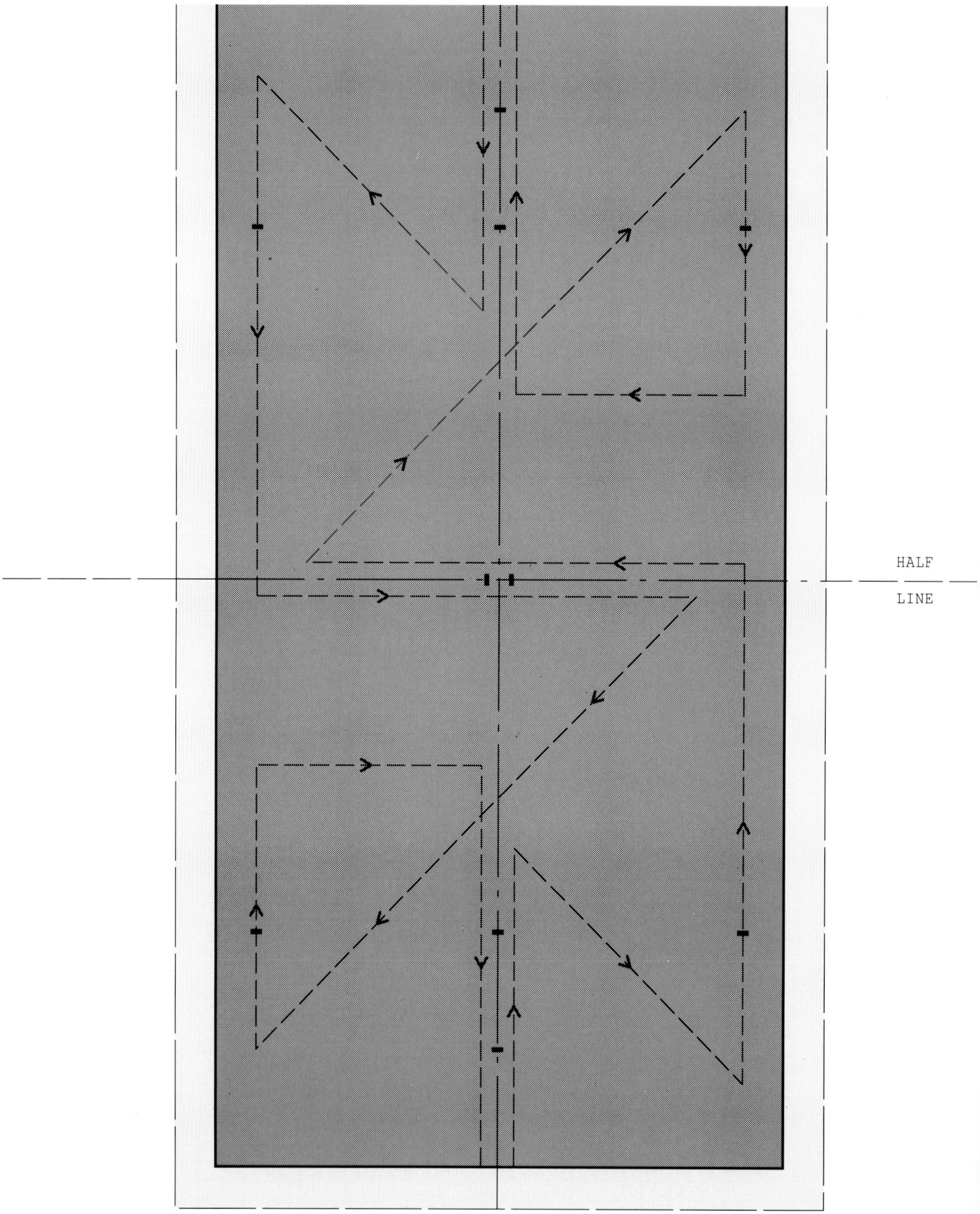

HALF
LINE

334

0 8 HORSESHOES AT 1/8" = 1'-0"

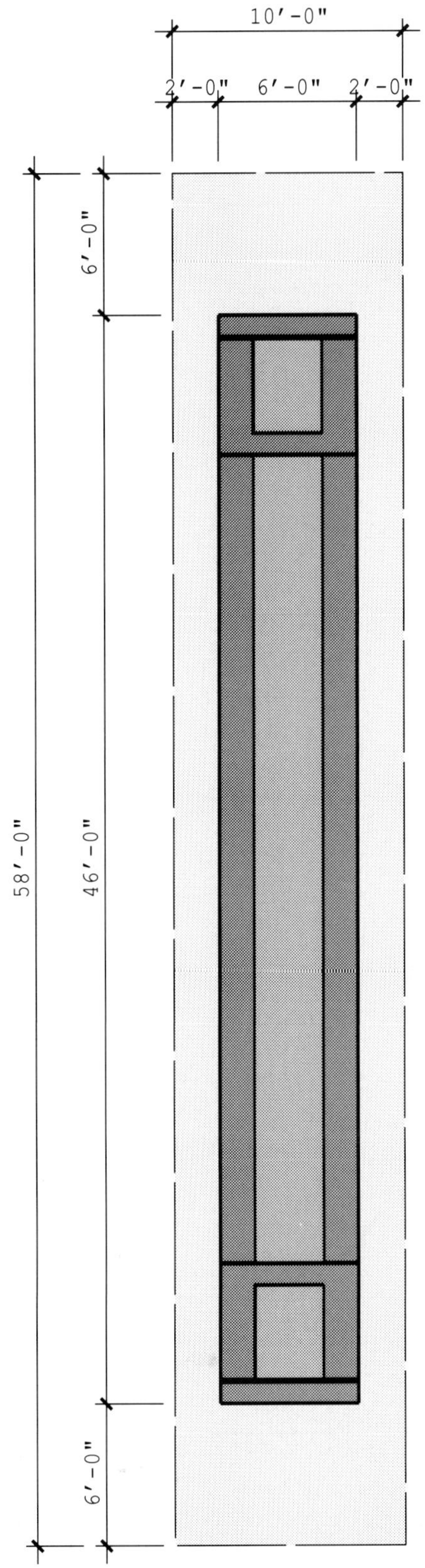
10'-0"
2'-0"
6'-0"
2'-0"
6'-0"
58'-0"
46'-0"
6'-0"

PLAYING AREA
276 SQUARE FEET

SAFETY AREA
304 SQUARE FEET

TOTAL AREA REQUIRED
580 SQUARE FEET

ROQUE AT 1/8" = 1'-0"   0 [   ] 8

36'-0"

3'-0"   30'-0"   3'-0"

3'-0"

66'-0"   60'-0"

3'-0"

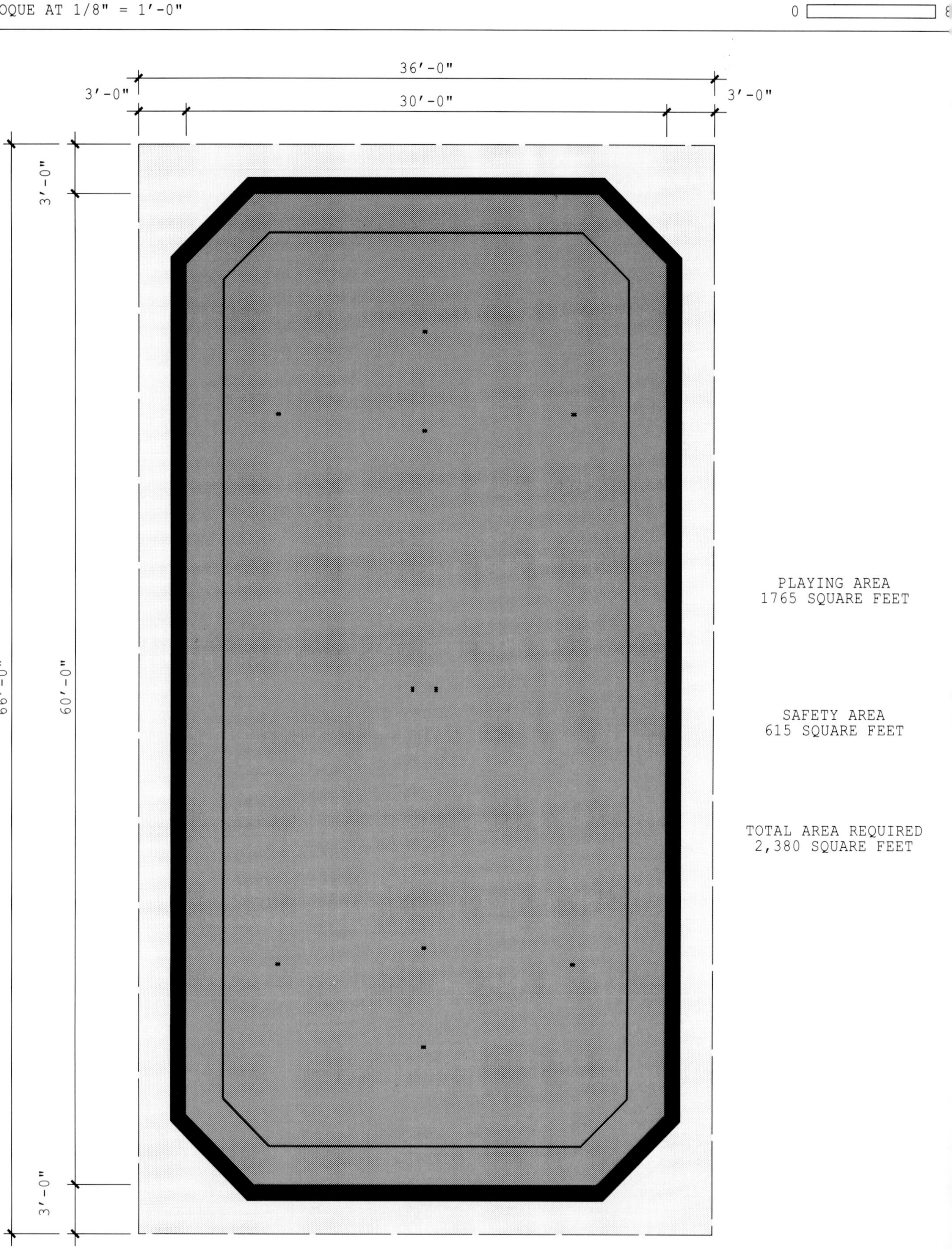

PLAYING AREA
1765 SQUARE FEET

SAFETY AREA
615 SQUARE FEET

TOTAL AREA REQUIRED
2,380 SQUARE FEET

0 10 CROQUET AT 1" = 10'-0"

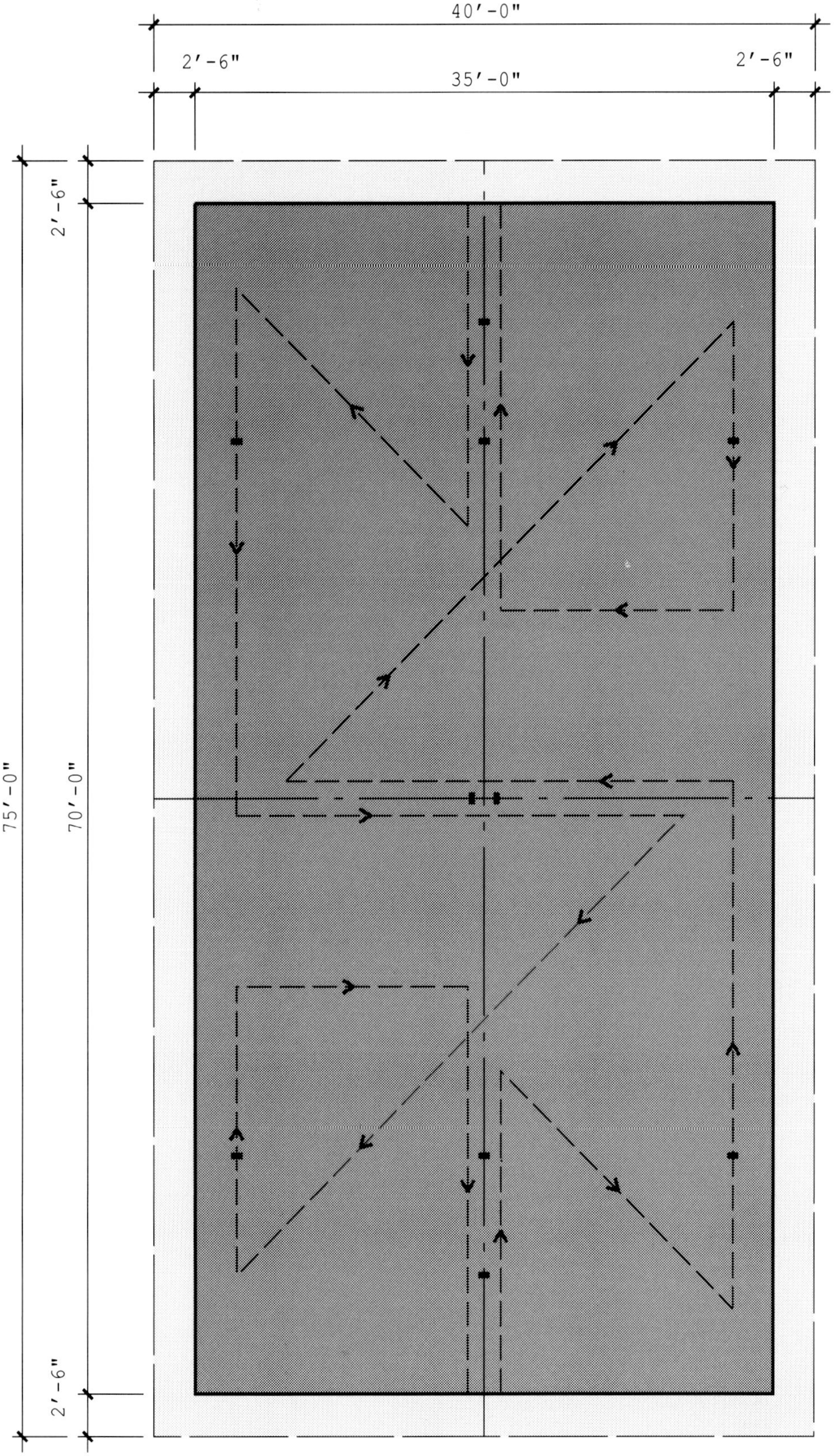
40'-0"
2'-6"
35'-0"
2'-6"
2'-6"
75'-0"
70'-0"
2'-6"

PLAYING AREA
2,450 SQUARE FEET

SAFETY AREA
550 SQUARE FEET

TOTAL AREA REQUIRED
3,000 SQUARE FEET

HORSESHOE AND ROQUE AT 1" = 10'-0"   0 ☐☐☐☐☐☐ 10

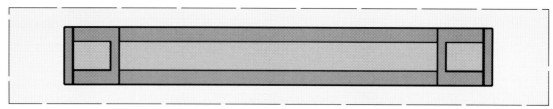

HORSESHOES

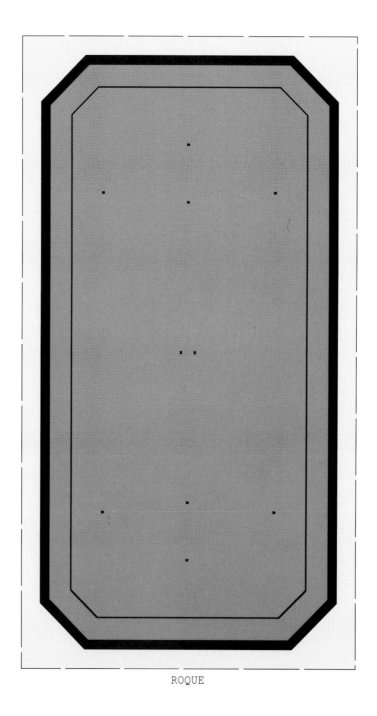

ROQUE

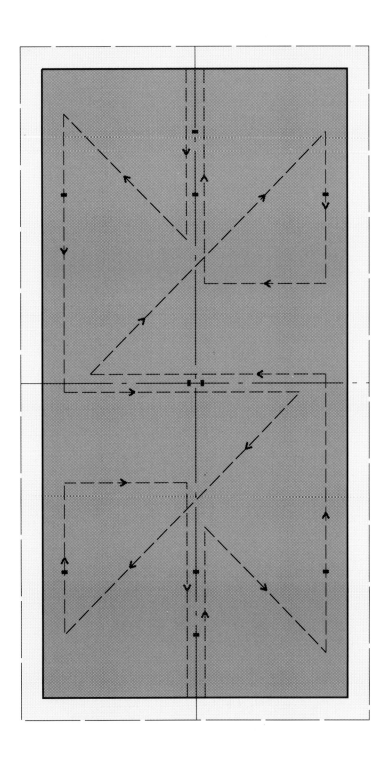

HORSESHOE AND ROQUE AT 3/32" = 1'-0"   0 8

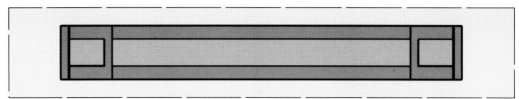

HORSESHOES

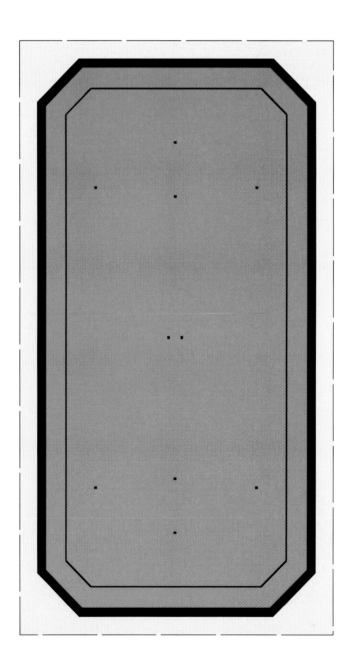

ROQUE

0 ▭ 16   COURTS AT 1/16" = 1'-0"

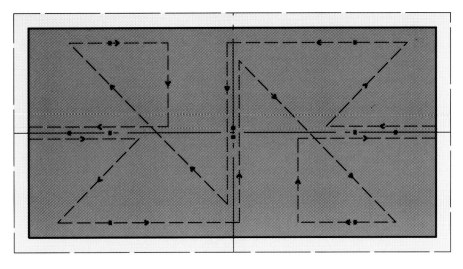

CROQUET

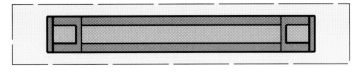

HORSESHOES

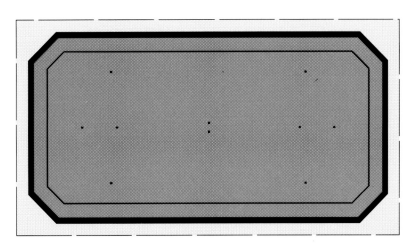

ROQUE

341

COURTS AT 1" = 20'-0"   0 ⬚⬚⬚⬚⬚ 2C

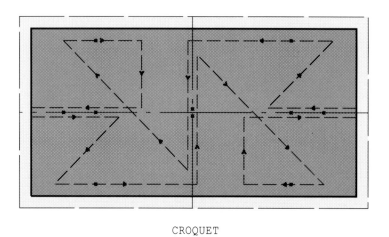

CROQUET

HORSESHOES

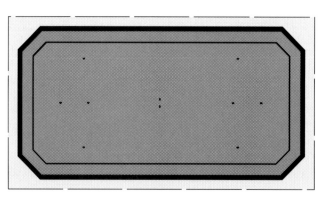

ROQUE

0 [========] 20

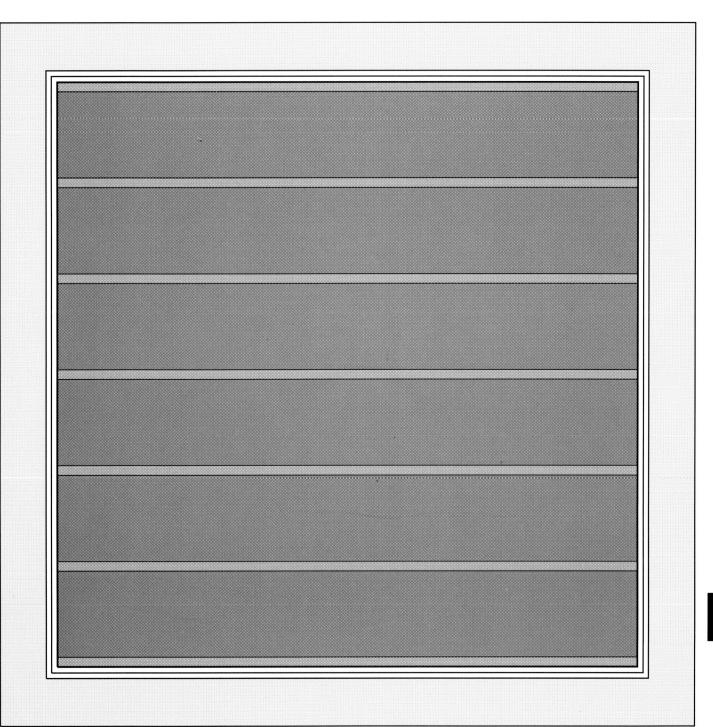

COURTS AT 1" = 30'-0"

0 ⬜ 30

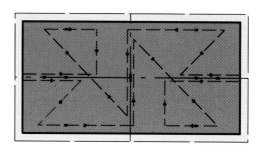

CROQUET

HORSESHOES

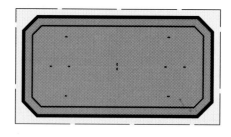

ROQUE

0 [ ] 30

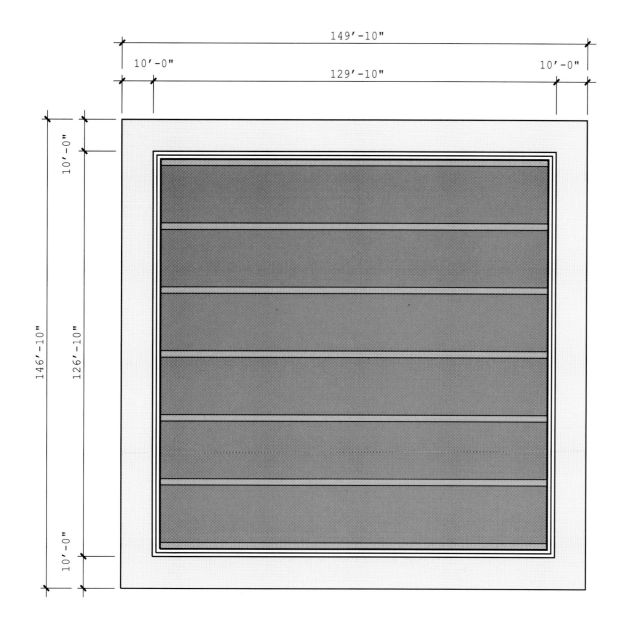

PLAYING AREA
16,467 SQUARE FEET

SAFETY AREA
5,533 SQUARE FEET

TOTAL AREA REQUIRED
22,000 SQUARE FEET

COURTS AT 1" = 40'-0"   0 ▭ 40

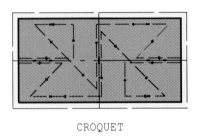

CROQUET

HORSESHOES

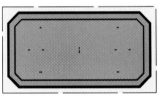

ROQUE

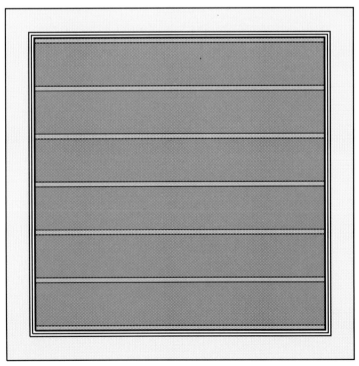

LAWN BOWLING

0 ☐ 20

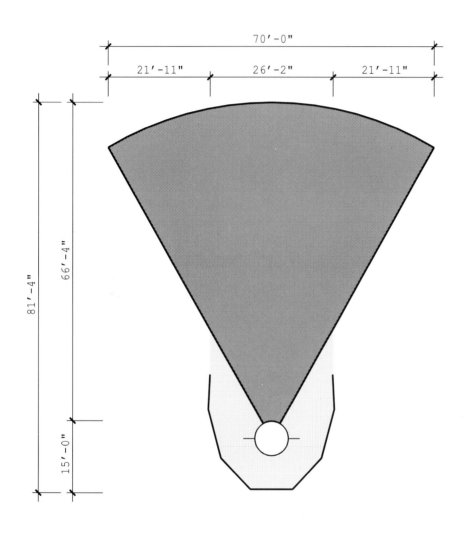

PLAYING AREA
2,560 SQUARE FEET

SAFETY AREA
490 SQUARE FEET

TOTAL AREA REQUIRED
3,050 SQUARE FEET

HAMMER THROW AT 1" = 20'-0"   0 [=========] 20

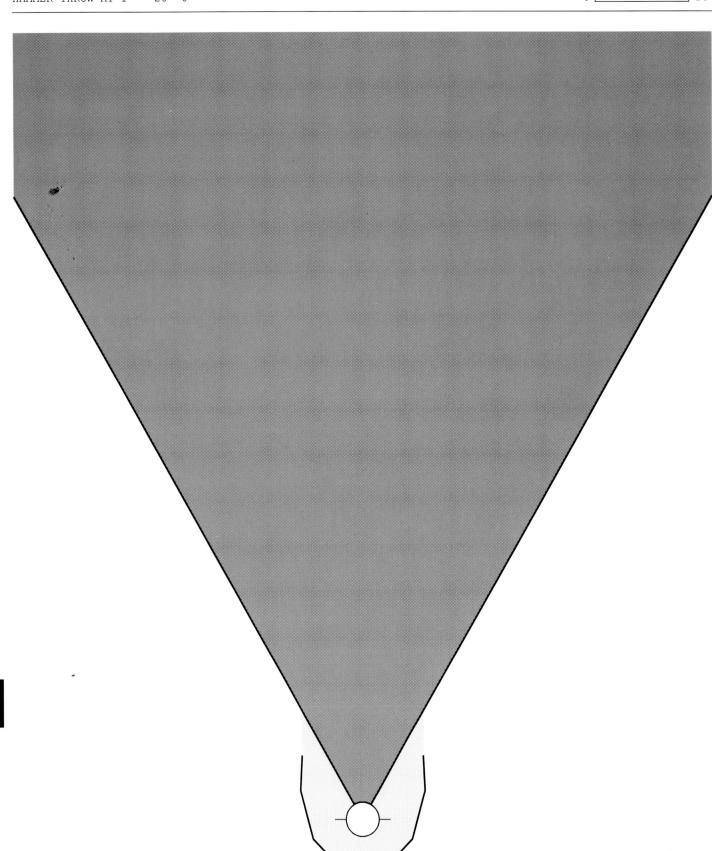

0 [＿＿＿＿＿＿] 20   DISCUS THROW AT 1" = 20'-0"

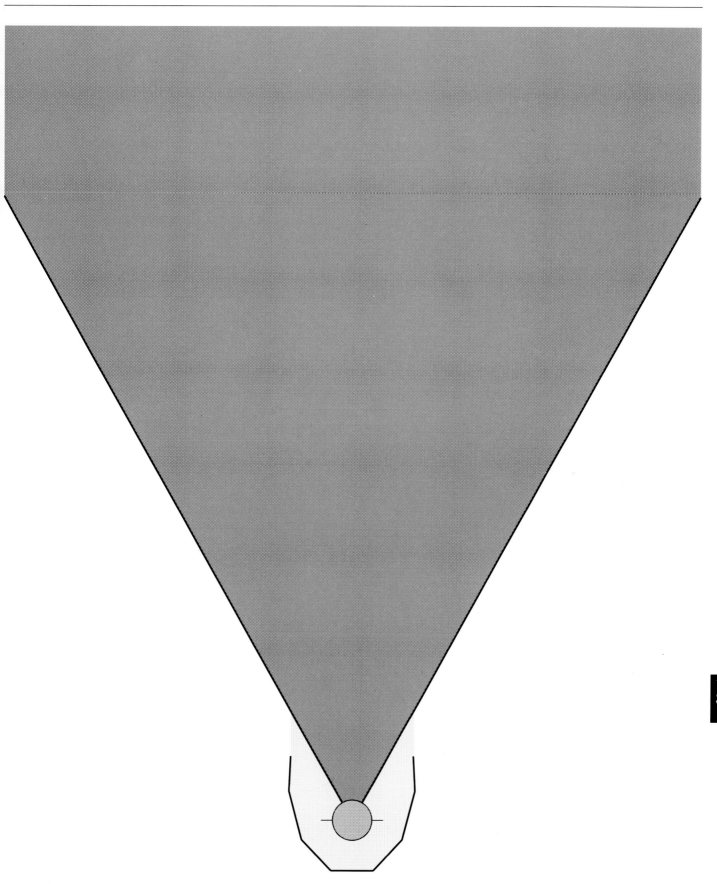

JAVELIN THROW AT 1" = 20'-0"   0 ▭ 20

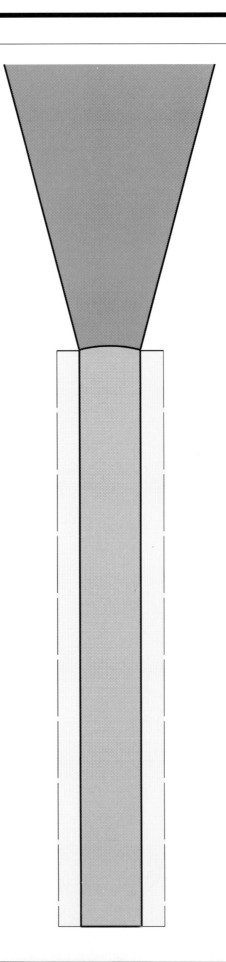

0 [   ] 20

LONG AND TRIPLE JUMP AND POLE VAULT AT 1" = 20'-0"

36'-0"

10'-0"   16'-0"   10'-0"

10'-0"

22'-0"

161'-0"

119'-0"

PLAYING AREA
828 SQUARE FEET

SAFETY AREA
4,968 SQUARE FEET

TOTAL AREA REQUIRED
5,795 SQUARE FEET

10'-0"

LONG AND
TRIPLE JUMP

351

HIGH JUMP AT 1" = 20'-0"   0 ⬜ 20

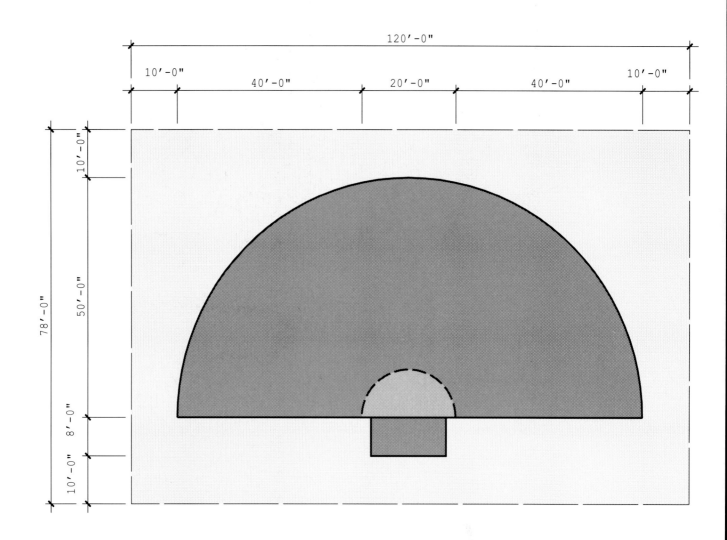

PLAYING AREA
4,035 SQUARE FEET

SAFETY AREA
5,324 SQUARE FEET

TOTAL AREA REQUIRED
9,360 SQUARE FEET

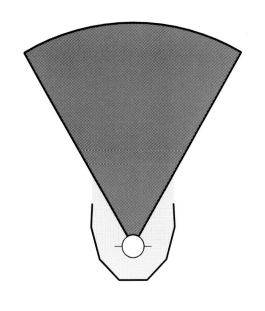

SHOT PUT

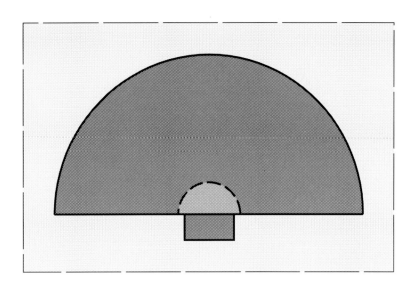

HIGH JUMP

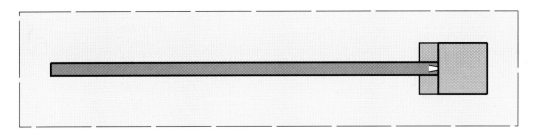

POLE VAULT

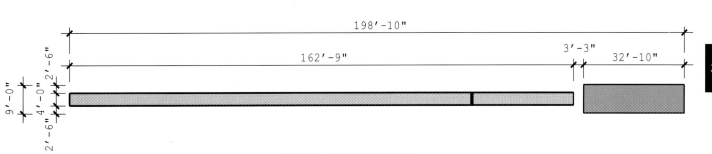

TOTAL AREA REQUIRED
959 SQUARE FEET

LONG AND TRIPLE JUMP

HAMMER THROW AT 1" = 30'-0"   0 [=======] 30

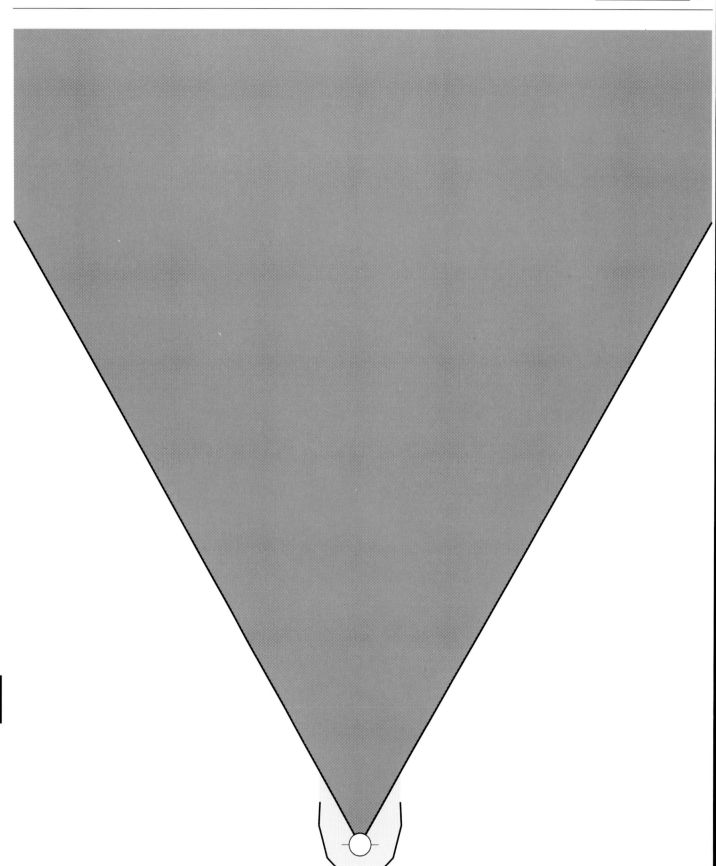

DISCUS THROW AT 1" = 30'-0"

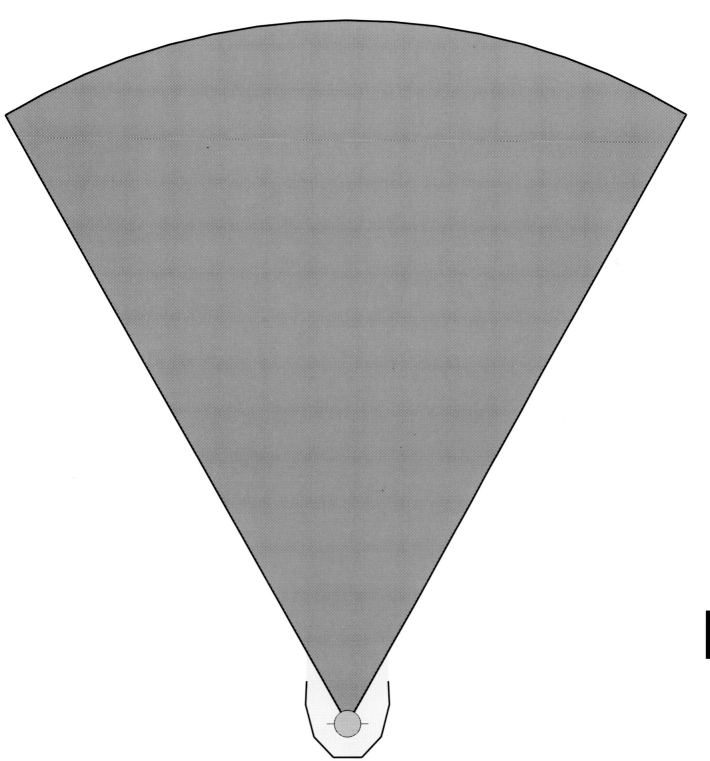

JAVELIN THROW AT 1" = 30'-0"

0 ▭ 30

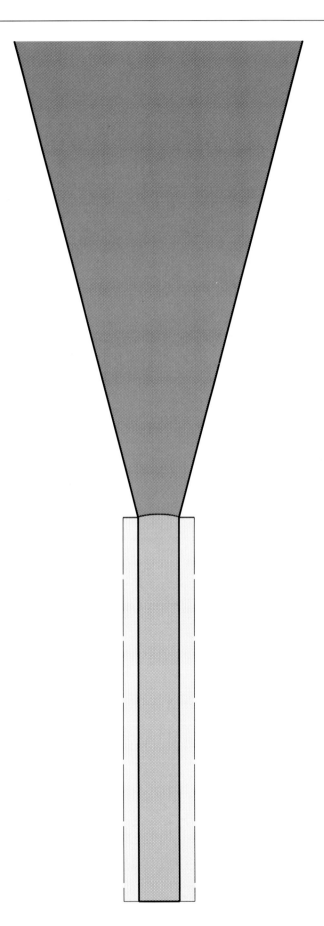

40

TRACK FIELDS AT 1" = 40'-0"

0 40

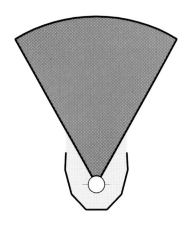

SHOT PUT

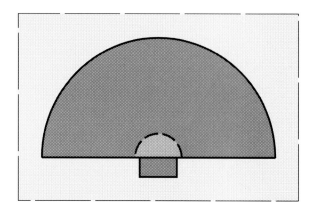

HIGH JUMP

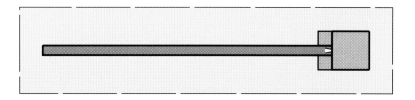

POLE VAULT

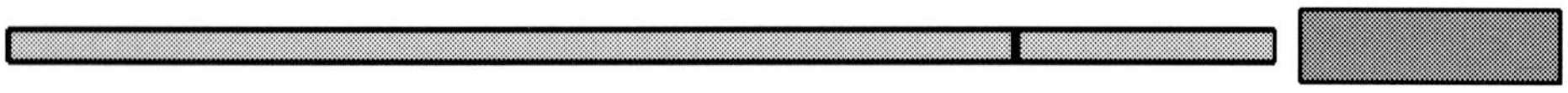

LONG AND TRIPLE JUMP

0 ▭ 40   HAMMER THROW AT 1" = 40'-0"

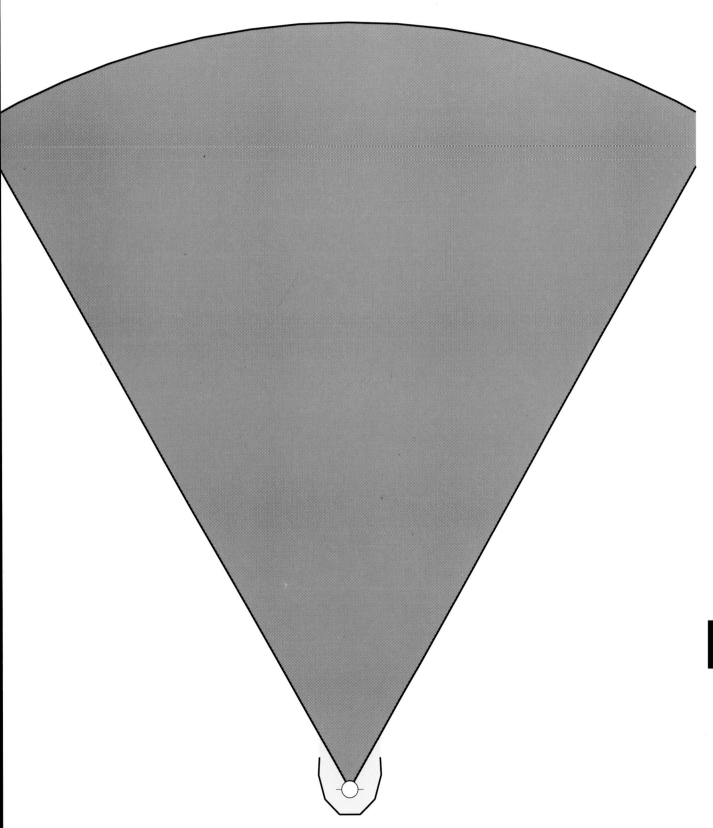

DISCUS THROW AT 1" = 40'-0"   0 ▭ 40

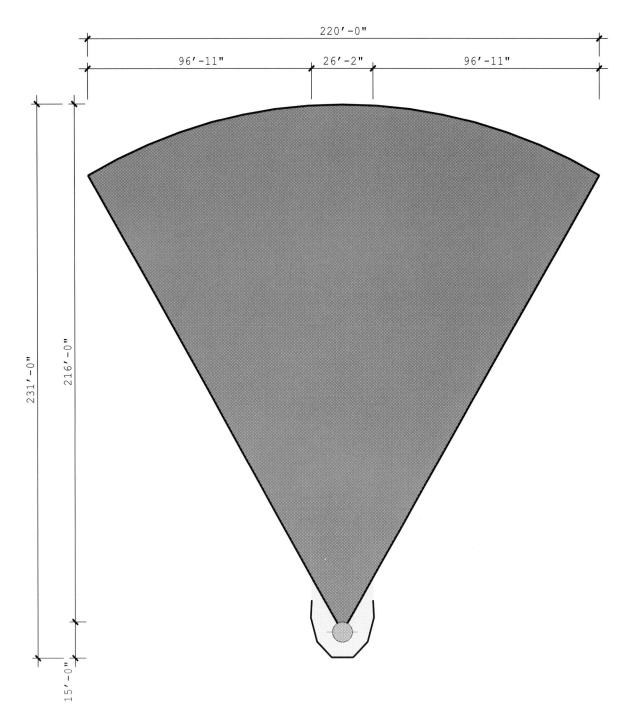

220'-0"

96'-11"   26'-2"   96'-11"

231'-0"

216'-0"

15'-0"

PLAYING AREA
25,307 SQUARE FEET

SAFETY AREA
494 SQUARE FEET

TOTAL AREA REQUIRED
25,802 SQUARE FEET

0 [   ] 40

JAVELIN THROW AT 1" = 40'-0"

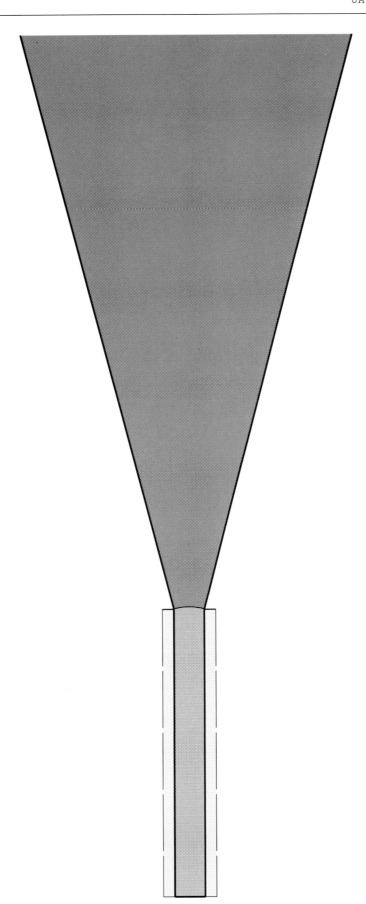

TRACK AT 1" = 50'-0"

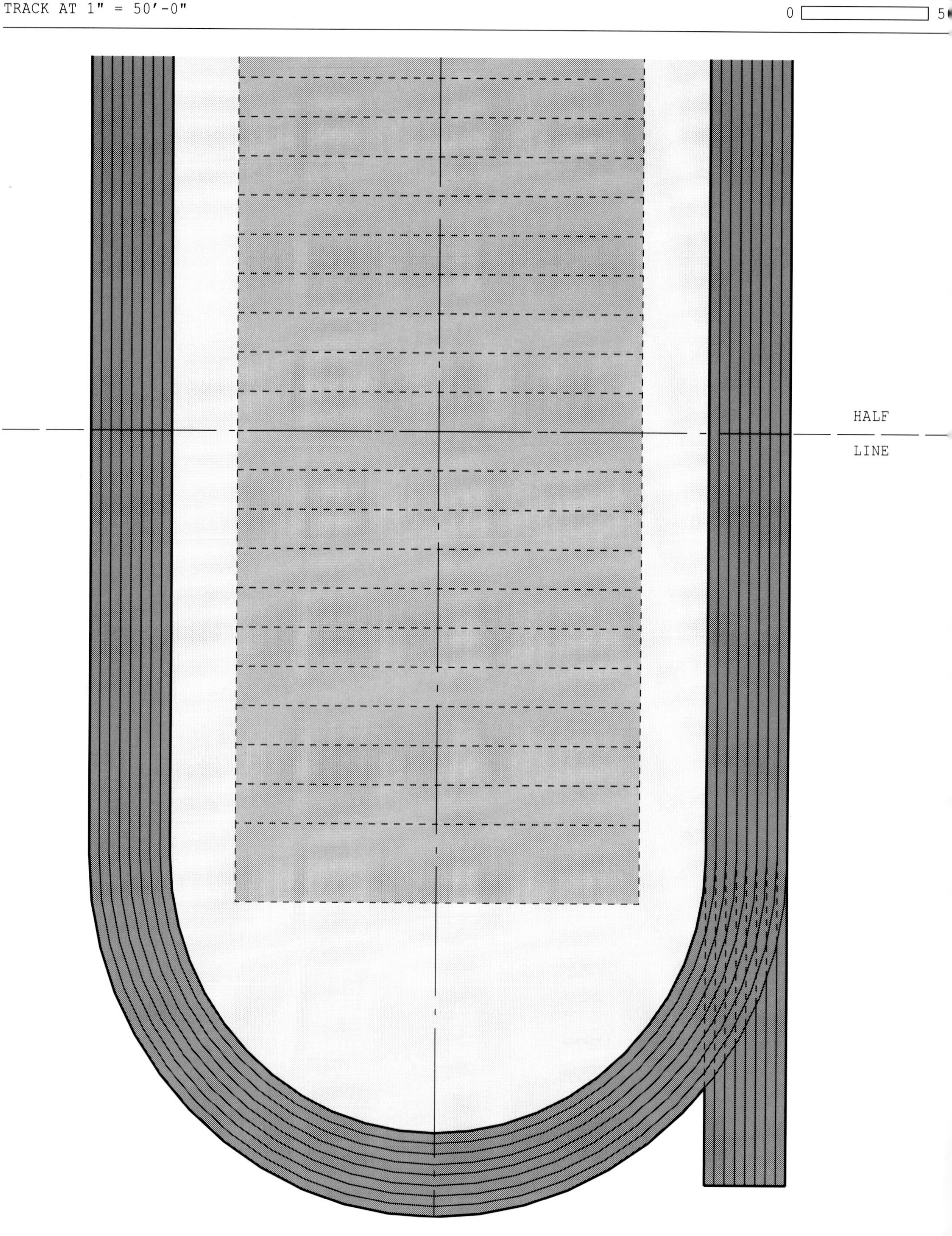

0 [====] 5

HALF

LINE

0 ▭ 50

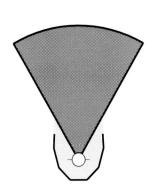

SHOT PUT

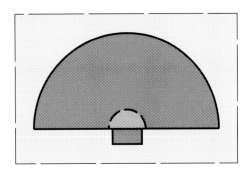

HIGH JUMP

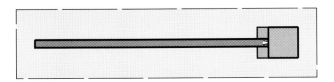

POLE VAULT

LONG AND
TRIPLE JUMP

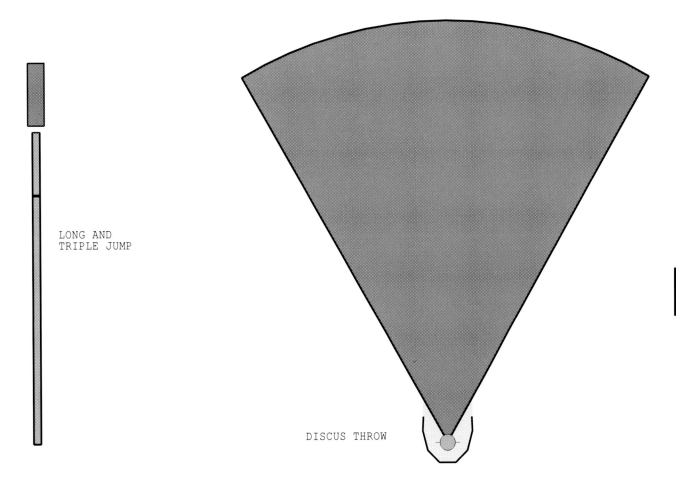

DISCUS THROW

HAMMER THROW AT 1" = 50'-0"   0 ⬜ 50

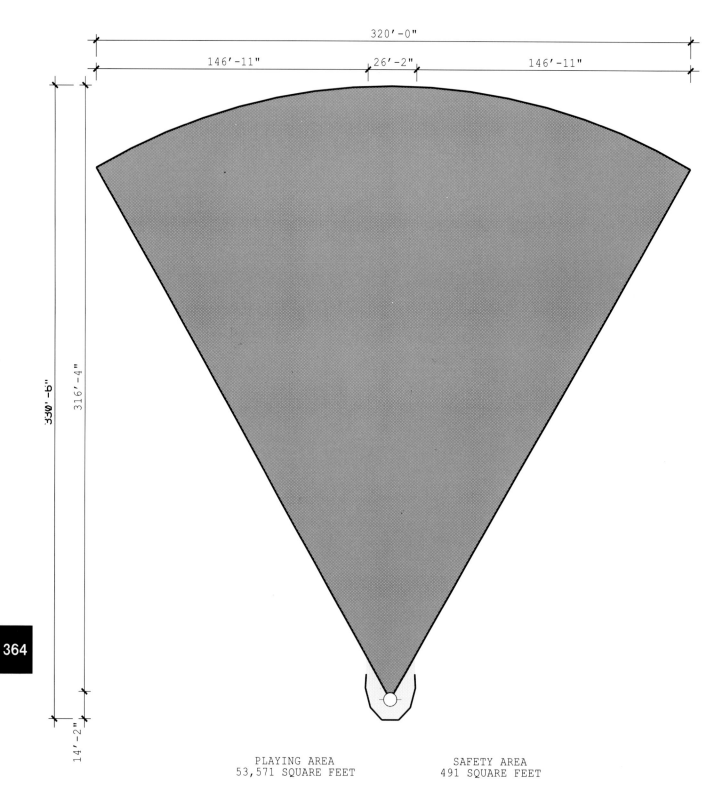

320'-0"

146'-11"   26'-2"   146'-11"

330'-6"

316'-4"

14'-2"

PLAYING AREA
53,571 SQUARE FEET

SAFETY AREA
491 SQUARE FEET

TOTAL AREA REQUIRED
54,063 SQUARE FEET

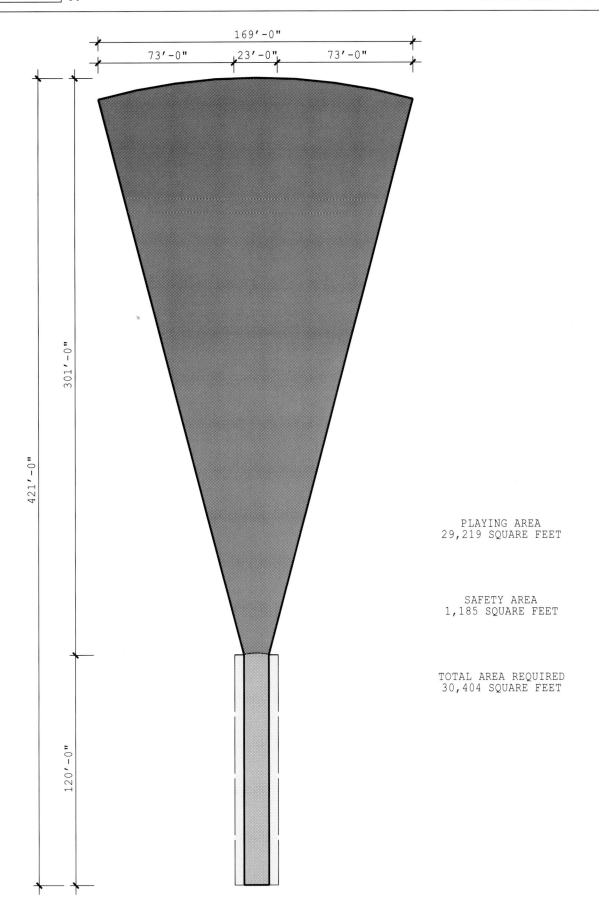

PLAYING AREA
29,219 SQUARE FEET

SAFETY AREA
1,185 SQUARE FEET

TOTAL AREA REQUIRED
30,404 SQUARE FEET

TRACK AT 1" = 60'-0"

0 [========] 60

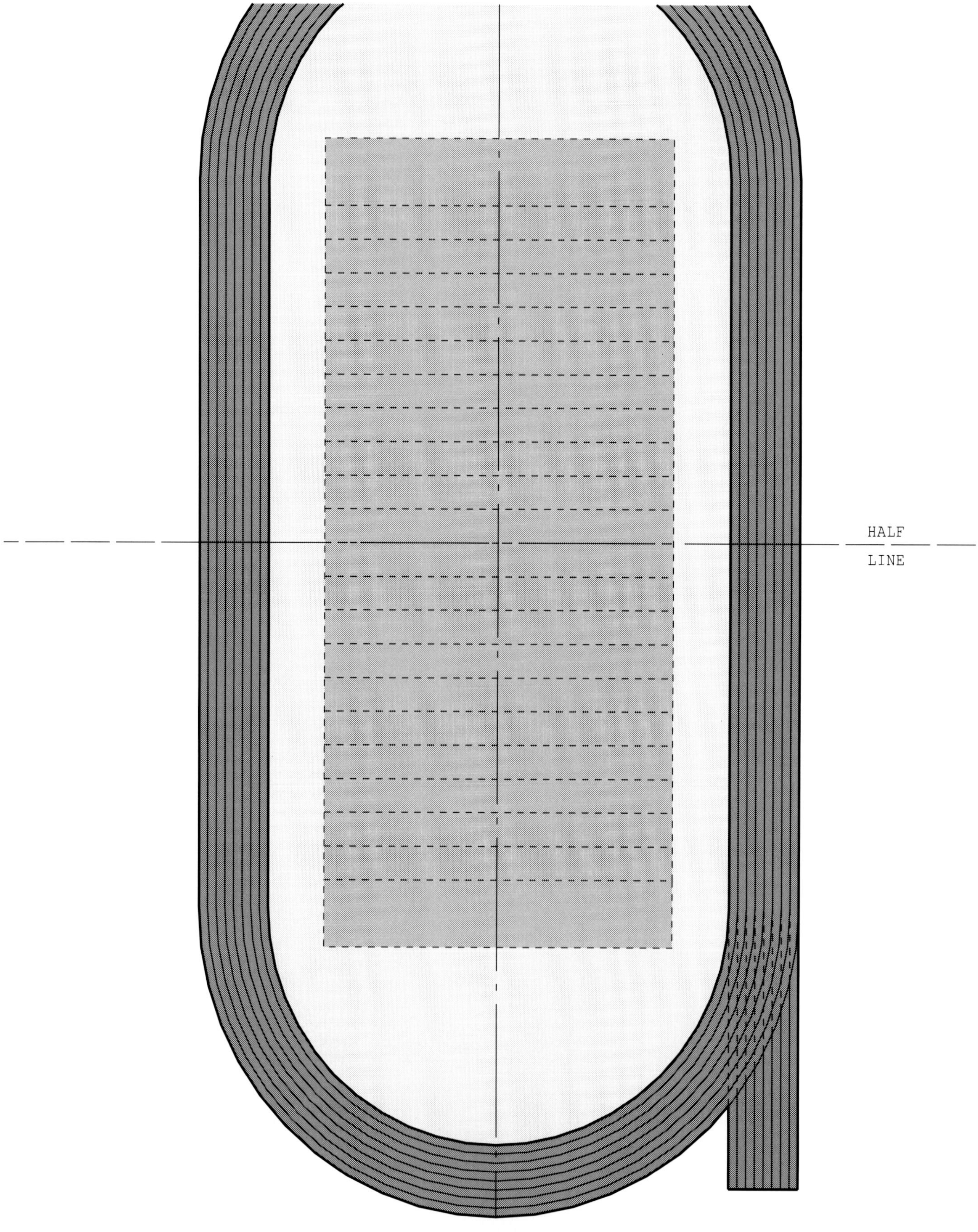

HALF
LINE

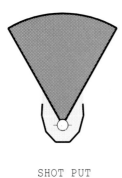

SHOT PUT

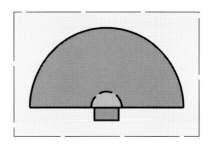

HIGH JUMP

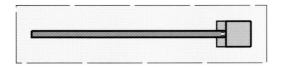

POLE VAULT

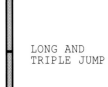

LONG AND
TRIPLE JUMP

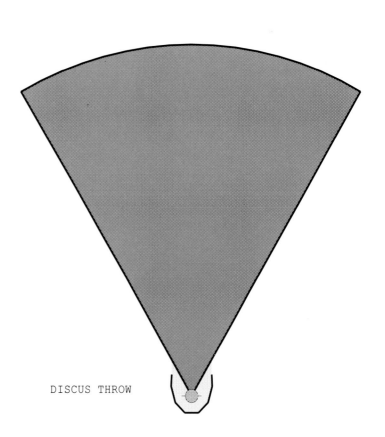

DISCUS THROW

HAMMER AND JAVELIN THROW AT 1" = 60'-0"   0 ☐▭▭▭☐ 60

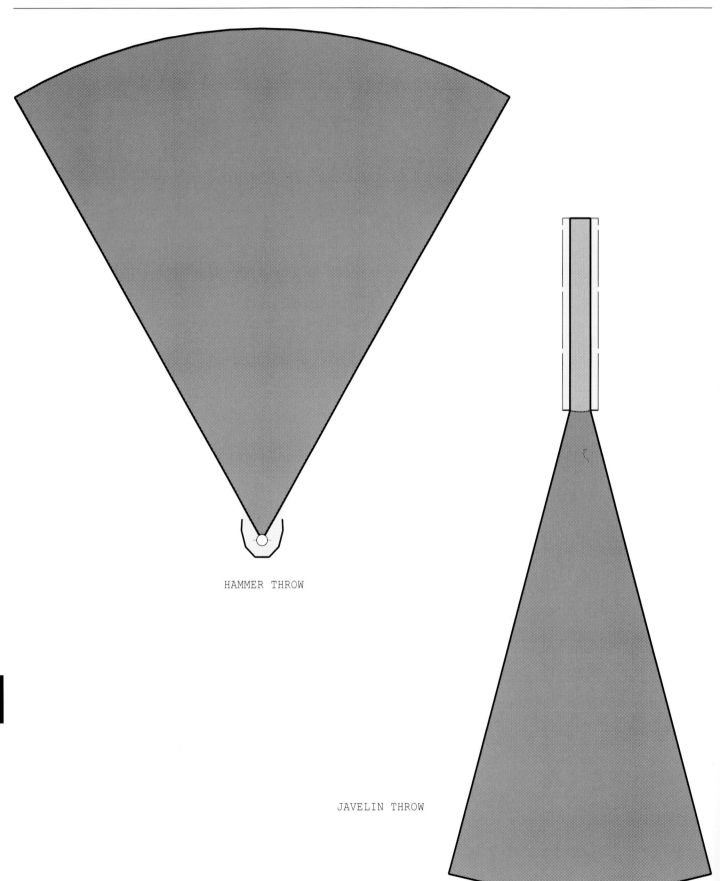

HAMMER THROW

JAVELIN THROW

1/4 MILE TRACK AT 1" = 100'-0"

276'-0"

32'-0"   212'-0"   32'-0"

138'-1"   138'-1"

600'-2"   324'-0"   449'-4"

138'-1"

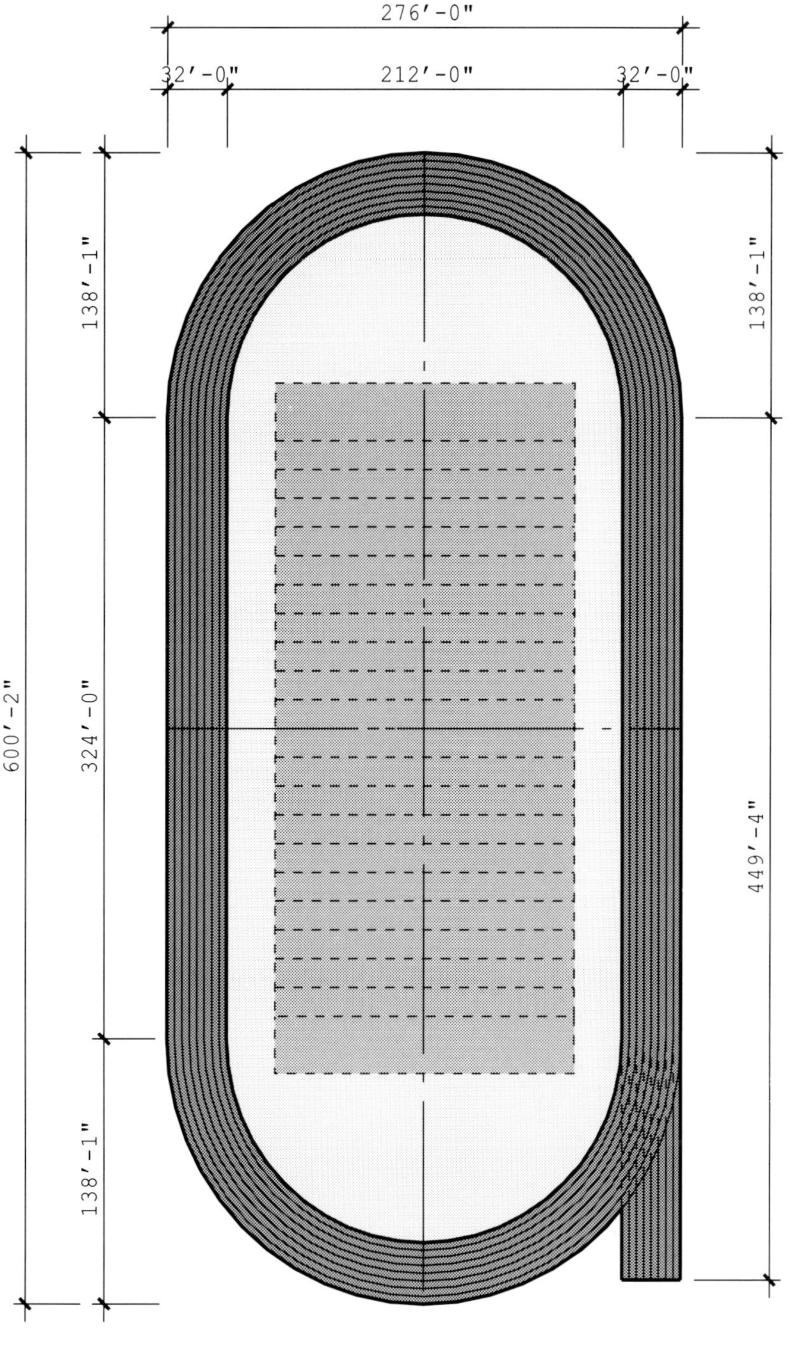

TOTAL AREA REQUIRED
150,934 SQUARE FEET
3.465 ACRES

TRACK FIELDS AT 1" = 100'-0"

0 ▭ 100

SHOT PUT

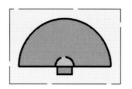

HIGH JUMP

POLE VAULT

LONG AND
TRIPLE JUMP

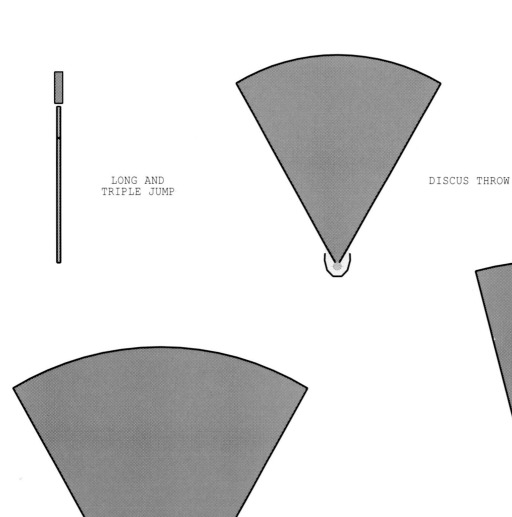

DISCUS THROW

HAMMER
THROW

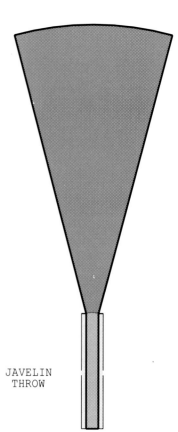

JAVELIN
THROW

0 [   ] 200

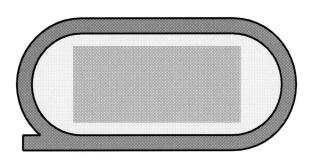

1/4 MILE TRACK

SHOT PUT

HIGH JUMP

POLE VAULT

LONG AND
TRIPLE JUMP

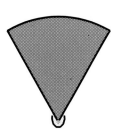

DISCUS THROW

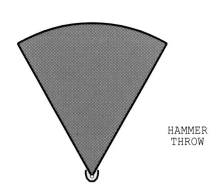

HAMMER
THROW

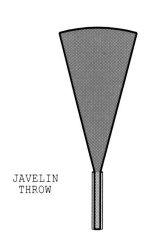

JAVELIN
THROW

ARCHERY AT 1" = 20'-0"

0 ⬛ 2

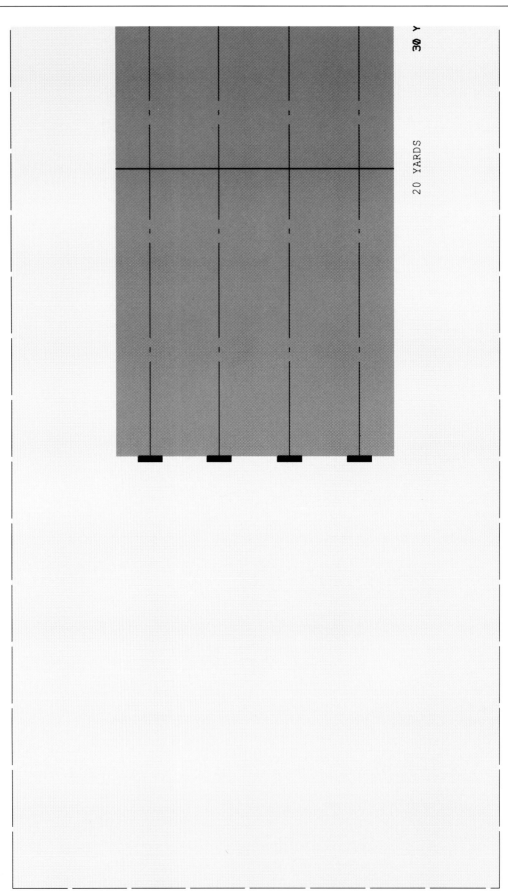

0 [   ] 20

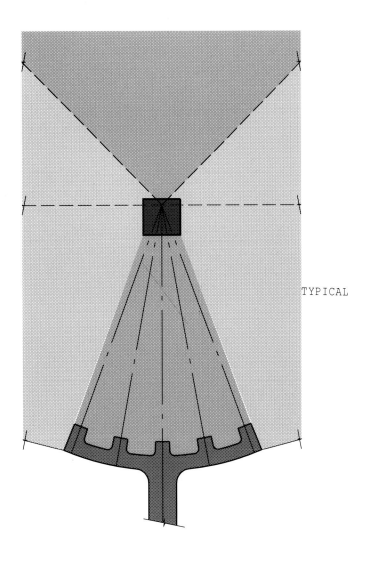

TYPICAL

SKEET AT 1" = 20'-0"   0 ▭ 20

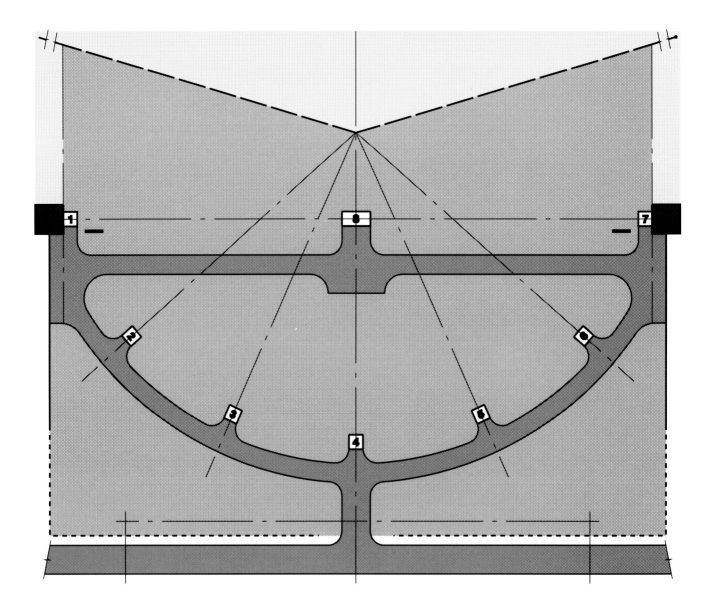

0 [========] 20

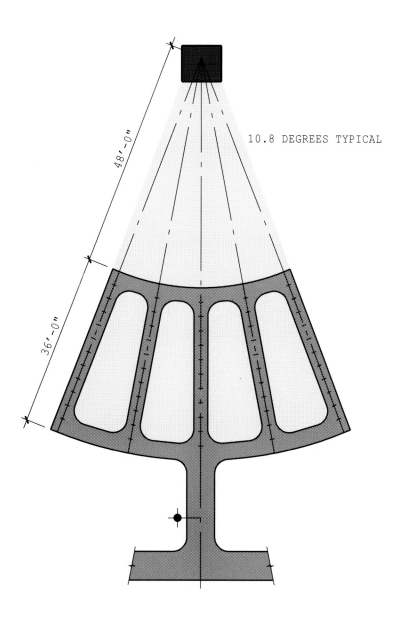

10.8 DEGREES TYPICAL

48'-0"

36'-0"

RANGE

COMBINATION AT 1" = 20'-0"   0 ⌷⌷⌷⌷⌷ 20

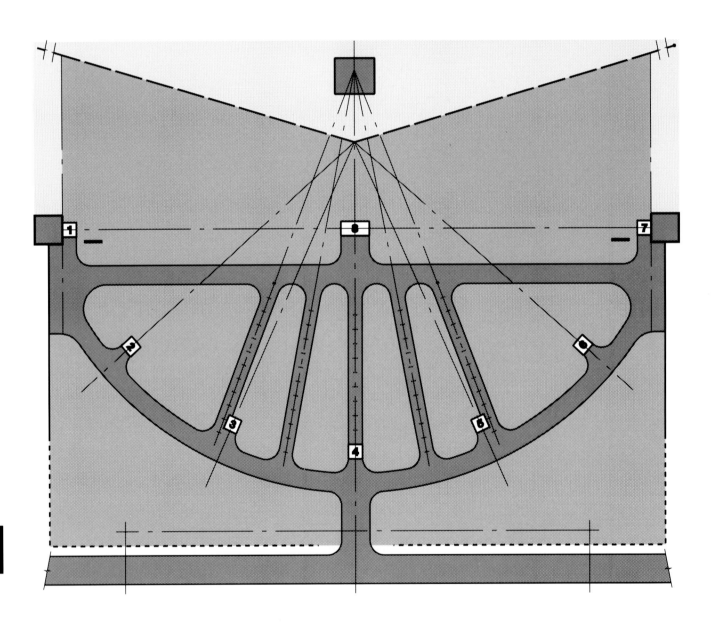

376

0 [_____] 30

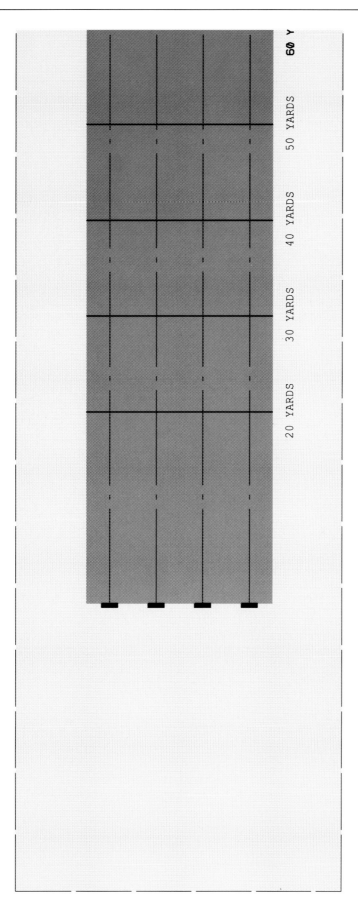

60 Y

50 YARDS

40 YARDS

30 YARDS

20 YARDS

RANGE AT 1" = 30'-0"

0 ▭ 30

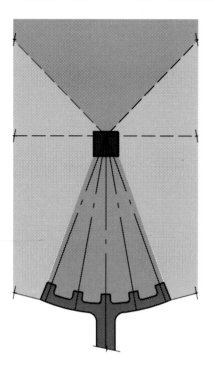

AUTOMATIC TRAP

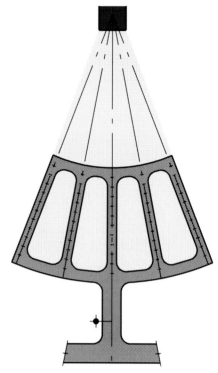

TRAP

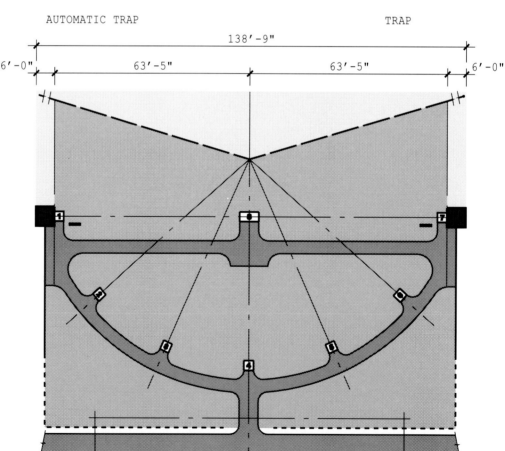

138'-9"

6'-0"　　63'-5"　　63'-5"　　6'-0"

SKEET

0 ▭ 30   COMBINATION RANGE AT 1" = 30'-0"

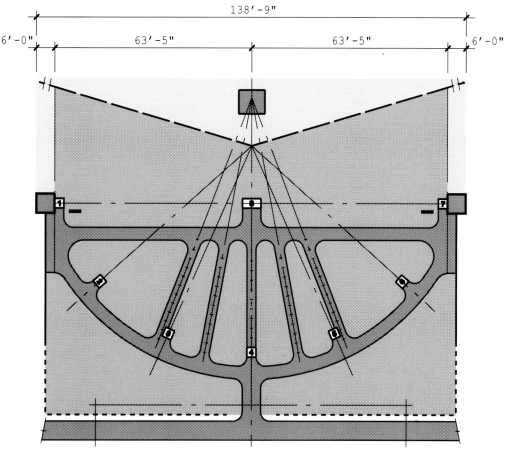

138'-9"

6'-0"   63'-5"   63'-5"   6'-0"

SEE TRAP AND SKEET
FOR INFIELD LAYOUT

ARCHERY AT 1" = 40'-0"   0 [========] 40

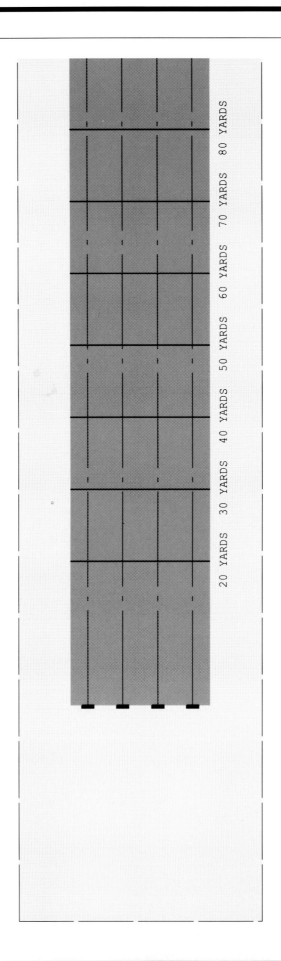

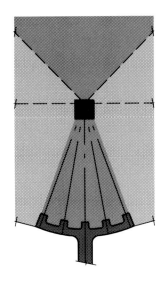

AUTOMATIC TRAP

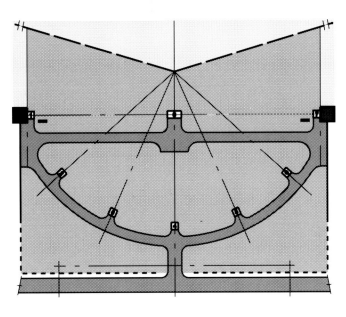

SKEET

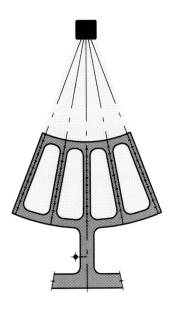

TRAP

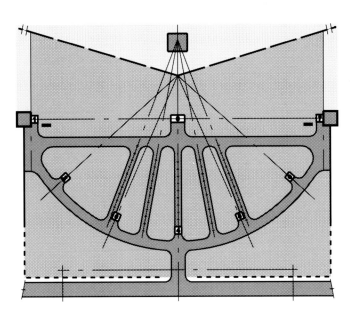

COMBINATION

ARCHERY RANGE AT 1" = 50'-0"

0 ⬜ 50

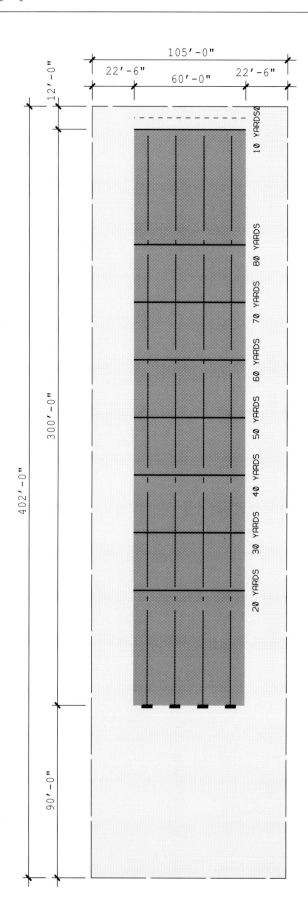

105'-0"

22'-6"   60'-0"   22'-6"

12'-0"

10 YARDS
80 YARDS
70 YARDS
60 YARDS
50 YARDS
40 YARDS
30 YARDS
20 YARDS

402'-0"

300'-0"

90'-0"

SHOOTING AREA
18,000 SQUARE FEET

SAFETY AREA
24,210 SQUARE FEET

TOTAL AREA REQUIRED
42,210 SQUARE FEET

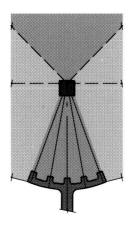

AUTOMATIC TRAP

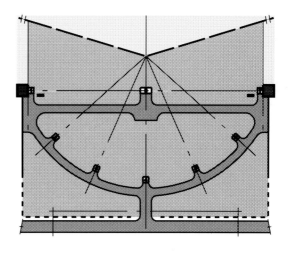

SKEET

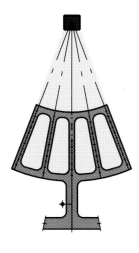

TRAP

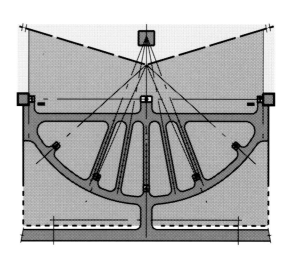

COMBINATION

RANGE AT 1" = 60'-0"

0 ⬜⬜⬜⬜ 6

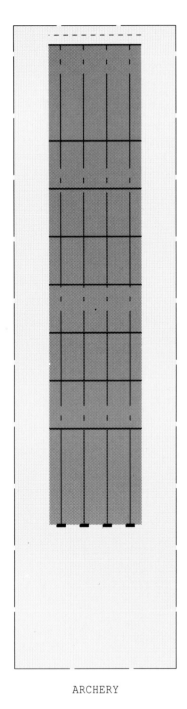

ARCHERY

AUTOMATIC TRAP

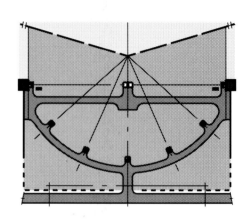

SKEET

TRAP

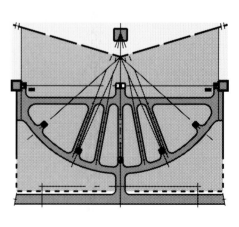

COMBINATION

0 [_____] 100

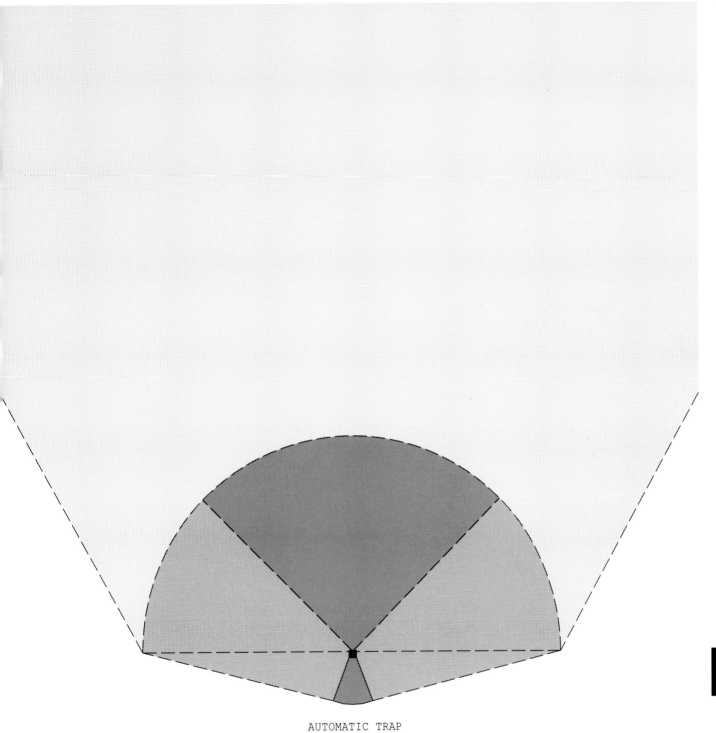

AUTOMATIC TRAP

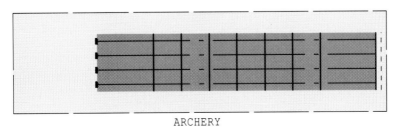

ARCHERY

SKEET AT 1" = 100'-0"

0 ☐☐☐☐☐☐☐☐☐☐ 100

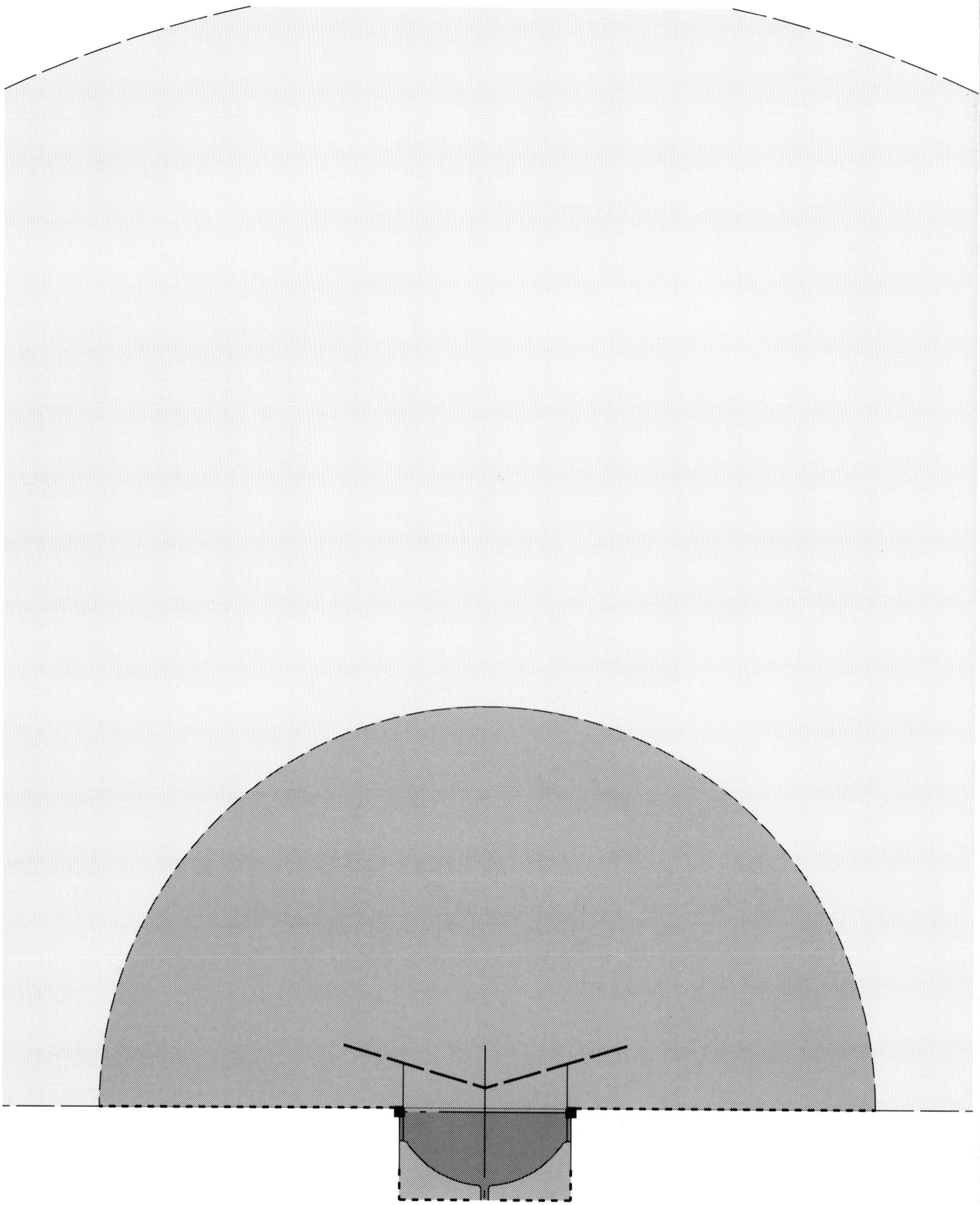

0 [   ] 100

COMBINATION AT 1" = 100'-0"

0 [======] 100

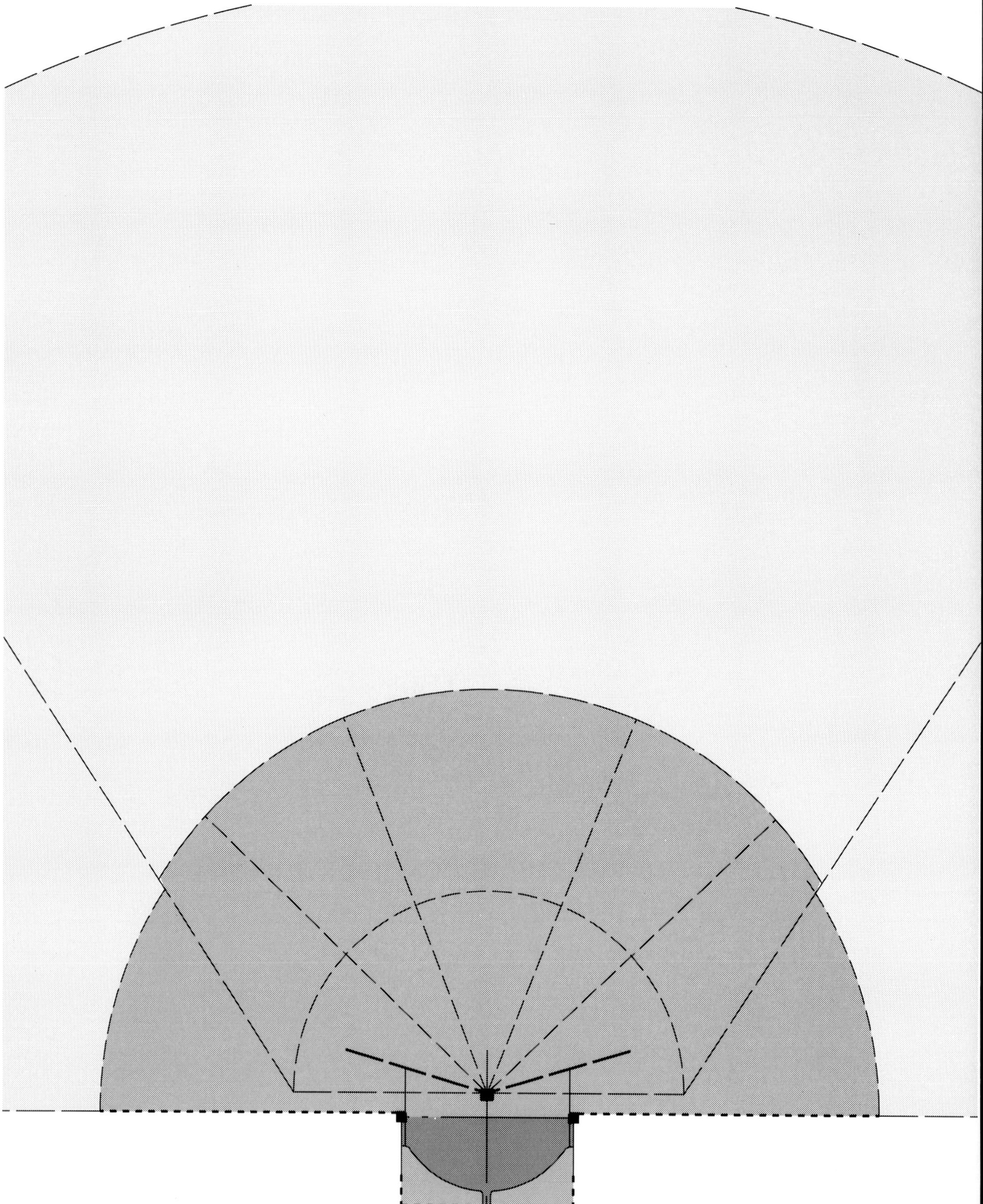

0 ☐▭▭▭▭ 200

RANGE AT 1" = 200'-0"

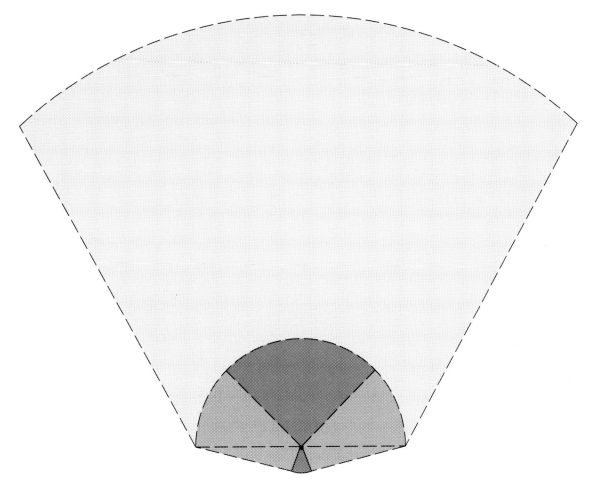

AUTOMATIC TRAP

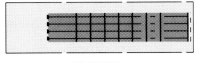

ARCHERY

SKEET AT 1" = 200'-0"

0 ▭ 200

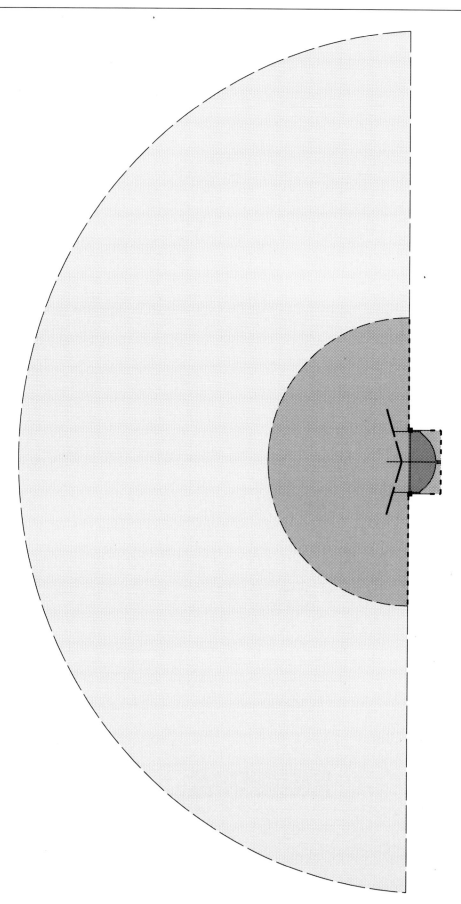

0 [========] 200

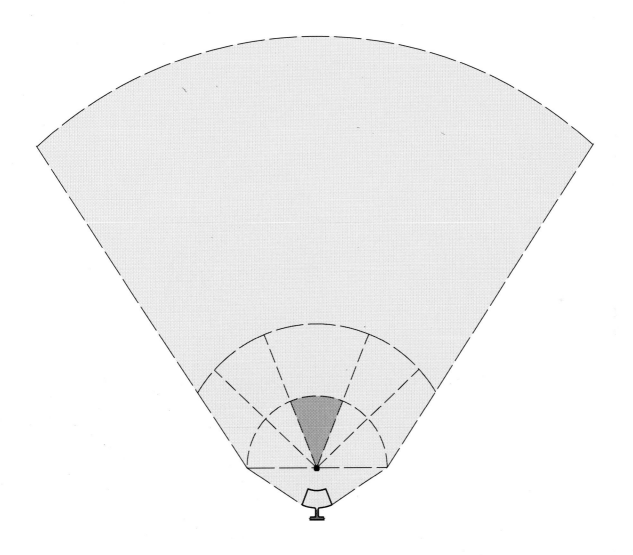

COMBINATION AT 1" = 200'-0"   0 ▭ 200

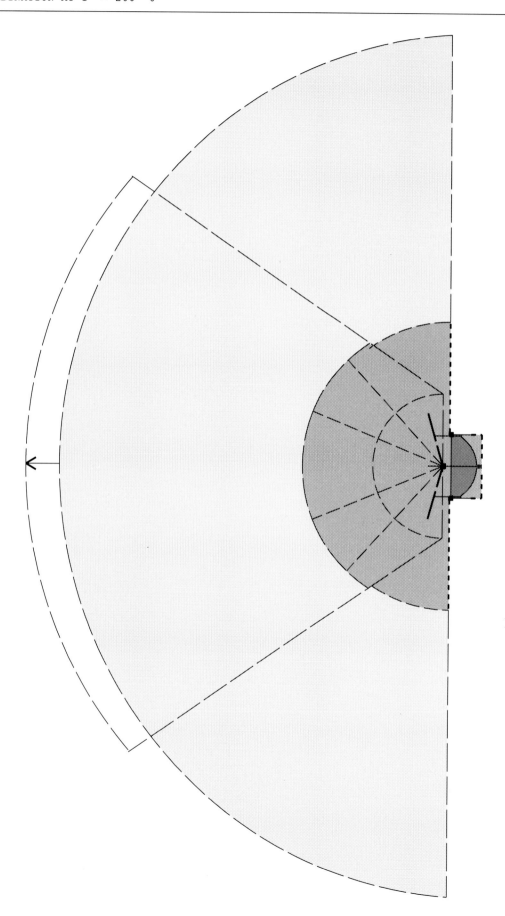

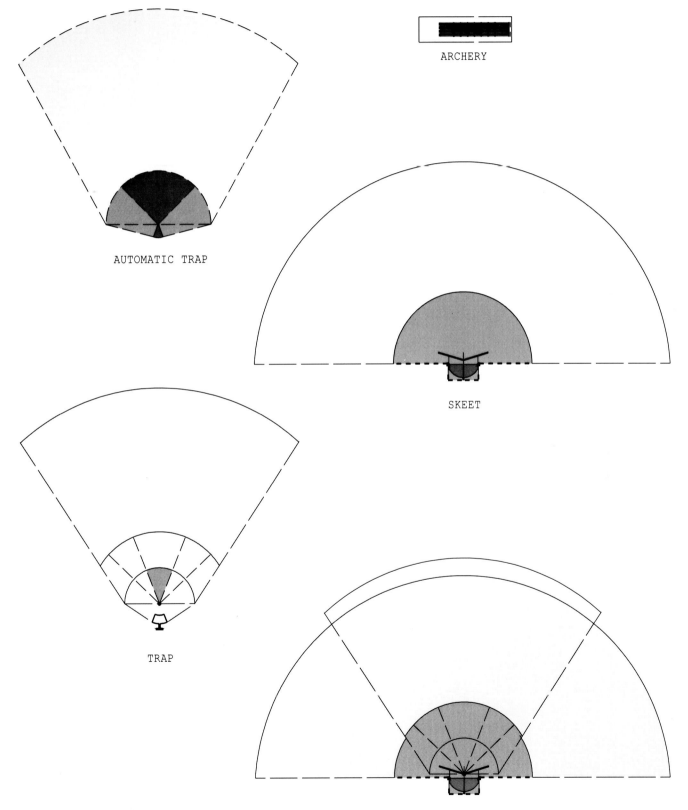

0 ▭ 400

RANGE AT 1" = 400'-0"

ARCHERY

AUTOMATIC TRAP

SKEET

TRAP

COMBINATION

RANGE AT 1" = 1,000'-0"   0 [_____] 1000

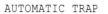

AUTOMATIC TRAP

SKEET

TRAP

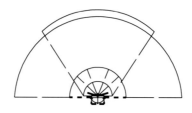

COMBINATION

0 ▭ 20

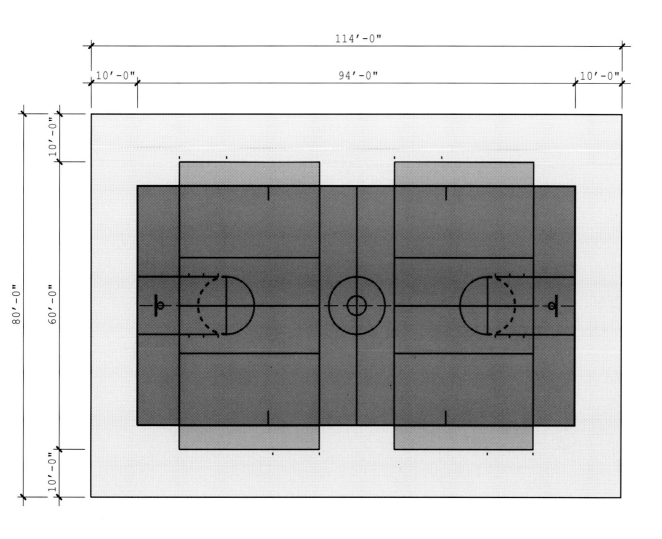

BASKETBALL/VOLLEYBALL

TOTAL AREA REQUIRED
9,120 SQUARE FEET

MULTIPLE COURTS AT 1" = 20'-0"   0 ⬛ 20

132'-0"

12'-0"   108'-0"   12'-0"

4'-0"

102'-0"

94'-0"

4'-0"

TENNIS VOLLEYBALL BASKETBALL
BADMINTON SHUFFLEBOARD

TOTAL AREA REQUIRED
13,464 SQUARE FEET

2 TENNIS COURTS AT 1" = 20'-0"

0 ▭ 20

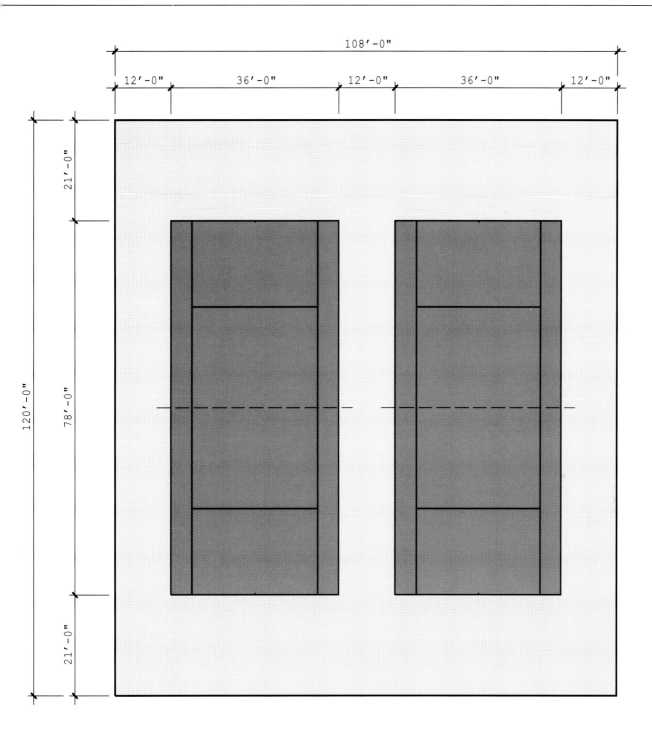

TOTAL AREA REQUIRED
12,960 SQUARE FEET

MULTIPLE COURTS AT 1" = 30'-0"   0 [   ] 30

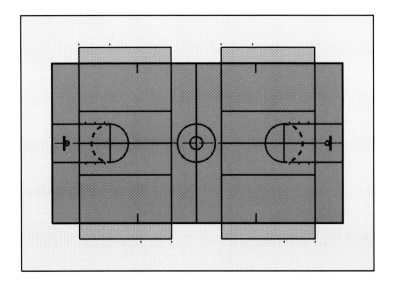

BASKETBALL AND VOLLEYBALL

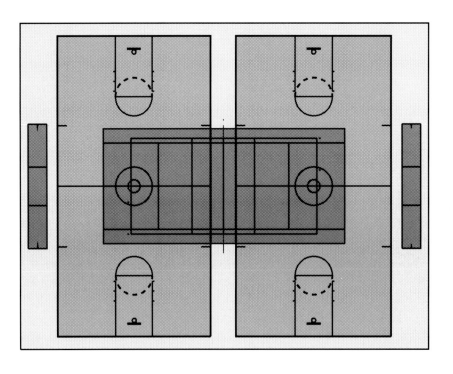

TENNIS, VOLLEYBALL, BASKETBALL
BADMINTON AND SHUFFLEBOARD

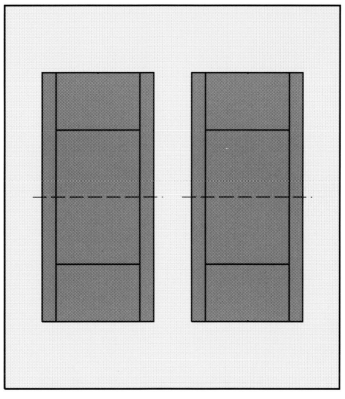

2 TENNIS COURTS

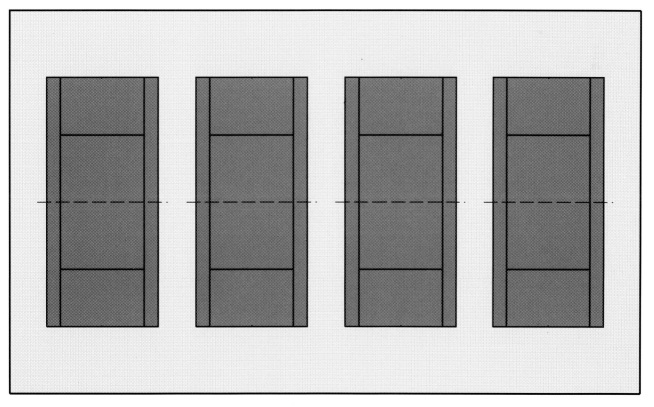

4 TENNIS COURT

MULTIPLE COURTS AT 1" = 40'-0"   0 ▭ 40

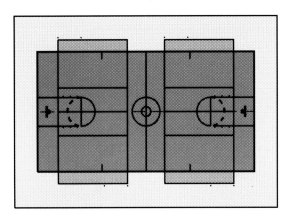

BASKETBALL AND VOLLEYBALL

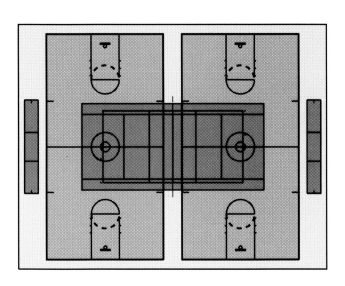

TENNIS, VOLLEYBALL, BASKETBALL
BADMINTON AND SHUFFLEBOARD

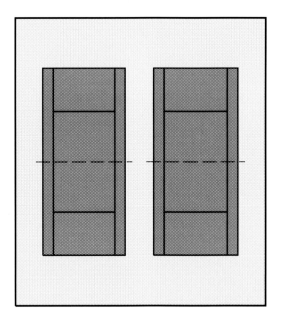

2 TENNIS COURTS

0 [   ] 40

4 TENNIS COURTS AT 1" = 40'-0"

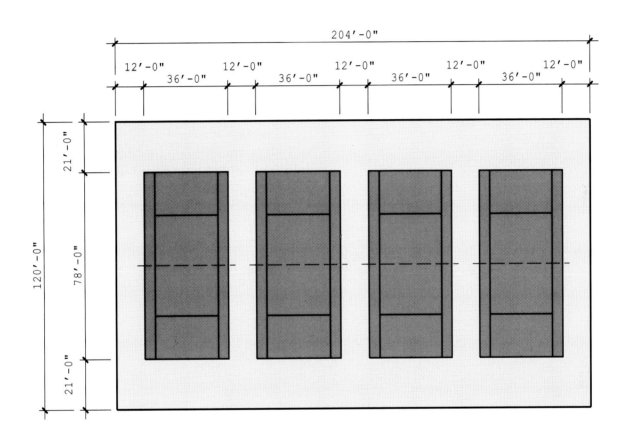

204'-0"

12'-0" 36'-0" 12'-0" 36'-0" 12'-0" 36'-0" 12'-0" 36'-0" 12'-0"

120'-0" 21'-0" 78'-0" 21'-0"

TOTAL AREA REQUIRED
24,480 SQUARE FEET

MULTIPLE COURTS AT 1" = 50'-0"   0 ▭ 50

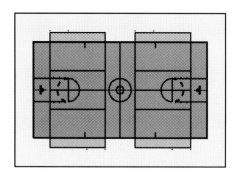

BASKETBALL AND VOLLEYBALL

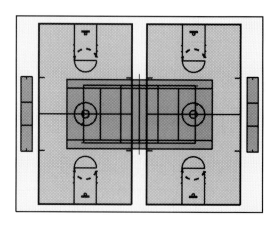

TENNIS, VOLLEYBALL, BASKETBALL
BADMINTON AND SHUFFLEBOARD

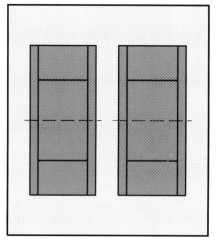

2 TENNIS COURTS

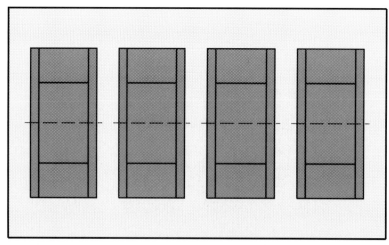

4 TENNIS COURTS

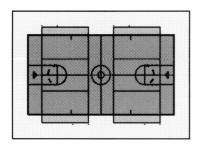

BASKETBALL AND VOLLEYBALL

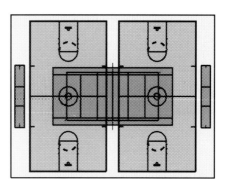

TENNIS, VOLLEYBALL, BASKETBALL
BADMINTON AND SHUFFLEBOARD

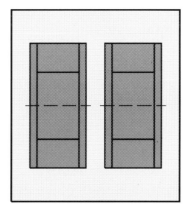

2 TENNIS COURTS

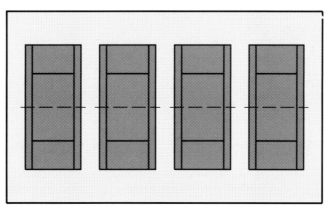

4 TENNIS COURTS

MULTIPLE COURTS AT 1" = 100'-0"

0 ⬜⬜⬜⬜ 100

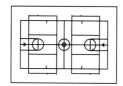

BASKETBALL AND VOLLEYBALL

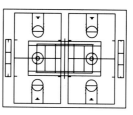

TENNIS, VOLLEYBALL, BASKETBALL
BADMINTON AND SHUFFLEBOARD

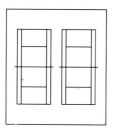

2 TENNIS COURTS

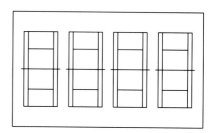

4 TENNIS COURTS

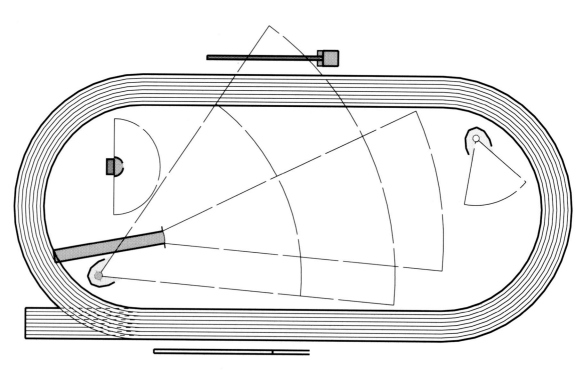

1/4 MILE TRACK

0 ⬜ 100

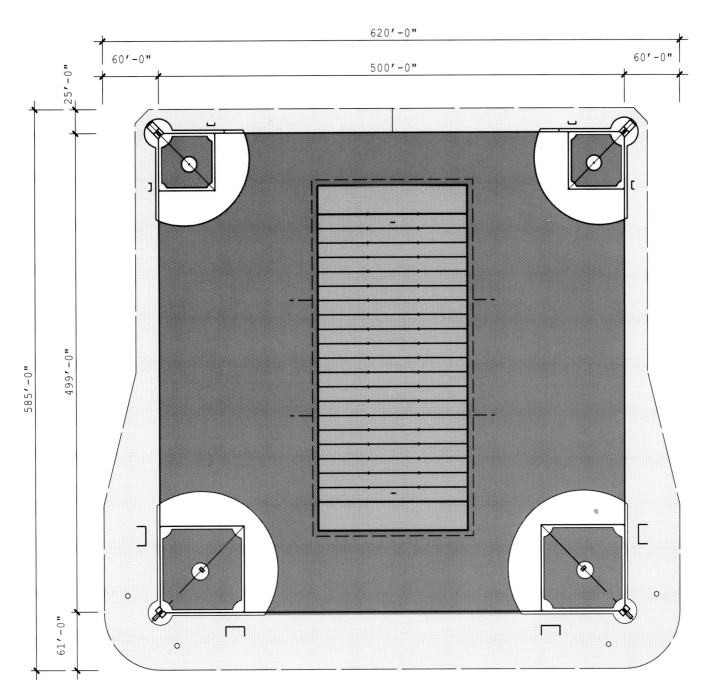

620'-0"

60'-0"

500'-0"

60'-0"

25'-0"

585'-0"

499'-0"

61'-0"

2 BASEBALL, 2 SOFTBALL
AND 1 FOOTBALL FIELD

4 BASEBALL FIELDS AT 1" = 100'-0"

0 ⬛▭ 100

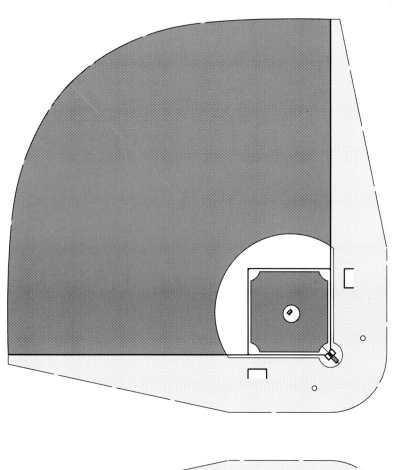
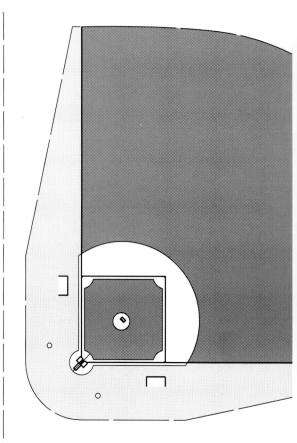
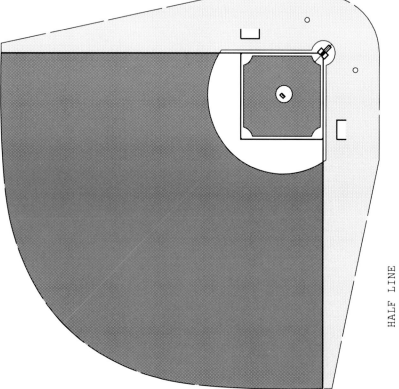
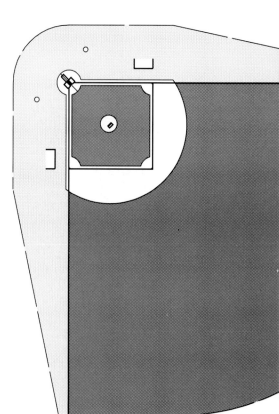

HALF LINE

0 [=========] 100

HALF LINE

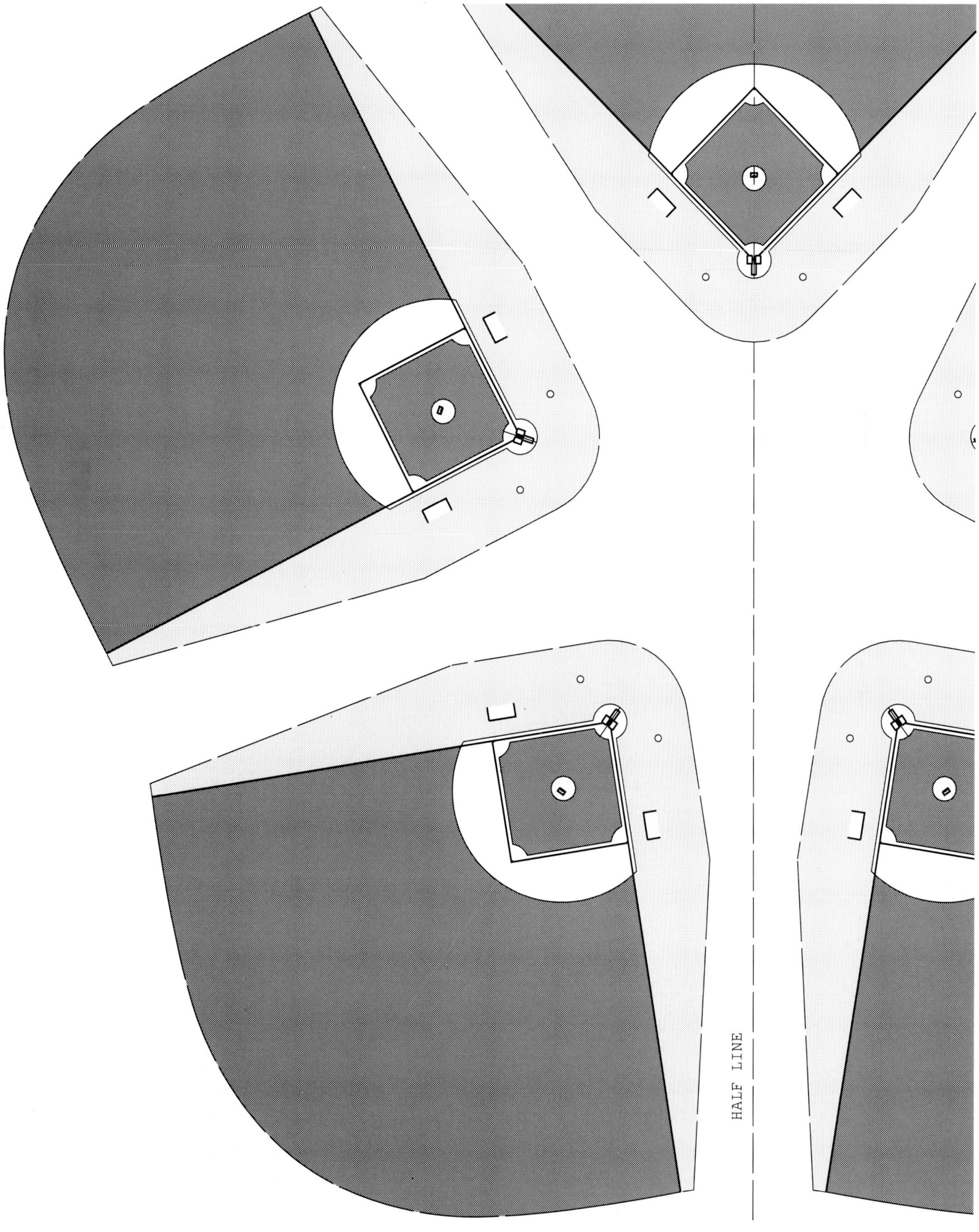

MULTIPLE COURTS AND FIELDS AT 1" = 200'-0"   0 ▭▭▭▭▭ 200

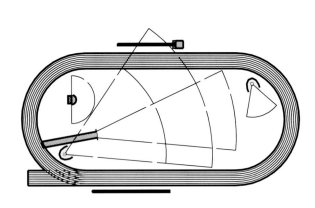

1/4 MILE TRACK

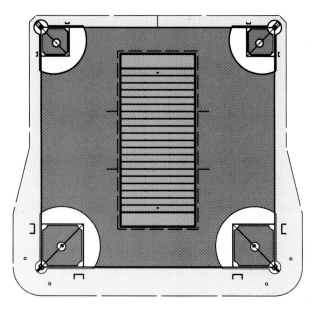

BASEBALL, SOFTBALL
AND FOOTBALL

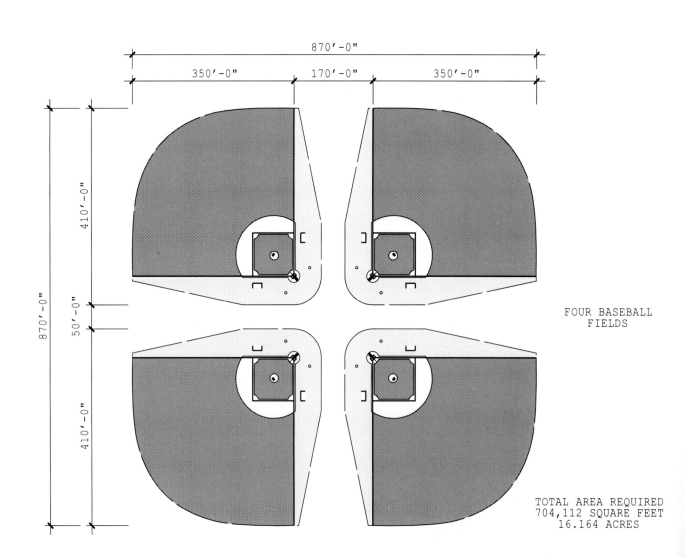

870'-0"

350'-0"   170'-0"   350'-0"

410'-0"

870'-0"

50'-0"

410'-0"

FOUR BASEBALL
FIELDS

TOTAL AREA REQUIRED
704,112 SQUARE FEET
16.164 ACRES

0 ▭ 200

5 BASEBALL FIELDS AT 1" = 200'-0"

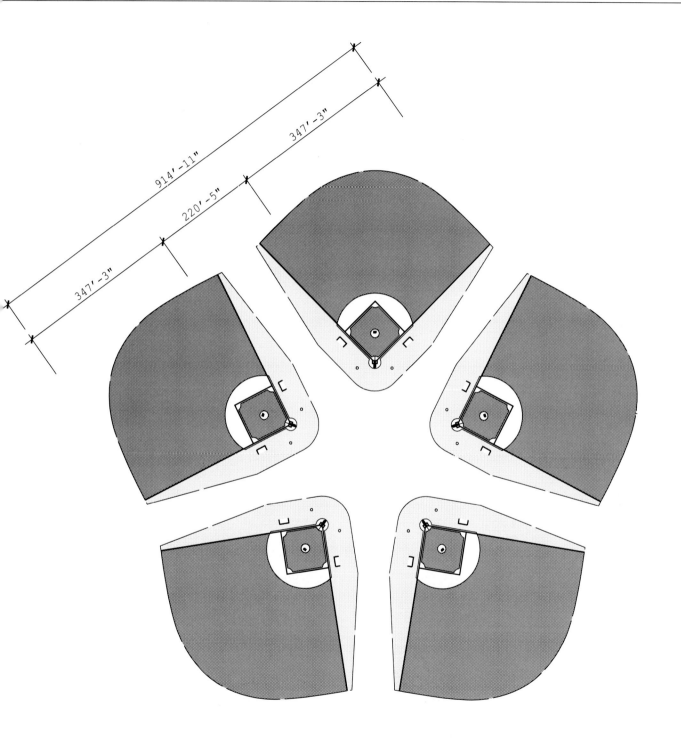

347'-3"

914'-11"

220'-5"

347'-3"

TOTAL AREA REQUIRED
916,730 SQUARE FEET
21.04 ACRES

MULTIPLE FIELDS AT 1" = 400'-0"   0 ▭ 400

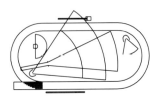

1/4 MILE TRACK

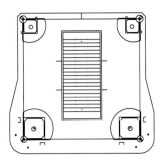

BASEBALL, SOFTBALL
AND FOOTBALL

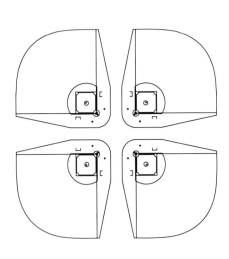

FOUR BASEBALL
FIELDS

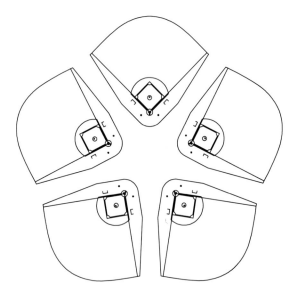

FIVE BASEBALL
FIELDS

0 ▭ 16

SIDE

PLAN

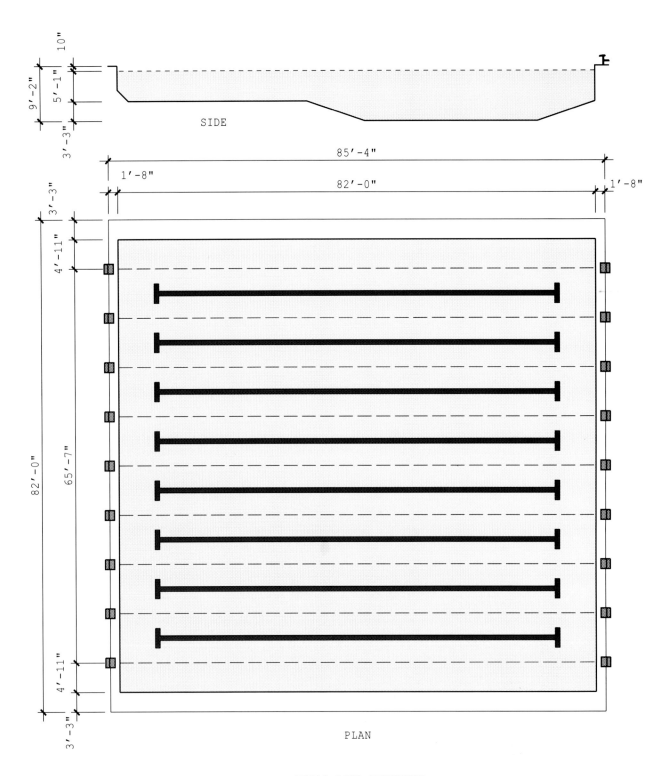

SIDE

PLAN

TOTAL AREA REQUIRED
6,996 SQUARE FEET

0 16

DIVING POOL AT 1/16" = 1′-0"

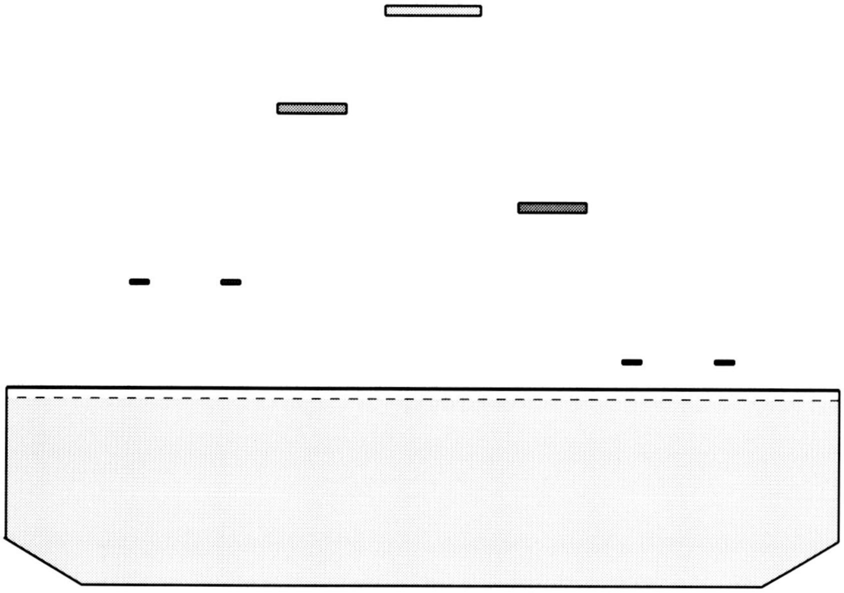

FRONT SECTION

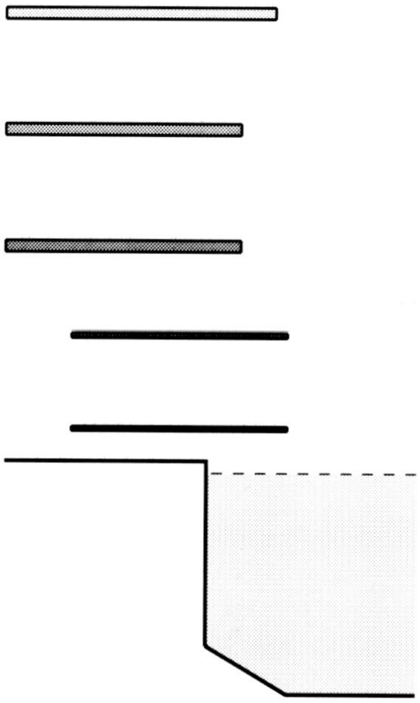

SIDE SECTION

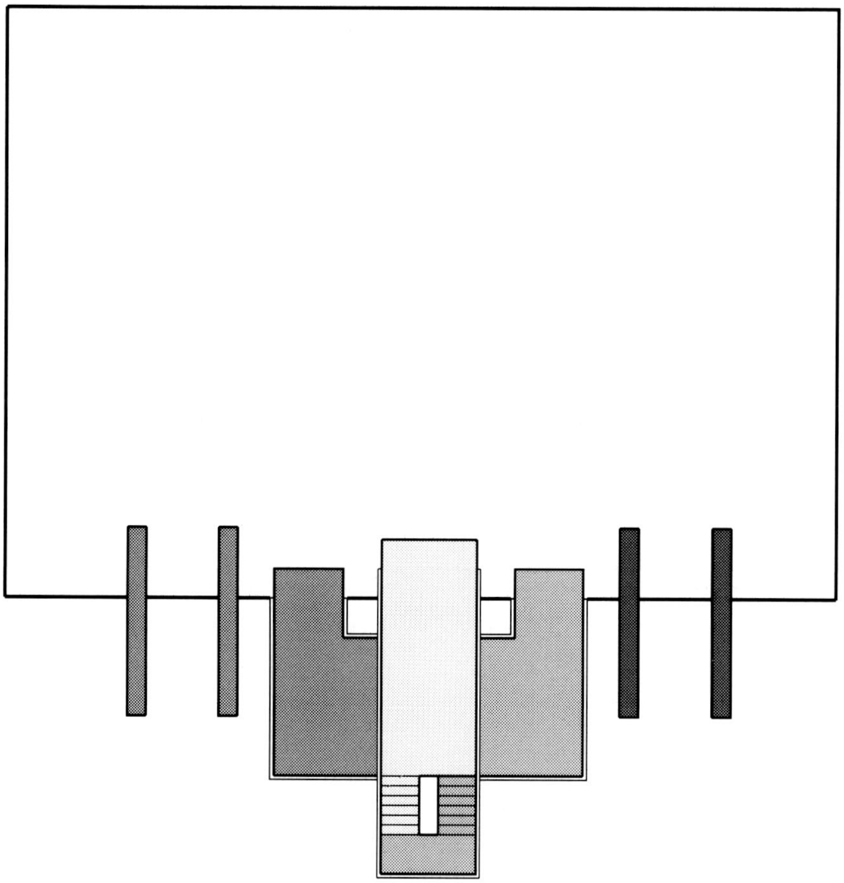

PLAN

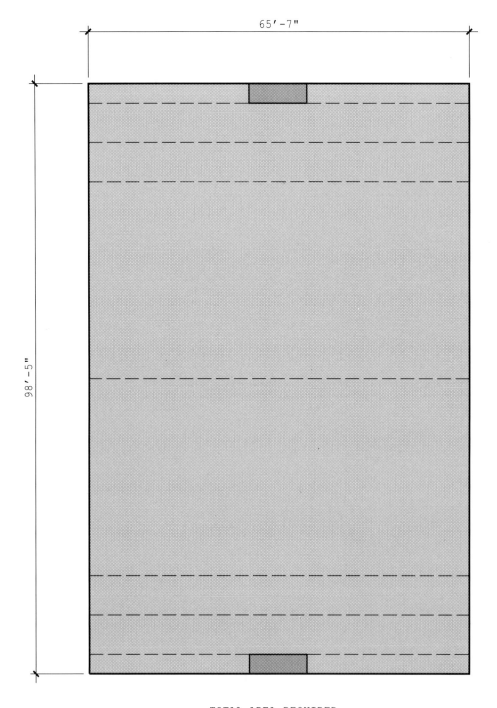

65'-7"

98'-5"

TOTAL AREA REQUIRED
6,458 SQUARE FEET

0 ▭ 16

HOCKEY AT 1/16" = 1'-0"

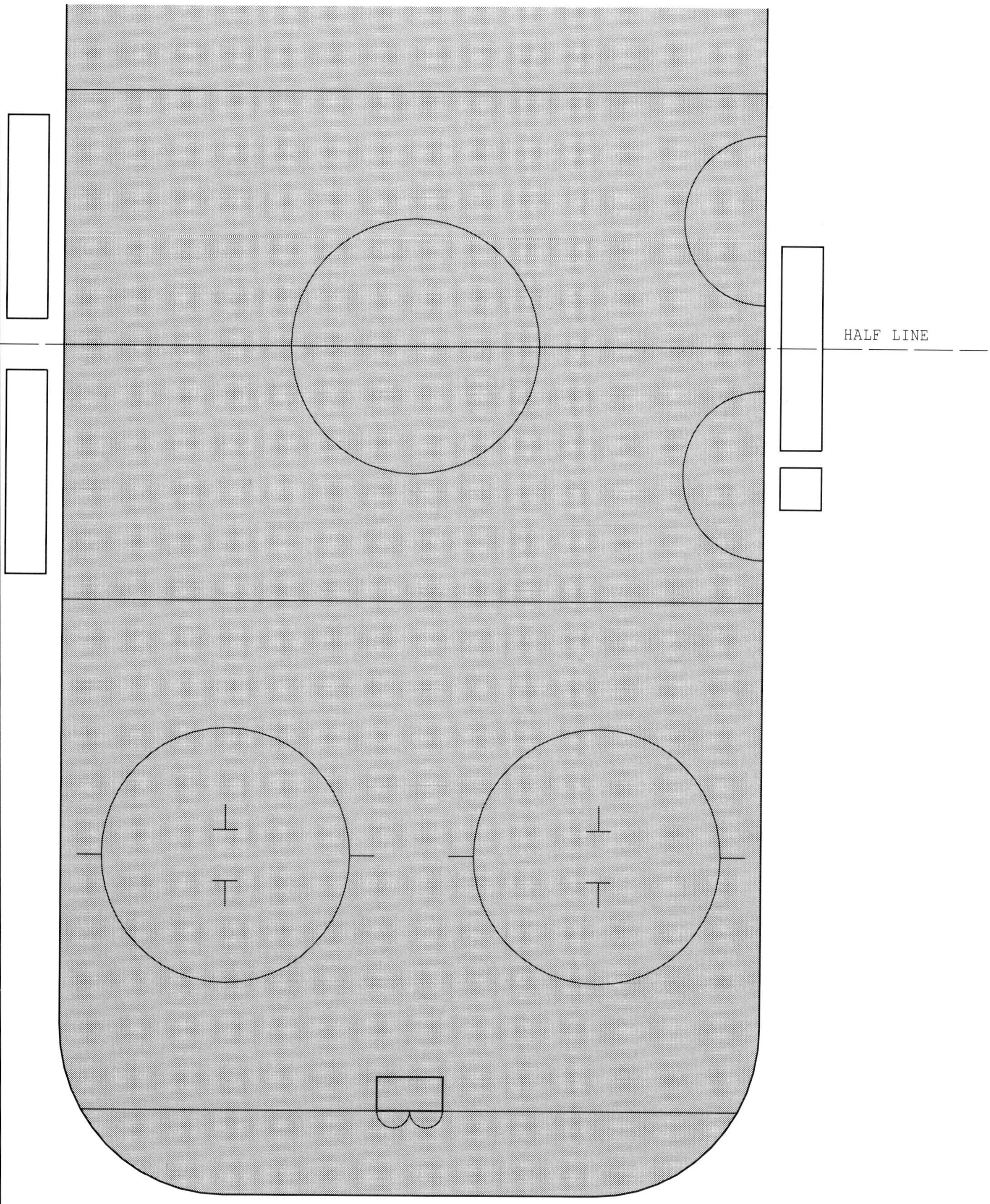

HALF LINE

50 METER POOL AT 1" = 20'-0"   0 [========] 20

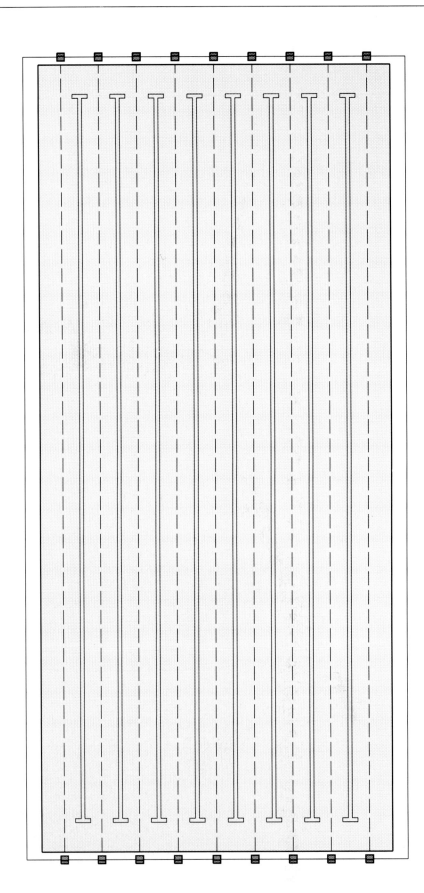

0 [   ] 20   25 METER AND WATER POLO POOL AT 1" = 20'-0"

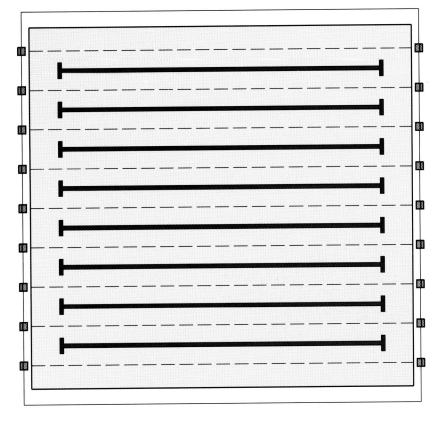

25 METER
POOL

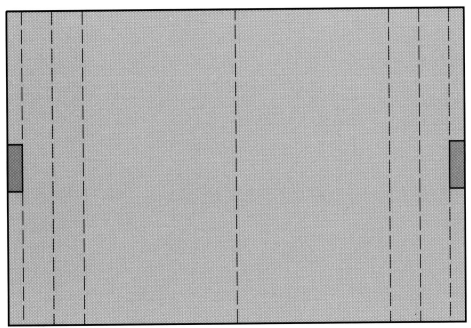

WATER POLO

DIVING POOL AT 1" = 20'-0"   0 ▭ 20

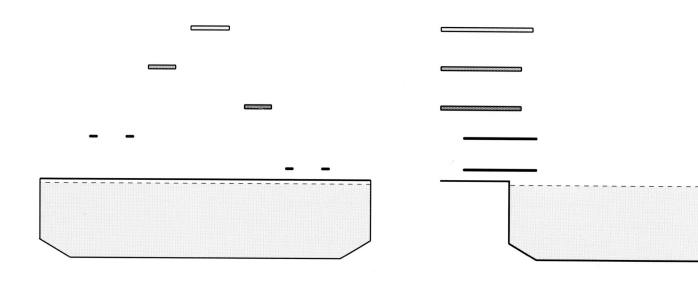

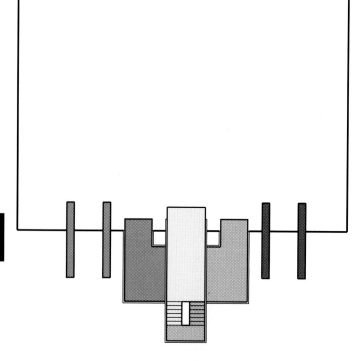

HALF LINE

50 METER POOL AT 1" = 30'-0"   0 ▭ 30

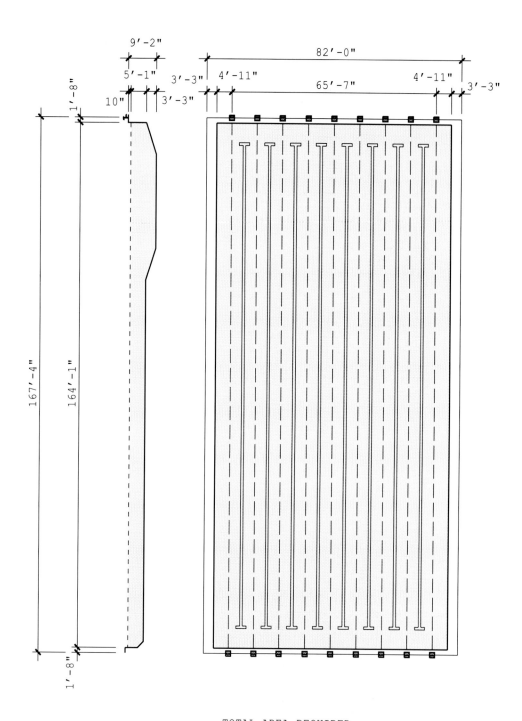

TOTAL AREA REQUIRED
13,723 SQUARE FEET

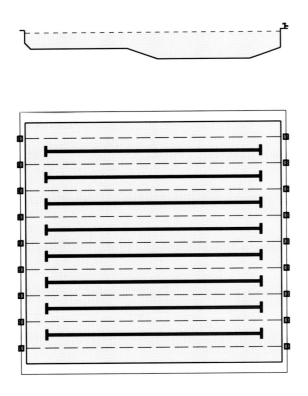

25 METER
POOL

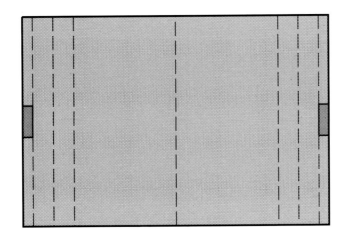

WATER POLO

POOLS

0 ⬜ 30

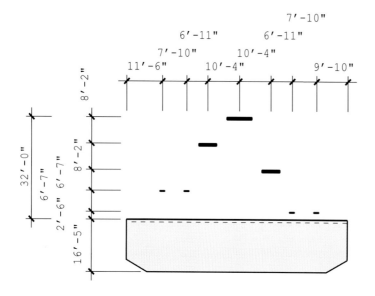

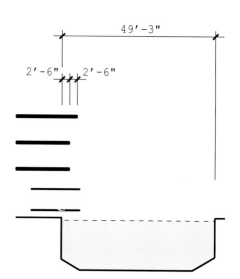

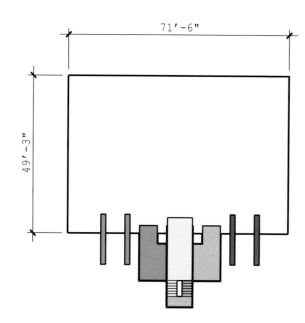

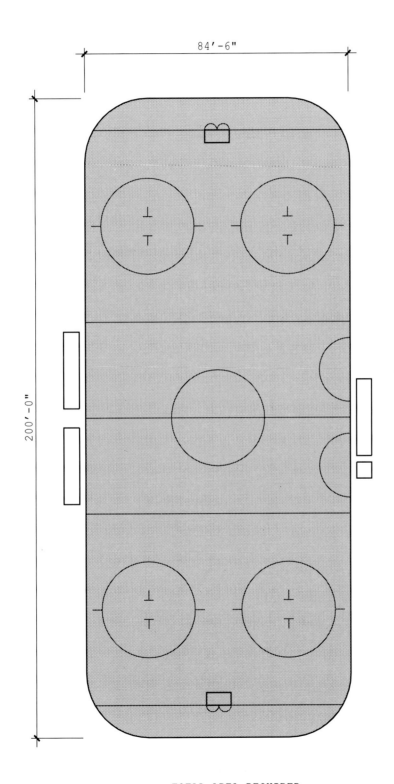

84'-6"

200'-0"

TOTAL AREA REQUIRED
16,631 SQUARE FEET

POOLS AT 1" = 40'-0"   0 [========] 40

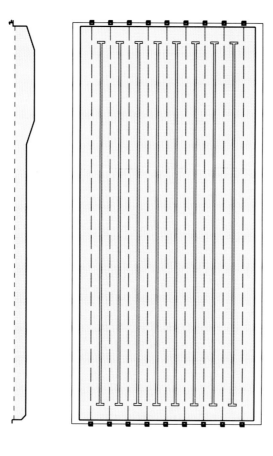

50 METER POOL

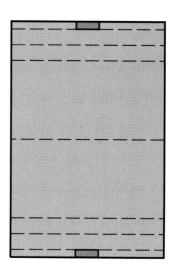

WATER POLO

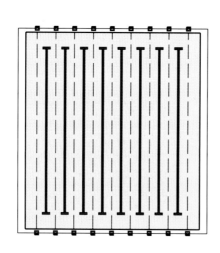

25 METER POOL

POOLS AT 1" = 40'-0"

0 [   ] 40

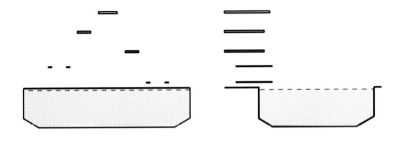

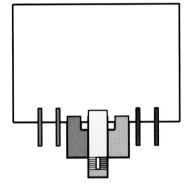

DIVING

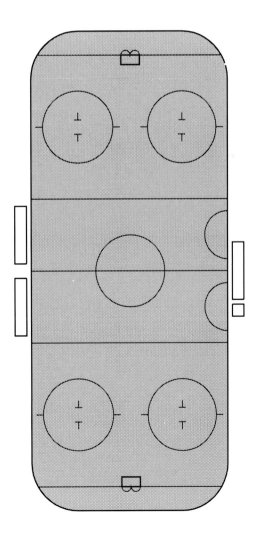

HOCKEY

0 ▭ 50

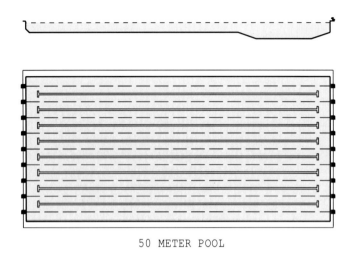

50 METER POOL

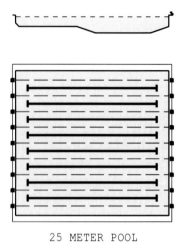

25 METER POOL

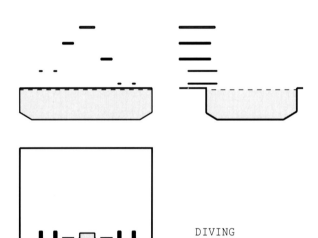

DIVING

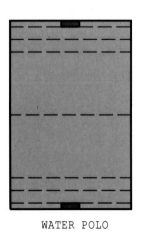

WATER POLO

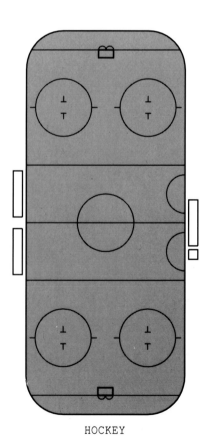

HOCKEY

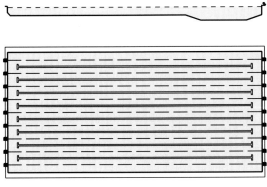

50 METER POOL

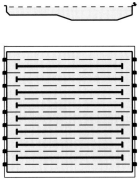

25 METER POOL

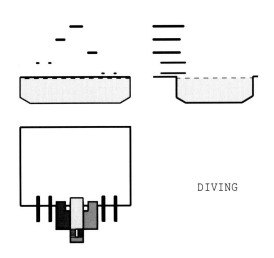

DIVING

WATER POLO

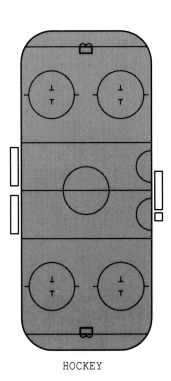

HOCKEY

427

POOLS AT 1" = 100'-0"   0 ⬜⬜⬜⬜⬜ 10

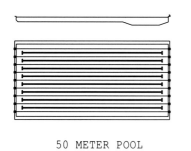

50 METER POOL

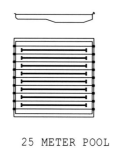

25 METER POOL

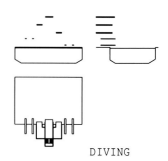

DIVING

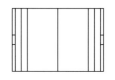

WATER POLO

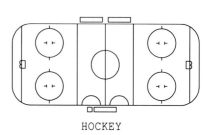

HOCKEY

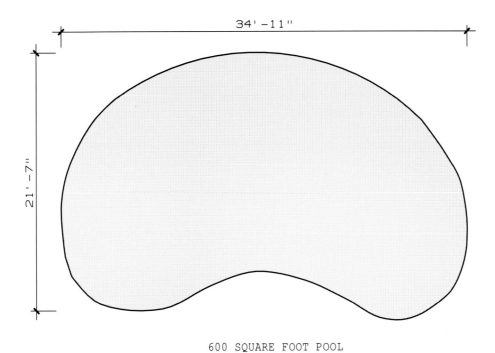

34'-11"

21'-7"

600 SQUARE FOOT POOL

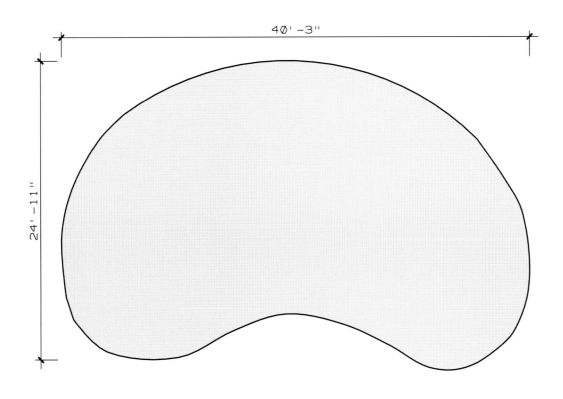

40'-3"

24'-11"

800 SQUARE FOOT POOL

KIDNEY SHAPED POOLS AT 1/8" = 1'-0"   0 ☐☐☐☐☐☐☐☐ 8

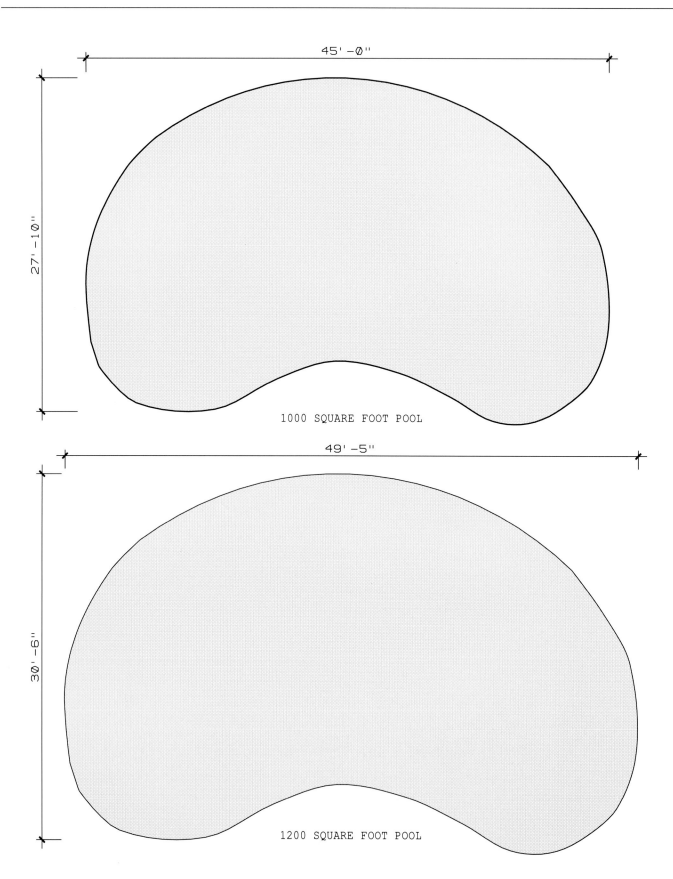

45'-Ø"

27'-1Ø"

1000 SQUARE FOOT POOL

49'-5"

3Ø'-6"

1200 SQUARE FOOT POOL

0 8 POOLS AT 1/8" = 1′-0"

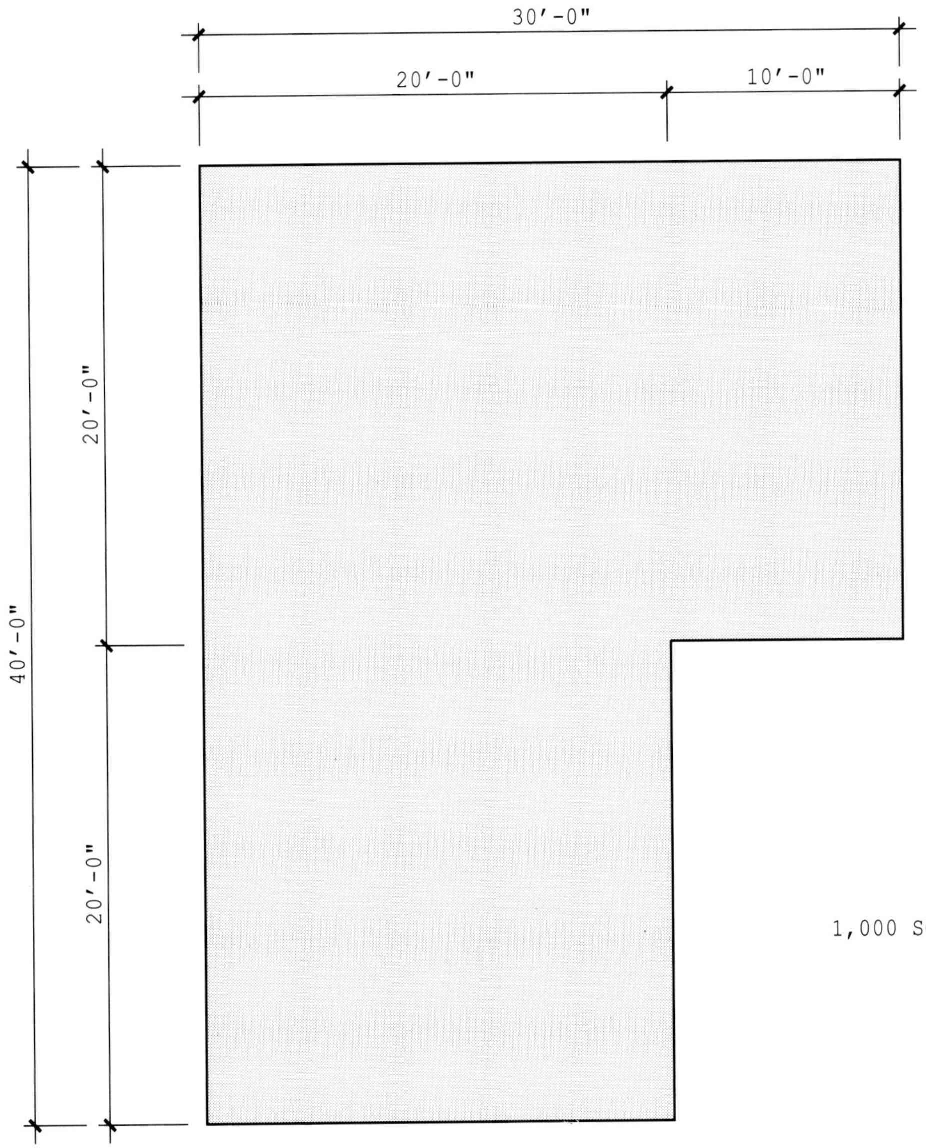
30′-0"
20′-0"
10′-0"
40′-0"
20′-0"
20′-0"

1,000 SQUARE FEET

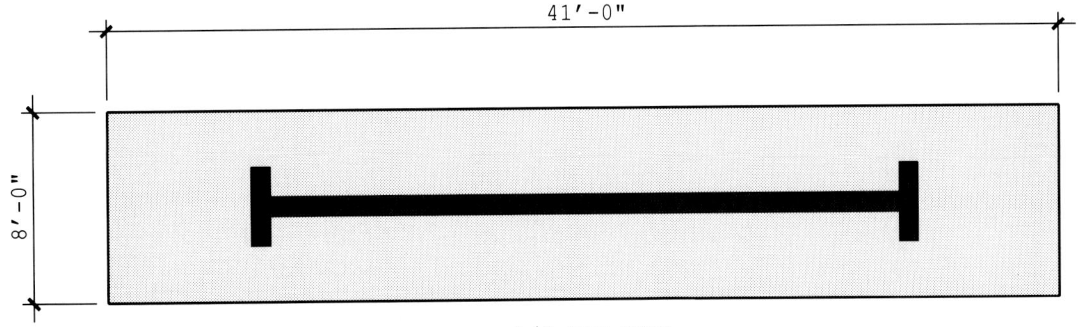
41′-0"
8′-0"

1/4 LAP POOL

328 SQUARE FEET

POOLS AT 1/8" = 1'-0"

0   8

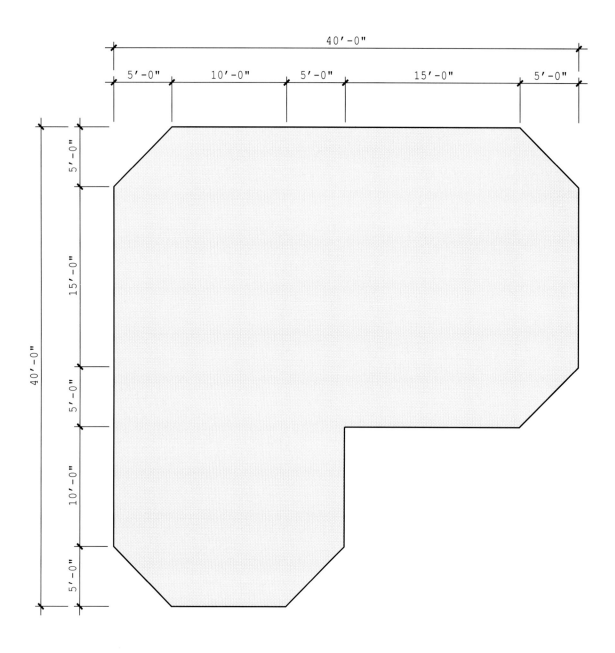

1,237 SQUARE FEET

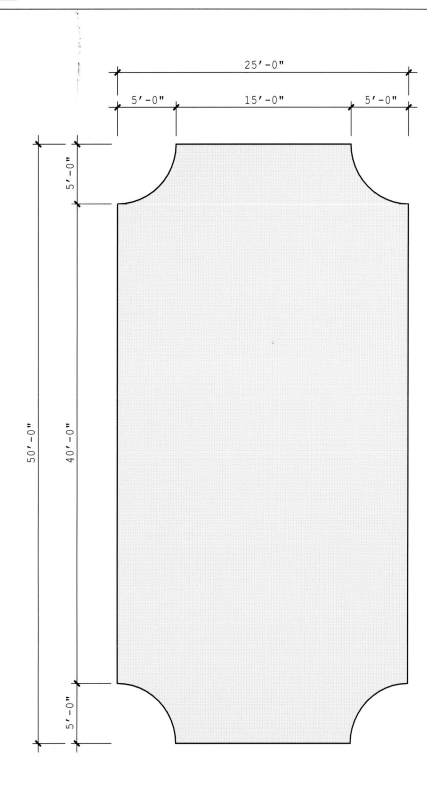

25'-0"

5'-0"   15'-0"   5'-0"

5'-0"

50'-0"   40'-0"

5'-0"

1,171 SQUARE FEET

RESIDENTIAL POOLS AT 1" = 10'-0"   0 ▭ 10

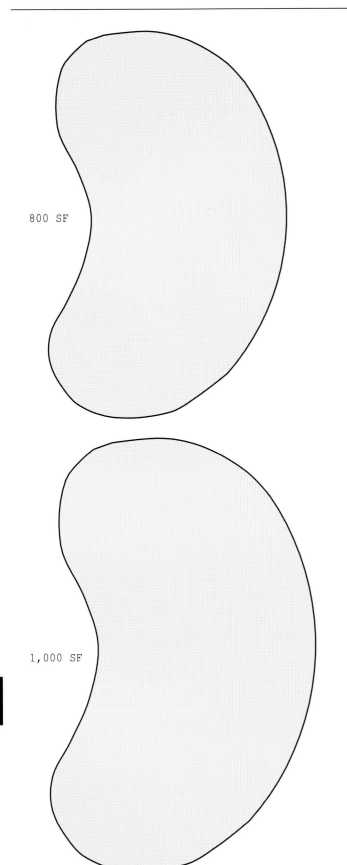

800 SF

1,000 SF

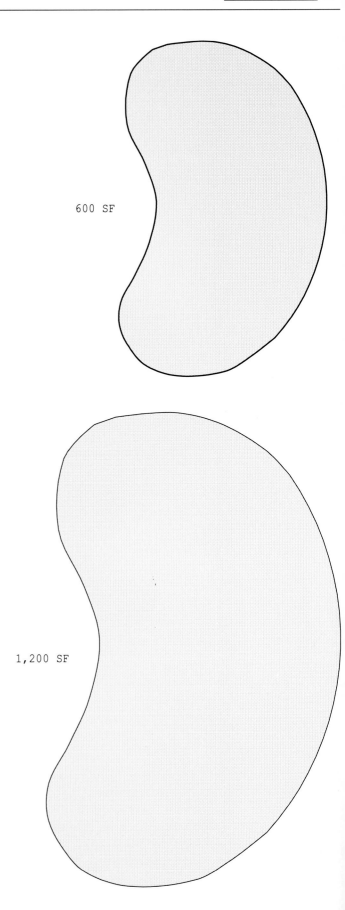

600 SF

1,200 SF

1,000 SQUARE FEET

1,237 SQUARE FEET

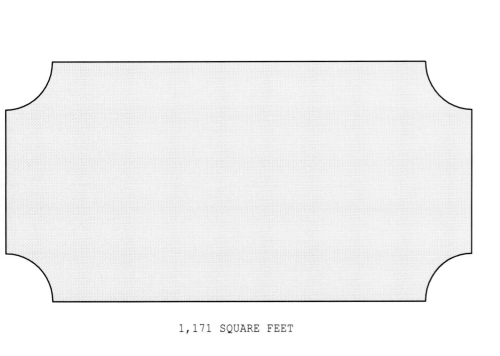

1,171 SQUARE FEET

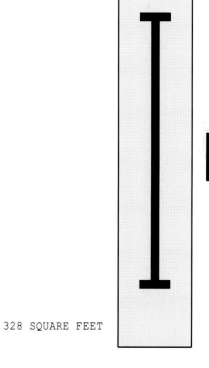

328 SQUARE FEET

LAP POOL AT 1" = 10'-0"   0 ▭ 10

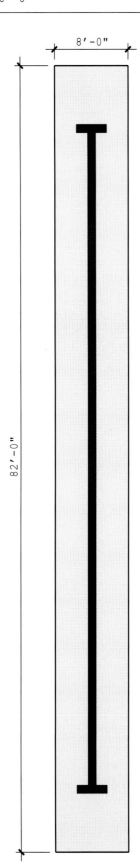

8'-0"

82'-0"

656 SQUARE FEET

0 ⬜ 8

800 SF

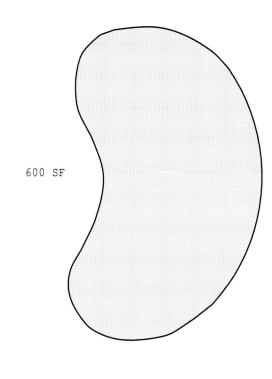

600 SF

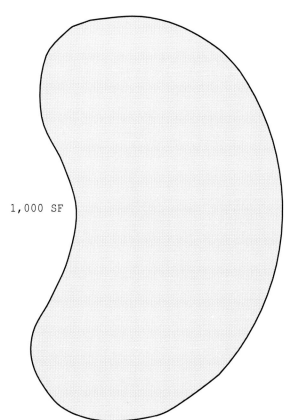

1,000 SF

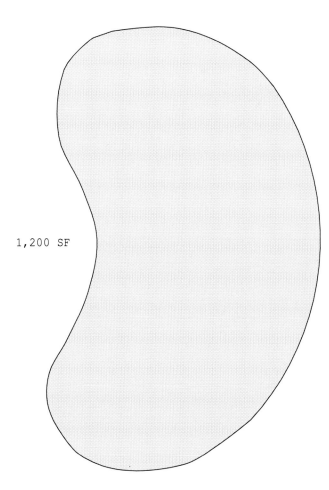

1,200 SF

437

POOLS AT 3/32" = 1'-0"   0 ▭ 8

656 SQUARE FEET

1,000 SQUARE FEET

1,171 SQUARE FEET

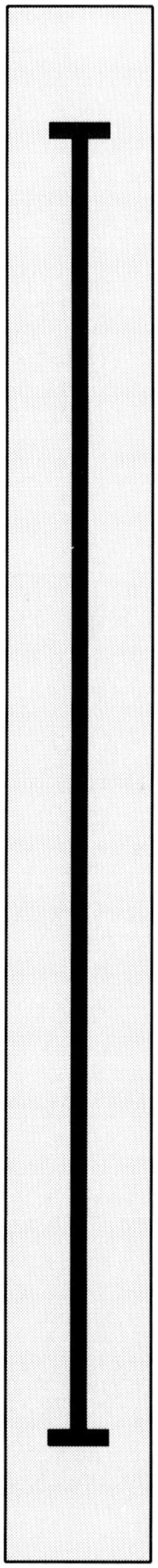

1,237 SQUARE FEET

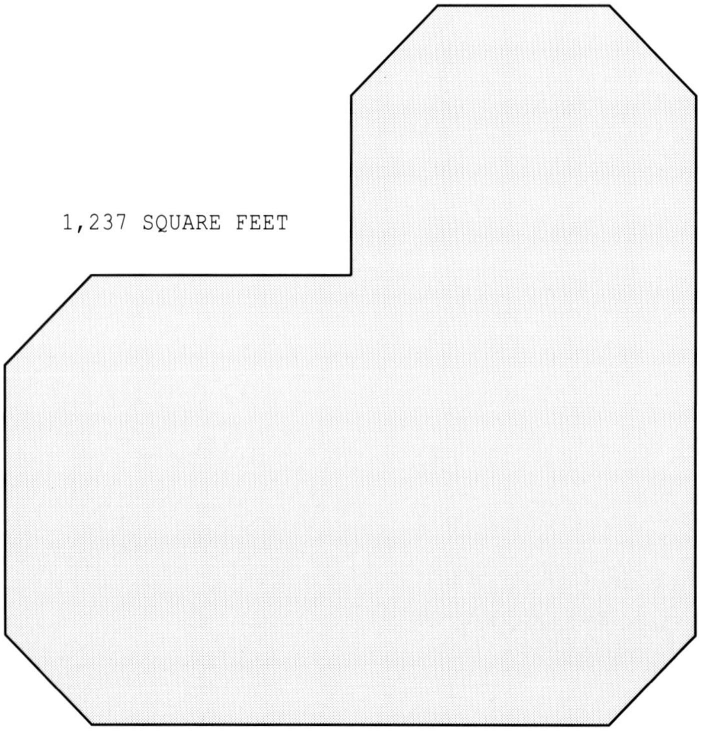

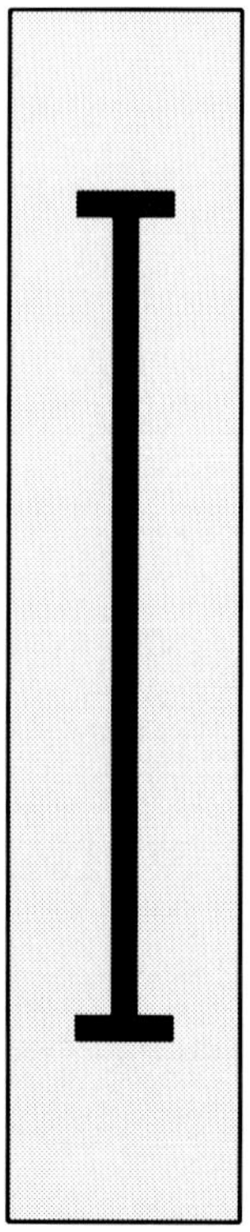

328 SQUARE FEET

0 ⊏———⊐ 16

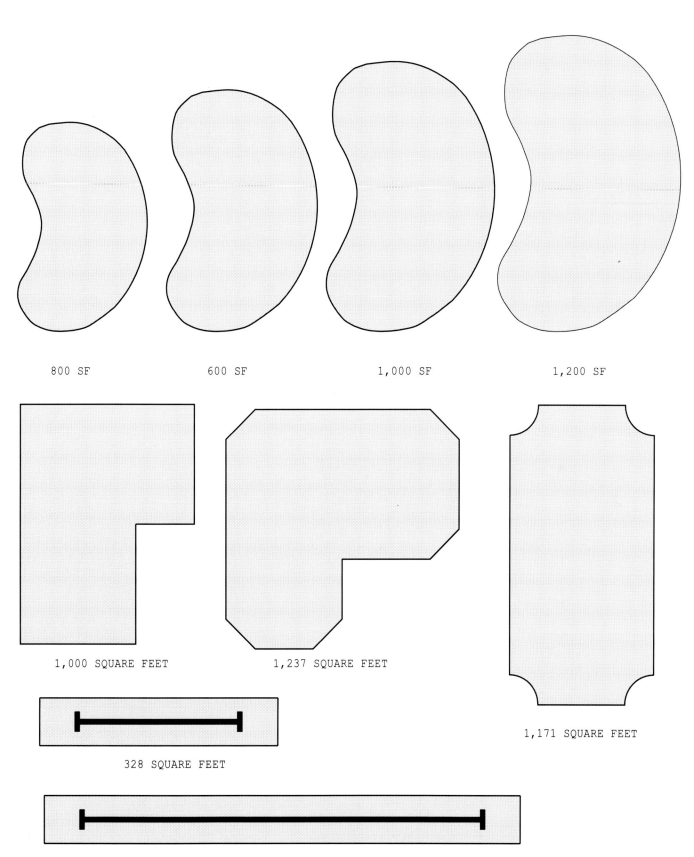

800 SF

600 SF

1,000 SF

1,200 SF

1,000 SQUARE FEET

1,237 SQUARE FEET

1,171 SQUARE FEET

328 SQUARE FEET

656 SQUARE FEET

POOLS AT 1" = 20'-0"   0 ▭ 2

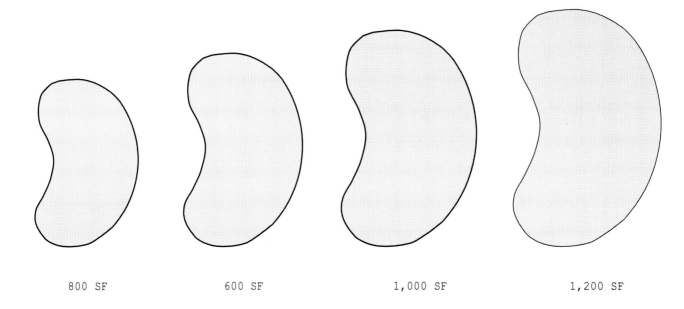

800 SF   600 SF   1,000 SF   1,200 SF

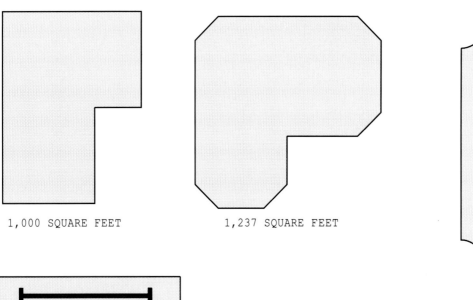

1,000 SQUARE FEET   1,237 SQUARE FEET

328 SQUARE FEET

328 SQUARE FEET

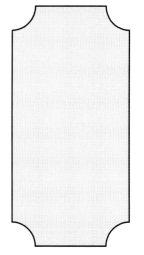

1,171 SQUARE FEET

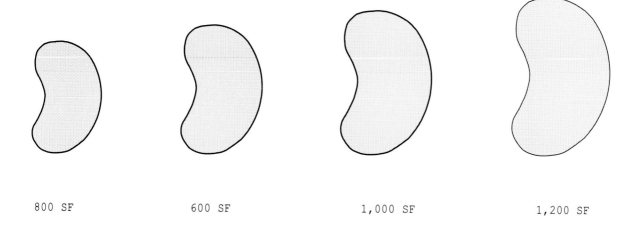

800 SF 600 SF 1,000 SF 1,200 SF

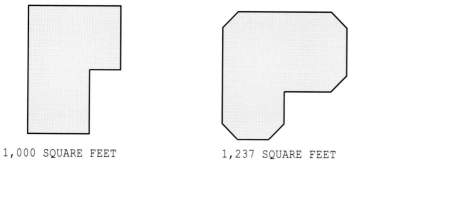

1,000 SQUARE FEET 1,237 SQUARE FEET

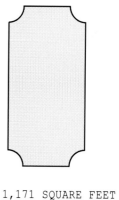

1,171 SQUARE FEET

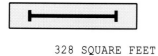

328 SQUARE FEET

328 SQUARE FEET

POOLS AT 1" = 40'-0"   0 ▭ 40

800 SF

600 SF

1,000 SF

1,200 SF

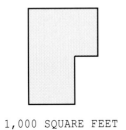

1,000 SQUARE FEET

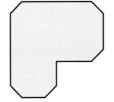

1,237 SQUARE FEET

1,171 SQUARE FEET

328 SQUARE FEET

328 SQUARE FEET

0 ▭ 4 SLIDE AT 1/4" = 1'-0"

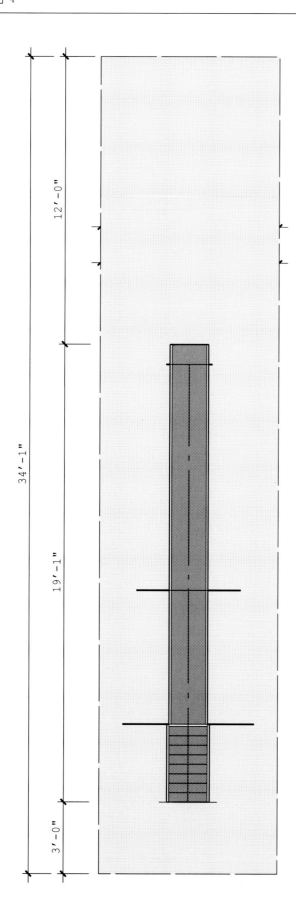

12'-0"

34'-1"

19'-1"

3'-0"

TOTAL AREA REQUIRED
261 SQUARE FEET

SWING AT 1/4" = 1'-0"

0 ▭ 4

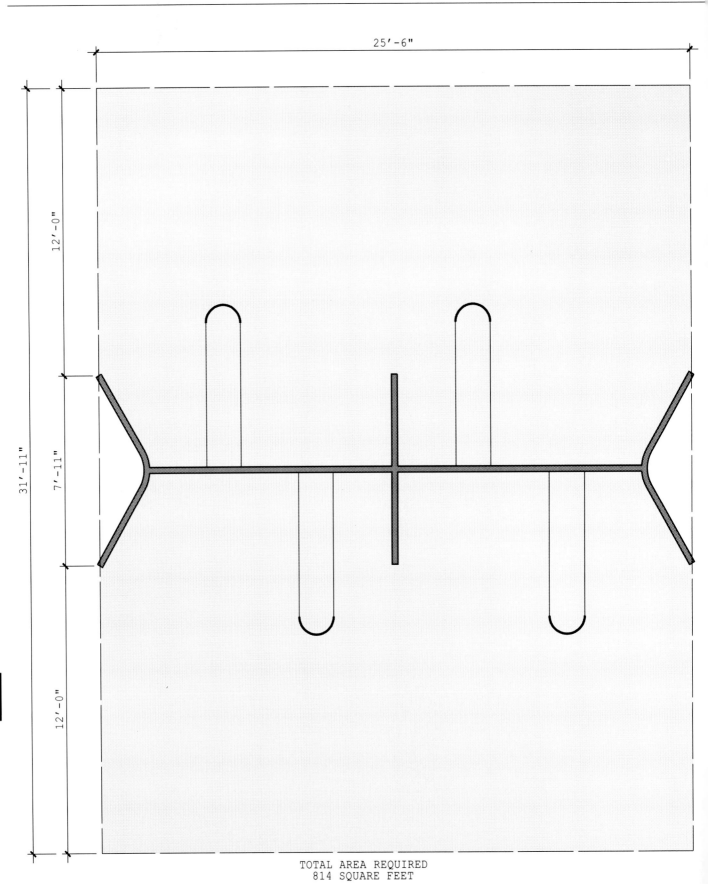

25'-6"

12'-0"

31'-11"

7'-11"

12'-0"

TOTAL AREA REQUIRED
814 SQUARE FEET

0 [   ] 4

24'-7"

6'-0"   12'-7"   6'-0"

14'-1"

6'-0"

2'-1"

6'-0"

HORIZONTAL LADDER

TOTAL AREA REQUIRED
346 SQUARE FEET

5'-0"   2'-0"   5'-0"

12'-0"

5'-8"

8"

5'-8"

SPRING TOYS

TOTAL AREA REQUIRED
119 SQUARE FEET

SPIN AROUND AT 1/4" = 1'-0"   0 ▭ 4

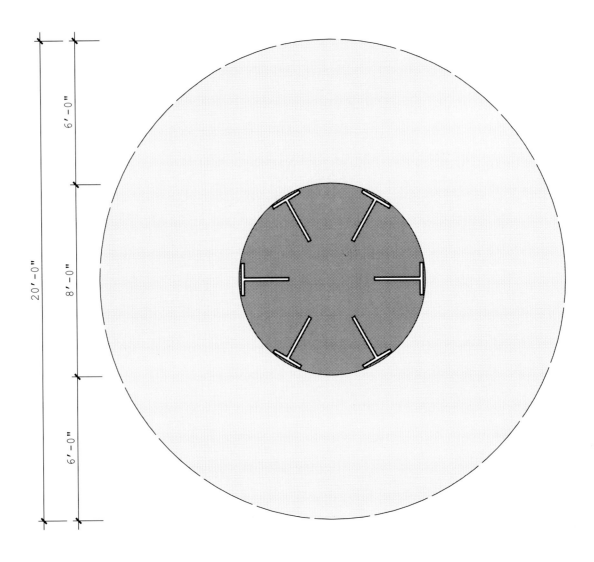

TOTAL AREA REQUIRED
310 SQUARE FEET

0 [_____] 4

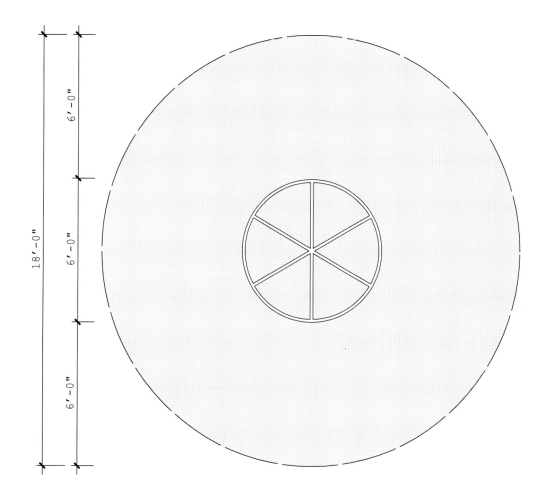

18'-0"

6'-0"

6'-0"

6'-0"

TOTAL AREA REQUIRED
252 SQUARE FEET

SMALL MULTIPLE PLAYGROUND AT 1/4" = 1'-0"   0 [========] 4

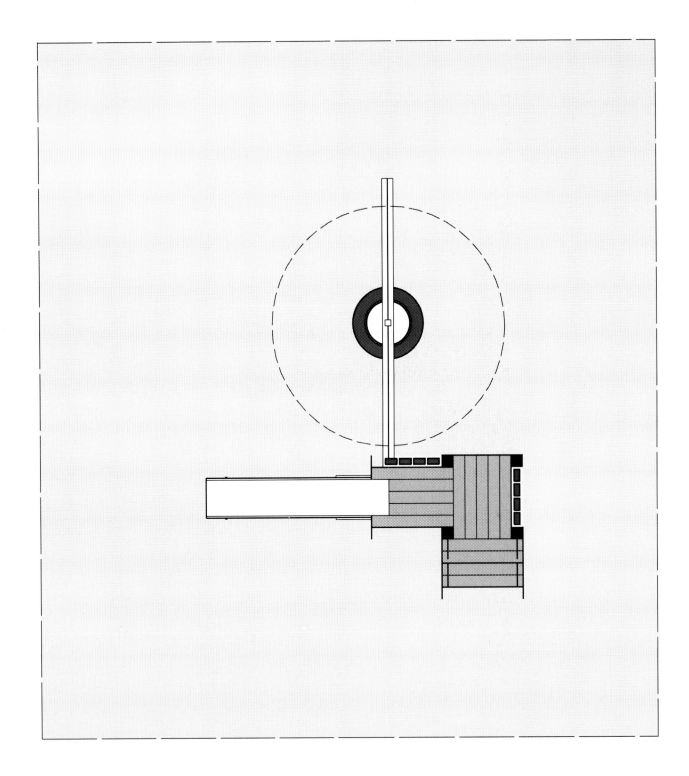

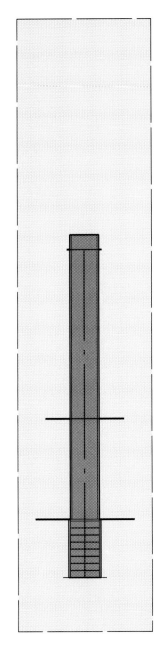

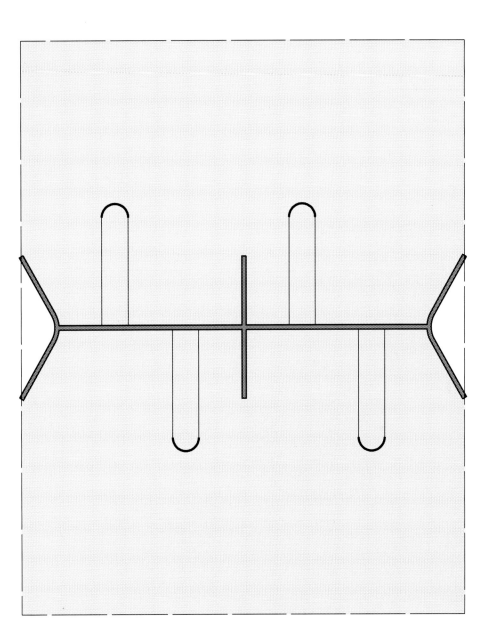

SLIDE   FOUR SEAT SWING

PLAY STRUCTURE AT 3/16" = 1'-0"

0 ▭ 4

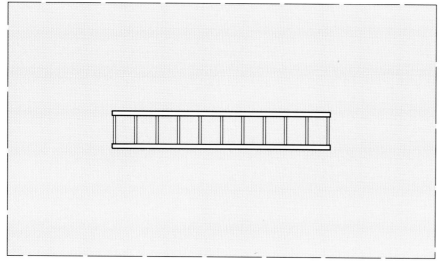

HORIZONTAL LADDER

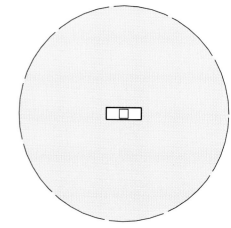

SPRING TOYS

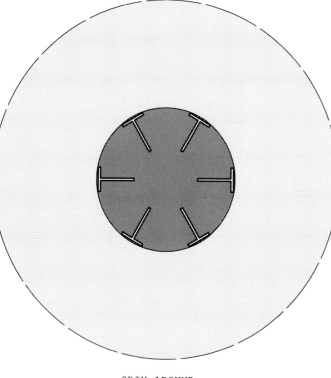

SPIN AROUND

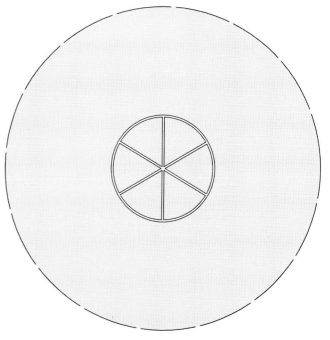

CLIMBING BARS

0 ☐☐☐☐ 4

SMALL MULTIPLE PLAY STRUCTURE AT 3/16" = 1'-0"

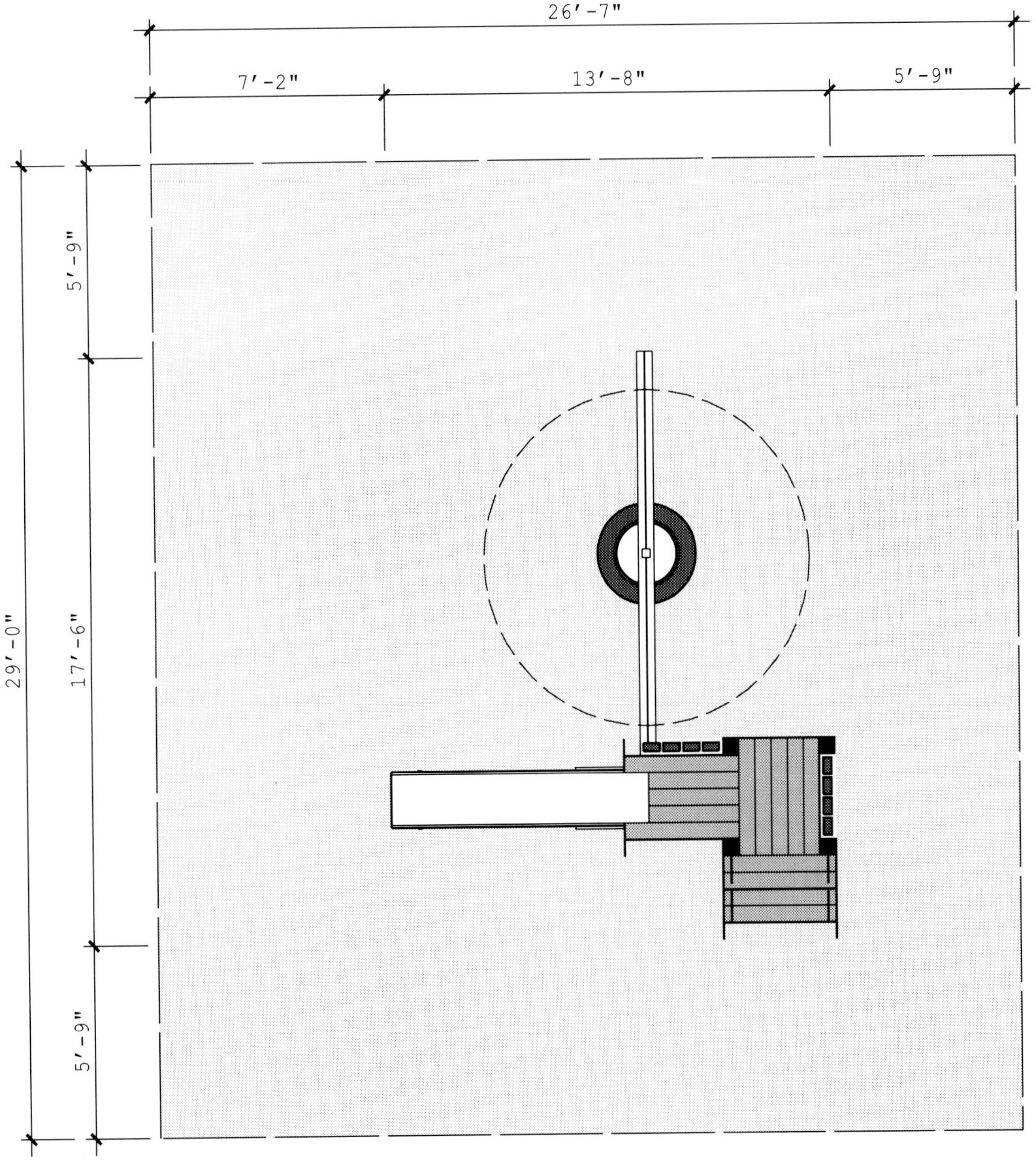

26'-7"

7'-2" 13'-8" 5'-9"

5'-9"

29'-0"

17'-6"

5'-9"

TOTAL AREA REQUIRED
771 SQUARE FEET

PLAY STRUCTURE AT 1/8" = 1'-0"   0 ⬜ 8

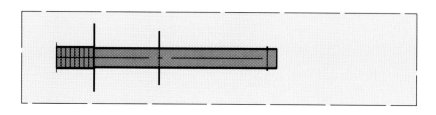

SLIDE

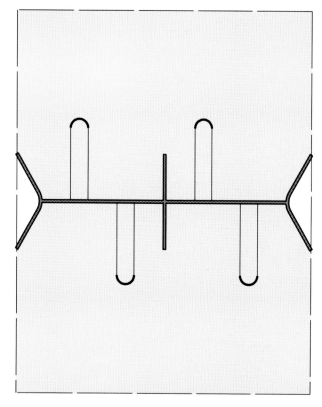

FOUR SEAT SWING

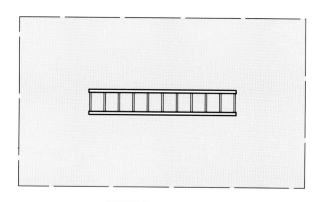

HORIZONTAL BARS

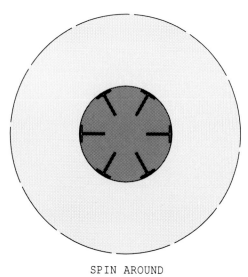

SPIN AROUND

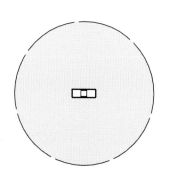

SPRING TOYS

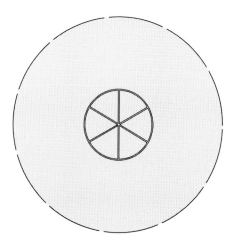

CLIMBING BARS

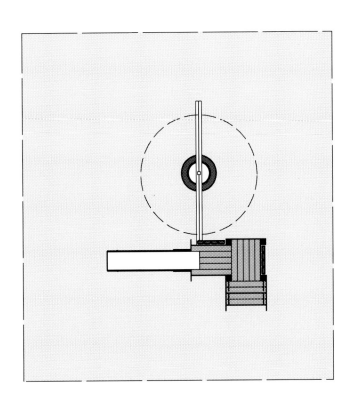

MEDIUM MULTIPLE PLAY STRUCTURE AT 1/8" = 1'-0"   0 ▭

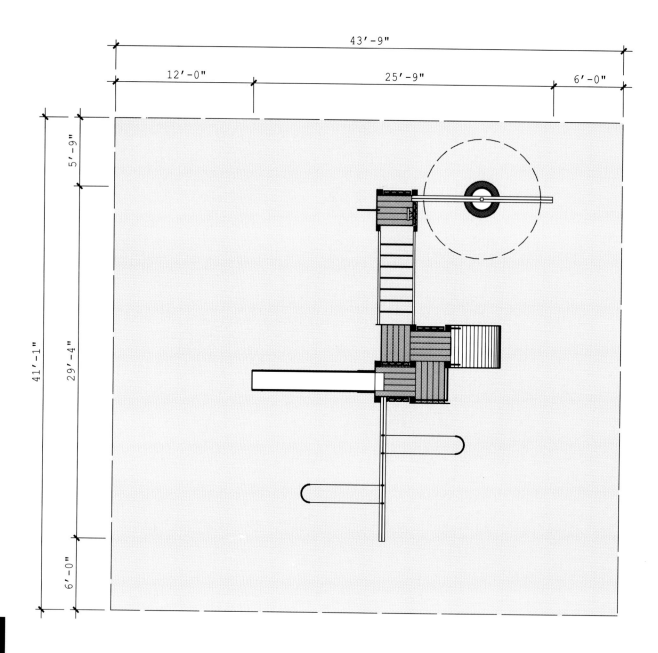

TOTAL AREA REQUIRED
1,800 SQUARE FEET

0   8

PLAY STRUCTURE AT 1" = 10'-0"

0 |==========| 10

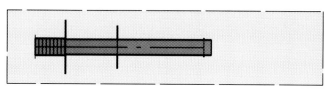

SLIDE

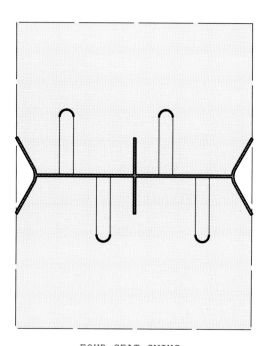

FOUR SEAT SWING

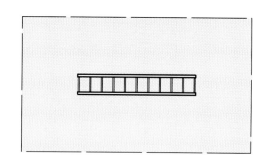

HORIZONTAL BARS

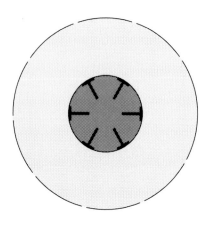

SPIN AROUND

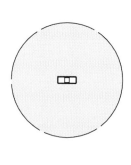

SPRING TOYS

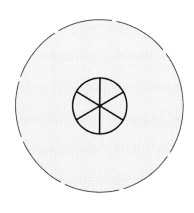

CLIMBING BARS

0 ▭ 10

MULTIPLE PLAY STRUCTURES AT 1" = 10'-0"

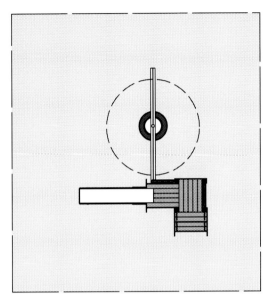

SMALL MULTIPLE PLAYGROUND

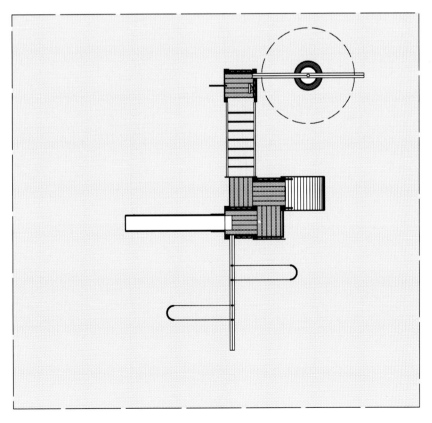

MEDIUM MULTIPLE PLAYGROUND

LARGE PLAY STRUCTURE AT 1" = 10'-0"

0 ▭ 10

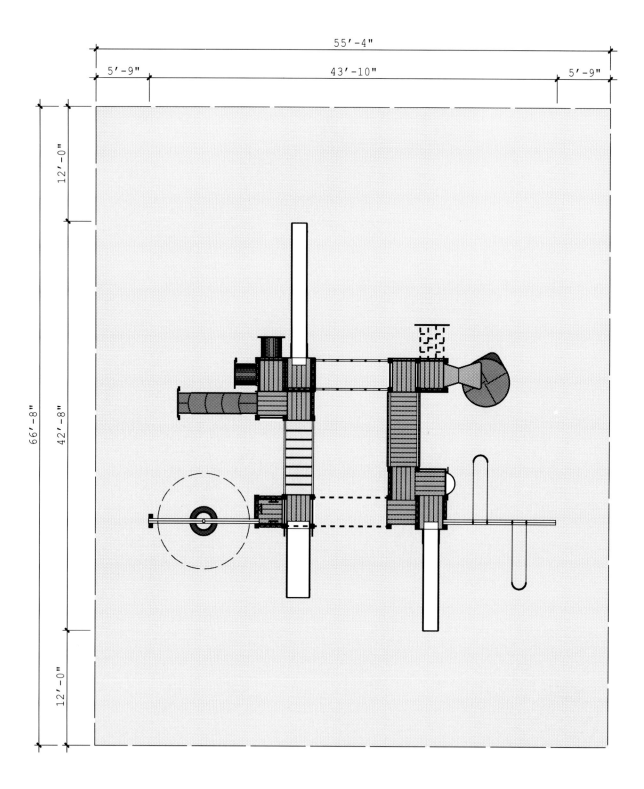

55'-4"

5'-9"   43'-10"   5'-9"

12'-0"

66'-8"

42'-8"

12'-0"

TOTAL AREA REQUIRED
3,692 SQUARE FEET

0 ⌷ 8 PLAY STRUCTURE AT 3/32" = 1'-0"

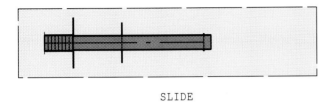

SLIDE

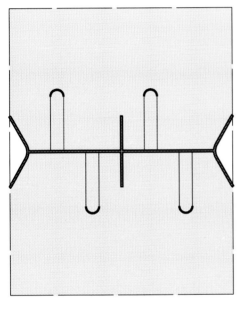
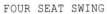

FOUR SEAT SWING

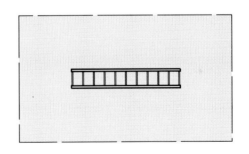

HORIZONTAL BARS

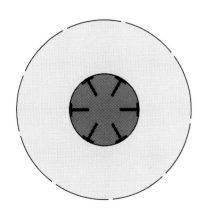

SPIN AROUND

SPRING TOYS

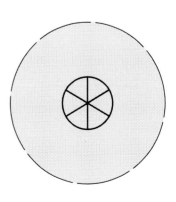

CLIMBING BARS

MULTIPLE PLAY STRUCTURES AT 3/32" = 1'-0"   0 ⬜⬜⬜ 8

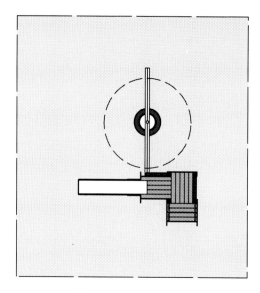

SMALL MULTIPLE PLAYGROUND

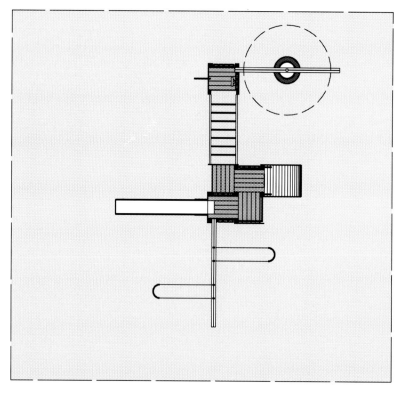

MEDIUM MULTIPLE PLAYGROUND

0 8

LARGE PLAY STRUCTURE AT 3/32" = 1′-0"

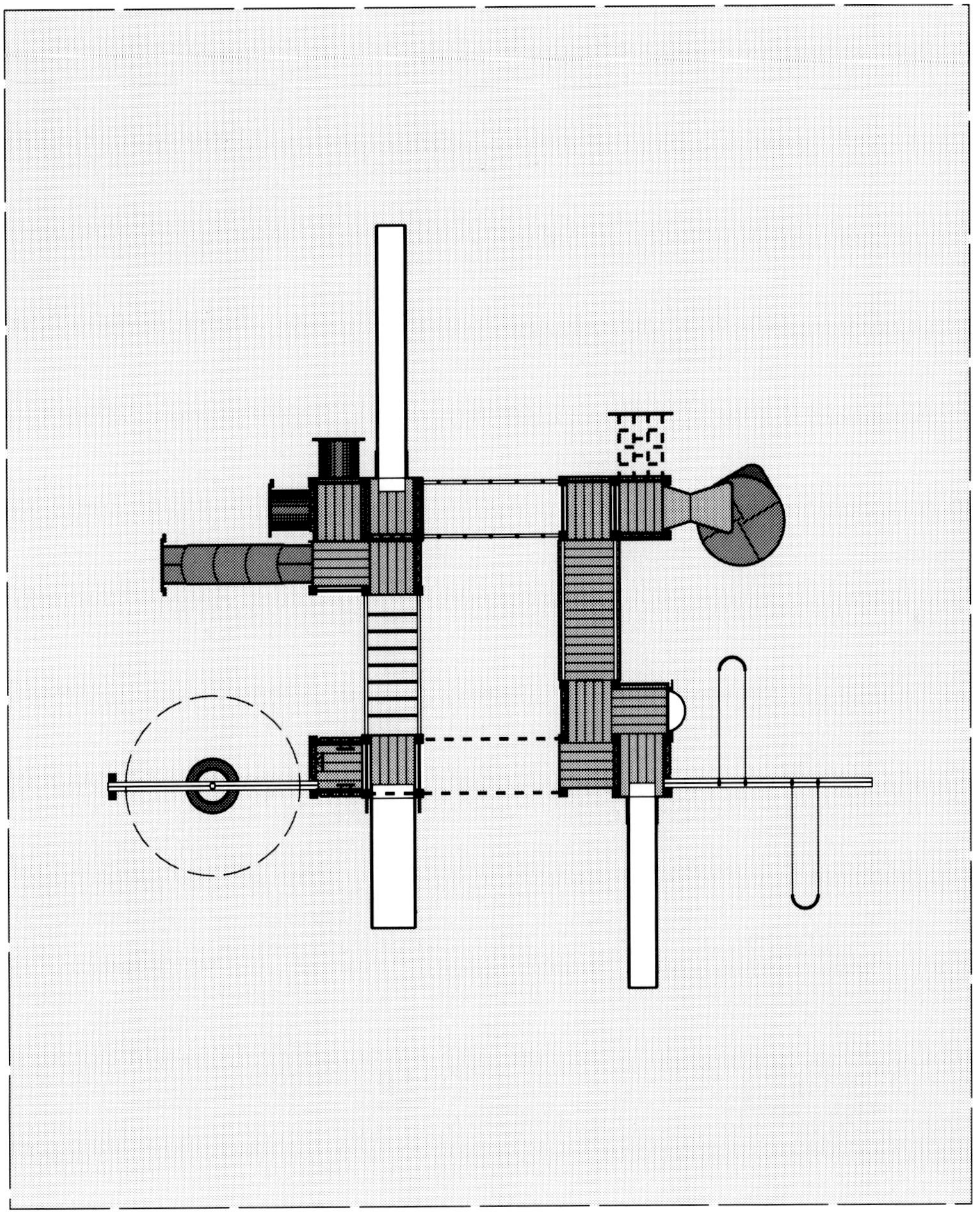

PLAY STRUCTURES AT 1/16" = 1'-0"   0 [▭▭▭▭▭] 16

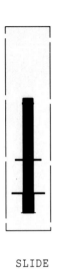

SLIDE

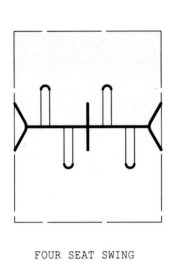

FOUR SEAT SWING

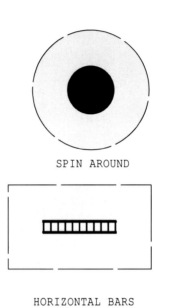

SPIN AROUND

HORIZONTAL BARS

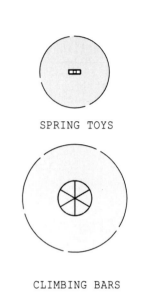

SPRING TOYS

CLIMBING BARS

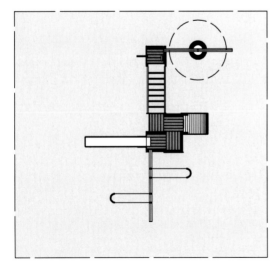

SMALL MULTIPLE PLAYSTRUCTURE

MEDIUM MULTIPLE PLAYSTRUCTURE

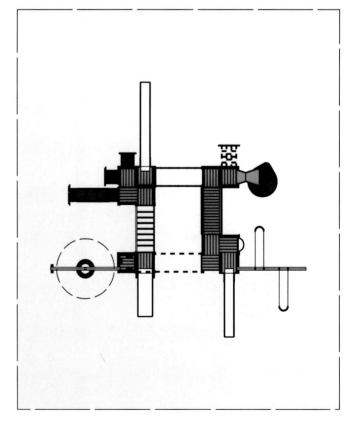

LARGE MULTIPLE PLAYSTRUCTURE

0 [ ] 20

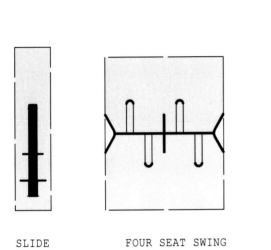

SLIDE   FOUR SEAT SWING

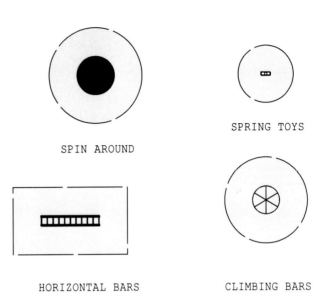

SPIN AROUND

SPRING TOYS

HORIZONTAL BARS   CLIMBING BARS

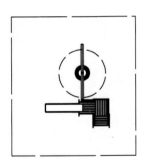

SMALL MULTIPLE PLAYSTRUCTURE

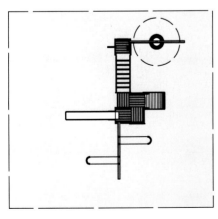

MEDIUM MULTIPLE PLAYSTRUCTURE

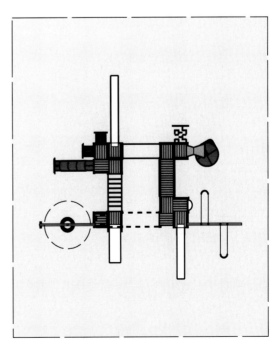

LARGE MULTIPLE PLAYSTRUCTURE

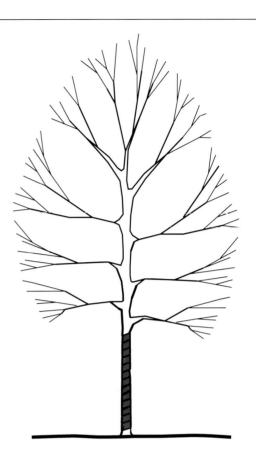

TREE VERSION 1	VIEW	PLAN	FRONT	SCALE	240	360	480	600
50' SPREAD		●			5	7	8	8
40' SPREAD		●			5	7	8	8
30' SPREAD		●			5	7	8	8
20' SPREAD		●			5	7	8	8

TREE VERSION 2	VIEW	PLAN	FRONT	SCALE	240	360	480	600
50' SPREAD		●			5	7	8	8
40' SPREAD		●			5	7	8	8
30' SPREAD		●			5	7	8	8
20' SPREAD		●			5	7	8	8

TREE VERSION 3	VIEW	PLAN	FRONT	SCALE	240	360	480	600
50' SPREAD		●			5	7	8	8
40' SPREAD		●			5	7	8	8
30' SPREAD		●			5	7	8	8
20' SPREAD		●			5	7	8	8

TREE VERSION 4	VIEW	PLAN	FRONT	SCALE	240	360	480	600
50' SPREAD		●			5	7	8	8
40' SPREAD		●			5	7	8	8
30' SPREAD		●			5	7	8	8
20' SPREAD		●			5	7	8	8

TREE VERSION 5	VIEW	PLAN	FRONT	SCALE	240	360	480	600
40' SPREAD		●			6	7	8	8
30' SPREAD		●			6	7	8	8
20' SPREAD		●			6	7	8	8

TREE VERSION 6	VIEW	PLAN	FRONT	SCALE	240	360	480	600
40' SPREAD		●			6	7	8	8
30' SPREAD		●			6	7	8	8
20' SPREAD		●			6	7	8	8

PLANT MATERIAL MATRIX

TREE VERSION 1	VIEW	PLAN	FRONT	SCALE	240	360	480	600
50' SPREAD		●			6	7	8	8
40' SPREAD		●			6	7	8	8
30' SPREAD		●			6	7	8	8
20' SPREAD		●			6	7	8	8

PALM TREE	VIEW	PLAN	FRONT	SCALE	240	360	480	600
30' SPREAD		●			6	7	8	8

TREE VERSION 1	VIEW	PLAN	FRONT	SCALE	96	120	128	192	240
50' HEIGHT			●		9	10	11	12	12
40' HEIGHT			●		9	10	11	12	12
30' HEIGHT			●		9	10	11	12	12

TREE VERSION 2	VIEW	PLAN	FRONT	SCALE	96	120	128	192	240
50' HEIGHT			●		9	10	11	12	12
40' HEIGHT			●		9	10	11	12	12
30' HEIGHT			●		9	10	11	12	12

TREE VERSION 2	VIEW	PLAN	FRONT	SCALE	96	120	128	192	240
50' HEIGHT			●		9	10	11	12	12

0 [   ] 20   TREES IN PLAN AT 1" = 20'-0"

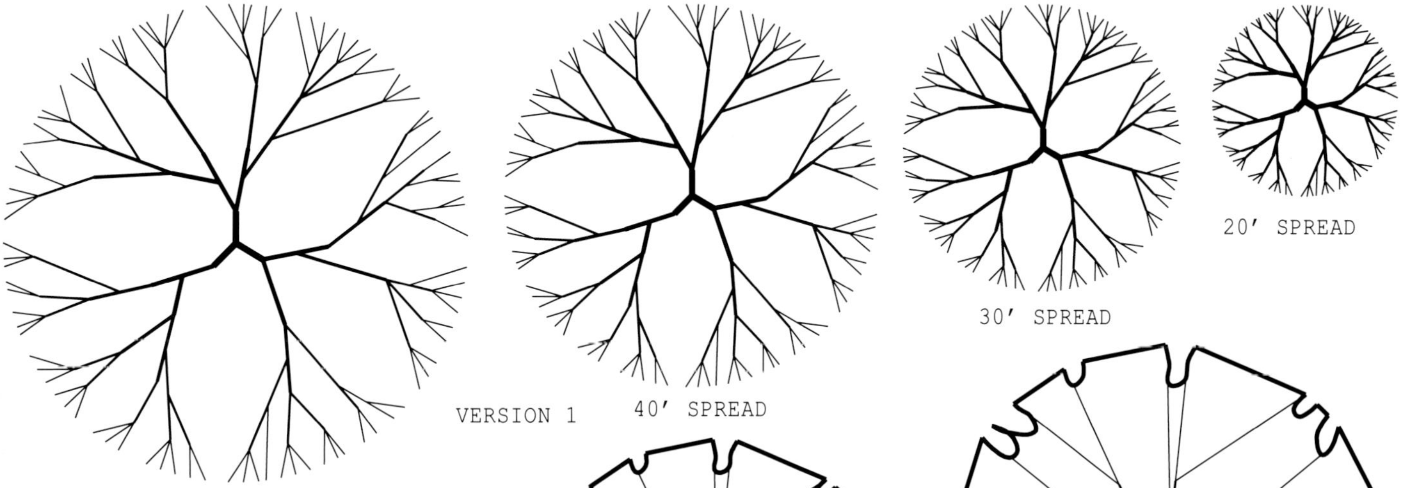

20' SPREAD

30' SPREAD

40' SPREAD

VERSION 1

50' SPREAD

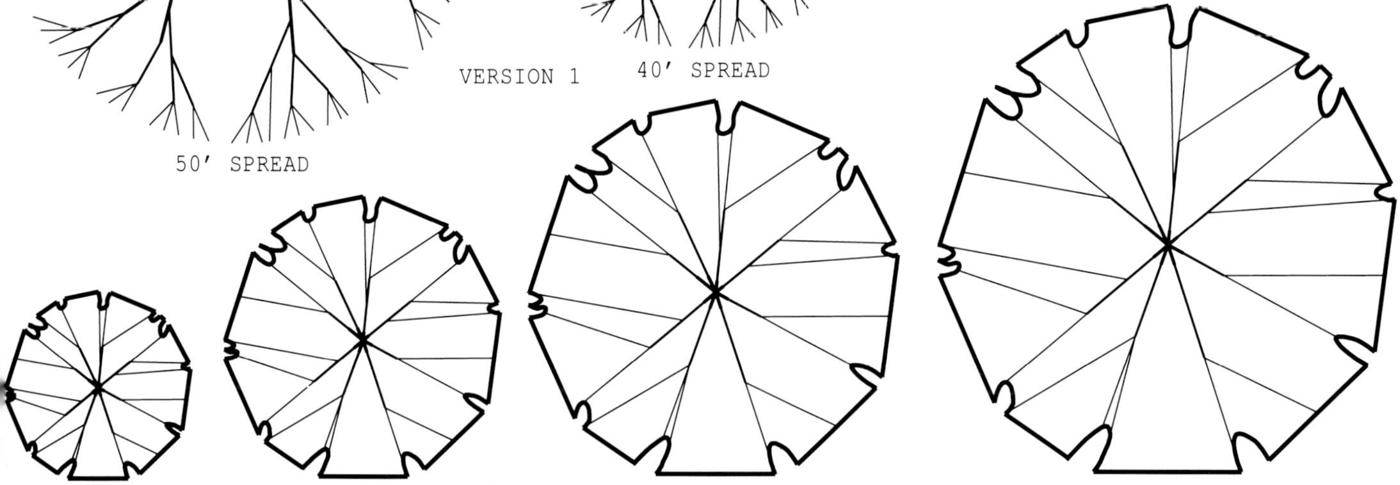

VERSION 2

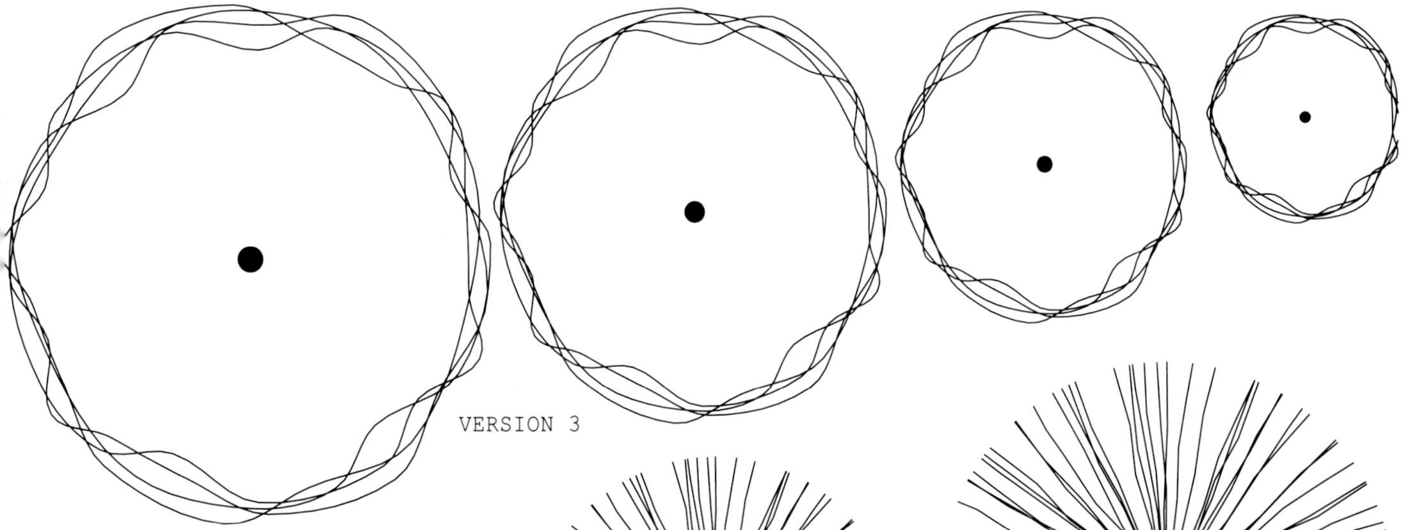

VERSION 3

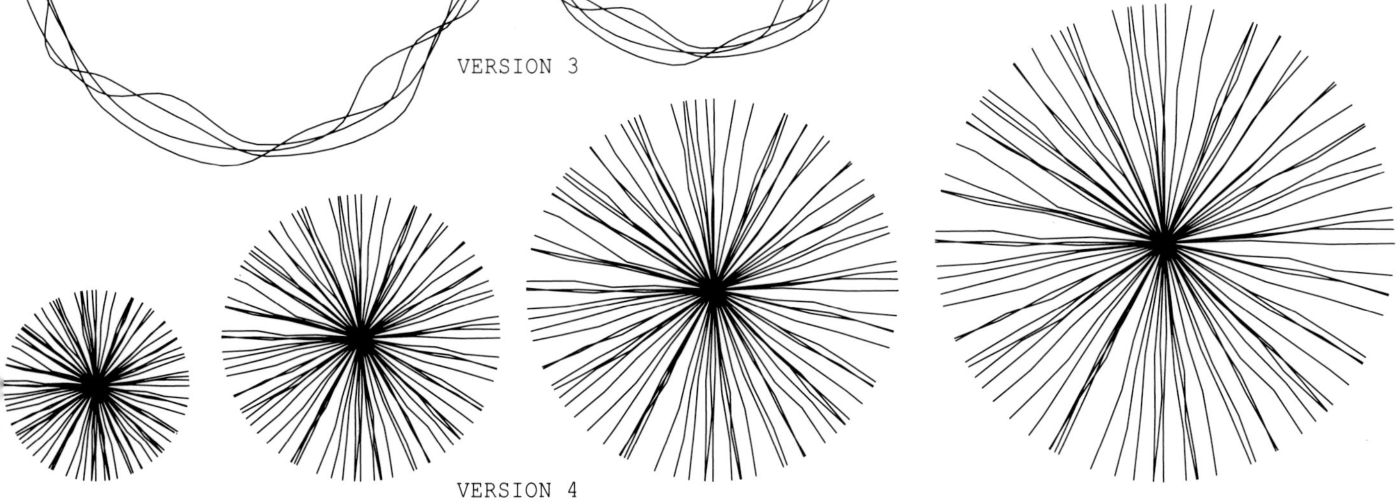

VERSION 4

TREES IN PLAN AT 1" = 20'-0"

0 ⬜ 20

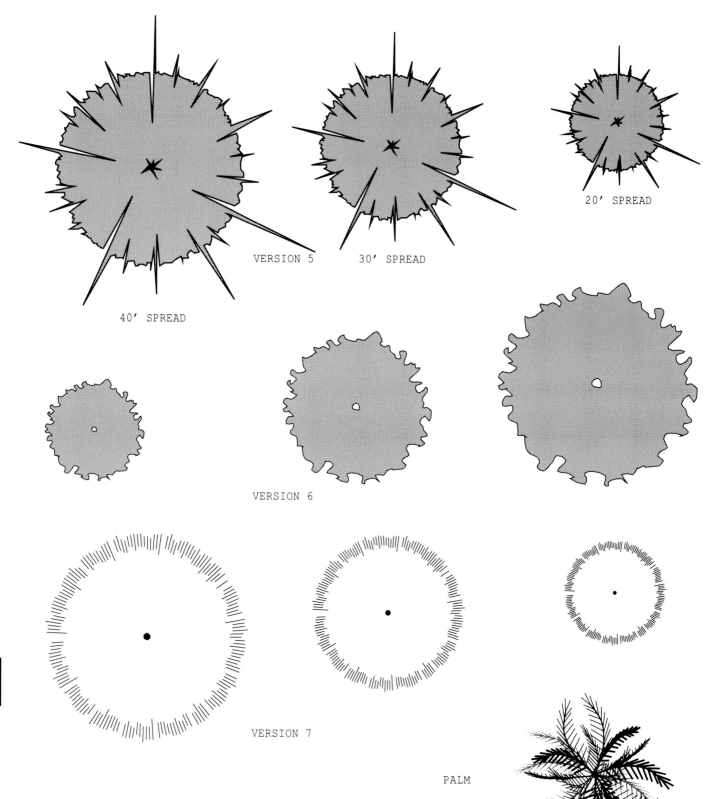

20' SPREAD

VERSION 5   30' SPREAD

40' SPREAD

VERSION 6

VERSION 7

PALM

0 ⬜ 30

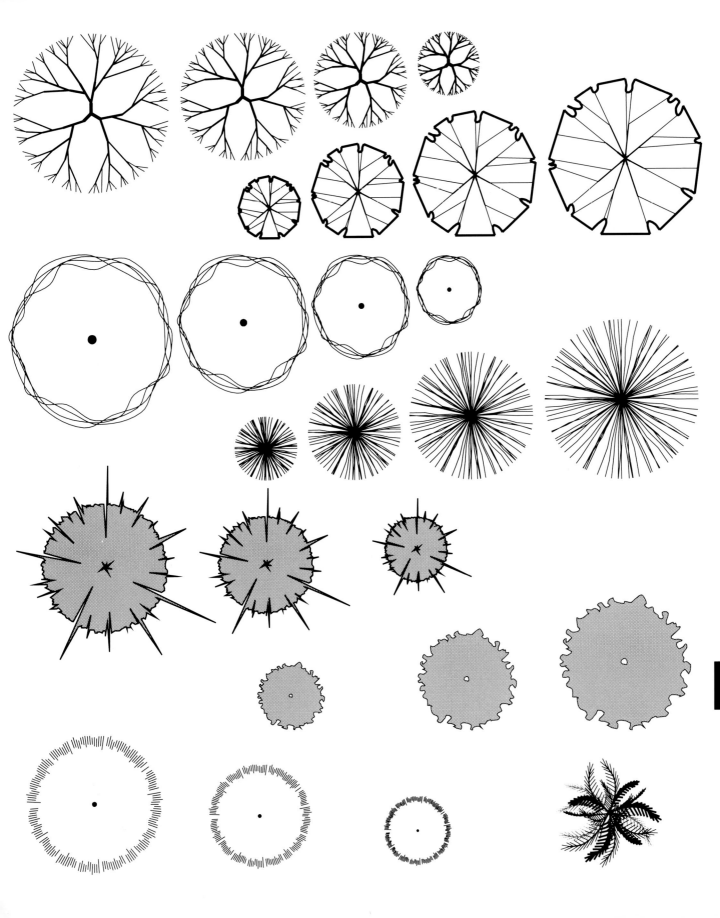

TREES IN PLAN AT 1" = 40'-0"   0 [＿＿＿＿＿＿] 40

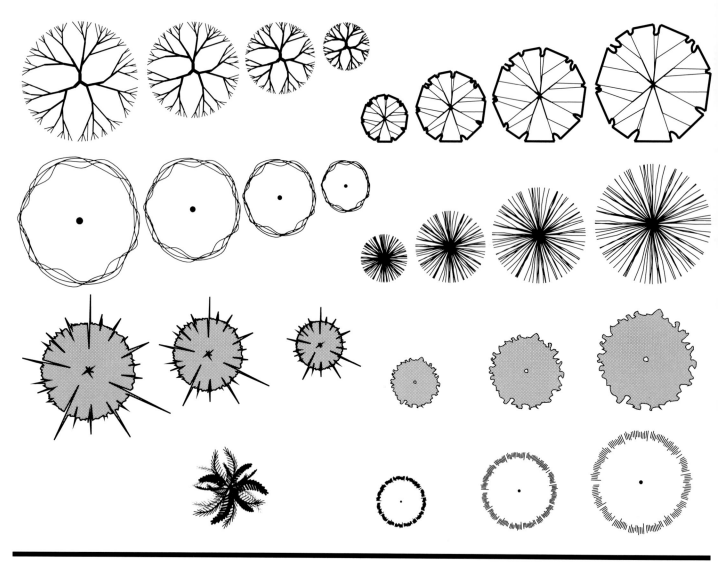

TREES IN PLAN AT 1" = 50'-0"   0 [＿＿＿＿＿＿] 50

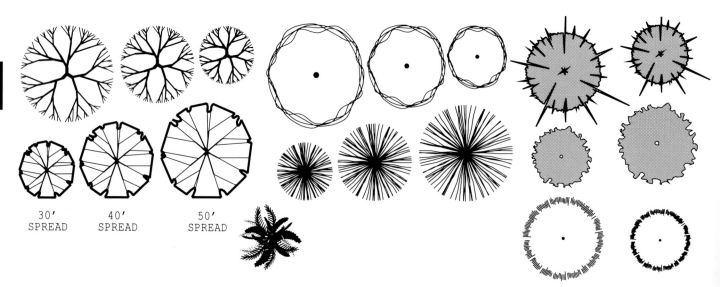

30'
SPREAD

40'
SPREAD

50'
SPREAD

0 ⬜========= 8

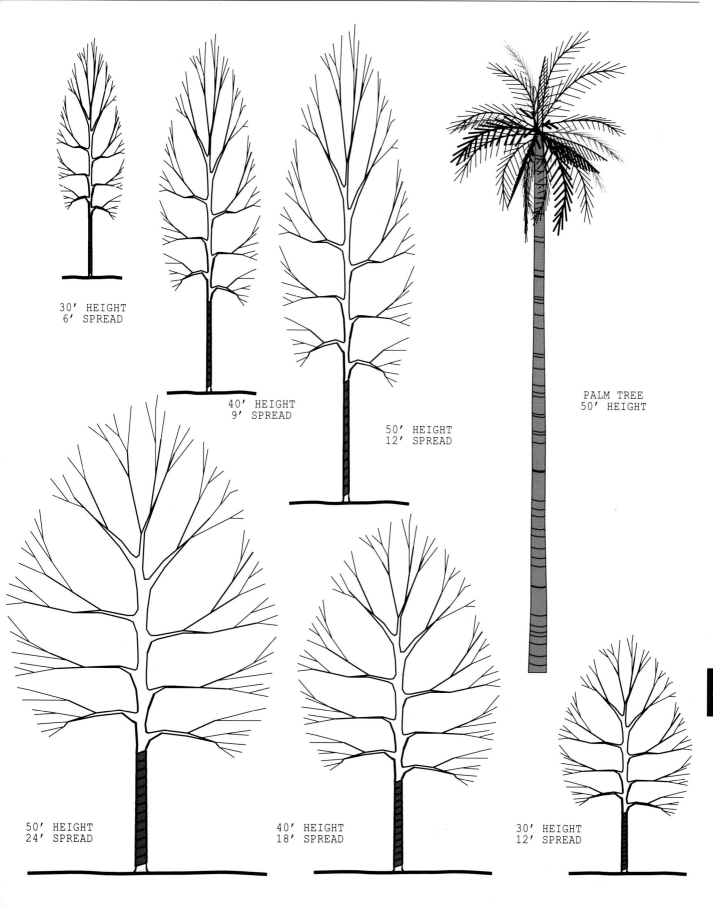

30' HEIGHT
6' SPREAD

40' HEIGHT
9' SPREAD

50' HEIGHT
12' SPREAD

PALM TREE
50' HEIGHT

50' HEIGHT
24' SPREAD

40' HEIGHT
18' SPREAD

30' HEIGHT
12' SPREAD

473

TREES IN ELEVATION AT 1" = 10'-0"   0 ☐────── 10

0 ⬚ 8   TREES IN ELEVATION AT 3/32" = 1'-0"

PLANT MATERIAL

TREES IN ELEVATION AT 1/16" = 1'-0"   0 ▭ 16

TREES IN ELEVATION AT 1" = 20'-0"   0 ▭ 20

476

TRAFFIC SIGNAGE	VIEW	FRONT	SCALE	24	32	48	64	96	120	128	192	240
STOP		●		481	483	484	484	484	485	485	485	485
YEILD		●		481	483	484	484	484	485	485	485	485
DO NOT ENTER		●		481	483	484	484	484	485	485	485	485
INTERSECTION		●		481	483	484	484	484	485	485	485	485
TRAFFIC SIGNAL		●		481	483	484	484	484	485	485	485	485
TWO-WAY TRAFFIC		●		481	483	484	484	484	485	485	485	485
SPEED LIMIT		●		482	483	484	484	484	485	485	485	485
WRONG WAY		●		482	483	484	484	484	485	485	485	485
ONE-WAY		●		482	483	484	484	484	485	485	485	485
RAILROAD CROSSING		●		482	483	484	484	484	485	485	485	485
NO PARKING		●		482	483	484	484	484	485	485	485	485
NO LEFT TURN		●		482	483	484	484	484	485	485	485	485
NO U-TURN		●		482	483	484	484	484	485	485	485	485

0 ⬛ 2

1'-7 7/8"

4'-0"

STOP

4'-6 1/8"

4'-6 1/8"

YIELD

YIELD

4'-0"

4'-0"

DO NOT
ENTER

DO NOT ENTER

4'-0"

5'-5 1/4"

INTERSECTION

4'-0"

5'-5 1/4"

TRAFFIC LIGHT

TWO-WAY
TRAFFIC

4'-0"

5'-5 1/4"

481

SIGNAGE AT 1/2" = 1'-0"   0 ▭ 2

SPEED LIMIT

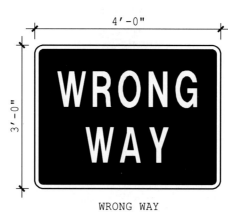

WRONG WAY

ONE-WAY

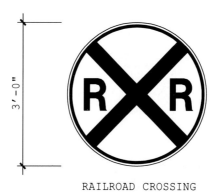

RAILROAD CROSSING

482

NO PARKING

NO LEFT TURN

NO U-TURN

0 ⬚ 2

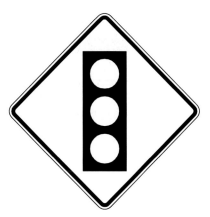

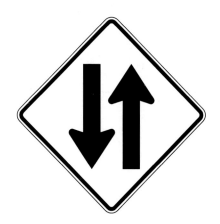

SIGNAGE

SIGNAGE AT 1/4" = 1'-0"   0 ▢ 4

 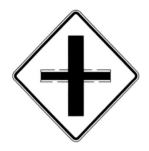  

SIGNAGE AT 3/16" = 1'-0"   0 ▢ 4

484

SIGNAGE AT 1/8" = 1'-0"   0 ▢ 8

0 [========] 10   SIGNAGE AT 1' = 10'-0"

0 [========] 8   SIGNAGE AT 3/32" = 1'-0"

0 [========] 16   SIGNAGE AT 1/16" = 1'-0"

0 [========] 20   SIGNAGE AT 1' = 20'-0"

485

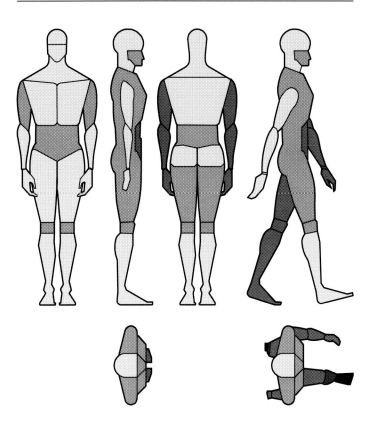

MEN	VIEW	PLAN	FRONT	SIDE	REAR	SCALE	24	32	48	64	96	120	128	192	240
STANDING		●	●	●	●		5	6	6	7	7	7	7	7	7
WALKING			●	●			5	6	6	7	7	7	7	7	7
SITTING		●	●		●		5	6	6	7	7	7	7	7	7

WOMEN	VIEW	PLAN	FRONT	SIDE	REAR	SCALE	24	32	48	64	96	120	128	192	240
STANDING		●	●	●	●		5	6	6	7	7	7	7	7	7
WALKING			●	●			5	6	6	7	7	7	7	7	7
SITTING		●	●	●	●		5	6	6	7	7	7	7	7	7

HANDICAP	VIEW	PLAN	FRONT	SIDE	REAR	SCALE	24	32	48	64	96	120	128	192	240
WITH CANE		●	●	●	●		8	8	9	9	9	9	9	9	9
IN WHEELCHAIR		●	●	●	●		8	8	9	9	9	9	9	9	9

0 [========] 2

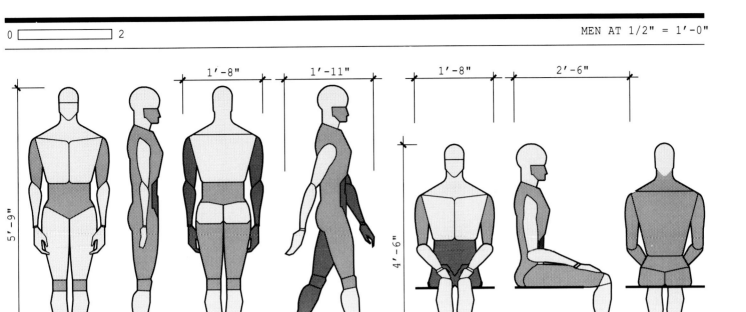

5'-9"

1'-8"   1'-11"   1'-8"   2'-6"

4'-6"

1'-8"

FRONT   SIDE   BACK   SIDE   FRONT   SIDE   BACK

PLAN   PLAN   PLAN

0 [========] 2

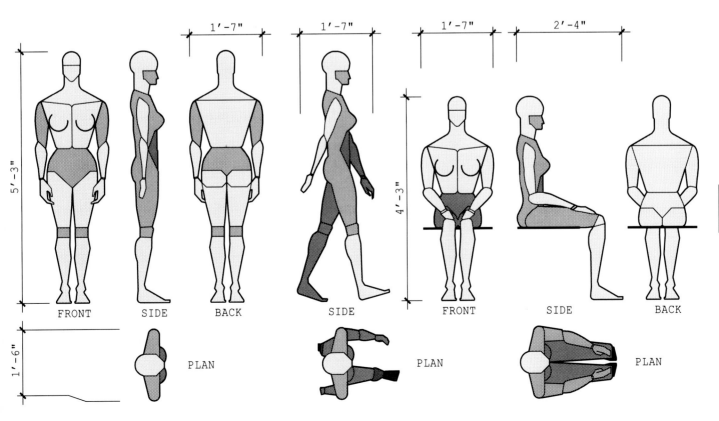

5'-3"

1'-7"   1'-7"   1'-7"   2'-4"

4'-3"

1'-6"

FRONT   SIDE   BACK   SIDE   FRONT   SIDE   BACK

PLAN   PLAN   PLAN

491

MEN AT 3/8" = 1'-0"   0 [   ] 2

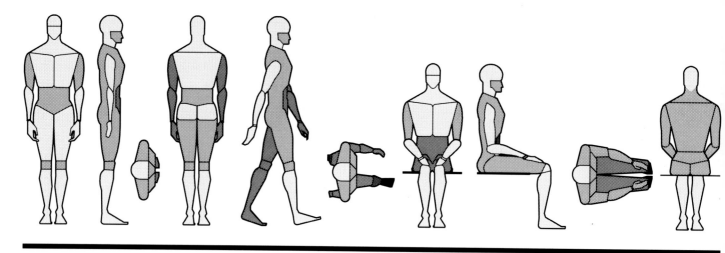

WOMEN AT 3/8" = 1'-0"   0 [   ] 2

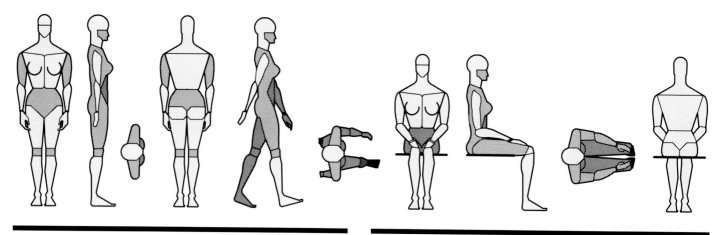

MEN AT 1/4" = 1'-0"   0 [   ] 4   WOMEN AT 1/4" = 1'-0"   0 [   ] 4

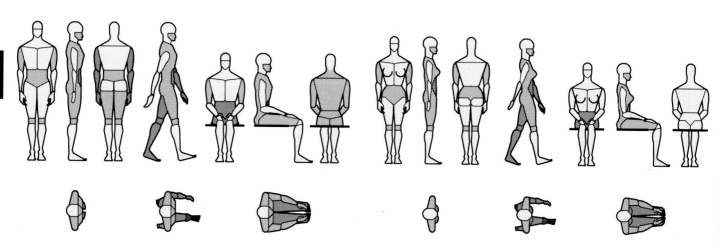

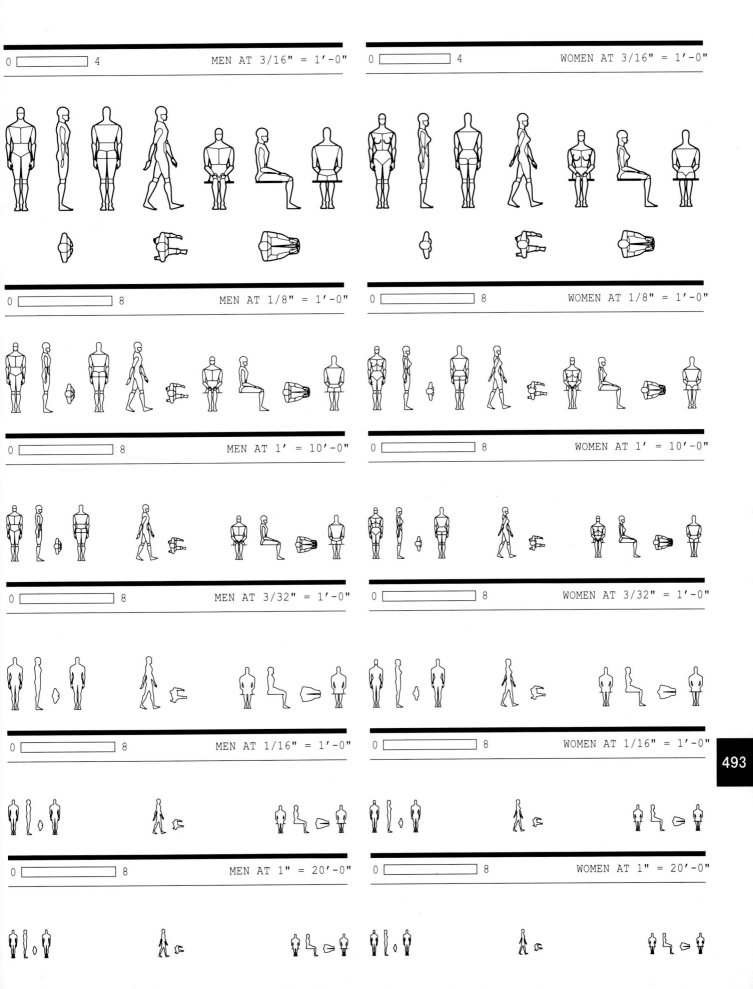

0 [____] 4   MEN AT 3/16" = 1'-0"

0 [____] 4   WOMEN AT 3/16" = 1'-0"

0 [____] 8   MEN AT 1/8" = 1'-0"

0 [____] 8   WOMEN AT 1/8" = 1'-0"

0 [____] 8   MEN AT 1' = 10'-0"

0 [____] 8   WOMEN AT 1' = 10'-0"

0 [____] 8   MEN AT 3/32" = 1'-0"

0 [____] 8   WOMEN AT 3/32" = 1'-0"

0 [____] 8   MEN AT 1/16" = 1'-0"

0 [____] 8   WOMEN AT 1/16" = 1'-0"

0 [____] 8   MEN AT 1" = 20'-0"

0 [____] 8   WOMEN AT 1" = 20'-0"

HANDICAP AT 1/2" = 1'-0"   0 ▭ 2

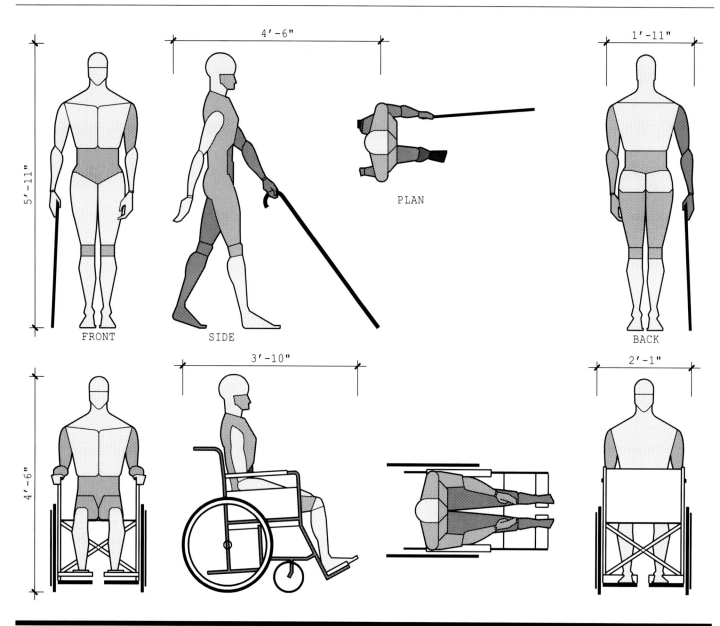

4'-6"

1'-11"

5'-11"

FRONT   SIDE   PLAN   BACK

3'-10"

2'-1"

4'-6"

HANDICAP AT 3/8" = 1'-0"   0 ▭ 2

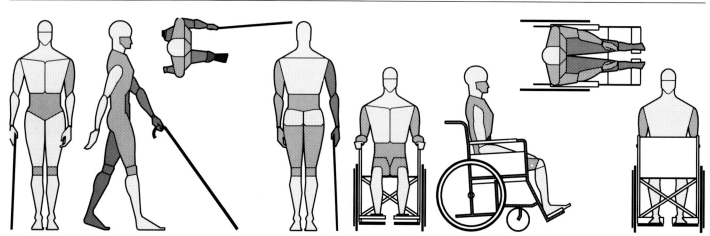

0 ▭ 4   HANDICAP AT 1/4" = 1'-0"

0 ▭ 4   HANDICAP AT 3/16" = 1'-0"

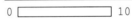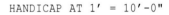

0 ▭ 8   HANDICAP AT 1/8" = 1'-0"   0 ▭ 10   HANDICAP AT 1' = 10'-0"

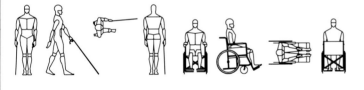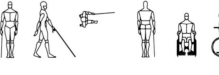

0 ▭ 8   HANDICAP AT 3/32" = 1'-0"   0 ▭ 16   HANDICAP AT 1/16" = 1'-0"

0 ▭ 20   HANDICAP AT 1" = 20'-0"

0   .5"   1"
1:1 12"=1'-0"

0   5   10   20
1:240 1"=20'-0"

0   1"   2"
1:2 6"=1'-0"

0   15   30
1:360 1"=30'-0"

0   2"   4"
1:4 3"=1'-0"

0   8   16   32
1:384 1"=32'-0"

0   6"
1:8 1-1/2"=1'-0"

0   10   20   40
1:480 1"=40'-0"

0   6"   1
1:12 1"=1'-0"

0   25   50
1:600 1"=50'-0"

0   6"   1
1:16 3/4"=1'-0"

0   15   30   60
1:720 1"=60'-0"

0   1   2
1:24 1/2"=1'-0"

0   35   70
1:840 1"=70'-0"

COMPLEX PLAN SCALES	VIEW	PLAN	3D	SCALE	SAME AS ENTRY
1:1		●			503
1:2		●			503
1:4		●			503
1:8		●			503
1:12		●			503
1:16		●			503
1:24		●			503
1:32		●			503
1:48		●			503
1:64		●			503
1:96		●			503
1:120		●			503
1:128		●			503
1:192		●			503
1:240		●			503
1:360		●			503
1:480		●			503
1:600		●			503
1:720		●			503
1:840		●			503
1:960		●			503
1:1,200		●			503
1:2,400		●			503
1:4,800		●			503
1:1,2000		●			503

SIMPLE PLAN SCALES	VIEW	PLAN	3D	SCALE	SAME AS ENTRY
1:1		●			504
1:2		●			504
1:4		●			504
1:8		●			504
1:12		●			504
1:16		●			504
1:24		●			504
1:32		●			504

GRAPHICS MATRIX

SIMPLE PLAN SCALES	VIEW	PLAN	3D	SCALE	SAME AS ENTRY
1:48		●			504
1:64		●			504
1:96		●			504
1:120		●			504
1:128		●			504
1:192		●			504
1:240		●			504
1:360		●			504
1:480		●			504
1:600		●			504
1:720		●			504
1:840		●			504
1:960		●			504
1:1,200		●			504
1:2,400		●			504
1:4,800		●			504
1:12,000		●			504

SQUARE AREA SCALES	VIEW	PLAN	3D	SCALE	16	24	32	48	64	96	120	128	192	240	360	480	1200
5 FEET		●			505	505											
10 FEET		●					505	506									
25 FEET		●						506	506								
100 FEET		●								506	507	507					
500 FEET		●											507	508			
1,000 FEET		●													508	508	
5,000 FEET		●															509
5,280 FEET		●															509
10,000 FEET		●															509

SQUARE AREA SCALES	VIEW	PLAN	3D	SCALE	64	96	120	128	192	240	360	480
5 YARDS		●			506							
10 YARDS		●				506	507	507				
25 YARDS		●							507			
100 YARDS		●								508	508	508

SQUARE AREA SCALES	VIEW	PLAN	3D	SCALE	2400	4800	12,000
5 ACRES		●			509	509	
10 ACRES		●				509	
25 ACRES		●					509
100 ACRES		●					509

CUBIC AREA SCALES	VIEW	PLAN	3D	SCALE	16	24	32	48	64	96	120	128	192	240	360	480
5 FEET			●		505	505										
10 FEET			●				505	506								
25 FEET			●					506	506							
100 FEET			●							506	507	507				
500 FEET			●										507	508		
1,000 FEET			●												508	508

NORTH ARROWS	VIEW	PLAN	3D	SCALE	NO SCALE
VERSION 1		●			510
VERSION 2		●			510
VERSION 3		●			510
VERSION 4		●			510
VERSION 5		●			510
VERSION 6		●			510
VERSION 7		●			510

COMPLEX PLAN SCALES - LARGE

.5" 1" 1:1 12"=1'-0"	0 5 10 20 1:240 1"=20'-0"
1" 2" 1:2 6"=1'-0"	0 15 30 1:360 1"=30'-0"
2" 4" 1:4 3"=1'-0"	0 8 16 32 1:384 1"=32'-0"
6" 1:8 1-1/2"=1'-0"	0 10 20 40 1:480 1"=40'-0"
6" 1 1:12 1"=1'-0"	0 25 50 1:600 1"=50'-0"
6" 1 1:16 3/4"=1'-0"	0 15 30 60 1:720 1"=60'-0"
1 2 1:24 1/2"=1'-0"	0 35 70 1:840 1"=70'-0"
1 2 1:32 3/8"=1'-0"	0 40 80 1:960 1"=80'-0"
1 2 4 1:48 1/4"=1'-0"	0 50 100 1:1,200 1"=100'-0"
2 4 1:64 3/16"=1'-0"	0 60 120 1:1,440 1"=120'-0"
2 4 8 1:96 1/8"=1'-0"	0 80 160 1:1,920 1"=160'-0"
5 10 1:120 1"=10'-0"	0 100 200 1:2,400 1"=200'-0"
4 8 1:128 3/32"=1'-0"	0 200 400 1:4,800 1"=400'-0"
4 8 16 1:192 1"=16'-0"	0 1000 1:12,000 1"=1,000'-0"

COMPLEX PLAN SCALES - SMALL

0 .5" 1:1 12"=1'-0"	0 5 10 1:240 1"=20'-0"
0 1" 1:2 6"=1'-0"	0 15 1:360 1"=30'-0"
0 2" 1:4 3"=1'-0"	0 8 16 1:384 1"=32'-0"
0 6" 1:8 1-1/2"=1'-0"	0 10 20 1:480 1"=40'-0"
0 6" 1:12 1"=1'-0"	0 25 1:600 1"=50'-0"
0 6" 1:16 3/4"=1'-0"	0 15 30 1:720 1"=60'-0"
0 1 1:24 1/2"=1'-0"	0 35 1:840 1"=70'-0"
0 1 1:32 3/8"=1'-0"	0 40 1:960 1"=80'-0"
0 1 2 1:48 1/4"=1'-0"	0 50 1:1,200 1"=100'-0"
0 2 1:64 3/16"=1'-0"	0 60 1:1,440 1"=120'-0"
0 2 4 1:96 1/8"=1'-0"	0 80 1:1,920 1"=160'-0"
0 5 1:120 1"=10'-0"	0 100 1:2,400 1"=200'-0"
0 4 1:128 3/32"=1'-0"	0 200 1:4,800 1"=400'-0"
0 4 8 1:192 1"=16'-0"	0 1:12,000 1"=1,000'-0"

503

SIMPLE PLAN SCALES - LARGE   SIMPLE PLAN SCALES - SMAL

---

0 ▓▓▓▓▓▓▓ 1"   0 ▓▓▓▓▓▓▓ 20   0 ▓▓▓ .5"   0 ▓▓▓ 10
1:1 12"=1'-0"   1:240 1"=20'-0"   1:1 12"=1'-0"   1:240 1"=20'-(

0 ▓▓▓▓▓▓▓ 2"   0 ▓▓▓▓▓▓▓ 30   0 ▓▓▓ 1"   0 ▓▓▓ 15
1:2 6"=1'-0"   1:360 1"=30'-0"   1:2 6"=1'-0"   1:360 1"=30'-(

0 ▓▓▓▓▓▓▓ 4"   0 ▓▓▓▓▓▓▓ 32   0 ▓▓▓ 2"   0 ▓▓▓ 16
1:4 3"=1'-0"   1:384 1"=32'-0"   1:4 3"=1'-0"   1:384 1"=32'-(

0 ▓▓▓▓▓ 6"   0 ▓▓▓▓▓▓▓ 40   0 ▓▓▓ 3"   0 ▓▓▓ 20
1:8 1-1/2"=1'-0"   1:480 1"=40'-0"   1:8 1-1/2"=1'-0" 1:480 1"=40'-(

0 ▓▓▓▓▓ 1   0 ▓▓▓▓▓▓▓ 50   0 ▓▓▓ 6"   0 ▓▓▓ 25
1:12 1"=1'-0"   1:600 1"=50'-0"   1:12 1"=1'-0"   1:600 1"=50'-(

0 ▓▓▓▓ 1   0 ▓▓▓▓▓▓▓ 60   0 ▓▓▓ 6"   0 ▓▓▓ 30
1:16 3/4"=1'-0"   1:720 1"=60'-0"   1:16 3/4"=1'-0"   1:720 1"=60'-(

0 ▓▓▓▓▓▓ 2   0 ▓▓▓▓▓▓▓ 70   0 ▓▓▓ 6"   0 ▓▓▓ 35
1:24 1/2"=1'-0"   1:840 1"=70'-0"   1:24 1/2"=1'-0"   1:840 1"=70'-(

0 ▓▓▓▓ 2   0 ▓▓▓▓▓▓▓ 80   0 ▓▓▓ 1   0 ▓▓▓ 40
1:32 3/8"=1'-0"   1:960 1"=80'-0"   1:32 3/8"=1'-0"   1:960 1"=80'-(

0 ▓▓▓▓▓▓ 4   0 ▓▓▓▓▓▓▓ 100   0 ▓▓ 1   0 ▓▓▓ 50
1:48 1/4"=1'-0"   1:1,200   1:48 1/4"=1'-0"   1:1,200
                      1"=100'-0"   1"=100'-0"

0 ▓▓▓▓ 4   0 ▓▓▓▓▓▓▓ 120   0 ▓▓▓ 2   0 ▓▓▓ 60
1:64 3/16"=1'-0"   1:1,440   1:64 3/16"=1'-0" 1:1,440
                      1"=120'-0"   1"=120'-0"

0 ▓▓▓▓▓ 8   0 ▓▓▓▓▓▓▓ 160   0 ▓▓ 2   0 ▓▓▓ 80
1:96 1/8"=1'-0"   1:1,920   1:96 1/8"=1'-0"   1:1,920
                      1"=160'-0"   1"=160'-0"

0 ▓▓▓▓▓ 10   0 ▓▓▓▓▓▓▓ 200   0 ▓▓▓ 5   0 ▓▓▓ 100
1:120 1"=10'-0"   1:2,400   1:120 1"=10'-0"   1:2,400
                      1"=200'-0"   1"=200'-0"

0 ▓▓▓▓ 8   0 ▓▓▓▓▓▓▓ 400   0 ▓▓ 4   0 ▓▓▓ 200
1:128 3/32"=1'-0"   1:4,800   1:128 3/32"=1'-0" 1:4,800
                      1"=400'-0"   1"=400'-0"

0 ▓▓▓▓▓ 16   0 ▓▓▓▓▓▓▓ 1000   0 ▓▓▓ 8   0 ▓▓▓ 500
1:192 1"=16'-0"   1:12,000   1:192 1"=16'-0"   1:12,000
                      1"=1,000'-0"   1"=1,000'-0"

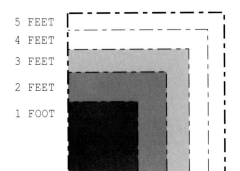

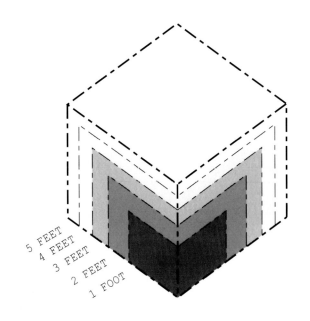

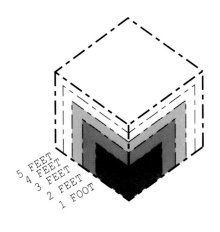

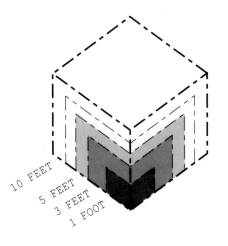

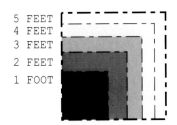

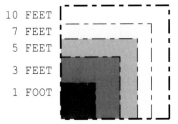

AREA AND VOLUME SCALES AT 1/4" = 1'-0"   0 [============] 4

10 FEET
7 FEET
5 FEET
3 FEET
1 FOOT
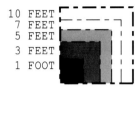

25 FEET
20 FEET
15 FEET
10 FEET
5 FEET
1 FOOT
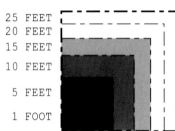

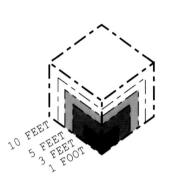
10 FEET
5 FEET
3 FEET
1 FOOT

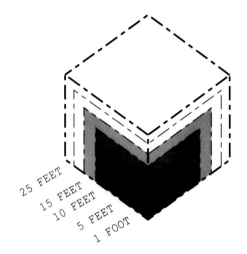
25 FEET
15 FEET
10 FEET
5 FEET
1 FOOT

AREA AND VOLUME SCALES AT 3/16" = 1'-0"   0 [============] 4

25 FEET
20 FEET
15 FEET
10 FEET
5 FEET
1 FOOT
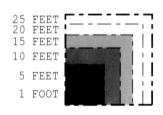

5 YARDS
4 YARDS
3 YARDS
2 YARDS
1 YARD
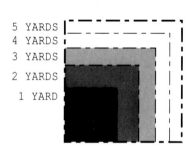

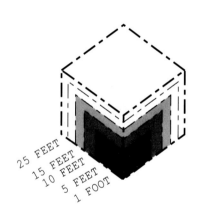
25 FEET
15 FEET
10 FEET
5 FEET
1 FOOT

AREA AND VOLUME SCALES AT 1/8" = 1'-0"   0 [============] 8

100 FEET
75 FEET
50 FEET
25 FEET
5 FEET
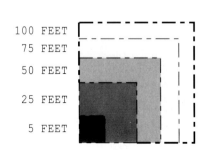

10 YARDS
7 YARDS
5 YARDS
3 YARDS
1 YARD
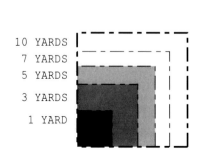

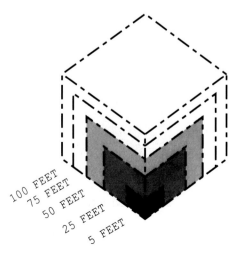
100 FEET
75 FEET
50 FEET
25 FEET
5 FEET

0 ▭ 4   AREA AND VOLUME SCALES AT 1' = 10'-0"

100 FEET
75 FEET
50 FEET
25 FEET
5 FEET

10 YARDS
7 YARDS
5 YARDS
3 YARDS
1 YARD

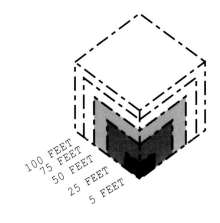

100 FEET
75 FEET
50 FEET
25 FEET
5 FEET

0 ▭ 4   AREA AND VOLUME SCALES AT 3/32" = 1'-0"

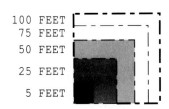

100 FEET
75 FEET
50 FEET
25 FEET
5 FEET

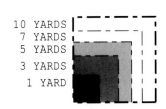

10 YARDS
7 YARDS
5 YARDS
3 YARDS
1 YARD

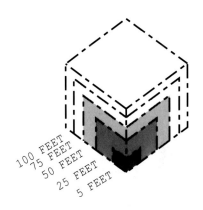

100 FEET
75 FEET
50 FEET
25 FEET
5 FEET

0 ▭ 8   AREA AND VOLUME SCALES AT 1/16" = 1'-0"

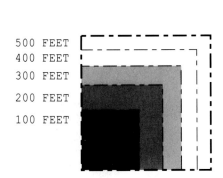

500 FEET
400 FEET
300 FEET
200 FEET
100 FEET

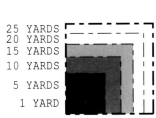

25 YARDS
20 YARDS
15 YARDS
10 YARDS
5 YARDS
1 YARD

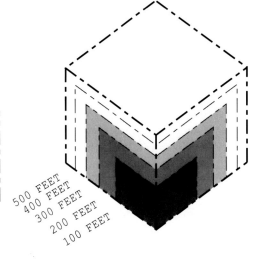

500 FEET
400 FEET
300 FEET
200 FEET
100 FEET

AREA AND VOLUME SCALES AT 1' = 20'-0"   0 ▭ 20

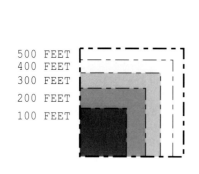

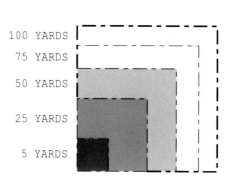

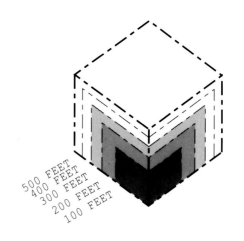

AREA AND VOLUME SCALES AT 1' = 30'-0"   0 ▭ 30

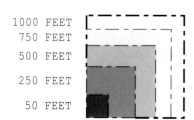

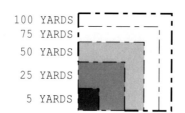

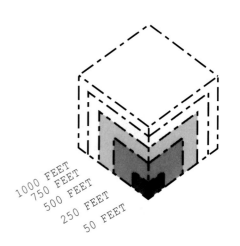

AREA AND VOLUME SCALES AT 1' = 40'-0"   0 ▭ 40

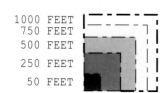

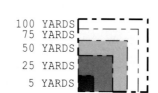

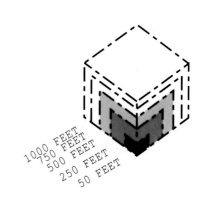

0 ▭ 100   AREA SCALES AT 1' = 100'-0"

5000 FEET
3750 FEET
2500 FEET
1250 FEET
250 FEET

5280 FEET
3750 FEET
2500 FEET
1250 FEET
250 FEET

10,000 FEET
7,500 FEET
5,000 FEET
2,500 FEET
500 FEET

0 ▭ 200   AREA SCALES AT 1' = 200'-0"

5 ACRES
4 ACRES
3 ACRES
2 ACRES
1 ACRE

0 ▭ 400   AREA SCALES AT 1' = 400'-0"

10 ACRES
7 ACRES
5 ACRES
3 ACRES
1 ACRE

0 ▭ 1000   AREA SCALES AT 1' = 1,000'-0"

25 ACRES
20 ACRES
15 ACRES
10 ACRES
5 ACRES
1 ACRE

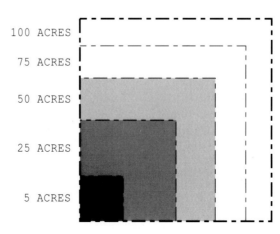

100 ACRES
75 ACRES
50 ACRES
25 ACRES
5 ACRES

NORTH ARROWS

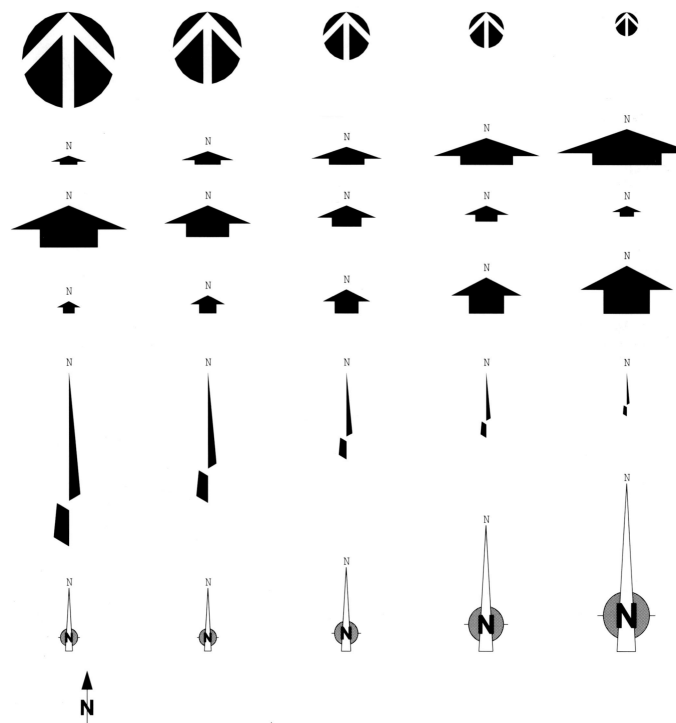

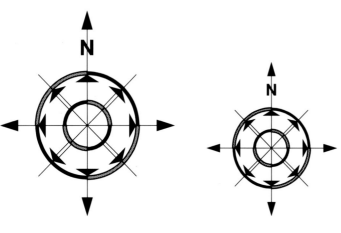